A LEGACY RECORDED
An Anthology of Martyrdom and Resistance

A LEGACY RECORDED

An Anthology of Martyrdom and Resistance

HARVEY ROSENFELD
AND
ELI ZBOROWSKI
Editors

MARTYRDOM AND RESISTANCE
48 West 37th Street
New York, NY 10018-7408

To the survivors of the Holocaust, whose
Spirit and Soul are embodied in
A Legacy Recorded

A LEGACY RECORDED
An Anthology of Martyrdom and Resistance

PRINTED IN THE UNITED STATES OF AMERICA
BY
ATHENS PRINTING COMPANY
New York, NY 10018-6401

ACKNOWLEDGEMENTS

Programs on Yom Hashoa V'Hagvurah, courses from grade school through graduate programs, an endless flow of the written and oral word—all these activities on behalf of Holocaust remembrance are taken for granted today. But it was the American Federation of Jewish Fighters, Camp Inmates, and Nazi Victims who did not take for granted these goals in the early '70s. While so many groups and individuals busy themselves with Holocaust activities today, it was only the Federation of Survivors that took the initiative and made its imprint on behalf of remembrance when nobody else did.

A *Legacy Recorded* is an anthology that eternalizes what the survivors, and in particular the Federation of Jewish fighters, have accomplished. The medium for this record is *Martyrdom and Resistance*, the internationally recognized periodical founded by the federation of survivors in the Fall of 1974. This anthology offers some of the representative articles that appeared during its first 20 years.

The production of this anthology requires thanks to many individuals. First, there are the writers of the articles presented during the 20 years of *M & R*. Then there are those who have contributed special articles for the anthology. Many deserving articles could not be included for lack of space, but many of them are cited in the introductions to each chapter of this book.

For these introductions to every chapter, we thank Prof. Henry Huttenbach. The cover that sets the dominant theme for the anthology, that of survivors, is that by Dr. Luba K. Gurdus. We also thank Jacob Felderbaum, who aided in the preparation of the manuscript.

Above all, we are grateful for the encouragement and support of Eli Zborowski, editor-in-chief of *Martyrdom and Resistance*, without whose commitment *A Legacy Recorded* would not have been published.

We also acknowledge the inclusion of those articles reprinted from other publications, in particular: Bryna Bar-Oni, "Remembering Hanukka," *Jerusalem Post*: Dr. Franklin H. Littell, "Why We Teach the Holocaust," *Jewish Exponent*; Eugenia Nadler, "Reflections at Yad Vashem," *Wiaomosci*.

HARVEY ROSENFELD, *Editor*

TABLE OF CONTENTS

M & R: Periodical of Achievement

By HARVEY ROSENFELD

Who was talking or writing about the Holocaust 20 years ago?

Indeed, discussions of the Holocaust or pleas for remembrance were then limited to a handful of scholars and to a few concerned survivors of the greatest atrocity known to mankind.

One of these individuals was Eli Zborowski, an *ish hazikaron*, a man of remembrance, whose spirit and being were entwined in not letting the world forget. He was instrumental in helping establish in 1963 the first regular Yom Hashoa observance in America, at the Young Israel of Forest Hills as a central commemoration for Queens, N.Y. Out of these observances came occasional publications and other materials dealing with remembrance projects and activities.

These publications were the seeds for *Martyrdom and Resistance,* which came into being in 1974. As president and founder of the then American Federation of Jewish Fighters, Camp Inmates, and Nazi Victims, Mr. Zborowski saw the periodical primarily as a vehicle for those most interested in remembrance. When it first appeared in September, 1974, the four-page format was designed to provide organizational news for several thousand members of the Federation, as well as to inform readers of remembrance activities and provide a roundup of contemporary historical reports.

A periodical for survivors: in the main, this was how the periodical was initially viewed by survivor and non-survivor alike. Writing for Israel's Ministry of Foreign Affairs, Dr. Abba Geffen, Director, complimented the new publication: "The publication is very timely for every Jew, especially the survivors of the Holocaust, who must never forget what happened in our generation—not to agonize on the bitter past, but to act, with confidence, that it will not recur. A bereaved nation, like a bereaved mother, cannot forget and cannot forgive."

Dr. Rosenfeld is editor of *Martyrdom and Resistance.*

As expected, the most applause came from survivors. In his enthusiastic congratulations, Ray Kantor, president of survivors living in Cincinnati, was "indeed happy to learn that at long last a publication of the survivors of the Holocaust, properly named *Martyrdom and Resistance*, made its debut." But Mr. Kantor wondered: "How did we ever do without it and for so long?" However, the important thing was that the survivor now had a voice and he was confident "The newsletter will prove to be a means of communication, an exchange of ideas."

It was not long, however, that the publication became more than a platform for survivors. The growth of *M & R* was remarkable. From a beginning readership of less than 5,000 survivors, the paper increased its circulation until it now stands close to 30,000. This includes researchers and scholars in Judaica; public and college libraries; rabbis, other religious leaders and organizations; and government officials. Readers are found throughout the U.S., Canada, Mexico, South America, Europe, Israel, South Africa, and Australia.

Interestingly, *M & R* has come to the attention of many who seem far removed from its concerns of the past or future. Among such 'unlikely readers,' was an individual in McIntosh, Minn., who ran Mudville Baseball Art, named for the legendary baseball town whose hero Casey struck out, and a reader in an Albuquerque, New Mexico, library, John Sandovall, who was inspired to write "Technology's Smile," a poem found in this anthology.

From its beginnings, *Martyrdom and Resistance* has received praise from professional journals, scholars, and community leaders. In 1976, for example, the prestigious *Library Journal* featured a review of *M & R* in its Magazines Section and said that the periodical "can be useful as a companion to studies in modern history."

As the oldest, continual periodical devoted to the Holocaust, *M & R* has, understandably, become a valuable resource for scholars and researchers. Its unique quality lies in the combination of news and features about *all* aspects of the Holocaust and resistance, including book and film reviews, reports about educational programs, and a presentation of survivor activities. There are other publications dealing with the Holocaust, but their formats are either geared to the educational aspects of the Holocaust, or are entirely devoted to scholarly pursuits, or are fragmentary in their reportage of the Holocaust. In short, *M & R* stands proud and humble to be the periodical of *record* for martyrdom and resistance.

From the groves of academia has come gratifying praise. One of America's most prominent sociologists, Dr. Marshall Sklare, Brandeis University, said the publication "will be of help to me in connection with my lectures on the American Jewish community." Dr. Lawrence L. Langer, on the faculty of Simmons College in Boston and author of a pioneering book *The Holocaust and the Literary Imagination,* predicted in 1977 that "such a newsletter is essential and will have a long and healthy life." Prof. David Wyman, the University of Massachusetts historian who authored the acclaimed *Abandonment of the Jews,* has made use of *M & R* in his research. References to articles in *M & R* fill the pages of David M. Szonyi's annotated bibliography and resource guide to the Holocaust.

And from Laramie, Wyoming, at the University of Wyoming, Prof. Christopher S. Durer, Chairman of the English Department, and Melville scholar, wrote us how "flattered and honored" he was that his article *"Moby Dick* and Nazi Germany" would appear in our pages.

When *M & R* completed its first decade, it took a major step in ensuring its permanent contribution to Holocaust research: the production of all back copies on microfiche with an accompanying index. The 76-page index has more than 3,000 entries divided into a Subject Index of 51 categories. The Index also includes Book Review Index, Poetry Index, and Movie Index.

Among universities now using this resource are Harvard University, the University of Texas, University of Toronto, City University of New York, Hebrew University, Emory University. The Library of Congress in Washington and the Royal Library in Copenhagen have also added the Index to their holdings.

Perhaps the most meaningful praise for a periodical came from a "colleague," a "fellow" periodical. In an article for the *Yonkers (N.Y.) Jewish Chronicle,* editor Carolyn Weiner, lauds *M & R* as "a living memorial to victims of Holocaust." The following lines open her discussion:

"Among the dozens of newspapers and magazines that cross my desk each month, there is one newspaper that never fails to move me tremendously. It is called *Martyrdom and Resistance* and it is the newsletter for the American Federation of Jewish Fighters, Camp Inmates, and Nazi Victims.

"It moves me, I believe, because unlike the televised Diary of Anne Frank' or 'Playing for Time,' or even 'Holocaust,' I feel the spirits of the martyred who, in a sense, live on through this extraordinary, informative newsletter."

Beyond all discussions of *Martyrdom and Resistance* as the periodical of record, one must keep in mind and not lose sight of the periodical's serving to put the deserved spotlight on the role of survivors in terms of their personal achievements, and in their advancing the cause of remembrance.

True, the periodical has outgrown its original, exclusive role as a voice for survivors and their organizations, but *M & R* is always aware that it records what the survivors have achieved after emerging as a Shearit Hapleitah, a remnant of a flourishing culture and heritage.

Turn the pages from our 20 years, and you will find the accomplishments of survivors, not only in keeping the spirit of remembrance alive, but as important if not more, their accomplishments in the gamut of human endeavor and creativity: the professions, business, education and all forms of community service, literature and other creative arts.

While *M & R* has attracted scholars and outstanding writers to its pages, it is the survivors who have poured their blood and emotions into these pages. Without them, *M & R* would be just another publication, albeit of much merit. And, more important, it was the survivors who charted the growth of the periodical. From my vantage point as editor, one cannot say too much about the leadership of editor-in-chief Eli Zborowski. Aside from the personal financing of *M & R*, he has guided the editorial development of the paper. He has encouraged and presented views often not in line with those of the "establishment." And he has to endure criticism, sadly, even from jaundiced survivors or survivor groups.

The achievements of the American Federation of Jewish Fighters are reviewed in this anthology. More than just a history of an organization, it is a tribute to Eli Zborowski's accomplishments. The words of Ralph Waldo Emerson are accurate in describing Eli Zborowski and the Federation: "An institution is the lengthened shadow of one man."

Two other survivors were very instrumental too in the growth of the paper. Marysia Felberbaum and Icek Shmulevitz were long-time members of the Editorial Board. Both are gone, but they will not be forgotten. Marysia was dedicated to the recording of survivor experiences and emotions. In addition to her prolific contributions, she "designed" the *Survivor's Corner*. Icek coordinated the Yiddish Supplement in the paper's formative years. Even when the periodical no longer carried Yiddish articles, he remained on the board and was always available with constructive thoughts and suggestions. As an outstanding journalist who articulated the sentiments and aspirations of survivors, he could speak with conviction and clarity about the direction of *M & R*. In short, his identification with *M & R* gave us status and widespread acceptability.

When one measures the achievements of *M & R*, one will speak long of its unique role in the observance of Yom Hashoa V'Hagvurah, its commemoration on the English calendar corresponding to 27 Nissan. Eli Zborowski has championed the centrality of Yom Hashoa, very often in the face of opposition. Because of his tenacity, and in his doggedly stating that position in *M & R*, Yom Hashoa V'Hagvurah is observed worldwide on 27 Nissan. What first began in 1963—in Forest Hills, Queens, N.Y.—eventually reached the White House, years later.

On this 20th-year celebration of *M & R*, we are not the celebrant accepting gifts, but we are offering this anthology in the cause of remembrance.

As discussed in another article in this anthology, the American Federation of Jewish Fighters, Camp Inmates, and Nazi Victims has passed from the scene. The publisher of *M & R* is the Martyrdom and Resistance Foundation. Beginning its third decade, *M & R* rededicates itself to serving all its readers.

A sampling of requests and thoughts from our public is reflective of the widespread interest in *M & R*:

A teacher at the Ulm American School in New Ulm, Germany, has requested materials or information for the teaching of a course.

Prof. Walter Renn, in the Department of History at Wheeling College in West Virginia, has asked for back copies of *M & R* for his book on postwar German attitudes and teaching of the Holocaust and Nazi persecutions in the Federal Republic.

Dr. Richard Mayer, dean of the College of Arts and Sciences in Aurora University, Aurora, Ill., has asked for a subscription to *M & R* to keep informed as he teaches a course on the Holocaust.

One Generation After, in Boston, reprints an article written by a seven-year-old, because "it shows that young children can be informed, have feelings about the Holocaust, and can express them."

The State Historical Society of Wisconsin aptly put the need for *M & R* in a 1979 article that appeared in its *News*. The sentiments are still very much relevant today. It begins by quoting Solomon Zynstein, then president of the American

Celebrating M & R Inaugural Issue (l. to r.) : Alex Schlesinger, New York State Governor Malcolm Wilson, Eli Zborowski.

Federation of Jewish Fighters, Camp Inmates, and Nazi Victims:

"The report of Solomon Zynstein . . . gives the greatest recommendation for the need of this newsletter (*M & R*) : . . . 'The ranks of the last survivors of the Holocaust, the last living witnesses of the Nazi atrocities, are steadily shrinking and with the passing of time there might be no one to remember and to remind the world not to forget.' When a piece of the current flood of neo-Nazi propaganda tells you that there was no systematic slaughter of Jews (or gypsies or Slavs) under Hitler, remember the ovens and gas chambers, emaciated bodies, and mass graves, lampshades made of human skin. And, above all, listen to the voices of these last survivors, for they are the tears and groans and prayers of the slaughtered multitudes."

A Holocaust Commandment: Hear the Voices of the Survivors!

Not unintentionally, this volume of writings on the Holocaust begins with the all too real phenomenon of the Survivors, for they have been touched by mankind's extreme power to commit the ultimate Evil—genocide, the Final Solution. They have inhabited the Kingdom of Death and lived to remember the martyrs, Six Million innocent Jewish victims of hatred. Their experiences of the Death Factories embody the Truth of Auschwitz, the mysterious meanings of the Holocaust.

While the remnants of the extermination camps still live in our midst, we have a solemn task to listen to the miraculous voices of the survivors. Those of us who seek to understand must use them as our guides through the inferno that was, but must never be again except as a permanent reminder of what happens when power is divorced from decency, when technology is devoid of humanizing morality. Like Virgil guiding Dante through a fictitious nether world, the Survivors will lead all subsequent generations into that all too real darkness of an actual past. Its cruel shadows extend permanently across mankind's remaining future.

The survivors of the Holocaust Hell have experienced the unimaginable, the inexpressible, the abnormal made commonplace. Their very existence, their decade-long silences, are often more eloquent, greater testimony than agonized pages of memoirs. But these imperfect fragments of the Holocaust Truth are our only hope of gaining access to the Holocaust Kingdom. And so we must preserve them, cherish them.

In her poignant statement, Lorraine Kaufman exhorts each survivor to pass on the legacy of Holocaust remembrances; in turn, Harry Cargas urges us to reach out and gather the harvest of Survivors' memories. History, the Holocaust Past, commands us to listen to the survivors, the Voices from the Holocaust Darkness. No other group of people has a greater moral imperative than they to their human experiences on all our consciousness by affirming the right to proclaim: "Mir szeinen doh!" They were THERE; they are *still* there; and they will continue to be witnesses as long as we recognize their triumphant presence amongst us here, today, and into every tomorrow.

American Federation of Survivors: A Legacy for the Generations

After the ravages of the Holocaust, the survivors were disinclined to discuss their experiences because of their social, physical and emotional states. Certainly, they made no attempt to unite to share common problems and concerns.

With the passing of time, as the experiences of the Holocaust became a tiny bit more distanced, a change took place. The first survivor groups were formed for purposes of friendship and fraternity. With family and friends murdered during the Holocaust, the survivors needed identification with those who had undergone similar experiences—if only just to talk and commiserate with. It was not surprising, therefore, that when survivor organizations were formed, and members and officers elected, they included those who had come from a common town, ghetto, camp, or in some cases, a region or country.

Perhaps the first and certainly most meaningful activity of these groups was a commemoration or observance, of the liquidation of a ghetto, an uprising or the like.

The survivors came to realize that they could make a more meaningful contribution by conveying the lessons of the Holocaust for the present generation and for the future. They became vigilant and spoke out when signs or acts of anti-Semitism appeared. They initated educational projects designed to inform the world of Jewry's most tragic days. In some communities, in fact, it was the survivors who organized the Yom Hashoa or Holocaust Remembrance days.

With more than two decades having passed since the Holocaust, it was becoming clear that the survivors had an important mission to accomplish that went beyond socializing with those from a common town or ghetto.

Eli Zborowski is editor-in-chief of *Martyrdom and Resistance* and chairman of the American and International Societies for Yad Vashem. He was the founder and first President of the American Federation of Jewish Fighters, Camp Inmates, and Nazi Victims.

The survivors realized that it was their sacred duty to make the world remember so that it could learn the lessons of the Holocaust. As the decades of the 70's began, there were recurring episodes of anti-Semitism and neo-Nazism throughout the world. Of equal concern and perhaps of more moment for the survivors was that more than 25 years after the Holocaust, the world hardly knew what a survivor was, what it meant to have endured the undescribable experiences from 1933-45. And most gnawing was the fact that the survivors had so much to offer the community, but there was no vehicle to channel the treasure. For the survivors themselves, there was the additional of agony of telling the story to their own children to avoid what was being called a "generation gap."

In 1971 an international conference of survivors in Israel discussed mutual problems. For years it had become painfully obvious that even in Israel, where so many thousands of the shearit hapleitah had made their home, there was little organized concern about the Holocaust. True, in 1953 Knesset had enacted the Law of Remembrance of Martyrdom and Resistance—Chok L'Zikaron Hashoa V'Hagvurah—that established Yad Vashem, the Remembrance Authority. It designated the 27th day of Nissan as the Annual Day of Remembrance—Yom Hashoa V'Hagvurah.

But in the main, Israelis preferred to look forward, not back to the tragedy of the past. Young Israelis were not learning the Shoa in the schools. More important, the united strength of the survivors was a resource that was not being utilized in Israel, in America, throughout the world.

It was a gathering of great importance, indeed, with almost no fanfare, no publicity. And the proceedings, like so much of the record of the Holocaust, was committed to memory.

Out of this conference emerged the World Federation of Jewish Fighters, Partisans, and Camp Inmates, which has been headed with much devotion through the years by Stefan Grayek. I myself spoke at the conference with great enthusiasm about the need for such a world federation of survivors. Most of the other participants from the U.S. were very active during the proceedings and were strong supporters of a world federation. Now it was time to coalesce the energies and resources of the survivors in America. Later that year, on April 7, 1971, a meeting was held in New York at the offices of the Anti-Defamation League of B'nai B'rith. In attendance were Rabbi Chaskel Besser, Abe Foxman, Seymour Robbins, Samuel Skura, Solomon Zynstein, and myself. What followed was the birth of the American Federation of Jewish Fighters, Camp Inmates, and Nazi Victims.

From its beginnings, the Federation was set up as an organization which would be an umbrella group to work with all survivor organizations.

FEDERATION OF SURVIVORS SOUGHT INVOLVEMENT WITH SURVIVOR GROUPS, JEWISH ORGANIZATIONS

Indeed, we strived for unity at the outset, but the Federation found unhappiness and discomfort even among those groups who joined the newly formed organization. We were an umbrella organization for survivors, but there were those who didn't like the umbrella, who felt that it was not protective enough of the special interests of each constituent member, who felt that the individual units would be swallowed up by the organization. But that never came to pass. As the Federation thrived, so did the individual units. The Federation serviced all of its members, as the constitutent members tailored their own activities and programs to meet their specific needs and requirements.

The Federation looked for the widest participation of the then-already-existing survivor organizations. These groups who supported the idea of federation and joined the umbrella organization are deserving of mention: Branch Masada 403 of the Farband Labor Zionist Order, Jewish Nazi Victims Organization of America, Fraternal Order of Bendin-Sosnowicer, Federation of Jewish Undeground Fighters Against Nazism, New Cracow Friendship Society, Lodzer Young Men's Benevolent Society, Warsaw Ghetto Resistance Organization, American Congress of Jews from Poland and Survivors of Concentration Camps, and the survivors-affiliate of the Jewish Labor Committee.

Not joining the newly created Federation was the World Federation of Bergen-Belsen, one of the oldest survivor organizations, whose leader the late Joseph Rosensaft had eloquently articulated the plight of the survivors before the public. With a solid record of achievement, the Bergen-Belsen group opposed the concept of the world federation of survivors and subsequently the American Federation. Whatever its reasoning for not joining, we respected the Bergen-Belsen decision and cooperated as much as possible with that organization and its leadership.

Cooperation was a keyword in the life of the Federation

of Survivors. Jewish organizations were delighted that there
was a vigorous organization of survivors ready to join forces
with others in serving the community. Whether it was on
behalf of Israel, Soviet Jewry, intergroup relations and tensions, the Jewish world knew it could count on the commitment, whether time, energy, or funding from the survivors.
Perhaps more significant, the Federation was set up so
that it could endeavor to work within and together with the
existing Jewish community in America. Just to mention a
few, the Federation cooperated with the Conference of Presidents of Major American Jewish Organizations (a later established organization) American Federation of Polish Jews,
ADL, American Zionist Youth Foundation, Memorial Foundation for Jewish Culture, National Council of Young Israel,
Yeshiva University, the Board of Jewish Education of Greater
New York, and the American Association for Jewish Education. The Federation had its home for several years in the
offices of the ADL and B'nai Zion. Reflecting this involvement
in Jewish communal life, the Federation was accepted as a

The objectives of the Federation were clearly stated at
the outset:

1. To hold the 27th of Nissan as Holocaust and Heroism
Memorial Day for Jewish organizations in the United States.

2. To establish a central place in New York for activities
on behalf of Yad Vashem, where Jewish organizations can
obtain informative and educational material on the Holocaust
and heroism.

3. To collect and record the names of those who perished
on Pages of Testimony to be kept in the Hall of Names in Yad
Vashem.

4. To carry on and expand the effort to instill consciousness of the Holocaust and heroism in universities and schools.

5. To collect oral testimony from survivors of the Holo-
caust living in the United States, under the direction of Yad
Vashem and the Institute of Contemporary Jewry of the
Hebrew University of Jerusalem.

6. To grant scholarships for research and publications on
themes connected with Holocaust and heroism.

member in the Jewish Community Relations Council of New York, joining some 25 major Jewish agencies in the central coordinating and resource body for the New York Jewish community.

A story on the beginnings of Yom Hashoa observance in the U.S. is presented elsewhere in this anthology. But what must be stressed here is that the observance of 27 Nissan as a national and world remembrance date became the number one objective of the newly formed Federation. On Yom Hashoa V'Hagvurah, 1972, it issued a joint proclamation with over 60 national Jewish organizations calling for the observance of April 11, 1972, 27 Nissan 5732, as the Day of Remembrance.

Special praise was given by the Department of Programs of the United Synagogue of America, citing the Federation "as the organization which brought Yom Hashoa to public prominence. It provides information on how to organize and observe this day of remembrance."

FEDERATION OF SURVIVORS FIRST ORGANIZED GROUP ASKING GOVERNMENT BODIES TO ISSUE PROCLAMATIONS

The Federation was the first organized body to ask government authorities to issue proclamations calling for the observance of Yom Hashoa on 27 Nissan. The Federation was cited in 1976 for its achievements in furthering Yom Hashoa observance in a resolution by the New York State Assembly calling for the adoption of a Holocaust Commemoration Day on 27 Nissan. The resolution also called upon the New York State Department of Education to inform all schools of Holocaust Commemoration Day and "that they be requested to duly commemorate the day so that the children of this state may know of the events of the not so distant past."

It should not go unrecorded that there was not full agreement, even divisiveness on the question of the date on which Yom Hashoa V'Hagvurah should be observed. From the start, the Federation believed that Jewish organizations worldwide should follow the position of the Israeli Knesset that observances will be held on the English calendar date corresponding to 27 Nissan. In so doing, the full symbolic value is evident: memorializing our martyrs on a date that falls between the heroism of the Warsaw Ghetto Uprising and the independence of the State of Israel, the phoenix arising from the Holocaust.

Those who questioned the observance on 27 Nissan were well-meaning and sincere. Be that as it may, years later there is no longer opposition. Yom Hashoa on 27 Nissan is as much an observance on calendars and on Hebrew *luachs* as other 'special days' that are to be marked and observed. What the Federation championed and has now been accepted by the 'other side,' reminds one of the words of the great literary figure Thomas Mann:

"We are most likely to get angry and excited in our opposition to some idea when we ourselves are not quite certain of our own position, and are inwardly tempted to take the other side."

But it takes more than a proclamation to sponsor a meaningful observance. And there were lengthy discussions by those who cared about remembrance on how best to convey the message. Sam Skura was involved in a variety of Holocaust remembrance activities, for Federation. But he came to realize that an observance, a lecture, a sculpture was simply not enough. Imagination was necessary.

FEDERATION COMMISSIONED YAD VASHEM TO PREPARE MOBILE HOLOCAUST EXHIBIT

Beginning in 1973, the Federation, with limited resources, was instrumental in disseminating material and information throughout the years on the Holocaust. The Federation commissioned Yad Vashem in 1972 to prepare mobile exhibitions on the "Holocaust and Resistance." These exhibitions circulated throughout the U.S., Canada, and South America in cooperation with other Jewish organizations.

The excitement attached to this creative remembrance tool was evidenced at the opening exhibit in Washington, D.C., when the admirers included U.S. Secretary of State Cyrus Vance and Nobel Laureate Elie Wiesel, in November, 1972.

Requests continue to stream in from organizations, both Jewish and non-Jewish, schools and colleges who seek to obtain the exhibit for permanent use.

The exhibit contains 33 boards of authentic photographs outlining Jewish history in Nazi-occupied Europe from 1933-45. Depicted through text and photos—many of them captured from the Nazis—are the periods of the rise of Hitler in 1933, the persecution of Jews and discriminatory laws, Crystal

Night, the outbreak of World War II, deportation, death
camps, resistance, and liberation. The documented exhibit
proves to the world that the Holocaust—in all its starkness
and inhumanity—was real.

Illustrative of the diversity of the users of the exhibit
was the sampling of requests received by the Federation in
May, 1977: a Hebrew day school in Nevada, a synagogue in
Mississippi, a college in Oklahoma, and a writer from Florida
who lectures to non-Jews.

The Federation also commissioned an illustrated booklet
on the "Holocaust and Resistance" by Israel Gutman, published
in English in Yad Vashem in 1972. To date more than
100,000 booklets have been distributed as a means of height-
ening awareness of the Holocaust and Resistance among Jewish and non-Jewish youth and the general public.

Two notable scholarly works were distributed by the
Federation: *Polish-Jewish Relations During the Second World
War*, by Emmanuel Ringelblum, published by Yad Vashem in
1974, funded by the Federation, and *Jewish Resistance During
the Holocaust*, published by Yad Vashem under the auspices
of the Memorial Foundation for Jewish Culture.

The publication of the Ringelblum classic was an inesti-
mable contribution to Holocaust literature. The Federation
made available to the English reader the views and appraisals
of Ringelblum, one of the most popular and beloved personalities in the entire Warsaw Ghetto. Ringelblum's contributions remain unparalleled in history and is still unique in the
annals of the people overrun and enslaved during World
War II.

THOUSANDS OF COMMUNITIES SERVICED
BY FEDERATION IN YOM HASHOA PROGRAMS

In the diverse, multifaceted institution known as the
Board of Jewish Education of Greater New York, then executive vice president, Dr. Alvin I. Schiff, never lost sight of the
Jewish youth. But he was worried that there was a lack of
materials and programs to inspire children to want to remember this awful period in the Jewish experience.

The Federation worked hard and creatively to meet this
problem. Not only did the efforts of the Federation result in
bringing the story of the *Kedoshim* to the youth, but it also
brought a marvelous, unforseen result. Identification with the
Holocaust became a source of Jewish identity. There were

youth who were completely alienated from Judaism. Learning of the Holocaust became a critical experience in discovering their own identity with the Jewish people. How was all this accomplished?

Yom Hashoa became the key. Every year during the Yom Hashoa period, the Federation distributed thousands of educational kits prepared by the Yad Vashem Holocaust Museum. For example, for the observance of Yom Hashoa on April 30, 1981, more than 26,000 posters, booklets, and program packets were distributed. Some 300 Holocaust and Resistance exhibits were sent to organizations, institutions, and groups, throughout the country, as far west as Washington State.

Members and officers of the Federation enhanced the observance of Yom Hashoa by visiting elementary and high schools, and colleges, or speaking of their experiences at community observances. This service was provided through the Federation Speakers Bureau.

Nothing could substitute for the lesson of remembrance personified by the presence and words of a survivor. It was the Federation that made it possible for people to learn, and it should be stressed that lessons were taught throughout the year, not just during the Yom Hashoa period.

Typical was the following letter received from a high school principal in New York in 1977:

"We are most grateful to the American Federation of Jewish Fighters, Camp Inmates, and Nazi Victims for making possible the unforgettable program in our school. Our students will not forget the words or the message of Mr. Skura. All the words that can come from the most eloquent history teacher or the most comprehensive textbook can not replace a survivor or have anywhere near the impact that a student gets from a survivor. Survivors are the real thing. Students who have heard the words of a survivor will never forget what the Holocaust was and what needs to be done to prevent the tragedy from happening again. Thank you, again, American Federation of Jewish Fighters, Camp Inmates, and Nazi Victims!"

But the classroom was not to be forgotten. The educational specialists in New York City's public high school were in close contact with the Federation in the late '70's, when the Holocaust curriculum was introduced into the schools.

Before material could be introduced to schoolchildren, there was a pressing need to ensure that the developers of the materials and the teachers themselves were well prepared.

How could Yad Vashem help? In 1972, the newly appointed
Chairman of the Yad Vashem Directorate, Dr. Yitzhak Arad,
gave a lecture tour at American universities under sponsorship
of the Federation. This highlighted a program held in cooperation with the American Zionist Youth Foundation. More than
50 campuses were visited. A similar tour had been undertaken
by Ambassador Katriel Katz at the time he was Chairman of
the Yad Vashem Directorate.

In addition, an all-day educational seminar was conducted for Jewish youth movements, with the principal
speaker, the late Ambassador Katz.

Meanwhile at the National Curriculum Research Institute
of the American Association for Jewish Education, the director, Dr. Hyman Chanover, was grappling with a problem. The
AAJE and the American Jewish Committee had sponsored a
workshop in 1973 featuring nine detailed papers that probed
psychological insights and instructional strategies on the Holocaust. But how would this innovative gathering transmit the
thoughts that had been explored? The Federation was contacted, and publication of the proceedings were realized
through funding in the form of a special "Teaching and
Commemorating the Holocaust" edition in 1974 of *The Peda-
gogic Reporter*, the AAJE journal.

The Federation was also busy at that time, in 1973, setting
up the Holocaust Studies Faculty Seminar at Touro College,
bringing together faculty, outstanding scholars, in the New
York metropolitan area, involved in the teaching and research
of the Holocaust.

ELI AND DIANA ZBOROWSKI CHAIR AT YU
IMPRESSIVE EDUCATIONAL ACHIEVEMENT

The most enduring educational project, however, has
been the establishment in 1975 of the Eli and Diana Zborowski
Professiorial Chair in Interdisciplinary Holocaust Studies at
Yeshiva University.

In the spring of 1975 the late Dr. Samuel Belkin, President of Yeshiva University, and other members of the administration, among them vice president Dr. Israel Miller met at
the main academic center with the officers of the Federation.
It had become evident that there was a burgeoning interest in
Holocaust studies, but where would the teachers and scholars
come from, to meet this critical need?

The chair was created at that meeting. It was the first time that American students were given the opportunity of investigating the Holocaust from the perspective of various disciplines on the undergraduate and graduate levels. Among the world-renowned scholars who have held the chair have been Prof. Lucy Dawidowicz, Prof. Erich Goldhagen, and Prof. Lucjan Dobroszycki. The chair has been instrumental in developing some dozen courses at YU, Yom Hashoa observances, an annual lecture series, and an annual summer institute on teaching the Holocaust.

This chair has spurred an ongoing, exciting Holocaust Studies program at YU that includes an archive collection, museum exhibitions, publication of the Heritage of Modern European Jewry series, and outreach and community consciousness activities.

The establishment of the chair was a proud moment for all survivors who had the opportunity to bring forth their experiences, abilities, and services to help shape the proper memorial so that the grim lessons of the past would never be forgotten.

Inaugurated by the Federation on the 30th anniversary of the liberation, the Holocaust studies program at YU continues to encourage young men and women to enter careers as specialists, researchers, and teachers in Holocaust studies, as professionals who would have the skill and dedication to create and perpetuate programs of enlightenment for synagogues, universities, elementary schools, high schools, and community centers of all kinds throughout the country.

One of its first projects, in 1976, was a colloquium on teaching the Holocaust featuring the difficulties in teaching Holocaust history, the psychological impact of teaching the Holocaust, and the theological issues to be raised. It had an enthusiastic participation of educators, through the cooperation of the Stone-Sapirstein Center for Jewish Education, the National Commission on Torah Education, and the New York Board of Education.

An intellectually exciting activity of YU's Holocaust Studies Program was the inaugural volume of the Heritage of Modern European Jewry Series. It is the English-language version of Rabbi Shimon Huberband's classic *Kiddush Hashem: Jewish Religious and Cultural Life in Poland During the Holocaust.* "As original, as penetrating as any documents from that time," said Elie Wiesel, "it will henceforth take its place as indispensable testimony of the Holocaust."

FROM THE PIONEERS OF REMEMBRANCE...

"It is ironic that the American Federation of Jewish Fighters forged the survivors as one 'people.' It is ironic because the Nazis did not divide the Jews either. Jews were all equal to them in that Jews were targeted for destruction. But, of course, the Federation of survivors did much more than make us one group again. The Federation showed that you could be supportive of your own group of survivors who all came from one region, but you could add to that by being one group united to advance the cause of remembrance."

— Rabbi Chaskel Besser

"The American Federation of Jewish Fighters, Camp Inmates and Nazi Victims and its organ *Martyrdom and Resistance* performed as a vital link and task in the commemoration of the Jewish past during the horror years of the Holocaust.

"There could not have been a more expressive and symbolic name for the organ of Jewish survivors than *Martyrdom and Resistance,* two expressions that really complement each other. Each martyr was also a resistance fighter, be it in an active way fighting as a partisan or military unit, or fighting for his or her survival, for members of the family, for a piece of bread, for an additional day of life in ghettos, hiding places, labor or death camps, fighting the major aim of the Nazis to exterminate Jews, first in Europe and then anywhere else.

"The Federation and its organ fought against the idea of 'sheep for slaughter.' The Jews were a fighting people, although with both hands and feet chained, in spite of the collaboration of all bystanding nations. The Jewish people fought for their survival in many ways with means mostly still not understood by the majority of those who were not present at that time.

"Be it only for the above reasons the Federation and 'Martyrdom and Resistance' earned their place of honor in recent Jewish history."

— Shmuel Erner

"The American Federation of Jewish Fighters, Camp Inmates, and Nazi Victims held its first meeting in Lou G. Siegel's restaurant in Manhattan. Those who attended, including myself, wondered what plans and programs we would carry out. Not long after that meeting, the idea and realization of *Martyrdom and Resistance* came.

"What the organization accomplished was awesome. It was the Federation that spawned the formation of many other entities engaged in remembrance and the perpetuation of the Holocaust story. In particular, special praise should be given to *Martyrdom and Resistance*, the publishing arm of the Federation, that so excellently articulated the narrative of the Holocaust and recorded the legacy: the story of the survivors and of survival."   — *Eugene Gluck*

"Today, as impossible as it may seem, people are denying that the Holocaust took place. People are saying the German nation is not guilty. The fact that we can refute all these nonsensical beliefs is because there was a group of survivors, the American Federation of Jewish Fighters, that years ago was collecting testimony, publishing books, educating students. We told the story, and this story will be preserved eternally."   — *Dr. Hillel Seidmann*

"The American Federation of Jewish Fighters united all survivors. We now could speak with one voice about the importance of remembering the Holocaust and about all matters that related to Jewish survival. When we spoke in an organized way, the message had a powerful impact on the non-Jewish community, on the non-survivors in our community, and, perhaps most important, on the second generation."   — *Sam Skura*

"We survivors were slumbering, apathetic about the cause of remembrance until Eli Zborowski woke us up and orchestrtated the founding of the American Federation of Jewish Fighters, Camp Inmates, and Nazi Victims. Our gains were modest in the beginning, and then came educational programs, Yom Hashoa observances, major publications, the founding of *Martyrdom and Resistance*. And now the growth of Yad Vashem through societies across the globe. We are not slumbering anymore."   — *David Weiss*

FEDERATION PERIODICAL, M & R, ATTRACTS
PRAISE, ATTENTION AROUND THE GLOBE

With all the breathtaking activity undertaken by the
Federation, it would not have sufficed if all this could not be
brought to a large and influential audience.

Although it cannot be called exclusively an educational
project, the inaugural in 1974 of a bi-monthly newsletter,
Martyrdom and Resistance, has had a tremendous educational
impact on the teaching of the Holocaust. An article on this
aspect can be found in this anthology.

But what should be recorded here are the names of those
who have played a role in the impressive development of this
periodical. And, again, it was the communal involvement of
the Federation that brought about the creation of *M & R.*
The *shadchan,* or the go-between, was Rabbi Marvin Luban,
then spiritual leader of the Young Israel of Forest Hills, N.Y.,
where the first organized Yom Hashoa observance began
in 1963.

I held conversations with Rabbi Luban about a compelling need to have a formal avenue of communications whereby
we could express our feelings, give direction to Holocaust
studies, inform the public on critical issues, and highlight
events the survivors sought to share with others and among
themselves. It was Rabbi Luban who introduced me to
Dr. Harvey Rosenfeld, who was editor of the National Council
of Young Israel's *Viewpoint.* American-born, he was more
conversant with Hamlet than Hitler. This is how Dr.
Rosenfeld was brought to the attention of the Federation,
and that's how *Martyrdom and Resistance* was born.

There are so many other individuals to thank, namely
those who have written for *M & R* throughout our existence.
Some of them are represented in the anthology. But we pay special tribute to the survivors in our first editorial board: Marysia
Felberbaum, Icek Shmulevitz, and Roman Weingarten. The
first two are no longer with us, but their contributions remain.
Marysia was an articulate force in seeing that the voice of
survivors had the proper forum in our paper. Her legacy
continues as her husband, Jacob, has assumed the duties of
managing editor. Icek, a skilled writer who was so sensitive
to the experiences and needs of survivors, guided our Yiddish

pages at the beginning, when that language was the *mama lashon,* the mother tongue of most of our readers.

FEDERATION IN PARTNERSHIP WITH YAD VASHEM IN MEMORIAL THROUGH PAGES OF TESTIMONY

The late Myron Zifsider was much like Icek Shmulevitz. He had lived through the Holocaust and was keenly concerned that the past not be forgotten. With complete devotion, he devoted the last years of his life to remembrance, and in particular the Pages of Testimony.

Many of the Six Million have no precise, identifiable resting place. Their only dignified and appropriate memorial is the Page of Testimony. The Federation collected more than 10,000 pages that have been added to those at Yad Vashem. To date more than 3 million have been recorded there; as large as the sum seems, the fact remains that some 3 million *kedoshim* are unaccounted for.

The pages not only eternalize the martyrs, but perpetuate the communities, organizations, and institutions destroyed during the Holocaust.

In our times when voices are raised denying or minimizing the Holocaust, there is a critical need of making the record as clear, exact, and complete as possible.

U.S. DEPARTMENT OF JUSTICE LOOKS TO FEDERATION IN PURSUING WAR CRIMINALS

We have always stressed remembrance although the vehicle for conveying the message varied. For the Federation, one avenue of remembrance was the bringing of former Nazi war criminals to justice.

The pursuit of former Nazi war criminals is not a question of revenge but an issue of justice and a sacred obligation to the martyred that their murderers not go unpunished. Who else but survivors can give identification and evidence regarding those crimes?

Elliot Welles is a survivor from the Riga ghetto. He knows how the martyrs brutally suffered before they perished, and he knows what the survivors endured and how the emotional scars remain. He has made a commitment that justice prevail.

He coordinated the efforts of the Federation in working

closely with officials at the U.S. Department of Justice and
the Immigration and Naturalization Service, in their efforts
to deport and prosecute the war criminals. *Martyrdom and
Resistance* has continually published lists of reported Nazi
war criminals in the U.S., including their alleged crimes,
with the hope that persons can verify the crimes and contact
the authorities.

In 1979 the Federation launched Project Justice as a
means of helping persuade the West German government to
extend its statute of limitations for prosecuting Nazi war
criminals beyond its expiration at the year's end. The Federation gathered thousands of letters petitioning the Bonn government, which finally extended the statute.

In 1983 the Federation joined the Jewish Community
Relations Council of New York at a reception honoring the
officials of the Office of Special Investigations (OSI) of the
U.S. Department of Justice. The close relationship between
the Federation and the OSI was noted as Yad Vashem medals
were presented to Allan A. Ryan, Jr., director, and Neil M.
Sher, deputy director, OSI, respectively.

IN THE SERVICE OF THE SURVIVORS

Yom Hashoa observances, pages of testimony, pursuit of
Nazi war criminals, etc.–indeed, the agenda of the Federation
was very busy.

Committees mushroomed as the Federation sought to deal
effectively with all problems affecting survivors. The Federation did not meet annually at winter resorts or in the playful
atmosphere of summer vacation spots but weekly at offices,
after "normal" business hours, after each survivors had put in
a hard, long day of work.

And even at work survivors sought to deal with the needs
of survivors. Survivors called: agonizing, lamenting. They
were not only emotionally and physically victimized, but they
were struggling in many instances to keep up with basic material needs. Sympathetically and patiently, survivor James
Rapp listened in his office and advised about reparations questions. In one instance, James Rapp and his Federation committee met with the West German consul to help settle delayed
cases and achieve improved and increased benefits. The meetings resulted in closer cooperation and coordination in this
area.

Because the overwhelming numbers of survivors resided

in the Greater New York Metropolitan area, the activities of
the Federation were centered in this region. On one level, the
Federation, cooperated with, was supportive of and encouraged
the smaller organizations of survivors, often made up of those
who came from various ghettoes and towns. The Federation
provided them with materials and programming ideas. Especially noteworthy was the encouragement the Federation gave
to the Federation of Former Jewish Underground Fighters
Against Nazism. Working closely with such heroic partisans
as Seymour Sewnek Robbins, Sam Mietek Gruber and Frank
Suchy Blaichman, the Federation contributed to the success of
the organization's programs, whether it was an annual dinner
or a memorial activity.

The federation of former partisans was the initiator
through its leader Frank Blaichman of the building, together
with the American Federation of Jewish fighters, a monument
at Yad Vashem, for the Jewish soldiers that fought in World
War II.

On another level, the Federation serviced survivor organizations outside the New York area. A network of survivor
groups has been functioning in Boston, Cincinnati, the West
Coast, Atlanta, Florida, and Tucson. The Federation also cooperated with local survivors groups that were not part of
the network, such as those in Chicago and Detroit.

FEDERATION, ISRAELI CONSULATE SCREEN
MAJOR DOCUMENTARY ON THE HOLOCAUST

Despite all its projects, notwithstanding the international
circulation of *M & R*, the Federation was often mistakenly
perceived as an endemic organization, with important but
limited concerns. Those who followed the growth of the Federation knew better.

Israel had produced a stunning Holocaust film, but wanted
American Jewry to experience the drama. Israeli Consul Shlomo
Levin joined Federation officers at a New York restaurant to
plan for the special occasion. Following weeks of excitement
and heightened interest in the Jewish community, the Criterion
Theatre in Manhattan was filled on April 28, 1975, for the
U.S. premiere of "The 81st Blow," shown under the sponsorship of the Federation, in cooperation with the Israeli Con-
sulate.

The showing of "The 81st Blow"—a documentary—was one
of the most talked-about activities in the Jewish organizational

calendar during 1975. In its impressive manner, the Federation brought together as sponsors the entire spectrum of Jewish groups. Interest was so heightened that the Criterion
Theatre could not accommodate the avalanche of ticket requests.

Once more, the Federation had been imaginative in putting the message across: Genocide must never happen again.
The Jewish people cannot remain without a homeland where
peace and security prevail. In short, the Federation had
sponsored the film to broaden the knowledge and understanding of that period to serve as a call to resist the ideology and
politics of anti-Semitism and hatred.

An emotional blockbuster produced by the Beit Lohamei
Hagetaot in Israel, the film is a two-hour documentary of
previously unreleased footage filmed by the Nazis. Preceding
the premiere, those at the Criterion heard a message on the
screen from former Israeli Prime Minister Golda Meir, under
whose patronage the film was shown. Some 50 national Jewish
organizations joined the Federation as sponsors of this historic showing. Following the premiere, the Federation made
the film available to organizations, synagogues, and other
groups.

The Federation took part in a number of other broad-
based projects, among them the International Year of the
Child in 1987, under sponsorship of the United Nations
UNICEF. The Federation cosponsored a memorial for more
than one million Jewish children killed during the Holocaust.
Dr. Eva Pallay, a leader in the field of Jewish education, per-
severed in seeing this project through. The memorial in Eisenhower Park, East Meadow, New York, was held during the
period of Kristallnacht observances. "One hopes that in this
International Day of the Child," Federation President Solomon
Zynstein said, "the memorial to these innocent victims will
serve as a vigorous recommitment that there will never be
another Holocaust."

The Federation met often as a group to solve common
concerns. These meetings also featured the participation of
world personalities who shared their experiences. The appearances of Leopold Trepper, leader of the "Red Orchestra," the
Soviet anti-Nazi ring during World War II, and World Federation President Stefan Grayek were memorable events.

The appearance of Mr. Grayek also underscored the role
that the American Federation played in acting on behalf of
the World Federation. The American delegation headed the
first delegation to Poland with a mission of improving rela-

tionships, securing documents for Yad Vashem and the Auschwitz Pavilion, achieving proper maintenance of the Jewish cemeteries, opening research materials to bona fide scholars, sponsoring forums and inaugurating programs to explore the 1,000-year Polish-Jewish heritage.

FEDERATION LABORS FOR ALL ISSUES THAT TOUCH ON JEWISH SURVIVAL

Yes, in order to prevent another Holocaust, the Federation was always ready to speak out on such issues dealing with Israel, Soviet Jewry, and anti-Semitism/neo-Nazism. When the halls of the United Nations resounded in shame in 1975 with its "Zionism Is Racism" resolution, it was the Federation that galvanized the survivor community with the appropriate support that told Israel of unshakeable support, in the fullest sense.

On the 30th anniversary year of liberation from the death camps, the Federation was honored at a testimonial dinner sponsored by the Greater New York Committee for State of Israel Bonds. The Federation also showed its solidarity for the State of Israel by marching as a group at the Salute to Israel Parades.

The participation of survivors on Solidarity Sundays for Russian Jewry was channeled through the Federation, who joined other member organizations of the Greater New York Conference on Soviet Jewry in marching for the rights of Soviet Jewry.

As survivors, we have never allowed anti-Semitic or neo-Nazi developments to fester. We have registered sharp protests and sought proper remedies. There were critical episodes, in particular the book of Northwestern University professor Arthur R. Butz denying the Holocaust and a neo-Nazi demonstration in Skokie, Illinois. In both cases, the Federation response was clear.

In a letter to Northwestern President Robert H. Strotz, Federation President Solomon Zynstein stressed, "The university cannot become a privileged sanctuary for the distortion of historic facts." The university head was asked to speak out and review the tenure of Prof. Butz.

The announced march of swastika-wearing Nazis through

Skokie generated an outpouring of wrath from survivors. The
setting was the Chicago suburb, heavily Jewish, with some
7,000 Holocaust survivors. The Federation joined the battle
and telegramed President Jimmy Carter, calling upon him to
request the Solicitor General to appeal an Illinois court decision that lifted an injunction against the march. The telegram
said, "The decision of the Illinois Supreme Court is a flagrant
disregard of the right of Holocaust survivors to live in an
atmosphere free of fear and oppression."

What has been discussed so far in this review of the
Federation does not take into account the participation of the
Federation in nationwide and international events, as the
World Gathering of Jewish Holocaust Survivors in Jerusalem,
or Washington, D.C., or the liberation of Auschwitz Conference, to name but a few. Moreover, to cite two examples, Mr.
and Mrs. Sam Skura and Mr. and Mrs. Marvin Zborowski
have furthered remembrance through setting up programs at
Hillcrest Jewish Center, Queens, and Queens College, respectively. These programs were aside from their contributions of
unlimited time and financial support for the Federation.

In addition, Federation officers and members were active
in furthering remembrance goals through membership in
such bodies as the U.S. Holocaust Memorial Council.

FEDERATION JOINS WITH YAD VASHEM IN REMEMBRANCE PROGRAMS AND PROJECTS

For that reason, many of the Federation leaders looked
to the premier force in Holocaust remembrance: Yad Vashem.
An article in this anthology by Eugenia Nadler gives one an
appreciation of this unique institution.

Yad Vashem was the natural link between the Federation
and the future. Many of the Federation programs have been
inextricably linked with Yad Vashem. Six newer projects
linking the Federation with Yad Vashem are the Valley of
the Destroyed Communities,the Monument to Jewish Fighters,
the International Center for Holocaust Teaching, Comprehensive History of the Holocaust, Rescue and Restoration of
Documents, and the Children's Museum.

To advance these and other remembrance projects, the
American and International Societies for Yad Vashem were
formed, reaching across the globe, as far as Hong Kong.

ACTIVITIES HIGHLIGHTED BY INITIATION
OF VALLEY OF DESTROYED COMMUNITIES

Groundbreaking ceremonies for the Valley took place in 1983 and the first section was opened on Yom Hashoa 1987 (5747). The Valley was inaugurated in 1992-5753 and eternalizes some 5,000 communities in 22 countries destroyed during the Holocaust.

To mark the 40th anniversary of the Allied victory over the Nazis, an international gathering in Jerusalem of the Congress of the World Federation of Jewish Fighters met in the spring of 1985. At that time the Monument to Jewish Fighters was dedicated. It honored the 1.5 million Jews who fought the Nazis as soldiers in the Allied armies and as partisans. The Federation project was co-chaired by Frank Blaichman, Sam Skura, and Miles Lerman.

A stirring talk was given by Mr. Blaichman, a former commander of a Jewish partisans unit who represented the Federation of Former Jewish Underground Fighters Against Nazism.

As was characteristic of its inimitable skill, the Federation brought together survivors and children who understood the importance of the project and participated in it with much devotion. The project was a tribute to the vision of Frank Blaichman, who would not rest until his dream of a monument to the Jewish soldiers and partisans became a reality.

Throughout the years the dreams of Frank Blaichman and so many others have been realized in the cause of remembrance, working through the American Federation of Jewish Fighters and now through Yad Vashem, and, more specifically, the American and International Societies.

Where do we go now? Where will our vision lead us?

In 1993 Yad Vashem marked its 40th anniversary: four decades of remembrance, life, and remembrance beyond the Holocaust. While the survivors still breathe, we will give life, double life to remembrance. We accomplished our remarkable mission as the American Federation of Jewish Fighters, Camp Inmates, and Nazi Victims. We now look to Yad Vashem, as partners in the never-ending obligation to ensure that the world will always remember our glorious but tragic past.

The impressive story of the American Federation, Jewish Fighters, Camp Inmates, and Nazi Victims has been told in the preceding pages. As indicated in that article, the organization took part in all major events and distinguished itself in those programs touching on remembrance.

What follows are excerpts related to these events and milestones, as articulated by the President of the organization, Eli Zborowski. While they are offered as the thoughts of one individual, they can be said to reflect the broad consensus of survivors and others sympathetic to their cause.

Although the preceding article is the history of an organization, one should not lose sight of the enormous contributions in a personal sense—beyond his role organizationally—of Eli Zborowski to remembrance. At Yeshiva University, where he established the chair in Holocaust studies, Mr. Zborowski urged the inauguration of a Yom Hashoa observance at the institution and then personally underwrote the costs of the program. In fact, the first speaker at its first Yom Hashoa observance was Prof. Elie Wiesel, a program also underwritten by Eli Zborowski. His dedication to the programs at YU have produced a vigorous curriculum of Holocaust study featuring interdisciplinary courses, publications, scholarly institutes, and outreach activities.

In more than 20 years that the Yad Vashem Mobile Exhibition on the Holocaust has been circulating throughout countless communities. It opened in November, 1972, in Washington, D.C., with the participation of Prof. Wiesel and Secretary of Defense Cyrus Vance. Again, Eli Zborowski covered the costs of the exhibit, and the followup expenses of maintaining, shipping, and conveying the exhibit to the various communities.

A short time later, again, it was the benefaction of Mr. Zborowski that produced a 1,000 sets of posters. And two years later, it was Eli Zborowski once more, with 1,000 more sets produced.

These are but a few examples of the dedicated support and resources that Eli Zborowski brought personally to the cause of remembrance during the achievement era of the American Federation of Jewish Fighters, Camp Inmates, and Nazi Victims.

THE EDITORS

LIFE IN A WORLD OF IRONIES

By ELI ZBOROWSKI

(The article followed the first Annual Dinner of the American Federation of Jewish Fighters, Camp Inmates, and Nazi Victims, 1976.)

More than thirty years after the close of the Holocaust we live in an age or ironies. The dissemination and publication of Holocaust-related materials have never been more widespread. A recent article in *The New York Times* featured the growth of Holocaust materials as a significant element in the publishing industry. "The Holocaust is neither a trend nor trendy; it has become a recognized discipline," according to the story.

Interest in the Holocaust has not been lost in Hollywood, as witnessed by the production of a multimillion dollar movie spectacular this year *The Voyage of the Damned*. On a more solemn level, the Music Council of The National Jewish Welfare Board has dedicated its annual Jewish Music Festival to the music of Jewish Resistance and Survival.

More and more colleges are introducing courses on the Holocaust. The same holds true for elementary and high schools initiating curriculums in this area.

All of this would serve to give survivors a sense of accomplishment and contentment. But we live in a world of ironies. In the midst of all these activities designed to make mankind remember the dark days of the Holocaust, we have a reverse, counteractive movement.

The most blatant example is the writing of a book by a professor at one of America's renowned universities, which brazenly, almost matter-of-factly claims that the Holocaust was a hoax.

Unfortunately, the Butz incident is not an isolated occurrence. Thousands of copies of the pamphlet "Did Six Million Die?" are being distributed in British schools. There are versions of this racist booklet in Dutch and German. In France, there is a growing demand for neo-Nazi literature. The situation has been worsening in Argentina.

The resurgence of neo-Nazism in West Germany has raised great concern.

A leading Anglo-Jewish newspaper warily noted this

perilous trend, and sadly pointed a finger of blame at the Jewish defense agencies who "are weak in tackling the issues involved in the renewed spreading of the anti-Semitic lies."

As survivors, we are aware of the ironies in our society, of the satisfying achievements in the midst of perilous circumstances. We ask ourselves whether we are doing enough to teach the young generation so that they will know what happened to our people, so that they can be aware of terrifying consequences of anti-Semitism, so that they can fully understand their responsibilities in response to the pain and suffering of their brethren.

As we approach Yom Hashoa V'Hagvurah, the 27th day of Nissan, which this year is April 15, we become regretfully aware how much more remains to be done. It is necessary to be able to fulfill the rabbinic dictim—"da mah shetashiv l'apikores"—know to answer the nonbeliever, those who doubt or deny the dimensions of the tragedy of the Holocaust.

No one should underestimate the value of observing Yom Hashoa. It has a powerful impact on both participant and nonparticipant. The young observe this day as a yahrzeit, a solemn day, a time of mourning, and will continue this observance each year for the rest of their lives.

ONLY A FIRST STEP

The observance of 27 Nissan, as well as the days preceding and following that date, are truly important, but it is woefully inadequate. It is a first step. To make people aware of the tragic past, there must be meaningful activities and programs throughout the entire year.

Despite the proliferation of Holocaust-related activities, there are still too many classrooms and campuses throughout the world where students have little knowledge about the Holocaust.

As survivors we fully realize how much remains to be done. We duly note how much has been done up to now and express our gratitude to all those who have helped and all those who have participated.

But in this world of ironies, one cannot rest complacently. With the arrival of Passover to be followed by Yom Hashoa V'Hagvurah how appropriate it is to rededicate ourselves to the betterment of the young generations and generations to come through the education of our children, as is written "And you shall tell it to your son."

ESTABLISHING A MEMORIAL REFLECTING THE HOLOCAUST

By ELI ZBOROWSKI

(The article deals with the aims and goals of the newly established U.S. Holocaust Memorial Council, established by President Carter in 1978.)

The Holocaust: is it a unique or universal phenomenon? What should we remember, and what is the lesson that humanity can draw from the tragic Nazi period?

To find this answer President Carter established a Presidential Commission under the chairmanship of the famed writer Elie Wiesel. The body was empowered to discuss, study, evaluate, and present appropriate recommendations to the Chief Executive of the United States. The Commission, its Advisory Board, and added advisors held very constructive discussions during a period of six months. These proceedings enabled victims and spokesmen of atrocities from other periods and war crimes in general to be heard in order to evaluate the connection between various tragedies of mass murder.

With the sensitivity of a survivor, I took part in all the meetings and listened attentively to every word and opinion.

WIDESPREAD ATROCITIES

During World War II the German armies occupied almost all of Europe, part of Africa. Wherever they were they brought suffering to the civilian population, not only as a result of war, but through the Nazi dogma of "obermenschen," which treated others as non-persons. The Nazi brutality was especially vicious in the occupied territories in the Soviet Union, where the partisans were strongest. We note and remember how inhumanely the Russian prisoners were treated and massively killed by the German captors disregarding all internationally binding conventions.

But all these crimes committed by the German armies under Nazi rule—which by itself cannot be forgotten or forgiven—are so different from that part of Nazi ideology that called for the obliteration of an entire people—the Jewish people. Unfortunately, they succeeded in destroying thousands of Jewish communities, with their unbelievably large numbers of six million innocent civilians: children, mothers, young and old, scientists and laborers, musicians, and the entire gamut of professionals. The only crime of these victims was that they were born as Jews or half-Jews, or of some Jewish blood. This is Genocide!

These Jewish sufferings, the Jewish tragedy under the Nazis was perhaps the consequence of centuries of teachings and preachings about the 'perfidy Jew' of 2,000 years ago. The fact that the free world around us stood by leaves a lot of unanswered questions.

The uniqueness of the Jewish tragedy, the especial nature of the Holocaust, is most dramatically seen in a small Warsaw museum, in the old, rebuilt part of the city, where two film strips are featured: the Warsaw Ghetto Uprising in April, 1943, and the city of Warsaw Uprising in August, 1944. The first strip ends with the destruction of the Ghetto—and this is the end of a once-flowering Jewish community with its 500,000 people and its cultural values. And this also symbolizes the tragic end of the thousands of Jewish communities destroyed by Nazis and their collaborators.

The second film shows destruction of the city: buildings turned to rubble, innocent killing of civilians, the evacuations; and later after the war's end the return of the brave and dedicated citizens to rebuild their city. And so with much pain but determination, thousands of towns and cities were rebuilt throughout Europe.

'DIFFERENT' CRIMES

Unfortunately, the Jewish communities remain destroyed, because the Nazi crimes against the Jews were of a 'different,' unprecedented nature in the history of mankind. These were the plans and actions of individuals whose knowledge derived from schools; their technology and science came from institutions of higher education. They attended churches at some time in their life; they played with their children on the same days they were burning Jewish children.

This is the unbelievable episode in human history. This is the Holocaust! The Holocaust is the tragic event that took place in our lifetime—and we, the Jews, were the victims of the world's impotency, of humanity's unpreparedness to prevent such atrocities. The Holocaust is a unique chapter in history that has to be remembered for what happened to Jews under the Nazi regime. It also has to be taught and remembered that Jews were persecuted for centuries, and yet remained as vibrant, cultural communities that contributed to the world's progress in all areas. The lesson has to be drawn that anti-Semitism is only a beginning, and it can lead to gas chambers and other forms of mass killings.

The President's Commission would not have fulfilled its mission in presenting a balanced picture and appropriate recommendations to Mr. Carter if it had not made the trip to Europe. We visited the sites of destruction in Poland and Russia, and were confronted with the enormity of the tragedy. To see Treblinka, documented as the place where 800,000 Jews were killed, to see 1,800 stones erected for each town or city, from which Jews were transported to the place of death transmits to us the uniqueness of the Jewish tragedy— namely, that together with the victims, 1,800 Jewish communities were erased.

To see this place of death of 800,000 innocent Jews and to hear about the heroic uprising that took place at such an isolated camp: this is the message of Jewish courage in the face of death. Our knowledge became deepened about the powerlessness of the Jewish people, about how they were forsaken: after visiting Auschwitz, after visiting the site of Babi Yar, and after many meetings in Poland and Russia.

The lesson to be derived from such a unique, historic tragedy is that it cannot happen again to any people on this world, and that Nazi ideologies have to be stopped at the beginning before it is too late.

TRANSCENDING ALL BOUNDARIES

We, former camp inmates and Nazi victims, together with you, our liberators, have a duty to bear witness, to leave a legacy behind for mankind that transcends all political, social or economic boundaries, so that the lives of our dear ones and the lives of all those soldiers fallen in action will not have been in vain.

You, who opened the gates of the death camps and the concentration camps as our liberators, have an obligation to remind the world of what you saw there.

FAITH IN HUMANITY

We, as survivors, who saw both faces of humanity, the darkest hour of human history and the most noble deeds of man, want the generations to come to draw a lesson from our experiences as to what racism, anti-Semitism, and hatred can lead to.

And we want our children to retell it to their children that after all our suffering, we have not lost our faith in humanity. Just the opposite.

While we call on all decent people never to forget and not to let the world forget the horrors of the past, we want to stress our belief in humanity and reaffirm our hope that a world of friendship, freedom, and coexistence can be built and must be built.

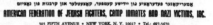

AMERICAN FEDERATION OF JEWISH FIGHTERS, CAMP INMATES AND NAZI VICTIMS, INC.

505 FIFTH AVENUE • NEW YORK, N. Y. 10017 • Tel.: 697-5670

President
ELI ZBOROWSKI

Vice President
BENJAMIN MEED

Presidium
RABBI CHASKEL BESSER
SEYMOUR ROBBINS
JOSEPH TEKULSKY
HARRY ZEGAS
SOLOMON ZYNSTEIN

Treasurer
ISAAC PULVERMACHER

Secretary
DR. HILLEL SEIDMAN

Fin. Sec'y
SAMUEL SKURA

Bulletin

April, 1972   Nisan, 5732

יום השואה
והגבורה

REMEMBRANCE DAY FOR JEWISH MARTYRDOM AND HEROISM
27th DAY OF NISAN

PROCLAMATION
DAY OF REMEMBRANCE — YOM HASHOA V'HAGVURAH
FOR JEWISH MARTYRDOM AND HEROISM
APRIL 11th, 1972 — 27th DAY OF NISSAN

WHEREAS, the Knesset of the State of Israel and Jewish Communities throughout the world have proclaimed the 27th Day of Nissan, corresponding this year to April 11, 1972, as a Day of Remembrance of the Martyrdom of 6-million of our people who perished in the European Holocaust and as a Day of Tribute to Jewish Herosim; and

WHEREAS, it is our obligation to perpetuate and keep alive the memory of our Martyrs - Kedoshim - and pay Tribute to our Heroes; and

WHEREAS, we remember the communities, synagogues and the public, cultural, educational, religious and benevolent instutions which were destroyed in an attempt to erase the name, the faith and the culture of Israel; and

WHEREAS, we pay Tribute to the Heroism of JEWISH SERVICEMEN, to the UNDERGROUND FIGHTERS, to the heroic stand of the besieged FIGHTERS OF THE GHETTOES who rose and kindled the flame of revolt in honour of their PEOPLE; and

WHEREAS, the ancient Jewish dictum "Thou shall tell thy son" offers meaningful assurance for Jewish survival in the tradition of our people; and

WHEREAS, our brethren in Israel and Jews throughout the world will gather on this assigned day to commemorate the Holocaust and pay Tribute to Jewish Heroism;

Now therefore, we - the undersigned - representing our organizations and The Jewish Community, proclaim the evening of Monday, April 10th, and Tuesday, April 11th, corresponding to the 27th Day of Nissan, as a Day of Remembrance and Observance.

We call upon all Jews to assemble in their synagogues and other appropriate places of assembly to commemorate the heroic deeds of our people in the European catastrophe.

This day must become of National Observance and Commemoration in our homes, in our synagogues, in our schools and any other places of assembly.

We call upon Rabbis and Community Leaders to make this day a Day of Observance for the entire community and to become **a permanent Day of Observance from year to year.**

Keep the Day of Martyrdom and Heroism holy.

REMEMBER THE 6-MILLION.

Light a memorial candle to their memory in your home on Monday evening, April 10th, 1972.

Front page of the 1972 American Federation Bulletin, forerunner of *M & R.*

A GATHERING IN JERUSALEM

By ELI ZBOROWSKI

(The remarks were made in 1981 at the dedication of the Heichal Shlomo Synagogue in Jerusalem, during the World Gathering for survivors and their children.)

By the grace of God I am privileged to stand witness today as a survivor of the most tragic period that befell our people. I, Eliezer Zborowski, the son of Moshe Zborowski, from the small town of Zarki, Poland, stand witness along with my fellow survivors in the eternal capital of the Jewish people. We are the surviving remnants of the once flourishing Jewish communities and are witnesses to the barbaric atrocities perpetrated by the Nazis against our people. It is our obligation, in the spirit of, "v'higadata l'vinchah," to retell our past as it actually happened for generations to come.

Here in the holy city of Jerusalem I have to recall that my father, of blessed memory, had escaped the Germans only to be killed by Polish peasants. While we remember that there were collaborators among the Polish people, we should recall that there were many righteous individuals like those who saved my mother, my brother, my sister, and myself.

We who have gathered together from the four corners of the earth are greeted here by the presence of the religious and lay leaders of Israel and the communities of the Diaspora and do now stand on the grounds of the Great Synagogues of Jerusalem. We acknowledge our presence here with thanks to the Almighty for having survived and for being able to fulfill our mission: to remind the world of the past, to draw the proper lesson, so that the future can be brighter for all of us by preventing similar atrocities.

The survivors hereby proclaim before the entire world that we will never forget our brethren who sanctified themselves during their lifetime and who did not separate themselves from our people when they fell before the despicable Nazis. While consecrating the name of Heaven and Israel, we pray that the blood of the Six Million Kedoshim not be covered up and that vengeance come upon the enemy.

We who came out from hiding, from the forests as partisans and from the death camps, have come to the State

of Israel, where the majority of survivors have found a home
and have helped build a united country.

We have come to the State of Israel and stand proudly
united in proclaiming our aims. We declare our solidarity with
Israel. We will always remember and are vigorous in our
determination that there will not be another Holocaust.

Valley of the Destroyed Communities at Yad Vashem.

THE OTHER FACE OF HUMANITY

By ELI ZBOROWSKI

(From an address at a 1981 conference of liberators of the Nazi death camps, sponsored by the U.S. Holocaust Memorial Council.)

We, the survivors of the Holocaust, are grateful to the soldiers of the Allied Forces who liberated us from Nazi tyranny. We owe our entire lives to you. As members of the United States Holocaust Memorial Council, we are privileged to greet you as our guests at this historic meeting of the liberators together with the survivors. We welcome you, who have come from far and near, to share with us a few days of recollection.

We who witnessed man's inhumanity to man also bear witness to the finest in man. We have seen both faces of humanity. We witnessed the German atrocities committed against innocent civilians, the murder of six million Jews, the destruction of hundreds of villages, and the complete destruction of the Jewish communities and their culture in Europe.

WITNESSING COURAGE AND BESTIALITY

We then lived to see the other face of humanity, the dedication to a common aim—the defeat of Nazism. We have seen the courageous soldiers who displayed heroism in saving us, the remnants of European Jewry. The Allied Armies crushed the Nazi beast and restored peace and freedom to a suffering, occupied Europe.

Yesterday we heard our Chairman, the renowned author Elie Wiesel, recall, in a way only possible for Elie Wiesel, the survivor's feelings at the moment of liberation. This morning we heard a most moving eyewitness account of Colonel Dr. Michael Chilczuk, who recalled what he had seen when he and his Polish unit as part of the Soviet Army liberated the concentration camp of Sachsenhausen.

We heard Rabbi Herschel Schacter, who as a young chaplain of the American Army was confronted with the indescribable reality of the concentration camp of Buchen-

wald. Rabbi Schacter moved to tears the generals and other
participants when he described the eyes of the skeletons looking at him in disbelief when he said to them in Yiddish: "Jews,
Jews, you are free. I am an American, an American Jew;
you are free, Jews."

We toast the brave and heroic armies of the East and the
West, the sons of those countries who laid down their lives in
their fight against Nazism and who gave us life once more.

We, Jews, the only people destined by the Nazis for a
final solution, were saved and Fascism was defeated thanks
to the Allied Forces, thanks to your bravery.

We are alive, yes, we are here, although only remnants of
the once flourishing European Jewish communities, and we
are here thanks to you, our liberators. . . .

RECALLING THE HEROES

I recall January 17, 1945, as the day when I was liberated
by the Soviet Forces led by General Vassily Petrenko, who
came from Moscow to participate in this conference, and
whose soldiers entered the death camp of Auschwitz on the
following day.

There were other heroic people during the Holocaust.
We recall the Partisans and organized resistance throughout
Europe that fought the Germans behind the front lines. We
remember the lonely battle of the Warsaw Ghetto and the
uprising in other ghettos. We recall the brave soldiers of the
Jewish Brigade. And we remember with special gratitude
and recognition those Righteous Gentiles who risked their
lives to save Jews.

GRATITUDE FOR RIGHTEOUS GENTILES

My family was saved by such heroic individuals in western Poland, and my wife, a child of 13, all alone, was saved
by a Polish woman in eastern Poland. We recall with over-
flowing joy the liberation, but, unfortunately, liberation came
too late for many suffering people, too late for my father. So
was the liberation too late for six million Jews and millions
of other victims.

Our meetings at the State Department are symbolic.
Today they are our hosts, while during the years of the
Holocaust, we were denied entry visas to the free world.

Today, we are grateful to all those countries who received us after the war and gave us a place to live so that we could rebuild our lives and our families and become once more, contributing members of society and, in countless instances, today's leaders and influential citizens.

REMEMBERING THE COMMUNITIES
THAT WERE ANNIHILATED

By ELI ZBOROWSKI

*(Remarks at the cornerstone laying ceremony in 1983 of
the Valley of the Destroyed Communities at Yad Vashem,
held during the World Assembly to Commemorate Jewish
Resistance and Combat During World War II.)*

It is because of the very existence and work of Jerusalem's Yad Vashem, fountainhead and inspiration for scores
of smaller Yad Vashems throughout the world—though perhaps known by other names—that the resolution has been
made to resist all acts of bigotry and persecution against
innocent people. This is the path for preventing another
Holocaust, be it against Jews or other people.

In this year of Jewish resistance we honor those who
fought during World War II. We salute those whose resistance
took many forms: in the ghettoes, in the forests as partisans,
in the camps as inmates—those who resisted wherever possible.
The world has forgotten to honor those who, faced with
almost certain death, resisted with arms. However elementary
their implements may have been, they resisted against the
might of the Nazi hordes, equipped with the most advanced
devastating weapons.

Not all resistance was physical. There were those who
helped one another in ways small and large—at the risk of
one's life. And there were countless thousands who surrendered their lives so that they could remain with their
families to the end.

And as we observe the 40th anniversary of Jewish
resistance, we remember the fight for life of every man,
woman, and child who perished at the hands of the German
Nazis and their collaborators.

The mere fact that some of us survived is living testimony
of the physical and moral struggle of the Jewish people during
the Holocaust.

We are gathered for the groundbreaking ceremony of the
Valley for the Destroyed Jewish Communities. It is most appropriate that in the year of Jewish resistance, we, the
generation of survivors, memorialize for all eternity the

Jewish communities that were annihilated during the Holocaust. . . .

It is envisaged that this Valley, when completed, will become a major national memorial not only for our times, but for generations to come. It is our hope that it will be completed successfully with the help not only of the people of Israel but of Jews, the world over, who will deem it a privilege to participate in this sacred task. . . .

And so, at this groundbreaking on the Mount of Remembrance, let us each, in his own way, take a silent oath to those who perished. In the face of intolerance and evil we shall not be still; in the face of bigotry, we shall speak out; in the face of violence, born of that evil and bigotry, we will resist.

At 2nd Annual Dinner, American Federation of Jewish Fighters, Camp Inmates and Nazi Victims, 1978. Honorees were Icek Shmulevitz and Sam Skura (l. to r.) : Federation president Solomon Zynstein; Mrs. Shmulevitz; Mr. Shmulevitz; Simon Weber, editor, *Jewish Daily Forward*; Eli Zborowski, dinner chairman. The dinner celebrated four milestones: 30th anniversary, State of Israel; 35th anniversary, Warsaw Ghetto Uprising; 35th year, liberation from Nazism; 8th anniversary, American Federation.

40 YEARS AFTER THE TYRANNY

By ELI ZBOROWSKI

(From a message at the Western Wall during the Israeli gatherings in 1985 to commemorate the 40th anniversary of Allied Victory.)

I share with you a great sense of privilege at being able to stand here with you, in front of the Kotel, at ceremonies marking the 40th anniversary of the end of Nazi tyranny—of the triumph of good over evil. Personally, I am overwhelmed with emotion and gratitude at being able to stand here with you in what is the holiest place for us, the Jewish people. . . .

It hardly seems possible that forty years have already passed: 40 years—so many thoughts. So many agonizing questions have passed through our minds in the intervening years —so many memories too, memories of those who survived, and of those who did not survive.

There are also memories of the brutal German war machinery, of sadism and savagery intermingled with memories of acts of self-sacrifice, courage, and love—memories of tears and tears of memories. . . .

I was liberated by the Soviet army on January 17, 1945, not far away from my home town. I vividly recall how I returned to an empty town and, while feeling sad at what I say, the full impact only hit me on May 9, 1945, when the Second World War ended, and I found myself in the city of Lodz. I was wearing the uniform of a soldier and was ready to fight the Nazi enemy while around me the city celebrated the end of the war. Only then could I cry. I recall that I, as a young man of 19, walked around the streets crying and feeling desolate because it was only then that I began to realize the full implication of what I had witnessed and so few of us had the good fortune, through the grace of God, to survive.

It was then that I began to comprehend the difference between the rest of the people around me who had reason to rejoice at the victory of the Allied forces over the German Nazis and us—Jews—and what had happened to our people after the attempt to annihilate us—the Jewish people. . . .

FIGHTERS AND THE MONUMENT

In paying tribute to all who fought Nazi Germany and their satellites, it is to the Jewish soldiers of all nations and especially to the volunteers from the Jewish Brigade in Palestine and to the Jewish fighters in the ghettos and forests of Europe to whom we owe our special gratitude, for it was they and only they alone who fought with special zeal and mission to save fellow Jews. All in total, one and one-half million Jewish fighters fought in the various Allied armies and in the partisan units. It is, therefore, quite fitting that the survivors of the former Jewish underground fighters have been instrumental in erecting the monument in tribute to the Jewish fighters during World War II which was just unveiled today in their honor on the Mount of Remembrance at Yad Vashem in Jerusalem. . . .

Forty years after the most tragic period of Jewish history we gather in the eternal capital of the Jewish people to express thanks to the Almighty for having lived to this day. We assemble here on the 40th anniversary of defeat of Nazi Germany to pay tribute to the brave Jewish soldiers, to the Jewish partisans and underground fighters of World War II. . . .

M & R at Fourteen

By Dr. Luba K. Gurdus

Mazel Tov!

Martyrdom and Resistance has celebrated 20 years. More than just a time of joy for the periodical, it is a season of joy and accomplishment for its thousands of readers, especially the survivors of the Holocaust.

Three decades after the end of World War II, *Martyrdom and Resistance* emerged from the pioneering stride of Holocaust survivors, united in the American Federation of Jewish Fighters, Camp Inmates and Nazi Victims. Increasingly mindful of the flagrant injustice of passing into oblivion, they were finally ready to raise a collective voice on behalf of their forcibly silenced brethren. Impelled by a consuming sense of mission and long-harbored urge to keep the promise, they decided to create a publication which would assist their effort and enhance the survivors' zeal to restore the dissipating history of the annihilated millions and bring their ordeal repeatedly to the attention of the world.

Martyrdom and Resistance, a modest four-page paper, made its first public appearance in September, 1974, hardly forecasting the spectacular expansion experienced in the ensuing years. From its inception, its destiny was interwoven with the growing interest in the Holocaust and its future was determined by objectives bound to touch a vital cord in every Jew. The issues of "martyrdom" and "resistance" consistently lingered on the minds of survivors, guarding the precious heritage of the lost martyrs and the innermost truth about their spiritual and physical resistance. Thus, *M & R* set out as an open forum for survivors, scattered around the globe and provided them with a vehicle for joint sharing and remembering. Dr. Harvey Rosenfeld, the periodical's editor, well aware of its aims and objectives, stresses that remembrance consistently was and still is its "keyword." The publication became a link between survivors, informing them of plans and projects of mutual interest and uniting them in the Holocaust-related activities, observances, gatherings and commemora-

---

Dr. Gurdus is a survivor and author of *The Death Train.*

tions for the lost millions and destroyed cradles of Jewish living and learning.

It is very fitting that the editorial board was composed of survivors. Working with Dr. Rosenfeld and survivor Eli Zborowski were Marysia Felberbaum, Icek Shmulevitz, and Roman Weingarten, all survivors.

The bi-monthly became a guide for its readers through the maze of scholarly, cultural, artistic and human-interest material; but at all times it remained a useful source of information about all generations of survivors. One of its compelling features is its "Survivors' Corner," solely devoted to "Voices of Survivors" including book reviews, articles, and excerpts from unpublished war manuscripts, diaries and poetry, plunging the readers into the past life and strife of the Holocaust.

The bimonthly's ambitious objectives are best demonstrated in the extensive subject Index of 1984, covering a decade of its existence. It is studded with entries to a variety of news of political, social, theological, cultural and other nature, dealing with the timely and sensational developments and touching on crucial issues of neo-Nazism and Nazi criminals and collaborators still at large.

What is very noticeable is the emphasis on survivors. Throughout the years, there have been more than 500 news stories and features on survivors: their experiences, reflections, and achievements after the Holocaust; observations by the families and children of survivors; and the activities and programs of survivor groups, notably the American Federation of Jewish Fighters, Camp Inmates, and Nazi Victims.

A special mention should be made of the consistent reporting on the lasting kinship with Israeli survivors and the close bond with Yad Vashem in all cultural endeavors and projects, including the jointly completed monumental memorial, The Valley of Destroyed Communities, supported by American survivors, headed by Eli Zborowski. Exhaustive coverage is also reserved for Holocaust education and news from the "Campus and Classroom . . ." The educators, contributing to the periodical, imply that the lesson of this major disaster with its flagrant violations, surpassing conventional injustice common to normative social systems, has an enormous impact on students and contributes to effective human rights education. They bring to the attention of the scholarly community the strides in methodology and the curricula developed in major national centers, namely the three volumes of The Human Rights Series published by The University of the

State of New York on "Teaching About the Holocaust and Genocide."

The bi-monthly's continuous growth is evident in all its sections, particularly in the consistently expanding media and book reviews. Relevantly, the many book reviewers, assigned according to their personal preference and expertise, also feature survivors, considered best qualified to provide a deeper insight into Holocaust memoirs and assess their documentary value. Similar considerations assure this section's particular merit for researchers, educators and students.

With its load of essentially varied information, the periodical is easily accessible. Informal and lively, it is not constrained by a rigid lineup of essays but marked by a flexibility of ever changing patterns of articles coupled with inserted sections of smaller items. In spite of continuously changing volume, the publication adheres to a set layout, conditioned by its purpose and direction.

During its 20 years of existence, *M & R* has become an accepted source of Holocaust reference material for libraries, public institutions, community centers, schools and the general public. It has tried to sensitize its readers to the meaning of martyrdom and resistance of six million European Jews during the long years of the Holocaust. It hopefully also enhances public understanding and recognition of the universal implications and centrality of the unprecedented event in human history. It reports on the crucial, Holocaust-related issues and acts as calendar for collective commemorations on a national and world-wide basis.

The bi-monthly developed into a meritorious resource due to the effort of Eli Zborowski, survivor, founder and editor-in-chief, whose exemplary dedication and commitment kept it well and alive. While other publications of similar nature, depending on public funding, were forced to fold after limited existence, *M & R* is consistently progressing and expanding. Its contribution to the preservation and understanding of the message and memory of the Holocaust cannot be over-estimated, while its reputation and popularity are already well established and a matter of pride and personal satisfaction to the editors, the editorial committee, and the many contributors. And, certainly, its most cherished readers continue to be the survivors, whose experiences and achievements have been realized as a legacy recorded.

FOR SOME MEASURE OF HUMILITY

By ELIE WIESEL

One generation later, it can still be said and must now be affirmed: There is no such thing as a literature of the Holocaust, nor can there be. The very expression is a contradiction in terms. Auschwitz negates any form of literature, as it defies all systems, all doctrines; to confine it to a philosophy is to minimize it, to distort it.

Ask a survivor, any one of them, and he will bear me out. Those who have not lived through the experience will never know; those who have will never tell; not really, not completely. Here you will find books to be of little help; paltry commentaries, they merely serve as guides. Between the memories of a survivor and their portrayal in words, even his own, there exists an unbridgeable gulf. The past belongs to the dead and the survivor does not recognize himself in the images and ideas which presumably depict him. A novel about Auschwitz is not a novel, or else it is not about Auschwitz. The very attempt to write such a novel is blasphemy, as is any attempt to explain or justify, for any explanation is a form of justification. Here ignorance borders on falsehood and deceit. This you must know, if you haven't understood it yet: Auschwitz means death, total, absolute death—of man and of all people, of language and imagination, of time and of the spirit. Its mystery is doomed to remain intact.

The survivor knows. He and no one else. And so he is obsessed by guilt and helplessness.

Bearing true witness: a painful and fearful task. For the fact that he has survived commands him to bear witness. But how can he speak up without committing treason against himself and others? A dialectical trap from which there is no escape: the true witness must be silent. Even if he succeeded in speaking the unspeakable, he would not be understood.

And yet, in the beginning, in a world still in ruins, he forced himself to come forth, and at least partially to lift the veil, not in an attempt to free himself of the past, but rather out of loyalty to it. In his eyes, forgetting meant that the enemy had won. The executioner always kills twice, the second time to cover all traces and evidence of his crime. To forget is to become his accomplice. One had to testify, in order that there be no forgetting.

A painful and thankless task, causing fear and remorse.
The words which the witness, strung together, the images
he summoned up seemed all too pale compared with their substance. The essence defied expression, resisted utterance, remained unspoken, on the other side; there was more intensity,
more weight, more truth in what he left unsaid. The panic
in the eyes of the old people, the whispers of children turned
old in the face of death, the silent solemn march of the
victims as though drawn to the flames and to the night; the
selections, the mass graves, those who said *Kaddish* for their
own death and for the living: he couldn't describe it and yet he
had to: A special language and vocabulary should have been
invented to say what no human being had ever said, nor ever
will.

Have you ever read, really read the stories told by the
survivors? They seem as though written by the same man.
Reluctant and fearful, he testifies quietly and says little; he
speaks in a whisper, as though guilt-ridden; he writes not with
words, but almost against them. Rather than communicating
the experience itself, he reveals his inability to fully express it.

The testimony of survivors inspired awe and humility.
At first, the question was treated with a sort of sacred rever-
ence. It was considered taboo, reserved exclusively for the
imitated. The great novelists of our times, the likes of Camus,
Mauriac, Faulkner, Silone, Agnon, were careful not to tackle
the subject. They acted out of respect for the dead as well as
the survivors. And they were also concerned about the truth.
In this peculiar domain, truth is stranger than fiction, which
they understood. Here, the imagination pales by the side of
reality. Their artistic and intellectual integrity barred them
from venturing on grounds haunted by so many ghosts and
buried under ashes.

The stories which were published resembled documentaries. These real-life stories could engulf the reader like a
nightmare, causing his heart to pound, instilling a feeling
of poignant excitement. This, one felt, was not an artist's
creation, but rather something transcending art and literature;
something altogether different. Following the protagonist in
his delusion of expression, one was carried away by his voice,
one tried to share his despair, but that was all. One remained
outside and behind. No one passed judgment; no one dared,
not yet. For want of a yardstick, a guideline, the survivor
was granted the right to forge his own style, to choose his
own form and mode of expression. A measure of humility still
prevailed.

But popularization and exploitation soon followed. And then, with the passing of time, it all began to deteriorate. As the subject became popularized, so it ceased to be sacrosanct, or rather was stripped of its mystery. People lost their awe. The Holocaust became a literary "free-for- all," the "no man's-land" of modern writing. Now everyone got into the act. Novelists made free use of it in their work, scholars used it to prove their theories, politicians to win votes. In so doing they cheapened the Holocaust; they drained it of its substance. The Holocaust was now a hot topic, fashionable, guaranteed to gain attention and to achieve instant success.

To ward off survivors' criticism, the exclusive right to that title was taken away from them. Suddenly, everyone began calling himself a survivor. Having compared Harlem to the Warsaw ghetto and Vietnam to Auschwitz, a further step has now been taken: some who had spent the war on a Kibbutz, or in a fancy apartment in Manhattan, now claim that they too have "survived" the Holocaust, probably by proxy. One consenquence is that an international symposium on the Holocaust was held recently in New York without the participation of any Holocaust survivors.

You are amazed? The survivors don't count; they never did. They are best forgotten. Don't you see? They are an embarrassment. If only they weren't there, it would be so much easier.

Please understand: I am not saying that the event should not be studied, explored and commented upon; quite the contrary, it should be. Nor do I deny the fact that some writers and scholars, including close friends, have helped to sensitize the rising generation to its various implication: their encounter with the Holocaust has profoundly altered their thinking, heightened their awareness and made their personal outlook more genuine. Some have become more religious and others less; all have moved closer to our people. I have nothing but respect for them, and they know it.

The profanity of facile and vulgar discussion I am referring to are the others, the majority, those in whom the themes inspire no humility. I am referring to all those who in their all-knowing arrogance becomes its profaners. They bring vulgarity into this domain too. They remind one of Job's false friends. Do you remember? Job suffers and it is they who speak. Worse yet: they explain his pain to him.

Yes, it is true, the survivors will soon be unwelcome, intruders. No more do we listen to them. Their assassins are now in the limelight. They are shown in films, they are scrutinized, they are humanized. They are studied at first with objectivity, then with sympathy. One movie shows a young Jewish girl in love with a militiaman. Another tells of the loves of a Jewish woman and a former SS. Gone are the days when the dead had their special place and gone the days when their lives commanded respect. People are more interested in their killers: so handsome and attractive, such a pleasure to watch. One forgets that there are still survivors among us. And that they remember. And that they know.

But then—who cares? Let their feelings be hurt. Their sensitivity is nobody's problem but their own. Their attitude exists among Jewish and non-Jewish intellectuals alike. They say it openly in journals and speeches. They blame the survivors for being obsessively attached to the past, for rubbing salt into their wounds, for engaging in self-pity, for exploiting their suffering. And to top it all, those who are so vulgar as to say this in public are the same ones who use the Holocaust in their own writings time and again.

For today a book about the Holocaust is a book like any other, produced by literary technicians. Anyone can write it: words, words which are carefully weighed, measured, borrowed for their market value, words distorted to satisfy some sort of thirst for vanity, or intrigue, or revenge. It is as though the survivors no longer existed.

And yet, they are there. And they hear you. And you are being judged by their despair.

M&R 2:5, Jan.-Feb., 1976
Reprinted by permission of *Shma* © Oct. 30, 1975

CHALLENGES FACING "SURVIVORS"

By Moshe Arens

... My family fled ... Riga, in what was then Latvia, on September 7, 1939, the seventh day of World War II, and found a haven in America. Less than two years later, on July 1, 1941, the German Army entered Riga, and within a matter of months my first home—family, friends, almost the entire Jewish community of Riga—was destroyed.

These were the days before the Germans had perfected the gas ovens for industrialized mass killings. The Jews of Riga were butchered. The killings began on November 29, 1941, at Rumbuli near Riga. The Jews had been herded into a ghetto shortly after the German occupation of the city. Now they were being transported to Rumbuli for the slaughter. In a blood bath that lasted several days: 30,000 of Riga's 40,000 Jews—men, women and children—were beaten and shot to death. By the end of the war, only one out of ten of the Jewish community survived.

Ever since, I have counted myself among the survivors of the Holocaust. Even though I did not witness the scenes of horror, I carry with me to this day the feeling that I was there at Rumbuli on those cold winter days and saw how thousands were ordered to undress, were beaten, pushed to the edge of forest graves dug by Russian prisoners of war, and slaughtered. This feeling has accompanied my waking hours, has entered my dreams at night. This memory has stamped my life and shaped my beliefs. It is with a sense of obligation to my people, born of this memory, that I have lived my adult life. And it is with this realization that I pledged to devote myself to the upbuilding of the Jewish State in Israel.

Does the Holocaust not carry a similar meaning to each and every Jew who was fortunate not to be in the slaughterhouse of Europe during World War II? The Haggadah, which we read each year at the Passover Seder, says: "In each generation must we see ourselves as if we had taken part in the exodus from Egypt." In an even more literal sense, ... in our time every Jew must see himself as a survivor of the Holocaust. We must feel as if we had been imprisoned in the ghettos, as if we had been through the slaughterhouse, as if we had been through the death camps.

We survived by the will of the Almighty—and were com-

61

manded to devote our talents and energy to following the
commandment: *"never again!"*

It was the last will and testament of the six million who
were murdered that we—the survivors—should build in our ancient homeland the secure haven for the Jewish people that
was not there when it was needed in the years of Hitler's
terror.

. . . And yet, the State of Israel was established only after
the Holocaust, only after the Jewish people came close to
being wiped off the face of the earth. And yet, Israel has
faced the danger of military defeat and destruction, by enemies
more numerous and better armed. And yet, to this day, Israel's
citizens are threatened by assualts on their physical security.

Could it have been different? You might reply: "What
is the use of asking rhetorical questions as to what might have
been?" And yet, these questions continue to haunt us—the past
is still the best guide we have to the future, to the future of
the Jewish people.

. . . Had the Jews of Europe heeded Ze'ev Jabotinsky's call
for mass evacuation to Palestine, hundreds of thousands,
maybe millions, would have been saved. Israel would have
attained independence earlier, possibly before the outbreak of
World War II. It could have provided a haven for the Jews
seeking to flee Europe. The fate of the Jewish people would
have been profoundly affected.

Much has been said recently about what might have been
done to save European Jewry during the years of the Holocaust. There are those who insist that nothing could have
been done. They must be reminded that when in April, 1943,
the revolt broke out in the Warsaw Ghetto, Hitler's armies
had already been beaten back at Stalingrad, Rommel had been
defeated in North Africa, and the Allies had attained superior-
ity on land, at sea and in the air. It was only then that Hitler's
machine of death was swinging into high gear.

The dimensions of the German onslaught on the Jews of
Europe were already known in 1943. If putting a stop to the
slaughter had been one of the strategic objectives of Allied
strategy, it is difficult to believe that many could not have been
saved. The fact is that it did not appear on the agenda of
Allied strategy. Did Jewish leadership in the free world exert
all their efforts to make the saving of the Jews in Europe a
central part of Allied strategy? Could this objective have been
attained with additional effort? We may never know the
answer to these tragic questions, but they will continue to
haunt us for generations to come. . . .

Let us stop for a moment and ask ourselves what might have been: if instead of the 260,000 Jews who left Europe for Palestine between World War I and World War II, millions had taken that path; if a concentrated effort by the American Jewish community had succeeded in making the saving of European Jewry a central aim of Allied war strategy in World War II.

The twentieth century will be recorded in history as a time when the Jewish people were almost destroyed, rose from the ashes of the Holocaust, and fought to reestablish their own state—the State of Israel. Much has been accomplished, much remains to be accomplished.

We like to pride ourselves on Israel's achievements. We want to believe that Israel is secure and, therefore, we sometimes belittle the difficulties still facing us. We are beleaguered by totalitarian states—most, hostile to Israel; many at war with us. We are surrounded by societies with long traditions of fanaticism, brutality, and intolerance. Day to day, we continue the fight for our security. . . . In these travails Israel needs support—moral, political, economic—and we are receiving such support from the American Jewish community on a scale without precedent.

This is the challenge that faces us: all of us survivors of the Holocaust. It faces us in Israel and you in America. It cannot be ignored. It has to be addressed. Means must be found—I say can be found—to meet this challenge. This is the test of our leadership and yours. It will no doubt be seen as such in future generations. It is a test we dare not fail.

M&R 10:4, Jan.-Feb., 1984

The above are excerpts from remarks by Israeli Defense Minister Moshe Arens, upon receiving an honorary doctorate from Yeshiva University.

TO MY FELLOW SURVIVORS:
AN OPEN LETTER

By HANNA HIRSHAUT

We devote our efforts and our energy to the preservation and sanctification of the memory of six million martyrs who perished during the Holocaust. We promise never to forget. We must go on with this work till the end of our lives and make sure that our children take over this responsibility.

At a meeting of the second generation of survivors, I listened to a young woman who said that researchers are beginning to gather information concerning survivors of the Holocaust . . . how they functioned and coped after the trauma . . . of all the horrors they witnessed and suffered.

This made me aware that the time has now come at the twilight of our lives to speak up and set the record straight. It is important that we leave our own evaluation of how we conducted ourselves and what we are leaving behind.

I think that probably nobody will do this more objectively and honestly than we, ourselves, looking at each other and coming to a conclusion that on the whole we are proud of our achievements and the way we conducted our lives under the most trying circumstances. Time has come to leave behind whatever feelings of guilt, inadequacy, and failure many of the survivors lived with up till now.

Look at the record. We were almost naked when we were liberated: be it from concentration camps, hiding, living on false papers or fighting in the forests. We were destitute with no money, no home, no possessions, no relatives, and no country.

History and literature tell us that after the enemy is defeated, the victors take revenge in every possible way. Look what happened. We could have, but did not, chase out the Poles from our homes and villages that they took over during our incarceration. Our possessions they robbed us of were never returned. We didn't take to the streets in Germany to kill, torture, burn, and rape or smash children against walls. We didn't even collect the thousands of tons of furs or trainloads of furniture and galleries of priceless art that were confiscated from every Jewish home that had anything of value. The amount of money and precious jewels will never be evaluated or accounted for.

64

To receive the meager tokens of restitution for lost health, we went to hell and back and waited for years for the decrees of German courts, and still many were rejected for no reason at all. Till this day the overwhelming majority of the survivors did not receive nor wanted reparations for murdered relatives.

There are those who ask, "Why didn't you take revenge?" The answers are many and probably each survivor had his own reasons. Some survivors may say: we were too weak and too sick to do anything in the very beginning after the liberation; but the most prevalent reasons are: we were not murderers, rapists, and thieves. Our moral and ethical background prevented us from becoming the beast that was dormant in the German Herrenvolk.

Our great heritage and moral dignity carried us through the ghettos and the concentration camps. The heroism of the martyrs and survivors is unprecedented. The self-sacrifices of parents for children, brothers for brothers, strangers for strangers and countless stories of self-denial in order to save a fellow man will never be fully known. With the exception of a few "rotten apples," the majority of the survivors can proudly take place in the "hall of fame" of the human race.

The struggles to start new lives, new families and new careers were both so braindraining and backbreaking because our new homes were now in another country and in settings of a different language. But we made it! Sure, most of us were deeply affected by the persecutions and hunger suffered during the Holocaust and many died since, as a result, but we tried to lead normal lives, many achieving the highest successes be it financial, academic, or scientific.

We brought up a second generation that we can be proud of, for they, too, strive for the highest careers and finest achievements.

We formed and joined community organizations and contributed to countless causes, never shrinking from responsibilities to do our best. The survivors were a contributing force wherever they settled—from South and North America, to Australia, from South Africa to Europe and, of course, Israel, where survivors as a group have made the most vital contribution in the fight for independence and in the defense of the Jewish homeland. In all these countries we never became a burden to the society.

The time has come to stress the positive in our lives instead of the sad and painful. The world around us has to understand that each one of us is in a way a hero, because

surviving in Nazi times was a superhuman effort. They tried
to annihilate the roots and branches. They tried to break our
bodies, our minds, our spirit. They succeeded in annihilating
the roots and many times in breaking our bodies, but the
branches survived and took new roots; and our minds and
spirit are strong and determined.

I wonder if the time hasn't come to tell our children and
our grandchildren about the great things in our past, before
and during the Holocaust, rather than constantly remind them
of sufferings.

Let's pick up our heads and let's help the new researchers
and historians to understand this phenomenon called "The
Survivor and the Holocaust."

Let us and other people stop asking the question: Why
did we survive and not the others? I don't think that there is
an answer, but maybe some Divine force selected us, as the
"chosen" inheritors of what once was the great European
Jewry and also to bear witness to the horrors of the Holocaust.

We are the phoenixes who burned, but rose from the
ashes, to carry the torch and to hand it over to the next
generation. The legacy we are leaving behind is rich in sufferings but also in triumphs and it should make our children
proud of us.

M&R 10:5, Jan.-Feb., 1984

REFUGEES

We were severed limbs of a tree
pick-up sticks to pyromaniacs
roasting our skin like marshmallows.
We were phantom arms and legs
of an amputee creeping
out of the smoking heap.
We were fevered by visions
of roots like fingers
implanted in the earth's belly.
Two by two, we boarded the boat
Noah's grateful beasts
to salvage what was left.
America! America! America!
We chanted the magic word of passage.
Our daughter sat quiet as baggage.

SONIA PILCER

M&R 2:3, Jan.-Feb., 1976

A SURVIVOR'S MEMORIES
REMAIN UNCHANGED

By Dr. Vera Laska

Twenty-four centuries ago, Heraclitus stated that the only constant in life is change. Yet, my memories do not change. They remain as a refrain that returns with the same tunes and images, with the same smell of scorched flesh and of bones that are glowing embers, with the same flames shooting towards a sky in search of God.

My memories remain unchanged. I cultivate them in solitude, for people around me nowadays would not understand them. I keep them as a bouquet of grotesque flowers, unknown on these happy and innocent American shores. They are called Auschwitz, Gross-Rosen, Nordhausen, Dora, and these are interspersed with weeds of cruelty, greed, and malice. They are all of various shades of gray, and the ribbon holding them together is black sorrow. I am mourning millions I never knew and those few dozen among them whose lives touched upon mine and whom I called friends, who were lost in the complex Holocaust called World War II.

My eyes have seen what can not be expressed in words, ever. Yet

That one triumph the gods bestowed upon men,
That only wounded can a heart claim victory.

Otakar Fiser: *Devisa*.

Just to die was a lark. It was the fear of dying, the steady, mental anguish visited upon us by virulent malevolence that time whipped into an agonizing ordeal, kneelhauling our souls day after day, without let-up, that was so hard. What made us endure it? It was partly the moral support that we gave each other. The five of us who stood so many *Appels* (roll calls) together were a closely knit unit: Olga, who managed to keep up her spirits and with it ours; her sister, Alice, who often saved her sanity with her lovely voice, singing us into dreams of the past; Verice, who even at the gates of hell preserved her purity and never succumbed to malice. We are all alive: in Canada, Yugoslavia, and in the United States. Nothing can ever come between us.

The fifth member was our camp baby Ribzili from

Rumania—all of 12 or 13 years old, she was not sure. She had bright, lively eyes, our Pygmalion, whom I taught to read the clock, who did not know the multiplication table; yet, she would compute with lightning speed the chances of survival, the fastest "organizer" with the instinctive shrewdness of two adults. I wanted to adopt her as my sister after the war.

I lost her in the madness of the last hunger march. We know that she survived the end of the war, but she disappeared and did not report at the checking point we all agreed on. Investigations in several countries were futile. Yet, she remains forever in our hearts as the breath of spring in our darkest winters.

How did I survive the physical and mental dehumanization? I believe through a fortuitous constellation of an originally healthy body, accidental luck, and, above all, strong will, that constructive force that rules emotions and guides intuition and imagination, and channels sentiments and temperament into a disciplined personality.

Those who despaired did not last long. Broken spirits could not protect abused bodies. Willpower, determination, even hatred, positive thinking, and mental energy were the lifelines of endurance, hence of existence itself.

There is not much use philosophizing, interpreting, or engaging in metaphysical speculation over the Holocaust. Such exercises limit the scope of communication to a select few. That also is the very reason I switched from studying philosophy to history. What is needed is the propagation of detached, stark truth, for facts are the clearest and most comprehensible carriers of the message, understood by all.

We who returned from the depths of hell, we the survivors, are standing guard that history should not repeat itself. But there are too few of us. You, the present and future generations, have to be the sentinels of human decency to prevent the recurrence of the obscenity of man toward man that was the Holocaust.

Of the handful of us who returned to life, some are broken in body and spirit. A few others are luckier. I know what is thirst, and hunger, cold, and fear. I know what life is all about, for I have tasted death. The experience did not break me. It made me stronger. While the black lace of sorrow will forever be draped over my heart, paradoxically I am capable of enjoying happiness more than those who did not savor the wages of fear.

I gained the gift of knowing how to live life to the fullest, body and soul. I carry in me constantly the awareness that I want to see and hear and know as much and as many people as possible, for knowledge is power and knowledge is happiness. Those who resist partaking in knowledge are the beggars of the world, cheating themselves of their share of humanity's bounties, and undeserving of the gift of life.

I consciously enjoy the sunrise at daybreak or the frolicking of the wind in the treetops. I rejoice over the laughter of a child and the beauty of a book. I am happy that I have food to eat and a clean bed to sleep in. I pity all those who do not know how to appreciate their plenties and, thus, shortchange themselves of so much gratification and pleasure. Above all, I cherish my freedom to listen and to speak without fear.

Those without a conscience had involuntarily taught me to deepen mine. The carriers of hate and evil elevated love and good into a sharper light. It is not enough not to be bad. Damn the neutrals sitting on fences, not minding other people's sufferings, for they are the cowardly henchmen of evildoers. Praying at times and places prescribed by custom to the God of your choice does not make you your brothers' and sisters' keeper. Only by reaching out a helping hand and by actively opposing wrongdoing do we earn the right to be called human.

Celebrate life as much as you can, without hurting others, for too much of it had been wasted through sheer madness. Place flowers of sympathy and sorrow on the nonexistent graves of millions who were annihilated through cruelty and with malice aforethought. Keep in mind the victims of the Holocaust and their bones scattered all over Europe, unmarked with crosses or David's star. For lest you forget, their sacrifices will have been in vain, and humanity will tumble into the abyss of evil again. Honor the memory of those fallen and strengthen your soul against a repeated bereavement of mankind so that you can look with a clear conscience into the eyes of your children.

Weep not for the survivors of the purgatory called Holocaust, for theirs is the ultimate glory in triumph: they outlived the evil of their tormentors, and by their lives overcame it; learn from them, for nobody, but nobody, knows how to savor the sunlight and the raindrops, the free flight of the birds, and the smile of the flowers as those who were once denied dignity, beauty, and the simplest things in life that make it worth living.

M&R 10:1, Sept.-Oct., 1983
Reprinted from Epilogue of *Women in the Resistance, and the Holocaust,*
Greenwood Press by permission of Vera Laska © 1983

A REUNION FOR THE GIRLS
FROM HAMBURG-SAZEL

By BERNICE LERNER

Their reunion is one filled with hugs, kisses and tears. Their ties are as close as blood relatives and as close as in the days in which they experienced the darkness brought by the Nazi Holocaust. They have since shared in *simchas* and stood by one another in times of tragedy, and they speak of their children as "our children." Theirs is a network whereby a group of approximately 30 women are closely in touch. And at the Cafe Baba, an American-Israeli Night Club, in Rego Park, Queens, they gathered to celebrate the 36th anniversary of their liberation from KZ Bergen-Belsen.

"Look at us, we're normal. Look around—normal human beings who produced normal, healthy children . . . and who have made something of themselves," spoke Sally Stern. "I think that it is quite an achievement." And she complimented Franka Gertel on raising three wonderful children. "In American families you would maybe find one child like those that she so beautifully raised."

I would say that nine out of ten of our children are professional people—doctors, lawyers, Ph.D.'s," said Franka. Around her were nods of confirmation. "And not that we pushed them . . . I did not encourage my daughter to go on and get a Ph.D.," said Helen Satler. "She saw how we were in a disadvantaged position in life and wanted to assure herself a better future."

Their children know what their parents went through. In Franka's case, she made sure to explain it to them in detail. She wanted them to know. Helen said she didn't need to talk to her daughter about it. She knew. When her daughter was in sixth grade, she was given an assignment to write a composition on "Freedom." "I could have written that composition . . . the way she expressed herself . . . it was as if she took the words right from me. 'What do you think, Ma. I live in this house, don't I.'"

One woman who had no children of her own was proud of Helen's daughter, her wonderful "niece." Her "lagerschwesters," (camp sister's) daughter was her niece. Relationships were formed when loved ones were lost. The relations

70

of adopted sisters who filled the void proved as full of love, trust and support as any real sister.

How could Helen forget that when she was imperiled while doing dangerous work and she cried out that she wanted to die—that the SS should kill her on the spot—that Franka and her sister formed a seat with their hands and carried her all the way back to the camp. And how could Franka forget that when she shared a bed with Isabelle, the poor girl suffered from an excruciating toothache, and the only medicinal comfort she could offer was being there to hold her. The many vivid memories are reinforced in their conversations.

From September, 1939, to August, 1944, these girls from Lodz and surrounding areas lived in the ghetto. In August, 1944, they were deported to Auschwitz, where all those who were not fit to work were "selected out" and sent to their deaths. As Germany needed slave laborers to step up the war effort, a group of girls, aged 12-25, were selected to work. They were sent to Hamburg, Germany, where they stayed in a renovated prison for four weeks before being taken to a labor camp twenty kilometers away—Hamburg-Sazel. They worked in many capacities. They were awakened at four in the morning and made to march to Hamburg to clean away the rubble left after the bombings. In so doing they were exposed to bombs, without the protection of air raid shelters. Many worked in Papnpitel, six kilometers from the camp, where they cleared away heavy railroad tracks in order to build quarters there for the SS. They worked with lorries, performing labor suited for strong men. In a brick factory, a Communist taught them the art of sabotage. By using the wrong ingredients the bricks would fall apart by the time they dried.

For nine months, 500 girls worked in Hamburg-Sazel. In April they were taken deeper into Germany while the Nazis fled, and came to witness the most extreme form of man's inhumanity to man. Ella Berenstein described the terror: "As we approached Bergen-Belsen the SS officers told us that this would be our end, that we would never come out of this place alive." "We saw the skeletons (*musselmanner*) with their gaping mouths . . . we saw half dead bodies dragging the dead to large open pits . . . and even people who still had life in them were burned. . . . We walked by the piles . . . piles of clothes, piles of shoes. . . . Piles of bodies!" Lice crawled the walls. The water which ran under the latrines to wash away the excrement was used for drinking. Typhus was rampant. Dead bodies that had lain for months were blackened. The

Nazis could in no way mask the destruction from the liberators —the enormity of the crime would be seen by the world. The evidence was impossible to deny and impossible to believe.

During these last days before liberation, hundreds among this group had died. Before liberation the Nazis baked crushed glass into loaves of bread for the starved people who had the strength to eat the poisoned food. Many more died. Franka estimated that even after the liberation on April 15, 1945, about 150 more girls from among their co-workers had died. A small number of survivors remain . . . and eighteen gathered at Cafe Baba.

Their husbands have their own stories to tell, having come, too, out of the depths of hell. And they have philosophies that are in accord with their wives' experiences. Abraham Stern expressed his thoughts and feelings: "We are quite comfortable now. But I often think—why couldn't we be less well off, all of us, but have more of our people with us, here."

At the reunion these beautiful, well-dressed women seemed so vibrant and radiant; in the presence of those with whom they knew there was total, unconditional understanding. When they meet at joyous occasions they remember. Sometimes they laugh when they talk about behavior that seems so odd now. "We laugh now, but it wasn't like that then." They cannot forget. At a wedding Ella would envision the scene her eyes witnessed the day before liberation. "It is always with me." On the occasion of a bar mitzvah Helen brought a potato to a friend who accused her of taking hers in camp. "I owed her a potato."

When Franka's husband died, her "family," the girls from camp, were there. They came in the morning and stayed with her until night.

When one of the girls approached another and told her that a third girl's husband lost his business, she gave $100: no questions asked.

"And that is how we are."

That they resisted and refused to succumb to the imposed process of dehumanization is inspirational. All of humanity has something beautiful to learn from this "family": girls with a common inexplicable past, spiritually bound together in the present and future.

M&R 8:14, Nov.-Dec., 1981

THE LOST LEGACY OF
HOLOCAUST SURVIVORS

By Dr. Abraham J. Peck

Among the most important examples of Jewish resistance during the Holocaust were the courageous and painfilled verses of the "Partisan Song," written by Hirsch Glick after the Warsaw Ghetto uprising. The "Partisan Song," as one of its stanzas read, "was written not in pencil, but in blood." It announced to the world (even earlier than Emil Fackenheim) that the Jewish people would live, and that despite the crematoria, they would neither give Hitler an immediate, nor posthumous, victory. "Never say," the song commanded, "that this is my final road, and that the light of day is banished by the clouds/The hour we have waited for is near/ Beneath our tread the earth shall tremble/We are here."

I would like to suggest that the phrase, "We are here" ("Mir szeinen doh," in Yiddish) may serve as an important key to understanding several ideological configurations of post-war European Jewry. Each of the configurations was interrelated with the others, but each had a distinct expression as well.

It meant, first of all, a clarion call to resist the death thrust of the Nazi sword against the heart and soul of Europe's remaining Jews.

It served as the fighting slogan of the widespread Zionist movement within the Jewish DP camps after 1945. Indeed, it served to emphasize that European Jewry would henceforth greet the future from a position of strength, of organization and attack—and not from a position dependent upon religious trust and faith. . . .

"Mir szeinen doh" had yet another meaning among post-war European Jewry. It was the unshakable belief of a group of survivors who felt that they had seen in the Holocaust, as one survivor stated, "the end of creation—not only an indelible memory of horror—but a 'permanent warning,'" that what he and others had experienced was a "pilot project for the destruction of humanity."

It is the final ideological expressions of "Mir szeinen doh," its creation and its subsequent encounter with the world, that is the essence of this essay.

I.

"Displaced Person is a savage euphemism," Marie Syrkin has written. "By now," she contends, "a DP is an almost forgotten term; so is DP camp." Yet the period between liberation and the establishment of Israel, during which survivors of the Nazi death camp became DP's, represents for Syrkin "a grim epilogue to the Holocaust and a coda to its meaning." Despite the obvious need for historians to understand and document the story of the Jewish DP's and of the Jewish DP camps in which they lived for periods of up to eight years and sometimes longer after 1945, precious little scholarly attention has been given to these areas. The reasons for such a state of affairs are numerous, ranging from the previous general inattention paid to the Holocaust (a phenomenon now corrected perhaps to excess) to the problem (especially in America) of linguistic competency among graduate students and even accomplished scholars, and to the very real problem of artificial periodization in which the twin pillars of Holocaust and redemption allow little room for intermediary self-standing research areas. . . .

Unpublished resource materials are vast, too vast to mention at this time. Published sources, many of them three decades old, are also available, including first-hand accounts of American Jewish army chaplains, reports of international visitors to the camps, descriptions of the camp newspapers, and reports of secular and religious efforts to educate Jewish children and adults, among others. One published source is worthy of mention by itself, namely the volume by Leo W. Schwarz entitled *The Redeemers*, published in 1953. *The Redeemers* stands as the only attempt thus far published to write the history of the displaced Jews and the camps in the American Zone. Schwarz apparently consulted a tremendous number of sources, but his book suffers from a fiction-like narrative, and displays little historical analysis and even less methodological concern.

Little is known, however, about the hopes and aims of the Jewish DP's beyond their need to leave "Galut Germany" for the land of *Eretz Yisrael*. They are usually portrayed as the passive objects of history, awaiting with resignation and despair the acting out of a drama in which they could play little if any role.

II.

Marie Syrkin is surely correct: DP is an almost forgotten term. After three decades or more as residents of numerous nations, primarily Israel and America, the Jewish DP's have evolved first into refugees, and finally now into survivors of the Holocaust. As survivors, they have become a much-studied group, both socially and psychologically. Psychiatrists conduct hours of research to study the effects of the so-called "survivors syndrome," of the transition from the harrowing experience of being an "individual in the concentration camp" to being the victim of the "concentration camp in the individual." Experts have found the survivors to suffer from a range of ailments, many psychological, the result of stress and suffering over a sustained period of time. The survivor is viewed as an emotional cripple, unable to function normally within society or family.

Survivors are also sought out by oral historians wishing to record their memories, and by school systems requesting their presence in classrooms where the Holocaust is studied and discussed. Interestingly, survivors' children and grandchildren, too, have become the objects of serious attention and study. The conclusion, both in Israel and America, is that the survivors of the Holocaust are walking cases of social and psychological abnormalities. It is a status now shared by their children and their children's children.

Yet, despite many such conclusions, the survivors continue to live, to function. Many have become successful professionally, and have found a place for themselves in their adopted surroundings. They have been steeled by the experience of survival to endure the slings and arrows of the uncertain world of trade and commerce.

Although many possess an external sense of success, the survivors remain a sub-group within the Jewish communities in which they live. They prefer to live in close proximity to each other, worship in their own synagogues, and participate in their own social organizations. And occasionally, when they are studied closely, certain feelings emerge about their relationship to the world, that vast body of humanity, Jew and non-Jew, which knew of the relentless Nazi drive to annihilate European Jewry. That sense, that the world knew, writes Dorothy Rabinowitz, "coexisted side by side with their perception that people (in America and elsewhere) rejected the facts about the Holocaust which had been published after 1945."

Other feelings, too, emerge which have to do with internal friction among the survivors who believe that, for many in their group, material well-being has become an end rather than a means. They feel that, because survivors have seen and suffered, "there should have come forward from among them a better sort of person, less selfish than the ordinary, perhaps; one more sensitive to humankind, one with spiritual goals that were a little higher than those of most people—otherwise, for what had they survived?"

The clearest voice among the survivors is that of Elie Wiesel. A voice of international significance, he supports the view that survivors are not normal. Survivors, for Wiesel, constitute a "separate, doomed, rapidly disappearing species, an isolated and tragically maligned species."

Maligned! "But how" we may ask. Wiesel responds: "After liberation . . . as they (the survivors) re-entered the world, they found themselves in another kind of exile, another kind of prison. People welcomed them with tears and sobs, then turned away." The survivors were "disturbed misfits who deserved charity, but nothing else."

What they wanted, according to Wiesel, was to "transmit a message to you, a message of which they were the sole bearers. Having gained an insight into man that will remain forever unequaled, they tried to share a knowledge with you, their contemporaries. But you discarded their testimony. . . ."

Because Elie Wiesel is not a historian, much of what he writes may very well be attributed to the creations of a fertile literary imagination. And because the survivors choose for the most part to remain silent beyond a few who write of their experiences in the Holocaust or in America, we who stand accused cannot really understand what Wiesel means when he writes of the message which the survivors looked upon as uniquely their own.

Perhaps a clue to the message could have been discerned in Jerusalem in the summer of 1981 when over five thousand survivors and many of their children met for the first and probably last time in history. The survivors gathered to hallow the memory of six million dead, to ask their children, who will survive them, to continue to bear witness for the six million, and to demonstrate in a quantitative sense, that revisionist historical efforts to prove the Holocaust a myth are vicious lies. "Mir szeinen doh" (We are here), the survivors repeated again and again, as did their children. But the message, the purpose, that which Wiesel calls "a legacy that could have changed the world," was not handed to the Second Generation. It is, I contend, the lost legacy of the *She'erit Hapleatah* (the Saved Remnant).

III.

We are not even certain when the term *She'erit Hapletah* came to be applied to those who survived Hitler's war against the Jews. It is a Biblical term which appears in *I Chronicles 5*, referring to the Jewish remnant that survived the Assyrian conquest. It appears in the list of survivors which was published in July of 1945. More importantly, it was the source of survivors' identity for those who survived the death camps, those who were partisans in the forests, and those who took refuge from Hitler in the deepest reaches of Russian Siberia. It was an identity which ultimately would give birth to a revolutionary ideology created from the inner being and experience of the *She'erit Hapletah*. . . .

In June, 1945, marking the liberation from Nazism, Dr. Zalman Grinberg, the earliest acknowledged spokesperson of the *She'erit Hapletah,* stressed the moral aspects of its existence: Hitler won the war against the European Jews. If we took revenge, we would descend into the lowest depths of ethics and morality to which the German nation has fallen during the past ten years. We are not able to slaughter women and children. We are not able to burn millions of people. We are not able to starve hundreds of thousands. . . .

Thus the nucleus of a philosophy of Jewish survival was being formed. But it would not develop on European soil. Despite the expectations of many, even of such a renowned interpreter as Salo Baron, the *She'erit Hapletah* would not, as had other previous generations of European Jews struck by the sword of hatred, cast off its tragedy and rebuild on European soil. . . . Instead, the *She'erit Hapletah* would journey back to the Jewish homeland, *Eretz Yisrael*, and rebuild their shattered remnants as other nations were doing in the aftermath of Nazism.

There was an anticipation, a nervous level of activity among the *She'erit Hapletah* in the months following liberation. The need for Palestine was clear, but so was the need for another source of purpose. . . . Menachem Sztajer grappled with the ultimate role and purpose of the *She'erit Hapletah*. In October, 1946, he challenged the survivors to decide for themselves. "Will it [*She'erit Hapletah*] simply mean an acci-

dental term for survivors of a destroyed people," he asked,
"or will it mean a revolution in Jewish history—a renaissance
in Jewish life?"

The ideology of the *She'erit Hapletah* was crystallized in
a series of brilliant essays by Samuel Gringauz in the years
1947 and 1948. Expanding upon the rudimentary ideology of
Jewish rescue and unification formulated by the partisan
fighter Abba Kovner, who in July of 1945 had spoken of the
need to "transform the Jewish tragedy from a sea of tears and
blood into a form of revolutionary strength," Gringauz added
a number of significant elements. "Today, the *She'erit Hapletah* has an ideology of its own," he wrote. "Ourselves the
product of a barbaric relationship of the environment to the
Jews, it is our task to create a more humane relationship to
the environment." This the *She'erit Hapletah* could do because, Gringauz asserted, "Our eyes are large and deep; for
they have looked on eternity."

Gringauz reiterated the need for European Jews to say
adieu to the discredited continent. "Our place is no longer in
Europe. We carry with us the legacy of our millenial history
to Palestine and America so that the secular continuity of our
ethical and cultural values may be assured." It was the
She'erit Hapletah, he maintained, who were the victims of
civilization. And it was they "who have been called upon to
discover the positive basis on which we can unite with it. . . .
Our tragedy must become the starting point of a new human-
ism." The Holocaust would be the starting point of a reorien-
tation of Occidental civilization, towards the cultural ideas of
the *She'erit Hapletah*. This ideal for Gringauz was no less
than a neo-humanism, the ideal of the moral and social perfection of humanity. . . .

By 1950, a deep sense of disillusion and disappointment
was already evident. In one of the last issues of *Undzer Veg*,
P. Pikatsch expressed a sense of disappointment. "We believed
that it was time to conquer evil and inhumanity," he wrote,
"that it would be a long time before bestiality would again
be able to conquer the idea of freedom." Instead, Pikatsch
found a different picture, in which the "spectre of hatred"
and the forces advocating the call to destruction and murder
emerged freely and openly to attack the democracies they so
hated. . . .

The voice of the *She'erit Hapletah* is today silent, its ideology non-existent. Beyond the solitary figure of Elie Wiesel,
it has been scattered to the winds of an all-too-immoral and
imperfect world. It was a voice that sought to give meaning

to the meaninglessness of survival, to help overcome the feeling of being "living corpses," at the mercy of an uncaring world. It was a voice that sought to change the direction of Jewish destiny and of human destiny, to steer a course towards the moral and social perfection of humanity. It was a prophetic voice, in tune with the Biblical voices of prophets in their quest for social justice. Finally, it was the voice of enduring legacy, established for the children of the *She'erit Hapletah*. Zalman Grinberg wrote that "we [of the *She'erit Hapletah*] live not for ourselves, but for our children, We can endanger our own fleeting existence, so that the security of coming generations may be insured."

But the voice is stilled, stilled because of the fear of "arousing disbelief, of being told 'your imagination is sick' . . . or you are counting on our pity, you are exploiting your suffering."

The question in this historic encounter of the *She'erit Hapletah* with the world must be—who is normal and who is not? Yet the answer is still not as important as the legacy passed on to the Second Generation, and the declaration by the children of the Holocaust that *"Mir szeinen doh."* That legacy must not be one of silence and it must not be one of fear. It should be the lost legacy of the *She'erit Hapletah*. It is a leagcy worth finding.

M&R 11:13, Nov.-Dec., 1984
Reprinted by permission of Shoah © 1984.

THE VICTIMS OF MENGELE

The 40th anniversary of the liberation of Auschwitz was on January 26, 1985. Newspapers across the world told of survivors who returned for official observances at the site of the largest of the Nazi death camps.

There were solemn ceremonies organized by the Polish Auschwitz Committee, including prayers and the laying of wreaths at an international monument near the ruins of the giant crematoria.

But the most poignant recollections and the center of media attention were related to the sets of twins, victims of Josef Mengele. They recreated the death march from Birkenau to Auschwitz shortly before the camp was liberated by the Russians.

They came not only to remember but to help lead an international effort to capture the "Angel of Death," who conducted experiments in generic engineering on twins and other inmates.

Their forum was at Yad Vashem, Feb. 3-6, entitled "J'accuse" (I accuse), the first international conference of Auschwitz twin-survivors. Some 100 of these twins, dwarfs, and others who survived the experiments gathered to give testimony before a six-member board of inquiry headed by Gideon Hausner, chief prosecutor at the Eichmann trial, now chairman of the Yad Vashem Council, and Telford Taylor, chief American counsel at the Nuremberg trials.

The horrific stories of the survivor's experiences were detailed, many never before recorded. Each tale seemed more gripping and more moving than the other. Certainly, few tales had the quality of the "bizarre" as that of Ruth Eliaz, who was forced to kill her baby, born while she was under the authority of Mengele. He was angered at not having noticed her pregnancy, which would have led to her gassing. Once she gave birth, she was forced to cover her breasts with tape so Mengele could see "how long a baby would live without food."

Mrs. Eliaz recalled: "The child got thinner and thinner, weaker and weaker. Every day Mengele would come and look at it."

Mrs. Eliaz was advised by a nurse in her bunkhouse to put the infant out of its misery. The nurse stole some morphine and syringe for that purpose. "You want me to kill my own child," Mrs. Eliaz responded. "I can't do it." But she did, as Mrs. Eliaz told a totally silenced audience in Jerusalem. "I murdered my own child. The next day Mengele came. He couldn't find my baby's corpse outside our blood. He cursed me for cheating him."

The convening of the session can be traced to the formation of "Candles," a recently founded organization of Auschwitz twin-survivors. And their testimony had a very deep effect on its members. As the *New York Times* wrote of René Slotkin, a twin who survived: "Just like Auschwitz changed me, I am not the same now after this meeting. It made me aware that there are others out there like me. This meeting unlocked things that we had been keeping inside ourselves. It will help us cope better, even though now we are hurting."

EMERGING FROM THE KINGDOM OF NIGHT

By ELIE WIESEL, Nobel Laureate

It is with a profound sense of humility that I accept the honor you have chosen to bestow upon me. I know: your choice transcends me. This both frightens and pleases me. It frightens me because I wonder: do I have the right to represent the multitudes who have perished? . . . It pleases me because I may say that this honor belongs to all the survivors and their children, and through us, to the Jewish people with whose destiny I have always identified.

I remember: it happened yesterday or eternities ago. A young Jewish boy discovered the kingdom of night. I remember his bewilderment, I remember his anguish. . . .

I remember: he asked his father: "Can this be true? This is the 20th century, not the Middle Ages. Who would allow such crimes to be committed? How could the world remain silent?"

And now the boy is turning to me: "Tell me," he asks. "What have you done with my future? What have you done with your life?"

And I tell him that I have tried. That I have tried to keep memory alive; that I have tried to fight those who would forget. Because if we forget, we are guilty, we are accomplices.

And then I explained to him how naive we were, that the world did know and remained silent. And that is why I swore never to be silent whenever and wherever human beings endure suffering and humiliation. We must always take sides. Neutrality helps the oppressor, never the victim. Silence encourages the tormentor, never the tormented.

There is much to be done, there is much that can be done. One person—a Raoul Wallenberg, and Albert Schweitzer, one person of integrity, can make a difference, a difference of life and death. As long as one dissident is in prison, our freedom will not be true. As long as one child is hungry, our lives will be filled with anguish and shame.

What all these victims need above all is to know that they are not alone; that we are not forgetting them, that when their voices are stifled we shall lend them ours, that while their freedom depends on ours, the quality of our freedom depends on theirs.

This is what I say to the young Jewish boy wondering what I have done with his years. It is in his name that I speak to you and that I express to you my depest gratitude. No one is as capable of gratitude as one who has emerged from the kingdom of night. . . .

M&R 13:16, Jan.-Feb., 1987
Excerpts from Nobel Prize Acceptance Speech

SURVIVORS' GRATITUDE TO ELIE WIESEL

By PAULA MANDELL

Many praiseworthy comments and editorials have been written about Elie Wiesel, but the action of the Nobel Prize Committee exceeds all those words. A distinguished body demonstrated that it recognized, understood and valued the experiences of the Holocaust survivors: experiences which in millions of words from pulpits, from podiums, and in the print media make one remember—not forget or obliterate what had happened. This serves as a warning to be alert and keep a watchful eye on the inequities around us. Unfortunately, far too many prevail. No one can identify more with the suffering than a person affected by the horrors of the Holocaust.

Because of Elie Wiesel, a measured blow was handed to the Arthur Butzes and Ernst Zundels, who claim that the Holocaust was a hoax—or to the likes of the French historian Robert Fourrison, who denies the Nazi crime and calls it a "giant historical lie."

Our lone voices were finally heard through Elie Wiesel. His thirty books were hailed as literature in its highest form. His crusade against human suffering and his denouncement of injustice were given a salute of honor and a bow of recognition by this august body who reveres man's elevation toward higher goals which ultimately lead toward the improvement of the human lot.

But how naive we were right after it all ended over forty years ago, believing that a lesson had been taught and mankind would open the gates to a world in which fairness, righteousness, and justice would reign. We were hopeful that a new era had begun and what we had endured had wiped the slate clean. With the consternation, however, we realize that this did not happen. In the words of Elie Wiesel, "There is so much injustice and suffering crying out for our attention: victims of hunger or racism and political persecution, writers and poets, prisoners in so many lands governed by the left and by the right. Human rights are being violated on every continent. More people are oppressed than free." He is one of us who from the podium and by his pen prodded the conscience of the world on the basis of his Holocaust experience to evaluate the sad status quo, to help rather than ignore, to reason rather than fight, to love rather than hate. We support Elie Wiesel in his fight for a better tomorrow. We, his comrades from the once kingdom of night, are not complacent. And if we tell and retell, write, or jot down our past experiences, we crusade for a better tomorrow.

Many scholars contemplate what impact the Holocaust will have on future generations. Will it figure as a unique and critical event in Jewish history? Will is be swept away and made to stand alongside the countless *hurbanim* (destructions) that befell the Jews throughout the history of the Diaspora? Will the ignorance of Jewish European history revive the question, "Why did they go like sheep to the slaughter?"

Understandably, we would like this cataclysm to stand out in Jewish history and occupy the first page. We would wish that the Holocaust remain the powerful and revered legacy it deserves.

We are gratified by the act of the Nobel Prize Committee toward one of us who so eloquently brought to light the unfathomable inhumanity of man against man and who with his message tried to mend the ills of the world. The Holocaust is perceived now through Elie Wiesel's profound works as a red light on the horizon of many colorless and wildly flickering lights—a beacon to inspire man, to promote justice and respect among all peoples.

VARIED FORMS OF SURVIVAL

By Sidney Schwimmer

To the layman, the term "Holocaust Survivor" is often narrowly interpreted as one who was interned in a European concentration camp during World War II, was able to escape death, and was released from his imprisonment at the war's end. This, however, is but one of many definitions. Forms of survival were multitudinous, and require clarification if one is to comprehend the complexity of the term "Survivor." First, one must answer the question: "Who is a Holocaust survivor?" And then one must analyze why one is categorized as a survivor.

A Holocaust survivor is defined as a person of Jewish faith or ancestry who dwelled all or part of the period between 1933-45 in a European country that was rulled or occupied by Nazis or their allies. He is, thus, defined as a survivor because he survived the Holocaust, regardless of whether he lived in Europe, part or all of the time, whether or not he was subjected to or was unscathed by Nazi atrocities.

To comprehend why some people survived and others perished, it is vital to know the time, place, political circumstances in the country of the survivor. Survival also depended on the personal circumstances of individuals.

There is a great distinction between the survivors who lived during the beginning of Hitler's persecution of Jews, 1933-40, or during part of this time and those who survived the entire Holocaust till 1945. The degree of the atrocities varied from one area or country to another.

In categorizing the varieties of survivors according to their whereabouts during the Holocaust, the following illustrate typical examples and shed light upon their survival patterns:

1) Individuals of Jewish faith or ancestry who, at the beginning of the persecution in 1933 and as late as 1941, were able to flee or emigrate from European countries to countries not under Nazi rule. These individuals did not experience or were not affected by the Holocaust.

2) Polish Jews who were able to escape between 1939-41. They fled to Russia, remained there till the end of the War, and later immigrated to other countries. Although they suffered great hardship in Russia with the rest of the citizens, they were never killed purely on the basis of their Jewishness.

3) Rumanian Jews who were not deported to K.Z. camps and who were liberated by the Soviets almost a year before the War ended.

4) Hungarian Jews (male) from forced labor camps who were sent in 1942 behind the front lines in the German-occupied Soviet territories and during 1942-43 became P.O.W.'s. They remained in the Soviet Union and returned to Hungary or emigrated after the War ended.

5) Hungarian Jews (males) from Hungarian forced labor camps who served inside the Hungarian borders and were exempt from deportation to Auschwitz during May-June 1944. They were later liberated in Hungary that year.

6) Hungarian Jews who lived in areas that were spared deportation. They were liberated in Hungary five months before the end of the War.

7) Jews from many European countries (primarily females), who managed to hide their Jewish identity and lived in places without being exposed as Jews.

8) Jews who managed to avoid the ghettoes or concentration camps and lived under an assumed name as non-Jews or Aryans with Aryan papers they obtained clandestinely.

9) Jews who lived part or the entire time in hiding or under the protection of a non-Jew.

10) Jews who for various reasons were exempt from ghettoes and spared from deportation to K.Z. camps at certain times and places because of their skill and indispensability in the German War machinery.

11) Jews who were under protection of foreign embassies or regulations.

12) Jews of the underground or partisans in the German occupied territories during 1942-44. This group included those in the Russian underground, among them some Jews from the Polish ghettoes who hid or escaped and were able to join the underground behind the battle fronts. They were liberated by the Soviets a long time before the War ended.

13) Jews who claimed they escaped from labor or concentration camps (even from Auschwitz). It must be viewed that such a possibility existed only at the time when the Germans were in the process of evacuation, especially during the turmoil that preceded the liberation. At any other time, such an attempt to escape led to almost sure death.

14) A small percentage of Jews, primarily from Poland, who, from the German invasion in Sept., 1939, until the end of the War, were in ghettoes, labor and concentration camps— and still came out alive. These survivors suffered the most, and

only they can offer a complete account of their plight for the entire period.

These categories of survivors merely constitute some basic varieties and should not be regarded as complete. Many other survivor categories existed–those whose experiences were similar to the ones I have cited, combined with other varieties of experiences, which could be specified ad infinitum. The categories selected represent the basic ones within my purview of experiences.

M&R 10:5, March-April, 1984

SURVIVING THE HOLOCAUST

By PROF. ROBERT MICHAEL

In a sense, we are all survivors of the Holocaust because we are alive today. We did not die in the Shoah. But there are concentric circles of survivorship. Those who had to confront the Holocaust, those who were there, those who directly experienced it, those who suffered at its heart and lived–they are survivors with a capital S.

And within fifty years they will all be dead, even the survivors of the Holocaust. Their anguish and their sadness, their horror and their revenge, their love and their courage will all be gone. All we will have left will be documents and data, photographs and film, and their words. The meaning of this evidence will be up to us.

Many of the survivor writers were very self-conscious about what they were doing. They realized that it was their pens that would lead to their eternal spiritual life, even if their temporal existence were to be cut short. Their documents were buried or smuggled out so that their tales would be told, so that their memories would be preserved, so that their defiance would be recorded.

This brings us to the problem of the accuracy of what the survivors report. Charlotte Delbo has written about Auschwitz, "I am not sure that what I have written is true (vrai). But I am sure that it happened that way (viridique)." The univers concentrationnaire can be experienced by no one except those who were actually there. But even they cannot tell us every-

thing that happened, let alone precisely what took place. Can
a grain of sand tell us everything about the Sahara desert?
Each person's experience is limited, and memory inevitably
corrupts what one has observed. Thus, there is no one version
of the Holocaust; there are as many versions as there are Survivors or were victims. Even "prisoners in the camp," said
Benedict Kautsky, "lived as if on different planets, depending
on the work they had to do." And most prisoners, writes Gitta
Sereny, "represent[ed] these events and their part in them with
a view to seeming—to themselves even more such as than to
others—what they would have liked to have been, rather than
what they were." Words themselves inevitably distort, as does
memory. In his book, Lawrence Langer says that any version
of the Holocaust can be only that, "a version, limited by memory, insight, and vocabulary." As Elie Wiesel says, "Every
witness expresses only his own truth in his own name."

Some Survivors' attitude to what they experienced
changed over time. They sometimes made opposite interpreta-
tions from those just after the Holocaust. But what does not
change are the devastating experiences themselves. They have
stayed always with the Survivors and through them they will
move into our lives to change them. May we all learn from the
Holocaust to live out our lives in the most life-giving, human,
loving ways we are able; and for those of us who believe in
a personal God, let us thus serve Him.

With Elie Wiesel, we must tell the tales of those who
died: to commemorate those millions of silent dead. So as not
to murder them twice by our silence. So that the Nazi goal
of total annihilation may be defeated. So that the truth may
be known and justice may be done. So that all human beings
may be helped to recognize their solidarity with all human
suffering. So that we can understand more fully that love of
God and love of neighbor mean the same thing. So that the
future, so potentially full of evil, may instead actualize Anne
Frank's dream that love, happiness, and beauty are real and
attainable. And though her belief that "whoever has courage
and faith will never perish in misery" was a fairy tale patently
false for the Jews murdered in the Holocaust, yet we must
believe that courage and faith can someday change the world
from its present course. We have no living alternative.

But this is not all. Knowing about and confronting the
Holocaust through the words of those who died and those who
survived can help us understand:

(1) That the Holocaust was a singularly Jewish experience with momentous consequences for mankind.

(2) The precariousness and vulnerability of life so that our reaction to the radical evil of the Holocaust will become the touchstone of our response to every denial of human rights, to every movement toward an unjust society where people are not respected for what they are.

(3) How to create a new environment where we and those we love can live without fear of tyranny and injustice.

(4) How bureaucratic organization, industrial management, scientific achievement, medical experiments, and technological sophistication were "rationally" used to dehumanize, diabolize, and destroy human beings.

(5) How the murderers could do their killing without allowing their "job" to affect the other aspects of their lives, how they could kill Jewish families during the day and love their own at night.

(6) That continuing to respond to the Holocaust with silence, without moral indignation and the action that follows from it, is to collaborate in the possible repetition, is to murder the victims a second time by condemning them to oblivion, by learning nothing from their deaths is to give Hitler a posthumous victory.

(7) That most of the leaders and the peoples of the West, including the Allies and the Vatican, refused significant help to the Jews of the Holocaust in part precisely because the victims were Jews (a) even after their initial incredulity wore off (b) even when there was little to lose by their words and actions (c) even though their professed wartime ideals, in supposed contrast to those of the Nazis, prized individual liberty and valued the lives of the oppressed.

(8) The impact of the Holocaust on, and the interrelationship between, our religious, political, moral and intellectual lives.

(9) How the Holocaust has affected our beliefs in and about God. How, for example, the existence of an omnipotent, omniscient, and, most important, an omnibenevolent Being is consistent with the murder of nearly 2 million children.

(10) The failure of most Christians to respond in a humane way to the needs of desperate, innocent people being murdered for no reason other than the fact that they were Jews and despite the fact that they were worshippers of the same God.

(11) How to use the Holocaust as a starting point in a new effort to build bridges of understanding between Christians and Jews so that never again will Christians be involved, and never again will such a Holocaust happen.

And so there may be ways of fighting the Holocaust retro-
spectively. For if the Holocaust is the victory of death over
life, of ugliness over beauty, of injustice over justice, of falsehood over truth, of hate over love, of evil over goodness, then
to remember is to give life a posthumous victory over death,
is to preserve the memory of those Jews who were so cruelly
murdered. In the post-Holocaust world we must remember
in order to achieve life, justice, beauty, truth, love, and goodness; to continue the fight to stay human in the face of the
forces always at work to coerce and persuade us into inhuman-
ness; not to let inhuman systems, like the Nazi *univers concentrationnaire*, come into existence in the first place.

M&R 10:5, Nov.-Dec., 1983

NEW FOCUS ON WOMEN'S
ROLE IN HOLOCAUST

By Dr. Luba K. Gurdus

Women Surviving: The Holocaust, a conference at Stern
College, in New York, will undoubtedly pass into the chonicles
of Holocaust studies as an important event. It came at the
time when the history of the Holocaust, gradually permeating
public consciousness, was badly in need of a deeper insight
and broader perspective. There is little doubt that the literature of the Holocaust is largely dominated by men. The Jewish
tradition of male spiritual leadership afforded male survivors
the authority to present the Holocaust experience from a
single perspective, denying women their history-making role.
This is gradually being adjusted. The recent flow of books,
TV features, plays and movies by and about Holocaust women
have focused the limelight on their experience.

The first major breakthrough came with Fania Fenelon's
TV feature "Playing for Time," followed by Kitty Hart's
"Auschwitz Revisited." Recently, Anna Sokolow's play "Hannah," about the wartime heroine Hannah Senesh, was an
exciting fare for theater audiences, and the memoir of Zivia
Lubetkin, "In the Days of Destruction and Revolt," was
adapted as primary source for the 40th anniversary commemoration of the Warsaw Ghetto Uprising. In addition, the

outpouring of women's writings, primarily personal accounts, brought to light uncommon acts of quiet sacrifice and heroism. The trauma of Holocaust women began to elicit fresh responses to a material becoming too stereotyped, accepted and familiar. It affords a much needed descent below the surface of the massive event, allowing a penetrating insight into a subject seemingly inpenetrable and inaccessible for human perception and reach.

While the history of Holocaust women is barely being transmitted, reputed writers, trying to weave the Holocaust experience into an accessible reality, reinterpret the issues and transfigure the facts for their artistic aims. The stories of women survivors became an easy prey for exploitation in popular stories stressing female vulnerability. An intellectual manipulation threatens to obliterate reality for romantic exuberance as in William Styron's *Sophie's Choice*.

The curiosity about women survivors is reaching a culmination point, and there is little doubt that the nature of the subject will attract further attention. Serious concern for this development and the various manifestations of gross distortion of fundamental facts and issues alerted the group of feminist scholars and survivors who gathered at Stern College.

The meeting was organized and headed by Dr. Joan Miriam Ringelheim, a Holocaust scholar and fellow of The Institute for Research in History. The two-day Conference focused its attention on experiences of women in ghettos, camps and partisan groups of Nazi-occupied Europe, trying to articulate the real issues and assess the impact of the experience on survivors. Their testimonies and comments became the factual basis for consideration and helped the participants to gain an insight into the complexities of the subject. Important data were emphasized and brought to the fore for a systematic development of a scholarly research agenda, incorporating a new humanities and feminist perspective.

It has been concluded that women were uniquely equipped to withstand the stress of dislocation, starvation, physical and mental abuse, and they function in spite of almost total loss of the traditional support structure. Women of the Holocaust have in many cases demonstrated indomitable courage, resilience, self-discipline, determination, and a deep sense of commitment. Quite remarkably, they also emerged with a capacity for humanity in a world of depravity and evil.

M&R 9:5, March-April, 1983

ON INTERVIEWING SURVIVORS

By Dr. Harry James Cargas

As survivors of the Holocaust now grow collectively older, many seem to be aware that if they do not tell their stories, the full truth of what happened at Auschwitz, at Buchenwald, at Dachau and at Treblinka may be in danger of being lost. Therefore, many of these women and men are more willing to share their World War II experiences for the record. As a result of this development, more and more individuals and groups are committed to taping interviews with survivors to bring a more complete history of the Holocaust into focus. It is my experience, as an interviewer of survivors, at first acting alone, and later as a member of the St. Louis Oral History Project (under the auspices of the St. Louis Center for Holocaust Studies), that too many interviewers may rush into a taping session before being adequately prepared to do so. Thus, the meetings become less useful than they might, even become counter-productive on occasion because a survivor might get "turned off" by the incident and refuse to be very cooperative on the first or even subsequent interviews. The seriousness of such an encounter cannot be overstressed, and neither can the preparation for it.

There are basically three time periods to look at: preparatory to an interview, the meeting itself, the follow up. Each is important and not to be slighted.

Before an interview, there is need for much preparation. Foremost is the need to know your subject. Study, in quite some detail, the history of World War II and the actual events of the Holocaust itself. (If you need a starting point, you can begin with Raul Hilberg's *The Destruction of the European Jews* or Nora Levin's *The Holocaust*. For additional suggestions you could consult my work published by Catholic Library World, *The Holocaust: An Annotated Bibliography* with 42 titles described.) To enter into a dialogue with a survivor while being basically ignorant of the events of the era about which you hope to be talking will inevitably prove disastrous.

Organize a series of questions that you plan to ask. These should be of two types: general and specific. Among the former might be such questions as "What has it meant to you to be a survivor?" "Are you angry today?" "Are you hopeful for the future?" "What has America meant to you?" "What does the State of Israel mean to you?" (This last is intended, of course, especially for Jewish survivors as will be a number of questions.) Of the more specific kind are: "When were you imprisoned?" "What was your family life like?" "How did you survive?" (This question must be asked in a particularly non-threatening way since survivors are sometimes asked this question in a tone which implies that the only way one could have continued to live was by cooperating somehow with the enemy. Perhaps a better way to phrase it would be "What were the circumstances that made it possible for you to live?"). Another important discussion prompter is this: "How has your experience influenced your religion?"

Try to obtain some good maps of Europe and of the areas, if you can ascertain them beforehand, in which your interviewee was raised, was imprisoned in a ghetto, was incarcerated in a camp, etc. A map illustrating placements of the various prison and death camps would also prove helpful.

Initial contact is probably best made with the prospective interviewee by letter. Explain what you want to talk about and what your qualifications are, which group you are associated with, etc. Give the person you are contacting the opportunity to refuse your invitation. There are some survivors who simply are unwilling, for a variety of legitimate reasons, to discuss the Holocaust, particularly with strangers. Allow for that with care so that you don't make them feel guilty for having turned you down. One of your goals is to help unburden these men and women, not to add to their enormous emotional load.

Follow the letter with a telephone call some three to four days later. If your person agrees to meet with you, arrange for a time and place. The location of the interview is important. It must be in surroundings in which both of you are comfortable. Almost always, in my encounters, I find that you will be invited to your interviewee's home. In general, that seems to be by far the very best site. Choose a time which will allow you a prolonged, no rush, uninterrupted visit—a time free from the bustle of scurrying teenagers, telephone rings and the like. Sunday morning is often a good choice.

Finally, as far as the preliminaries are concerned, be fully prepared. Know your subject, as previously indicated. If possible, take two tape recorders which are in tested working order and be sure to have more than enough cassettes with you. It is discouraging to be in the middle of a very sensitive dialogue and have to interrupt it because you failed to have the adequate amount of tapes. You can almost never "pick up again where we left off" on a subsequent visit. One other point of preparation: be prepared to be shocked, to be bored (by a repetition of stories, by autobiographical details which may have no bearing on what you are trying to do–although you can be fooled on what turns out, finally, to have value), to be fully trusted (with all of the baggage that goes with it), to be only partially trusted (by a skeptical survivor who may want to know why you are really doing this–what's in it for you?). Your task is to listen. Prepare yourself to listen well.

Now we come to the actual interview. It is important that you go alone for your appointment. Another person, even a friend of the person you are visiting with, can prove quite distracting. You are attempting to build up a relationship with your person, and another individual simply breaks the mood too often. You are asking the survivors to trust you and that is difficult enough. To ask that such trust be extended to another may be unrealistic. The only time a third person might be in on an interview is, if that person is a spouse of the interviewee. Very often the spouse too will be a survivor and some of the best sessions I've heard are with a wife and husband. The interaction between the two of them may at times prove extremely informative.

You can begin the discussion by showing the maps which you brought, asking the survivor to indicate places of autobiographical importance to her or him. Let them teach you. Do not go in like the big Holocaust expert, even if your knowledge of the field is wide. You don't know what this individual went through and you wish to find out. If you are perceived as a know-it-all or as one who is interviewing only to validate certain preconceived theories, your encounter is doomed.

After a few minutes around the maps, or however you begin, it might be a good idea to play the tape back to your interviewee. There is something comforting, less threatening to the person when the voice can be monitored. Somehow a little of the mystery of technology disappears and any elimination of barriers is to be welcomed.

Several important "don'ts" must be stressed. First, don't be in a hurry. Show that you are relaxed. Help create a calm atmosphere. This will allow for a much better climate of response to you and therefore to your questions. Second, unless specifically asked, do not "help" a person who is groping for words, struggling for language. Just take it easy. The word being searched for eventually comes. If you don't come off as a language expert or a superior (therefore threatening) intellect, you won't run the risk of a wrong, even insulting guess, or of planting your ideas into the minds of the speakers. Third, don't interrupt the flow of words to ask for clarification, to get the spelling of a word, to ask for a repeat of a word you don't understand. Make a note and come back to your new questions later. Finally, don't stick rigorously to the order of questions you have prepared. Answers to some of your questions will, if you are alert, lead to new queries which you will wish to put to them. Do so and later come back to those still to be covered from the list you brought with you.

Now a few "do's." Do allow for pauses and for silences. Oftentimes a person will have a better answer to your inquiry than the first one given. Or a reformulation, an elaboration, will bring out wonderfully new and thoughtful information. Stacatto interviews, quick question followed by quick reply in rat-at-at-at fashion, are the worst kind. Media interviewers are terrified of pauses, of "dead air" on their programs. That's why most of them are so vacuous. But you don't have to be in a rush; important answers usually take time. Another do: do pay attention to what your interviewee is saying. Many of your best questions in the session will be based on something which your new friend has just said. Follow the lead and go with it. You can always return later to your prepared questions. Also, in paying attention, you may find that you will better be able to get at what is meant as well as what is said. For example, sometimes someone will say something like, "I don't want to talk about it" in a way which is actually testing you. What may be meant is "I do want to talk about it if you think you can take this dreadful account." Be alert for this kind of statement. If a person says, "It isn't important but . . ." this may well be a signal that it is indeed important to the narrator. Follow it through. Also keep an eye on the tape. Don't let the best part of the interview be lost because the cassette was used up eleven minutes earlier! Do be certain to get the correct spelling of family names, place names, foreign expressions used during the interview. There will be time to do that towards the end, from your notes, as the encounter is winding down. Do ask to see any artifacts, documents or letters that your person might be willing to share with you, and ask for the stories behind each. Finally, do learn when *not* to turn off the tape recorder. Sometimes a few of the best insights will be given you as you are saying good-bye at the door. You may hear, "Oh, I forgot to mention . . ." or some such lead in. Get it on tape. It could be of great value in the interview.

And last there is the post-interview period, the follow up. Immediately as you can, after your visit, try to recall if anything of importance was said before the tape recorder was started or after it was turned off. Note down on paper anything that might prove of value later. If you were shown artifacts, describe them, comment on the way they were presented, etc.

You should begin to transcribe the tape, verbatim, as soon as is convenient. One reason is that you will still have the rhythm, the pronunciation of the survivor's speech fresh in your mind. This may be necessary for understanding certain terms and expressions which the recorder may have fuzzed. And, remember, the tape is actually the document you had sought. It contains so much, much more than any transcription because it has tone of voice, silences, sighs, weeping—so much more is communicated via the tape than via the typewriter to someone who wasn't there.

Members of the St. Louis Oral History Project have found that surivivors welcome follow up phone calls from interviewers. After all, new friendships have been made; a bond ought to be kept up. Very personal secrets, in many cases, were revealed during the discussions and to drop the relationship immediately may result in feelings being seriously hurt. When appropriate, a New Year card or a birthday greeting (you'll probably have that anniversary on your tape) is recommended.

One important caution remains. No individual should interview survivors too often. I know one man who had wide experience in doing interviews with writers (which he published) and with the famous and not so well known on his television programs (covering a 7-year period). He interviewed twelve survivors in two and a half months for a projected book and he was absolutely burned out. Some of his tapes have yet to be transcribed (after over four years) and the book is going nowhere. My suggestion is each interviewer limit the number done to about two or three per year, spaced at least several months apart. The dialogues are very emotionally draining. This is perhaps more apparent regarding the survivors, but observation proves this to be true of the inquiries as well.

M&R 8:5, March-April, 1982

SPEAK UP BEFORE IT IS TOO LATE

By Lorraine Kaufman

It has often been said that there is nothing worse for a parent than to bury a child. But there is something worse—to have your child murdered and then to have the ashes used as fertilizer for the Polish and German countrysides: no burial, no tombstone, no exact date of the *yahrzeit*. And this is what happened to many of your younger brothers and sisters.

I have come to talk about children: the slaughtered, the survivors and the generation after, for these are the children of the Holocaust.

The slaughtered—1,500,000 children murdered by the hands of merciless SS men.

The survivors—those, like many of you, who miraculously survived the Nazi death machine.

The generation after—children like myself, the sons and daughters of survivors.

These are all the children of the Holocaust, Jewish boys and girls who were ruthlessly annihilated as part of Hitler's plan to make Europe "Juden-Rein." They were 1,500,000 children: children who didn't live long enough to taste the sweetness of life, who knew only the cruelty and bitterness of their executioners. They were 1,500,000 children: murdered before they could dream, murdered before they could achieve, murdered before they could understand. And most certainly we have not forgotten those children who were never given the opportunity to breathe their first breath. These are the slaughtered children who we remember today with tears in our eyes and bitterness in our hearts.

But we cannot bring these children back. I could tell you that the world has not forgotten these children. But that is not the truth. Most of the world has forgotten their death and the atrocities committed against them—we have not forgotten them—those of us who gather today and say Kaddish for these children have not forgotten. But we are so few in number and fewer each year. I ask you: Who will say Kaddish for these slaughtered children 30 years from today?

That is up to you, the survivors. You are the second group of Holocaust children. You are the ones who entered the concentration camps and ghettos while you were children

96

and teenagers. Once liberated you realized that your childhood
had been destroyed beyond the barbed wire. You were the children who survived. You know intimately of the brutality, of
the death marches, of the selections, of the hunger and the
beatings and of all the horrible realities of the Nazi death
camps. You are survivors of a time in history that is the ultimate proof that man's inhumanity to man can be greater than
that ever imagined, a moment in history when a Jewish life
was worth less than a used cigarette.

But you survived. From behind the barbed wire of Bergen-
Belsen and Dachau and from the Nazi created hell of Maidanek
and Chelmno, the living dead began to live again. Your
struggle to become human again has been an overwhelming
success. You have undertaken awesome responsibilities. One
of the largest is that you have chosen to bring children into
this world, and many of your children are now married with
children of their own. But some of you have neglected the most
important responsibility: the responsibility of telling your
children about your experience in the camps and about the
slaughter of your families and friends.

You were eyewitnesses to the greatest crime ever committed in the history of mankind. You must speak for the
dead, particularly for the 1,200,000 slaughtered children, for
the dead cannot speak for themselves. You know the incredible
truth. How can you let the world forget? How can you let
your children forget?

For thousands of years the history, customs, joys and
tragedies of the Jewish people have been passed from parent to
child, from one generation to the next. But many of you have
broken with this tradition because for the last 35 years you
have been silent. The most sickening and tragic period in Jewish history is buried beneath your silence—a silence that once
was understandable but today has become dangerous.

Some of you have made sure that your children have
viewed Jewish history with one eye and, therefore, half a heart.
You have told us so much about the Exodus of the Jews from
Egypt but so little about the liberation of the Jews from Nazi
death camps. You have told us so much about the flood but
we know so little of the fires: of the fires in the ghettos; of
the fires that destroyed some of the cities, towns and villages
in which you were born; of the fires that burned the flesh of
the grandparents, aunts, uncles and cousins. . . .

You have told us more about Haman and the Persians
than you have about Hitler and the Nazis. While many of you
have remained silent, the world around us has not. Open your

eyes to the reality of today: a reality where anti-Semites across the world are advocating that the slaughter of 6 million Jews never happened, that the Einsatzgruppen never killed, and that places like Sobibor and Auschwitz exist only in the minds of the Jews.

This is what has become, of your silence. We have been waiting. Your sons and daughters are saying that the time has come to pass the torch to the generation after. So that we may pass this torch to our children, the tragedies that befell our parents must now be brought into the open. We must be taught all about the murdered and the murderers. We must be taught all about the hatred called Nazism. You must teach us so that we, your children and your grandchildren, will be able to recognize such a danger should another Hitler rise again. You must teach us so that we can understand the effect of your experience in our lives.

Finally, you must teach us so that in 30 years it will be the children of survivors, your children, the generation after, who will stand before this monument and say Kaddish for the slaughtered.

You, as survivors, must come to understand that no history book, no film, no one can ever explain to your children what happened to you. Only you can do that. You must come to understand that your children will not judge your actions during the time you spent in concentration camp. No one can stand in judgment.

Finally, you must come to understand that your children need to know the whole truth. Though the truth may be painful, your pain will pass, but the truth about your experiences will live forever in the hearts and minds of your children, of your children's children and of the generations to come.

If there is no one standing before this monument 30 years from today, then I will know you continued your silence.

If you think the world has learned a lesson from the horrors of Auschwitz, you are sadly mistaken. Today, we are also honoring the memory of those Jews who died in the defense of Eretz Yisroel. Thirty-two years of statehood and four wars later, Jews in Israel are still being killed because they are Jews. Those who hate continue to hate.

Your generation knows the truth about the murdered and the murderers. My generation is waiting to hear your truth. We are still waiting.

M&R 7:9, Nov.-Dec., 1980

APPELFELD'S AGE OF WONDERS

The Age of Wonders. Aharon Applefeld, Tr. Dalya Bilu. David
Godine, 1981, 270 pp. $12.95.

Reviewed by DR. MARK W. WEISSTUCH

The Age of Wonders, Israeli author Aharon Appelfeld's
second novel to appear in English, is the strangely moving
story of a survivor. It is primarily a book of memories. The
memories it deals with though are not of persecution, deportation, starvation, beatings and concentration camps. Such
unfathomable Holocaust experiences rest at the center of the
novel but are never mentioned. Instead, Appelfeld is concerned
with the sense of loss engendered by the Holocaust. The shape
and technique of the work underscore this intent.

The book is divided into two sections. The first part, like
Badenheim 1939, the author's previously translated work, is
set in ante-bellum Europe, a time when the Jews of Europe
stood poised on the edge of the abyss, but many were looking
the other way. It describes the perplexites, anxieties and
frustrations of a well-to-do Jewish Austrian family caught
in the grip of mounting anti-Semitism. The vision of this world
is shaped by the instinctive, often poetic, perceptions of Bruno,
the eleven-year-old son. His evocative first-person narration
renders a profound image of unrelenting physical and spiritual
disintegration. It is the picture of a world coming undone as
swiftly as pulling the thread out of a button.

At first, the impending doom is dimly discerned, nothing
you could put your finger on, only subliminal suggestions of
dislocation. Gradually, as the net inexorably tightens, Bruno's
observations become sharper and more palpable. His thoughts
become suffused with dire premonitions—"The feeling that we
were doomed seeped through me like a thick liquid" or "everything around us was in a state of gray, drugged despair and
the bitter smell of the approaching end was already in the air."
Such insights bring about the premature end of his childhood
innocence.

The dominant figure in Bruno's life is his father. Appelfeld's sensitive study of his deterioration provides a compelling portrait of the contradictions of the assimilated Jew. A
writer of modest repute, he was a friend of Stefan Zweig and
a zealous admirer of Franz Kafka, whose themes filtered

through his works. A., as he is referred to, saw himself first
and foremost as "an Austrian writer." "No one," he exclaims,
"will deny me this title." Long ago he rejected his Jewish
origins and now he vehemently attributes all the travails
suffered by Jews to the uncultured, alien *Ostjuden* and the
self-interested, narrow-minded "petit-bourgeois Jews."

When the plague strikes, though, he himself becomes the
victim of anti-Semitic literary criticism. As his reputation
crumbles, he stubbornly refuses to relinquish his faith in
Austrian decency and reasonableness. He denies the obvious
pressures, nurturing instead illusions of security. His rage
turns inward, manifesting itself in self-contempt and a de-
meaning increased hostility toward Jews. Humiliated by
strangers, ignored by former colleagues, rebuffed by old
friends and stung by the contempt in his wife's eyes, he collects
the tattered remnants of his self-respect and flees to a mistress
in Vienna.

The enigmatic bond between father and son leads to the
second section of the book entitled "Many Years Later When
Everything Was Over." Bruno is thirty years older, the same
age his father had been when the world collapsed. He has
been living in Jerusalem, choked by a barren, loveless mar-
riage. He is drawn back to his home town by some publisher's
renewed interest in his father's novels. This public resurrection of his father prompts a need to purge his memories. Sunk
in an embracing melancholy, he wanders through the town
searching for shards of his past.

What he encounters are stranded ghosts and emotional
cripples, twisted and distorted half-lives—an embittered, reclu-
sive Jewish Jew-hater; his former housemaid, once sensual,
now a slovenly prostitute, guilt-ridden for abandoning a Jewish lover during the deportations; a fey band of "mongrel"
half-Jews obsessed with their inferiority; a cowardly convert
consumed with self-hate. The lofty Austrian culture to which
his father sacrificed his dignity is revealed in the vacuity of a
popular striptease singer and the inane cavorting of the Singa-
pore Midgets.

Bruno's return visit reaches an oblique climax when he
recognizes his own sad fate—he has inherited an empty legacy.
His life is drained and unfurnished, destined to a dull expect-
ancy. This alienation is emphasized by the shift in the second
section to a detached third-person voice and the flat mono-
chromatic tone of the narration. It is confirmed, too, by the
final image of the book: "He stood still for a long time, empty
of thought or feeling. His eyes focused vacantly on the blink-

ing railway signal, waiting for the brass plate to fall and the
whistle of the engine to pierce the air."

Appelfeld has wrought a poignant threnody of the survivor's enduring trauma. His prose is apt and restrained and
never judgmental.

M&R 8:2, March-April, 1982

ODYSSEY OF A SURVIVOR

By Bread Alone: The Story of A-4685. Mel Mermelstein, Auschwitz
Study Fund, 1979. 290 pp. $12.95

Reviewed by DR. LUBA K. GURDUS

One should read Mermelstein's book *By Bread Alone* not
only for its story but also for its ideas. The book's narrative
is a fusion of facts and inferences, leading at times to meaningful conclusions. All along the author, enlightened by the
wisdom gained through the perspective of time, raises questions; and though he chides himself for hoping to answer them,
he cannot resist from drawing various deductions.

One of the questions is the feasibility of escaping from
the Holocaust. Mermelstein is obviously obsessed by this haunting idea and deplores the "innocence of the crowds" who have
permitted themselves to be herded to Auschwitz. At the same
time, he is aware of the fact that non-compliance with Nazi
orders was dangerous and seemed self-defeating when a glim-
mer of hope still existed, though "hope was on the side of
submission."

The author recounts the past of Munkacs, Hungary, and
describes the troubled history of the region which passes
through a number of political crises. Against this background
he portrays the changing fortunes of the local Jews, including
his family and himself at the carefree age of sixteen. With
bitterness and contempt he mentions the Hungarian Arrow-
cross bandits who assisted the Nazis in rounding up Jews but
does not omit to quote the friendly attitude of the Ruthenian
peasants.

He concludes with apprehension that the irony of it all
rests in "the binding power of Jewish family bonds," which
prevented Jews from exploring possibilities of escape and

became a great asset for the Nazis, resolved to annihilate
them. Mermelstein is, therefore, grateful to his father, who
warned him and his brother, Lajos, not to stay together as
not to watch each other's suffering and become the enemy's
prey. In his own survival, he sees his father's "prophecy
fulfilled.

The author's imaginative power contributes to a vivid
narrative that arouses the reader not only to think but to see.
Leading the reader through his odyssey, he shows his numerous scenes of great impact. One of them is the "danse
macabre," in Auschwitz, when hundreds of naked men, forced
to run in endless circles around flaming pits, are being tossed
into fire, writhing and moaning. Also gripping is his detailed
description of the "Revere Block" in Buchenwald's Little
Camp, from which he was liberated on April 11, 1945. Stricken
by typhus, Mermelstein stayed there through the last stage of
his ordeal, confined to barracks, lined with shelf-like bunks,
each holding five inmates. There he was lying, "lice-ridden,
shivering with cold, starved for a bite of food."

By Bread Alone poignantly pictures his perennial bouts
with hunger which eventually caused his sliding to the state
of a musselman. Only thanks to his friends and a compassionate camp assistant was he able to hold on. The author provides useful information about the camp hierarchy and the
degenerate camp officials who gratified their sadism and lust
for murder by torturing Jews.

The book is a concise and sincere statement of facts which
seem never to reach the level of stereotype. The author is careful not to overload the reader with too much technical detail
and substitutes the extraneous data with photos, inserted
between the pages. They provide documentary evidence and
help to visualize the scope of the mounmental event of which
Mermelstein's story is an important component.

The book has generated great response and meaningful
comment. Among those who have tried to denigrate and
undermine its impact was a so-called "Revisionist Group,"
known as the Institute for Historical Review, in Torrance,
California. In 1980, the group challenged Mermelstein "to
prove that Jews were gassed in the gas chambers in Auschwitz." He filed a lawsuit against them and in December, 1981,
he received a "Resolution" from the Council of the City of
Los Angeles, resolving the issue in his favor and stating unreservedly that "the Holocaust is not reasonably subject to
dispute."

ANYA: STORY OF SURVIVAL

Anya. Susan Fromberg Schaeffer. Macmillan, 1974. 489pp. $8.95.

Reviewed by BARBARA KESSEL

I picked up the book *Anya* by Susan Fromberg Schaeffer
on a Saturday afternoon and until I finished it, I only put it
down when I was forced by hunger pangs to eat or to carry
out some vital chore. And even when I put it down, it never
left my mind. *Anya* is a novel written as an autobiography of
a woman from her childhood in Vilno, through the hell of the
concentration camps, continuing the story of the war's aftermath and ending in 1973 when Anya is 52 years old.

The 489 pages fill a lifetime in very vivid detail. It is a
pity that the word "vivid" is so over-used because it describes
this book exactly. This is so lifelike a recounting that I find it
difficult to believe it is a novel. At the very least, Ms. Schaeffer
must have based it on lengthy conversations with very real
people. It describes more closely than I ever thought imagin-
able the situations that many experienced and it explains—as
far as possible—how they became the kind of people they are
today. It explains their devotion to their children, their clan-
nishness, their love of Israel, their fear of certain nation-
alities, their hatred of others, their wisdom and their strength.

The book is very powerful, not in the sense that it
manipulates the reader's emotions as a book like *Love Story*
does, but it is powerfully evocative. It creates a very real
world in the reader's imagination. It is a difficult book to read
precisely because as much as it is a novel, it is a true story.
There may not have been anyone named Anya Savikin Lavin-
sky Meyers in "real life," but her autobiography truly belongs
to thousands of survivors.

Anya's childhood was a happy one. She had a loving
family, two brothers and a sister, two loyal housekeepers who
were more like cousins, a medical school education, and a pleasant group of friends. She was courted very persistently by a
young man from Warsaw and finally married him. Their
child put an end to medical school but Anya adjusted. Then
the war came and the tenor of her life changed entirely. She
watched every member of her family being killed except her
child, whom she was forced to hide with a Gentile family. She
survived the camps through ruse and luck. The poverty and
suspicion that were the war's legacy required a continuation

of cunning and good fortune, and Anya made it to America having found and reclaimed her child. There, she built a new life for herself from scratch and lived to watch her daughter grow away from her and become a person in her own right. There is little self-pity in the book, little philosophy. There was simply no time for it. Anya spent her days figuring out how to make it to the nighttime, and her nights were spent shoring up energy for the next day's struggle. Not until later in life, in America when she is settled and comfortable, does the book begin to ask questions and even this is the shortest section of the narrative. The most striking, educational sentence—to me—is, "I ask myself, 'What for? What is it for? To do so much and have it all taken away, to be taken away from everything and yet, I do not want to die; I want to live.' "

This book is really about survival, about the instinct, the need to survive even when the things going on around you make you ashamed to belong to the human race. Anya says her daughter gave her the impetus to struggle on, yet there are other characters in the book and in life who did not have any family left and still fought literally tooth and nail to live. One review said that this book is about "our ability to love, to make commitment." I do not think so. I think this is a trivial conclusion. I think Americans want all books to be about love, or perhaps the reviewer has to believe this book is about love in order to retain his sanity, or perhaps he just doesn't understand. This book is about survival. Survival sometimes makes no sense, so no review can go beyond that statement or the review will become nonsensical.

REMEMBERING HANUKKA

By BRYNA BAR ONI

December in Byten, a small town in Eastern Poland, was not the time of year we children particularly looked forward to, except for Hanukka.

For weeks before, my sisters Yentle and Henya busied themselves putting in the storm windows, spreading a kind of dry moss with a sprinkle of colored tissue paper strips on the window sills, between the window panes. They saw to it that all cracks were sealed, doing the best they could to prepare the house for winter before the snow set in. Father spread bales of straw over the potatoes, carrots, beets and radishes in the cellar to prevent the frost from rotting them. He saw to it that the yard was well stocked with fire-wood, to keep the family warm during the long winter.

In December, our little town lay sleepily under its heavy blanket of snow, and the frost drew magical patterns, fingerings of branches on the window panes. The prisma of icicles hanging over the brows of buildings made the little town look like a labyrinth of castles, or crystal chandeliers giving out a shimmering of light and rainbow colors at sundown, when the amber skies foreshadowed the biting winds of the next day. At night the strong wind howled in the chimney like a pack of hungry wolves.

Later on, during my two years with the partisans in "Wolves Lair Woods" when I escaped the liquidation of our Ghetto by the Nazis, the howling of the wolves reminded me of those windy, wintry nights. But then I was secure and happy with my family and friends.

December was the time when the geese we raised were put in a pen to be fattened for the gribenes we would eat on Hanukka with the latkes. On Sundays, the entire family was busy shredding heads of cabbage and layering it in barrels with cranberries and cherry leaves. Our young and healthy appetites loved a feast of sauerkraut and potatoes.

We children used to coast down the snow-covered hills on our sleds, and went skating on the river Szczara. In the evenings, we used to do our homework by the white, tiled stove in the middle of the house. Yentle and Henya used to spend the long winter nights reading, studying the Bible and arguing over the various commentaries. My Hebrew teacher, Jankel, used to be the authority in their Bible discussions. Besides, he was courting my sister Henya. He liked to play chess with her, but she was too tough for him to beat.

After a day's work in our grain mill, Mother sometimes succumbed to the local life-style, finding relaxation by sitting at the stove plucking goose feathers for the quilts and pillows she was preparing as a trousseaux for us girls. Sometimes, we kids pitched in too, and one of us used to read aloud the melodramatic novels like "Rebecca," which had just become popular. We devoured these books romanticizing about the places and people vicariously experiencing their happy and sad situations, having pity and sympathy for them and thus making the long winter bearable.

Hanukka, children loved. Each evening, as we lit the candles, we received our "Hanukka gelt" and raced to our friends to use the shiny pennies for the Hanukka game of spinning the "dreidel" (top). We silently prayed "Gimel-take it all."

On Saturday night, Yentle and Henya used to hold their annual Hanukka party at which they raised money for Israel. They belonged to the Revisionist Organization, were disciples of Zev Jabotinsky. The first latke was auctioned, going to the highest bidder with great fanfare. As the party went on, the stacks of pancakes gradually diminished.

I remember our last Hanukka party before the Holocaust. I gave a speech in Hebrew, comparing the Maccabees with Trumpeldor. I have forgotten my Hebrew, I'm afraid but I can still remember that I began with *"Ein davar—tov lamut bead artzeinu"*—"Never mind, it is good to die for our country." Trumpeldor's famous last words.

Today, I light my Hanukka candles sadly, weighed down by all those memories. Gone is my childhood and gone is the *stetl*. My family lies in a deserted mass grave, martyrs—not heroes. . . . —and quietly flows the river Szczara.

M&R 6:6, Nov.-Dec., 1979
Reprinted from *Jerusalem Post*, 1979

THROUGH A SURVIVOR'S EYE

One of The Holy Cast: Judaism and The Holocaust Through The Eyes of a Survivor. Isaac C. Avigdor. Judaica Press, 1987. 384pp. $18.

Reviewed by DR. JONATHAN ROSENBAUM

Few events in history have been documented as fully as the mass murder of European Jews by the Nazis. Thousands of memoirs of eyewitnesses, numerous reels of film, almost the entire archives of the Third Reich, oral histories of survivors and liberators, and even the testimony of perpetrators have reconstructed the all-but-successful attempt at genocide with a precision that is both overwhelming and necessary. With such a vast corpus of information, it is easy to question why

yet another memoir should be published. What more is there
to say and how can it be said in an original way?
The author of the volume under review, Rabbi Isaac C.
Avigdor of Hartford, addresses this question and provides as
response a volume which in form as well as content possesses
many qualities which shed new light. Avigdor has composed
not simply an autobiographical memoir, but a series of
vignettes of an exceptional family's survival and loss in times
of hope and cataclysm. His book is worthy because it leaves
us with a feeling of triumph as well as a deep understanding
of the catastrophe.

Isaac Avigdor is the son of Rabbi Jacob Avigdor, who
served as the communal Rabbi of Drohobycz-Borislaw in
Galicia. The senior Avigdor was a rarity in the thriving pre-
War Jewish communities of Eastern Europe. Educated in the
intensive rabbinic traditions which immersed the student in
Talmud and Bible, but which generally eschewed secular
studies, Jacob Avigdor might well have become a typical
Eastern European Jewish scholar had he not married a woman
with a special outlook. Rechel Braindel was a graduate of the
European *gymnasium*, and through a prenuptial agreement
she required her future husband to adopt the study of secular
subjects. A brilliant student, Jacob Avigdor accepted this
challenge and, later, when the Polish government required
that all communal rabbis be graduates of the *gymnasium*, he
was one of the few who qualified. In 1933, he became a still
rarer phenomenon: he received the Ph.D. degree at the University of Lvov (Lemberg), an accolade which was almost
unknown within the Eastern European rabbinate.

Jacob Avigdor was, thus, a man of both worlds: the
intensively Jewish and the intellectually secular. He even
served as a chaplain in the Polish army before the Second
World War, receiving the rank of major. With such creden-
tials, he would become a very wanted man under the Nazis, yet
he survived the war by more than twenty years and ultimately
went on to lead the Jews of Mexico, adopting Spanish and
publishing several of his more than thirty books in it. Among
his most important writings was a forty-page rabbinic respon-
sum (an answer to a question of Jewish law) which served as
the foundation for freeing thousands of women to remarry
after the Holocaust by setting down rules of evidence based on
the conditions of mass murder which would allow them to be
declared widows.

The author provides us with these facts and many more
in a style which is both precise and personal. His work is not

meant as an exhaustive study, a full course meal from appetizers to after-dinner drinks. Rather, it is a series of hot and cold delicacies which together comprise food for the spirit as well as the intellect. The book is divided into four parts: "Memories from the Valley of Death," "Moments of Holiness Year Around (sic)," "Memorable People," and "Milestones in the Family."

The first section, which represents almost half the book, provides an understanding of the metamorphosis through which this survivor and so many others have come. Despite his heroic efforts which clearly saved both family and friends, Isaac Avigdor, our author, could not bring himself to discuss fully his experiences until many years after the physical horror had ended. His moving chapter about his mother is especially illustrative.

Avigdor follows these narratives with an imposing section of short sermons on each major holiday of the Jewish year. One might expect these to be dry and technical. They are aimed at the knowledgeable Jewish layman and each provides a lesson from the recent, terrible past as well from an ancient text. The thoughts are witty and often inspiring, but they do require a reasonable knowledge of Jewish lore and literature.

Two short sections conclude the work: a collection of appreciations of special persons whom Avigdor has known and a series of thoughts on recent special occasions in the life of the Avigdor family. The appreciations include persons who have played especially important roles in recent Jewish life, the most well known of whom is certainly Aliza Begin, the wife of the former Prime Minister of Israel. Mrs. Begin came from Drohobycz and she and her husband were married by Rabbi Avigdor's father. The author describes the wedding in detail and in doing so provides certain new historical facts about the development of a central figure in recent Jewish history.

The book is not flawless. It possesses the occasional stylistic errors which one would expect from an author who is not composing in his native tongue (e.g. "my . . . disability to write" or the redundant "False Lies"). However, the book is an inspiration to survivors who have not yet spoken, a memorial to the martyrs who cannot speak, and a source of understanding to future generations who will want to know the past so that they can prevent its repetition.

WHEN WE ARE GONE

The world is waiting
breathlessly
for the last of us
survivors
of the great murderous fit
to vanish
and to become
a legend.
The world is ready
to shake off
the last vestiges
of ashes
from its feet.
The world is eager
to quell
the feelings of guilt
to drown its conscience
in another purifying myth
catharsis necessary for the mob
lusting for blood.
When we are gone
the world able to deny at last
the reality of
Auschwitz
Bergen-Belsen
Majdanek
Treblinka
will shroud the shameful images
from its collective mind.
When we are gone
the world's gigantic wheels
imbued with hatred
will go on blindly
unchanging
turning
grinding
growing receptive
to the next onslaught. . . .

YALA H. KORWIN

M&R 8:14, Nov.-Dec. 1981

THE GUARDIAN OF A LIFE THAT HAS DISAPPEARED

By Dorothy Fuerst

Like fireworks exploding simultaneously, the photographs taken by Dr. Roman Vishniac of a world destroyed by the Nazis are now being exhibited in Amsterdam, London, Paris, New York. The Jews he depicted are seen again: old Jews walking the snowy streets of Cracow with books under their arms; young Jewish girls lining up shoes at a summer camp; a professional water carrier balancing pails on a yoke across his shoulder.

Dr. Vishniac remembers them all and that last one mentioned in particular. He himself had tried to carry water on a yoke but spilled too much and the customer would not pay him. Obviously, carrying water was a skill that had to be learned. Dr. Vishniac remembers the young, destitute coal carrier, too, in another picture. He has an impish smile, belying his ragged clothes and the hernia Dr. Vishniac tried to alleviate with a truss. He remembers them all. They are all his children.

They have emerged, the people of this doomed world, to reach us, and they do, to speak to us once again of the world they inhabited; to show us how they made their sparse living; how intensely they studied Torah; how they feared the future; how they despaired of hope.

Dr. Vishniac protographed them always with a hidden camera, without poses, without artifices so that the truth would be recorded, that the photographic record would destroy the myth that the Jews were rich and manipulated the money centers of Europe. Nevertheless, he became a target for recording the truth. He knew this and many times had to run from the police because, in spite of his best efforts, his camera had been detected. The authoritarian Polish government of the 1930's jailed him eleven times for photographing the poverty and the discrimination the Jews were subject to.

Dr. Vishniac began his odyssey in 1933, starting in Poland, continuing over the Carpathian mountains on foot, unobtrusively photographing a farmer surrounded by his few geese, children at play, children squeezed into wooden pews, following the *rebbe's* lesson in their books. He went through Czechoslovakia and Hungary, then back up to Poland again. He lived and worked in Berlin, but between 1933 and 1939 he

110

returned repeatedly, taking 16,000 pictures of this doomed people.

The last year he was able to photograph was in 1939. At the outbreak of war he fled ahead of the advancing Germans. In France he hid some of the prints of his pictures, taking many others with him to New York. After the war, many prints were returned to him from their hiding places; and now he lives with these 2,000 pictures that were saved. They surround him in his apartment in New York. Dr. Vishniac has blown some of them up, almost life size and mounted them and he watches them go about their business in Cracow, Warsaw, Lublin, and points in between.

Decades after his arrival in the United States, his friends, his family, this doomed world he photographed is emerging from his apartment, to be recognized, to be remembered. November, 1983, saw the publication of Dr. Vishniac's book, *A Vanished World*.

What would they say, these people of the pictures, if they could speak to us? According to Dr. Vishniac, who lived among them, whose guardian he is, they would want to be conscious of our Jewishness, to stick together, to know that the impossible once happened, to make sure that a Holocaust never happens again. This is the message of the pictures.

M&R 10:6, Nov.-Dec., 1983

THE WHITE KERCHIEF

By LUSIA PILCER

It was after Yom Kippur 1942 when the ghetto of Czenstochow started to have 'selections.' The purpose as we knew it at the time was to separate the young and healthy who could work while the children and the elderly were sent to different camps. Living on Aleja 1 above the marketplace where the selections were held, we could see everything. I stood watching from our window as the people passed by. We shouted to each other, "Look, there's our friend. He's lucky. He went to the right side." We saw friends, relatives, even my first cousin and closest friend, Lilka, pass by. I was relieved to see her chosen to join the right side which we somehow sensed, though we did not know for sure, was the safe side. Every few days, the German Commander Degenhart and his helpers emptied the streets, house by house.

At home, we slowly prepared for the selection. Since we knew that our street would be last, we spent the days talking, not knowing if we would ever see each other again. My parents gave me some jewelry that I could sell if I needed food. We sewed it into the lining of my clothes. My mother also forced me to take a bottle of raspberry juice from my grandfather's factory. Later, it would be doled out by the teaspoon to those who were ill. We advised each other and hoped that my fictitious papers that said I had worked cleaning army barracks would convince Germans that I could be useful to them. I remember knitting woolen gloves for my young brother Miecio for the coming winter as we waited.

When our time came, we lined up in winter coats without fur collars (we had been forced to give them to the Germans some time before). I was wearing my new fur-lined boots. My mother had dyed her few streaks of grey, hoping that she would look young enough to work. In the last minute as I was about to leave, she put a white kerchief over my head.

At the gate where the selections took place, I showed my papers but they were torn into pieces. We were all sent to the left side, clinging to each other. My mother was weeping because she had hoped so much that the papers would save me.

Suddenly, we saw a German soldier walking through the lines shouting, "Where is the girl in the white kerchief?" Seeing me, he pulled me out of the line, I was frightened and started to cry, fearing that he wanted to take my boots. I didn't even say goodbye to my parents. I followed blindly behind him. He led me to the other line on the right side and left me there. I felt an arm around me and it was Lilka, who tried to quiet my tears. We held each other, crying, as I told her what happened. At that moment, I thought to myself that it was my mother's white kerchief that was her gift of life to me.

I went through many selections afterwards but always with a belief that I was somehow protected and no harm would come to me because I was wearing the kerchief. I only lost it when we heard the Russians had come to Czenstochow, and we ran from the *lager*. Maybe my mother felt that she had finished her job. But I often wish that I still had the white kerchief so I could feel her protection over me.

M&R 5:5, Sept.-Oct., 1978

IT WAS JANUARY 18, 1943

By MARYSIA FELBERBAUM

In the Warsaw Ghetto, calm reigned in the deserted, snowy streets. Actions eased for a while, yet the enemy couldn't be trusted. The weary, emaciated remnants of a people of the Ghetto sought shelter in bunkers, underground passages and attics from the cruelty of the tyrant. Only some were still employed in the German-run "shops" and outposts. Everyday at dawn, silently, as if they were shadows, the workers moved through the empty streets, uncertain whether they would return "home" at night.

And fearful premonitions tore and tormented our souls, expecting the oppressor's wrath to unleash any moment. Suddenly at daybreak, piercing voices resounded all around. Jewish policemen, down in the courtyard, yelled: "Action! Action! Get out!" Terror seized me! Would the end be drawing near? There was dreadful panic.

Quickly, the women, children, and the elderly began leaving for refuge in the bunker underneath the building. Shooting was heard all over. The SS-men were fast approaching.

Unexpectedly, rumors spread that acts of resistance were taking place on Nalewki and Niska Streets. The news sounded incredible. However, even more incredible appeared the sight of a tremendous sack, filled with ammunition, carried by two young boys. We watched stunned. Yet, as unbelievable as it seemed, it was happening. And one's heart pounded fast, and joy lit a face. . . . Not ever again shall the enemy succeed without impunity in destroying the innocent! The fateful moment arrived! Soon the entire Ghetto would flare up in revolt against the mighty forces.

Sudden silence ensued in the courtyard. The SS-men stormed in! Instantly they ravished the victims in their bestial claws. Appalled but resigned, we realized that our fate was sealed.

My brothers and I and thousands of others were marched in military order, escorted by gendarmes, with their rifles pointed at us. It was a sunny, beautiful morning. Abundant tears drenched my face while bidding farewell to the empty buildings and deserted streets. Soon we reached our destination, the Umschlagplatz (assembly place for deportation). As the gates to the gehenna opened, a most horrifying sight struck our disbelieving eyes: SS-men, tremendous "peitches" (whips) in hands, mercilessly smote the victims as they entered. Hundreds, compressed into a shapeless mass, writhed in agony at the feet of the beasts. And "peitches" wriggled, and shots resounded, and chaos pervaded.

Little children and mothers, husbands and wives, torn apart from each other, were shoved and hurled into the trains headed for Treblinka. Ferocious, heartbreaking shrieks of the unfortunate, crammed in the freight cars, reverberated. The shooting, screaming, yelling and shouting, mixed with the shrilling roar of the madness-ridden SS-men, drove one to insanity. The shapeless mass wiggled back and forth, as if prodded by a devilish power. Here and there, one hit by a bullet slid down and was trampled. A young man next to me, badly wounded, cried out, bent his shoulders, and moved on supported by the crowd.

Sunddenly, the shapeless mass surged forward. We found ourselves in front of the huge building. With difficulty we forced our way inside through a window. Propelled by the crowd, we landed on the upper floor. In the undescribable turmoil it was humanly impossible to grasp what was happening. Here again, rageful SS-men, howling savagely, drove their prey to the trains. And their "peitches" whistled, viciously, pitilessly striking the half-conscious victims.

Unexpectedly, it calmed down. Cringed and shivering violently, I stopped in a corner of the huge hall. I was alone! The crowd disappeared, and so did my brothers, I rose to my feet quickly and frantically began calling their names. But only the echo reverberated in the empty, huge hall. . . . Abram! Beniek! Seconds, minutes passed. Bewildered, I paced the hall. Then suddenly, as if from afar, I heard their voices. Within seconds, my two brothers and I were together again.

A veil of darkness embraced the Umschlag. The enormous halls filled up again with freshly captured victims. Evidently the intensity of the action did not diminish. Transports streamed in continually. The place was jammed, and one had to struggle for a tiny spot on the floor to kneel or to crouch.

It was late at night already. Some people exhausted, fell asleep. They breathed rhythmically, just as if they were in their own homes. I remained awake. Noiseless, I lifted myself up and crawled to the big window nearby. Outside, the night was moonlit, snowy-white. Silence reigned all around. Down there silhouettes of the guards moved slowly. I could hear the cracking of the snow under their heavy boots. In my despair,

I uttered faintly: "How magnificent is the world and life and yet, how unjust and unfortunate is my lot . . ."

Silence reigned over the gigantic hall at daybreak. The cold was beyond bearing. All windows were coated with thick frost. We felt deserted and separated from the rest of the world. The SS-men had not arrived.

Some people contemplated breaking out. They had brought tools along when captured and hoped to dig an undergroud passage from the basement to the outside. Determined to challenge fate, old, young, male, female, all offered help in this herculean undertaking. Hours of hard labor, indescribable exertion followed, but to no avail. Walls were too thick and impossible to penetrate, and time was running out. The Germans would be arriving any minute. Just as soon as the risky undertaking was abandoned, the shooting outside started again. The cellar became the main target. Quickly the Germans blockaded the entrance and shots reverberated every now and then to remind us of the threatening presence of the SS.

We squeezed deeper into the darkness of the underground and waited. Hours dragged out tediously while we debated what to do. Some people had a lot of money and valuables. They deliberated over bribing the SS-men to gain freedom.

Somehow rumors reached us that no selections or transports would take place that day. Because of freezing temperatures, the Germans couldn't run the trains to Treblinka. The good news was indeed encouraging, yet one refused to be optimistic. Nature couldn't remain favorable for long. As night fell upon us again, the SS left.

Stillness reigned all around when suddenly, overpowered by some optimistic thoughts, and as if guided by bizarre premonitions, we began to wander the cellar hallways again. Our aim was to reach the upper level of the building. Led by intuition, or "good spirits," straggling through the winding passages, we unexpectedly arrived at a staircase towering above us. Right at the foot of the staircase stood a Jewish policeman who guarded the exit of the building. Controlling the gate to freedom, he, for money, permitted some to make their way out of the Umschlagplatz.

My brothers and I watched astounded. We dared not approach the Nazi collaborator. We had no money and couldn't bribe him. Yet, our hearts palpitated as if expecting the improbable to happen. Suddenly, as if floodlit, illuminated with bright sunshine, the staircase became the scene of a strange incident.

A tall woman appeared on top of the staircase. Her pale face, disorderly hair, tattered coat, right hand hanging immobile, profuselyl bleeding, and the thin stream of blood, flowing down the stairs were a terrifying sight. Evidently, she got hurt while fleeing. Thus, the bribed policeman, frightened, left his post and ran to help the injured victim.

Shocked, my brothers and I, without a second's delay, grabbed the unexpected chance. As soon as the policeman turned around, we jumped on the staircase. Taking gigantic steps, as if driven by a superhuman force, we advanced, higher and higher, till breathless and close to collapsing, we reached the roof of the Umschlagplatz.

We glanced for a moment, confused and impatient. Our target was the adjacent Werterfassung, the center where Germans collected the plundered Jewish furniture. In order to get there, a very high wall had to be scaled. We stood by the wall helplessly, together with our escapees. There was no time to waste since we were exposed to the German guards in the street below. Every second counted now!

Suddenly, Beniek decided to climb the wall. Supported by Abram, he struggled to get to the top. Unbelievable as it seemed, within seconds he stood on the roof of the Werterfassung. As Abram lifted me, I labored with all my strength, clinging onto some crevices. I made it to the top, even though my face, hands, and knees were bleeding, and my clothing was tattered.

Abram remained beneath and helped other to scale the wall. However, soon he had to join us on the roof. Quickly, we rushed downstairs. We had to hide at once!

Suddenly, some strange voices resounded outside in the hall. "Come out of your hideouts. The action is over. You can go home now!" We listened, astonished, not able to determine what was happening. We hesitated. The calling, however, didn't stop. It sounded rather so persuasive and luring. We left our hideout. How we regretted our hasty decision! We were immediately surrounded by Jewish police. For no apparent reason they searched for women; men were free to leave. The trains to Treblinka were running again.

I was trapped again! Separated from my brothers, I was dragged to the police chief and then pushed into line with the others just captured. Astonished, I watched Abram getting through to the police chief who recognized him as his old friend. I heard Abram begging for my release. The chief remained insensitive to the pleas. He yelled that his mother was taken away too. Why then would he care about an old friend's sister? And so, resigned, I just stood there, fearful, trembling. Something strange happened! A young man appeared right in front of me. He grabbed my arm, pressed a card into my hand, and quickly pulled me out of the line. Unnoticed we ran downstairs and then through a long corridor. Breathless we stopped at a door. Amazed, I recognized my savior, with whom I was acquainted some time ago. He was employed in the Werterfassung now. Therefore, he could provide me with an employee card, which was indispensable, had I gotten caught again. My rescuer led me into the Werterfassung kitchen. Delightful soup moistened my parched lips and dry throat.

My brothers Benick and Abram joined me soon, and the three of us, reunited, set out for home. Under the protective shadows of night, we hoped to reach the bunker safely. We moved in silence from street to street, holding on to the walls of empty buildings. The cries of the unfortunate thronged in the trains, mournfully echoed from afar. We shuddered! Our legs barely carried us through the lifeless streets as we finally trudged up to our home and bunker beneath.

And the tale of our miraculous escape was told and retold till late into the night. Only a few hours remained till daybreak. We could rest now, until unpredictable fate would strike again.

M&R 9:7, Jan.-Feb. 1983; 10:8, Sept.-Oct. 1983

WHEN THE WARSAW GHETTO BURNED

By MARYSIA FELBERBAUM

Those were the days when the German army stood at the gates of the ghetto. The enemy, powerful, equipped with the most modern, sophisticated weapons, was ready to enter and extinguish the remnants of the dehumanized, the emaciated. But, suddenly, an unbelievable happening took place. Jews, in their despair and lonelinesses, threw themselves into battle. The ghetto lit up in bloody flames. The Aryan Warsaw and the world watched, indifferent!

The spectacle went on for weeks, Jews, hiding in the Aryan sector, watched, heartbroken, astounded, disillusioned, in silence. . . . Jew hunting kept many busy. Szmalcowniks and all sorts of blackmailers were roving the streets madly, searching for Jews who had a chance to escape from the inferno nearby. In streetcars one could hear lively conversations among the passengers watching the burning buildings on the other side of the walls: "Pluskwy, koty sie smaza!" (The bed-bugs, the cats are roasting.) And funny, sarcastic remarks passed from mouth to mouth. Sometimes they would spot on a roof of a building a woman with a child who preferred, to being consumed by fire, death by jumping to the ground with her offspring.

And one wondered whether such horrifying scenes would evoke pity or perhaps cause one to shed a tear. Instead, to no surprise, the Germans were earning praise: "They certainly are doing a good job for us"—would be the usual remark. The Jews, indeed, would never return to claim their homes, businesses, properties. Eventually the Poles would be the benefactors of this carnage.

Moving in the city streets was dangerous, especially for those with false identifications. People just paid more attention to who is who, particularly when someone with Semitic looks came into sight. After all, it was mostly the Poles, not the Germans, who were efficient in discovering a Jew. The Pole, expertly and easily, could detect the despair and hopelessness etched on a Jewish face. Hence, Jew-hunting was after all a not too difficult venture.

One late afternoon I was returning home. Suddenly I heard voices behind me: "To ona, Zydowka" (This is a Jewess!). There were five of them, children, around eight or nine years old. Dressed shabbily, in dirty clothes, they encircled me. Screaming and yelling, they wanted to draw the attention of passers-by and the police. Knowing that they were looking for money, I quickly threw them my wallet and ran away, leaving the youth-gang behind. Only one block away from home, I didn't dare to return to the apartment fearing the band would follow me. Thus, I ran up to the attic of the building, climbed a beam supporting the roof and settled behind it.

Soon I heard rumbling on the staircase. One just marveled at how well those youths knew the art of hunting a Jew. On the way up, they stopped on each floor to check for open doors behind which the expected prey could have taken refuge. Finally, they came to the attic; amazed, I watched from above how careful the area was examined. Disappointed, they left, sliding down the banisters.

My fears, however, weren't over yet. Obviously I was dealing with very experienced and well-trained szmalcowniks. Not wasting much time, they returned very soon. Speedily

they reached the attic without stopping on every floor as
before. Wild fury must have possessed them. Madly, they
were overturning each broken, old piece of furniture. Screaming and pushing each other—they searched every corner. The
elders must obviously have worked diligently on educating
their offspring in the "dignified" art of blackmailing and
stealing.

And the ghetto burned, and the brave and the last fought
the uneven battle they knew from the onset was lost. And the
fires spread day and night, consuming more and more of this
cursed, isolated island of death and bestiality. . . .

One day I received news from my younger brother Beniek,
who jumped off a death train to Treblinka and was hiding with
Mrs. Wojciechowska. I decided to see him. It was a sunny,
warm afternoon as I boarded the trolley heading toward
Wojciechowska's place. From the moment I entered the street-
car I experienced a strange feeling. Instinctively, I felt that
somebody was watching me. Within a short time I reached
my destination, crossed the huge court of the building, not
even turning my head once. However, the fear that I was
followed didn't leave me. As I ran up the staircase, I heard
someone following me. Still, I got to the door of the apartment,
entered the kitchen, and quickly ran into the next room where
my brother was hiding. . . .

Surprised, I found a young, handsome man, in his early
thirties, dressed exquisitely. I realized immediately that I was
dealing for a change with a sophisticated type. He asked for
my documents, looked at the kennkarte (I.D.), and immediately declared that it was falsified, and my appearance
seemed Jewish.

In this most critical situation, with Beniek hidden in the
next room, I decided to get the blackmailer out of the apartment and bargain with him outside. We walked out together
and got to a crossing where a German stood guard. My persecutor adamantly claimed that I was Jewish and that he could
right away give me away to the German with an instant death
sentence, without too many questions asked. I cried bitterly,
fearing that those were my final moments. I pleaded with him
for mercy. Finally, he agreed to take me to his friend's house
located nearby and settle the "case." . . . I followed him. The
friend, a young boy, fourteen perhaps, opened the door of the
attic apartment. "Zlapalem drugiego kota dzisiaj!" (I caught
another cat today!), announced my "charming" companion.
The seemingly innocent young boy, shook his head, as if wondering at the older friend's "achievements."

Now the blackmailer asked sternly for money and any valuables I had on me. I gave him my brother's expensive attache case and a thousand zloty, quite a sizeable amount. Visibly pleased, he was about to leave; however, he did not forget to ask me to return the next day and disclose any known addresses of rich friends hiding with Poles. On his way out he abruptly pulled me over to the only window in the attic and ordered me to look out.

One could never forget the view that struck my bewildered eyes. The ghetto in flames was a terrifying sight, an indelible vision one could never eradicate from a memory. And my captor growled viciously: "nobody of yours will ever come out of there! you will be left alone, all alone in the world!" Sadistic hatred emanated from his voice. Finally he left. I stood at the window, astounded, petrified. . . .

And the ghetto burned. The fires raged wildly, as though revolting in anger and bitterness against unfathomable injustice and shattering silence of the world. . . .

M&R 11:6, March-April, 1985

WE ARE THE SURVIVORS

We are all that are left
of a multitude of people,
Who without clothes to protect themselves
marched proudly to their deaths.
Never uttering their fears,
only the sacred words of prayer.
We are the survivors,
that never knew the horrors of the
death camp,
the smell of gas reaching open nostrils,
the point of a gun on barely covered bones,
and the doom that a pair of black
boots brought.
We never saw our families taken away
in trains never to return,
or fall bleeding and dead in open pits,
knowing we would join them shortly.
We never experienced the pain,
but six million did.
And in their sacred memory,
we must never allow ourselves to forget.

M&R 6:5, March-April 1960   MICHELLE PRICE

THE LITTLE ORPHAN

Tell me, little girl, pray say,
Why your sorrow, fears?
Your large, black and lovely eyes
Why always full of tears?

I bear a sorrow, aye I bear,
I to no one in the world can call,
Father, mother have been killed
When I was still quite small.

Grandma, grandpa, too, are slain
In the wood where the large trench turned,
Brothers, sisters of my faith
In one room they all were burned.

Our goods and all for which we toiled
From all our Jewish people there,
The Nazi took away from us
And sent us forth to death, despair.

Like an abandoned stone I'm left,
And I am quite alone,
I have remained quite desolate
Sans family or home.

Sorrow I bear and bear
That in the world alone am I,
My dear ones murdered, doomed to die,
When I was still so small.

FRUME GOLKOWICZ-BERGER
TR. DR. PERCY MATENKO

M&R 9:5, March-April, 1983

REUNION FOR CAMP INMATES
AT SPECIAL JERUSALEM INAUGURAL

27 NISSAN 5747—This was a special time for survivor Solomon (Sam) Gross, who was in Israel for Yom Hashoa V'Hagvurah. More important, he was on hand with his wife for the inauguration at Yad Vashem of the first unit of the Valley for the Destroyed Communities. Mr. Gross is on the Executive Committee of the American Society for Yad Vashem.

But Mr. Gross certainly had an unanticipated experience beyond anything that he could have imagined. It was a reunion with a close friend, inmates at a German workcamp, 46 years ago.

It was during a visit to the Jerusalem Museum that Mr. Gross spotted what he thought was a familiar face among people seated in front of the building.

After walking on a few steps, Mr. Gross turned back and in wonderment asked the familiar face: "Are you from Poland?"

"Yes," came back the response.

"Are you, perhaps from Klobuck?" Mr. Gross probed further.

"Yes," again, came the response.

"Then, please, show me your hands," Mr. Gross pleaded with the man, who was bewildered at this point.

Shortly, "the man with the hands" identified himself as Mr. Swierczewski.

Mr. Gross mumbled one more query: "Are you Marek?"

That's all that was needed. The two men fell into each other's arms after a 46-year absence.

A native of Chrzanow, Poland, Sam (Shlamek) Gross was detained in November, 1940, in the Zwangs Arbeits Lager Sakrau in Germany. It was there that a friendship developed between the boy and the man, Marek: two, who sustained each other with moral support.

During one crisis point, Mr. Gross confided in Marek that he was planning to cut off his finger as a means of being permitted to leave the camp and return home.

"You are young . . . you will survive," Marek pleaded with Sam. "Why ruin your two healthy hands?"

But in a twist of irony, it was Mr. Swierczewski, who cut off his finger three days later. He received word from home that his child was dying and his wife was beside herself

122

in helplessness. If he cut his finger, he thought, he could return and help them. It was futile. They both perished.

Through the years, Sam Gross had terrible, haunting memories of a friend who talked him out of committing an act of folly, and then the friend disregarded his own advice. Forty-six years had passed, with nary any communication between them. Sam Gross entered the United States and Swierczewski rebuilt his life in France, residing in Paris.

But they finally did meet again, as Sam Gross came to Yad Vashem to remember. How symbolic it is that they met, remembered as they reunited in Jerusalem, the united, eternal capital of the Jewish people.

M&R 14:8, Sept.-Oct. 1987

SURVIVAL AS "ARYAN"

By ROSE GREENBAUM-DINERMAN

. . . My goal was the village of Yavorovo, where I hoped to get in touch with the Polish family, Soldanski. I had been given the name by a Jew in Exczegowo, who told me the Soldanskis were friendly toward Jews. . . .

I knocked on one of the doors. It was opened by a young Pole. I greeted him calmly and told him a fictitious tale about my family having been deported by the Germans to perform slave labor. Having escaped I was now seeking a place to stay for the time being. He asked me to come inside, where I met three of his younger brothers. I gathered from their conversation that they were five brothers, all living under this roof. Their parents were dead.

The oldest brother, who came home several hours later, was not averse to helping out a Polish woman who managed to escape from the German clutches. On the contrary, he deemed it a patriotic act. He volunteered to provide me with false identification papers. As one who escaped German slave labor, I could not use mine. . . .

My first few days in the Soldanski household passed without incident. It occurred to me that my life was entering a period of relative security. I might, in my new guise as a

Christian, survive the Nazi deluge. But fate willed it otherwise.

Of the five Soldanski brothers, the oldest displayed the most kindness, while the youngest proved the most hostile. He began arousing his brothers against me, warning them of the terrible consequences owing to the fact that I did not possess the proper papers. The situation became so aggravated that the oldest took me to his cousin, reputed to be a Communist. But it became immediately apparent during our conversation that the Communist was at the same time a vicious anti-Semite. "The only positive thing the Germans are doing," he said, "is killing Jews." I did not remain there very long. The host told me to take my things and leave.

. . . Soldanski led me out on the road and pointed to a house in the distance whose owners were always in need of help. The woman of the house hired me without any preliminaries. I worked very hard. I carted heavy buckets of water from the well, did the laundry, washed the floors, and fed the pigs. During my leisure time I knitted sweaters. Exhausted, I slept poorly.

But here, too, my employment was brought to a sudden end by circumstances beyond my control. One day, returning from the shed where I milked the cow, I heard unfamiliar voices in the room. I stopped to listen. They were talking about me. My hands, they were saying, were very delicate; how come I never complained of the hard work. I must be Jewish, they concluded.

. . . I was wrung out, physically and spiritually . . . I entered the forest and began seeking a stout branch from which to hang myself. . . .

An urge to live seized hold of me. "You must live"—my mother whispered. I rose with great effort. My legs were still, and I rubbed them furiously to restore the circulation of the blood. I seized hold of a tree to keep from falling. My eyes were filled with tears, but I felt a reawakened desire to live. . . .

After walking a short distance, I spied a house and knocked on the door. "Jesus, be praised!" I said as the door opened. I was invited inside and treated to a large bowl of food. Eating my fill, I thanked my hosts and left.

I walked a long time until exhaustion overwhelmed me. I saw a trim little white house and started toward it. What made me feel salvation was there I don't know. Was it fate? An accident? But there, in that trim little house, I found what I was seeking. The wonderful people who lived there took me in and gave me shelter.

I will not take up space here to describe my stay with the Polish family Ostrowski. During my stay with them, I was surrounded by warmth and friendship. Nobody in the family knew I was Jewish until the day the Russian patrols first entered the village, and I revealed the secret to my hosts. After the liberation of the village, I decided not to put off returning to Gombin. In our letters, my brother and I vowed to go back to Gombin as soon as the war ended and wait for each other in my parents' house. Pan Ostrowski tried persuading me not to go; the highways were clogged with military vehicles and unsafe for a young woman. But I was very eager and found it impossible to put off.

Old Pan Ostrowski escorted me to the highway and helped me get on a Russian military truck that was heading in the direction of Gombin.

M&R 14:5, Nov.-Dec. 1987

STORY OF KIELCE: CEMETERY AND A SURVIVOR

By DOROTHY FUERST

This is the story of one town, deep within Poland, the cemetery near it, and, above all, of one man who made a difference. From one perspective it is the story of all cemeteries across Eastern Europe, desecrated and violated; and of all their nearby towns, bereft of Jewish life. From another perspective, it is the story of a unique event and a unique person who persisted. In the end, there was a change in a monolithic government and a monolithic church to redeem the cemetery near the town, Kielce from which he, William Mandell, had come.

Kielce, 180 kilometres from Warsaw, is in the heart of Poland. There never were halcyon days in Kielce; there was poverty and there were pogroms but, for the most part, 25,000 Jews worked, lived Jewish lives, experienced the normal joys and sadness of life, and in the course of time died a natural death. There are no Jews in Kielce any more. Their ashes and their bones lie in Treblinka, not in the cemetery of

Kielce, though their cemetery has served as the burial ground
for the Jews of Kielce.

In 1943, the Nazis forced 45 remaining little Jewish
children, the youngest of whom was 10 months, to the cemetery, to shoot them down, as they ran and hid among the
graves. They were buried in a mass grave, the 45 little children of Kielce. No transportation to Treblinka was necessary.
One more time, in 1946, the cemetery of Kielce was to receive
Jewish dead. Two hundred Jewish survivors returned to their
town, to search for their own, to pick up old threads of their
former lives, maybe because they did not know where else to
go. In that post-war purely Polish pogrom in 1946, 42 Jewish
survivors of the Holocaust were killed and were buried in
the town cemetery. Then the Jews of Kielce left their town
and their cemetery and their dead.

In 1981 William Mandell, a native of Kielce, now living
in New York City, felt a need to return to see, to have one
more look at the town he had come from. There were no Jews
in Kielce any more. He found that the synagogue building
still stood, but had been converted to a Polish state archive.
So he turned to the cemetery hoping there to find a Jewish
presence. Instead he found Polish youths playing football
among the graves, discarded vodka bottles, gravestones vandalized, broken, gone. The Jews of Kielce, like the Jews buried
in cemeteries throughout Eastern Europe, had been violated
one more time, but in their case William Mandell made a
difference.

However, William Mandell's efforts were successful in
Kielce only because at that time there was a tri-partite repre-
sentation dealing with Polish authorities. The goal was the
restoration of Jewish cemeteries. The three groups are the
World Federation of Jewish Fighters, Partisans, and Camp
Inmates, World Federation of Polish Jews, and World Jewish
Congress.

He returned to New York. The cemetery, the desecration,
and the violation did not leave his mind, and he could not
leave it. There was some help from friends, but he provided
the driving force himself. He remembers, "We wrote in the
Jewish papers what we found in Kielce. Then we had our own
lawyer and we wrote registered letters to the Polish government, to the Polish representative to the United Nations, to
the Polish ambassador in Washington, with copies to Ambassador Jeanne Kirkpatrick, Senator Moynihan, to Senator
Javits and to the Pope."

No answers came back, but some ripple must have come

from some place. A year later, drawn back again to Kielce
and to the cemetery, William Mandell returned to Kielce and
the cemetery with his daughters. Three changes had taken
place. The mass grave of the massacred children had a long
piece of concrete around it, the vandalized monument to the
victims of the pogrom had been repaired, and 130 gravestones
had been returned as a supposed monument erected to the
memory of the children. However, no child's name was memorialized.

The major work was still to be done. The cemetery was
still desecrated, had not yet been redeemed. William Mandell
returned to New York, organized, collected money, provided
the force, time, energy, resources and, above all, the compul-
sion to see the job done and on August 23, 1987, the cemetery
of Kielce was finally restored, rebuilt, redeemed.

William Mandell had been determined to turn the attention of the world to the cemetery of Kielce, and indirectly to
the desolate cemeteries throughout Eastern Europe. Seventy-
six Jews from Canada and the United States, former residents
of Kielce, and/or their children were to be present. But William Mandell wanted a Polish presence too, in confirmation and
in dedication. Six days before the dedication ceremonies he
traveled ahead to Warsaw, to invite the bishop to be present
at the dedication ceremony. Others came too.

On August 23 eight hundred people: Jews, Poles, the
foreign press, the Catholic Church, Communist officialdom,
came to Kielce, to recognize, to confirm the redemption of the
Jewish cemetery, the work of William Mandell. It was in the
month of Elul and Rabbi David Blumenfeld, whose father,
also a rabbi, born in Kielce, put on a tallit and blew a shofar,
a call to God of the Jewish presence, in front of the synagogue,
now a Polish archive. Then *El Mole Rahamim* was chanted,
then kaddish, and finally Hatikvah.

After that the group moved to the cemetery. It was Jewish territory now. William Mandell turned the key to the
recently built gates and spoke in dedication and commemoration. The bishop, too, spoke there, a few words in Hebrew,
in acknowledgement to "our older brothers, the Jews, from
whom our Christian religion comes" and finished in greeting
'Shalom U'vraha.' Again the rabbi said El Mole Rahamim,
a verse of Tehilim; candles, hundred of yahrzeit candles were
lit. "Again we said Kaddish together, again we sang Hatikvah
together," remembers William Mandell. Then, before parting,
William Mandell gave the key to the cemetery gate to the

Polish authorities for safekeeping and to keep the cemetery
safe.

The dead of Kielce have their peace again. The high walls,
that William Mandell had built, 275 cm high, protect them;
the Magen David, the Shield of David on the wrought iron,
look in and look out: in on the graves in allegiance and out at
the Polish world in separation. What William Mandell accomplished also gives proof that there is a hope for the future.
Despite past despair and gloom, present-day Polish authorities
are striving to repair and restore—just like the Kielce cemetery—the broken relationship between Jews and Poles.

M&R 14:5, Nov.-Dec. 1987

FROM THE PIONEERS OF
REMEMBRANCE...

A hearty mazel tov to the American Federation of Jewish
Fighters, Camp Inmates and Nazi Victims, Inc., and
Martyrdom and Resistance and to its leadership, Eli Zborowski, the founder, and Dr. Harvey Rosenfeld, the editor,
on your twentieth anniversary.

The vital agenda pursued energetically and successfully
for 20 years by *Martyrdom and Resistance*—Holocaust remembrance and education, fighting anti-Semitism, supporting persecuted Jewish communities across the globe, helping
to bring Nazi war criminals to justice, and standing by
Israel in her fight for security and peace—epitomizes the
program of survival and renewal crucial to our community.
The aims and goals of *Martyrdom and Resistance* represent
the "tachlis" of our time in Jewish history, and their achievement will help insure Jewish continuity. We are proud to
walk this road together with you, for the sake of our martyrs,
our survivors, our children and our entire people.

ABRAHAM FOXMAN
National Director
Anti-Defamation League of
B'nai B'rith

II. The Genocidist State: The Third Reich

Of all the legacies of the 13-year Nazi regime, genocide—the systematic extermination of European Jewry—will be remembered the longest. Though hundreds, if not thousands, of books and articles have appeared seeking to probe the causes and consequence of the rule of Nazism, an overwhelming number unavoidably find themselves enmeshed in the Nazi/German involvement with the Jews. Three themes have elicited intense debates and bitter controversies: 1) Hitler's direct connection to the Final Solution; 2) the place of anti-Semitism in Nazi ideology; and, 3) the relationship of genocide to totalitarianism. In the last two years, a fourth and very divisive issue has rent the ranks of West German historians and commentators, namely, the question whether the crime of the extermination of the Jews was unique or simply one terrible example of state criminality that had been preceeded and followed by equally onerous instances of mass slaughter initiated by other governments.

The Third Reich was the 20th century's great crucible of social tension and resolution. No mind seeking to be in tune with the major themes of the contemporary world can afford to ignore the historic lessons locked in the history of Germany between 1933 and 1945, least of all the Jews, its foremost victims.

Along with the articles in this section, the reader would do well to read these scholarly articles: *The Crime and Punishmen of I.G. Farben* (Joseph Borkin, 5:2 Nov-Dec. 1978, Review, Charles R. Allen, Jr.); *The Holocaust in Historical Perspective* (Yehuda Bauer, 5:2 March-April 1979, Review, Monty N. Penkower); *The Holocaust: A History of the Jews of Europe During the Second World War* (Martin Gilbert, 12:2 March-April 1986, Review, Dr. Charles Patterson).

THE SUPPORTERS OF HITLER

Who Voted for Hitler. Richard F. Hamilton. Princeton University Press, 1982. 664 pp. $50.

Reviewed by CHARLES R. ALLEN, JR.

Let there be no mistake whatsoever about the importance of this work by Professor Richard Hamilton in bringing to bear new data and significant insights into the question as to who really did vote for Adolf Hitler and the NSDAP in a series of elections that witnessed the fatal plunge of Germany —and the world—into a maelstrom of fascism, war, and the Final Solution.

It is necessary to recall the electoral gains and losses that Hitler underwent in his march to power. By 1930, the Nazis became the second largest national party. In 1932 a crucial series of voting brought them in July 37% and then a loss, in November, to 33% of the total votes cast. After Hitler was named chancellor by Hindenburg, the last so-called "free" elections were held (of course, they were not free in any sense) on March 5, 1933, when the Nazis pulled 43.9% of the total vote. On March 24, 1933, the Nazi-packed Reichstag slammed through the Enabling Act which effectively ended any further pretensions about parliament as polity and laid down the foundations of the Hitler dictatorship.

There are other figures to recall: The participation of the national German electorate was quite high from 1919 until the final act of 1933. It ranged from 77.4% of the eligible vote (1924) to the highest, 88.7%, on March 5, 1933! (In the United States where, presumably, the experience in basic democratic processes, like national elections, is on a higher plane, the usual proportion of turn-outs to eligible voters over the past century has been rarely over 50%.)

Moreover, on March 5th, the SPD and KPD, the German Left (a powerful force in the Weimar Republic) polled 30.6% of the total vote or 12 million votes even though most of its leadership was already in concentration camps, its various units outlawed and scattered by the Hitler terror and, most tellingly, the two forces irreconcilably at odds to the very last Nazi imprisonment of their numbers.

When exercising the vote and in the teeth of a raging terror (by late 1932, the SA had won the battle of the streets in most German cities), an overwhelming majority of Germans did not vote for Hitler.

But enough—some 17.2 million—did support the Nazi Party so that Right power brokers forced his accession. The question has long been argued: Who did vote for Hitler? And Professor Hamilton painstakingly—largely by assiduous, detailed research among the official registries of voting from 1919 to 1933 in Germany—comes up with answers as well as sharp reflections on their implications.

In the course of his multi-levelled statistical analyses, the author challenges certain time-honored assumptions (which have since the 1930's been the received wisdom of most scholars, Left, Right, and Center).

He begins by attacking primarily what he terms "the centrist position" which is comprised of two parts, the first social (class), the other "social psychological."

This theory holds that "the social structures of advanced capitalist societies change in such a way as to worsen, absolutely or relatively, the position of the lower middle class."

The centrist theory further holds that the petty bourgeoisie "reject their traditional parties and turn to the parties or movements that promise a restoration of their former position."

It should be pointed out that during the 1930's and after the Second World War official Communist theoretical writings took a similar position. R. Palme Dutt, for example, whose 1935 work *Fascism and Social Revolution* happens to contain many useful insights, despite stilted jargon and patently propagandistic nonsense, embroidered the "centrist" position yet more. In bad times, argued Dutt, the lower middle classes— the small shop keepers, the civil servants, teachers, lower middle white collar workers, etc.—were declassed and driven into "the lumpen proletariat and demoralized working class" which in turn soon became "dominated by the petit bourgeois."

The wrangle of the Left did not prevent latter-day liberal academics from taking this wholly untested hypothesis and, elaborating monumentally on it, creating veritable "schools" of thought that derived solely from it. The works of Erich Fromm (from his 1941 *Escape from Freedom* to his last work, *The Anatomy of Human Destructiveness,* 1973), William Kornhauser (*The Politics of Mass Society,* 1959) and Martin Lipset's highly influential *Political Man: The Social Bases of Politics,* 1960 have been the progenitors of this position. One will find the writings of William Shrirer, John Toland, and Holocaust scholars such as Raul Hilberg, who unquestioningly make this assumption.

Virtually all start from the premise that the petty bourgeoisie at a time of cataclysmic economic crises shortly emerge as the essence of a fascist mass base and, indeed, were the foremost support and cutting edge for Hitler and the Nazis. Professor Hamilton demonstrates quite persuasively that such was by no means the case during the period 1919-1933 before Hitler's final take-over. As nearly as he could tell from his exhaustive research (and eminently rational thinking about his materials, facts and figures), the petty bourgeois or identifiably "mixed voting districts" did not—so long as they were able to vote—desert their customary party ranks for Hitler and the NSDAP. Nor did solid, clearly demonstrable working class districts in the significant cities; on the contrary, as the crises escalated, they closed ranks and came out even more vigorously for either the SPD (Social Democratic Party) or the KPD (Communist Party of Germany).

Not that Hitler did not receive votes from these groups; in certain cases, he clearly did—but not significantly so as to support this long-held truism that the lower middle classes were the base of support for those who voted for Hitler.

What Hamilton unarguably demonstrates in the truly massive voting districts which were crucial in building Hitler's power base is that the "educated" and affluent middle, upper-middle and clearly upper classes in Germany—as the crises mounted—did desert former party loyalties and did vote in disproportionate measure for Adolf Hitler and the "program" of the NSDAP.

The author analysed voting records of 14 cities. Berlin was the largest, most cosmopolitan. There "the highest levels of support for the (NSDAP) came from the upper- and upper-middle-class districts . . . probably exceeding 60%." In Berlin's working class districts "strong support for the . . . Left" was clear through 1919-1933. But with this crucial distinction: "a fair-sized minority" among working class voters had always supported Conservative and nationalist parties. By 1932, it was among these workers that crucial defections to the NSDAP took place, running from 20% to 25% of the vote. As nearly as can be determined the "mixed" districts (workers and lower middle class) did not so behave this way but showed the smallest such losses. This refutes the presupposed wisdom of a petty bourgeois base for the NSDAP. There are powerful implications to ponder here.

M&R 10:2, Sept.-Oct. 1983
(First of a Two-Part Series)

KRISTALLNACHT: A GERMAN CATHOLIC RECALLS SADLY

By HUGO FRICK

You can believe that this was not an easy task for me; tears always come into my eyes when I think of the misery of these people and also of the shame we did in our name to the German people. The evening before (November 8), we all were unsuspecting. About 11:00 p.m. there began a terrible noise and commotion. SA and SS men in uniform, all personally known to us, appeared in front of our door and began to demolish the house of Loehnberg's across the street from us. All windows were smashed, doors broken in, and then the house was entered. Furniture and other articles were thrown into the street, and even the food that was found was thrown out and trampled upon. And these poor people had next to nothing to eat any more because the stores for some time were not allowed to sell to Jews. The two old ladies, Mrs. Loehnberg and Mrs. Lebenberg, both old and grey, were driven out of the house in a brutal way; scantily dressed, they ran crying pitifully up and down the street.

My father had already gone to bed. He woke up from the loud noise, he looked out of the window, and when he saw what was happening he began to shout and wanted to open the window to tell the Nazis to stop. My mother stood behind him. I can still see how she held him back, because she was afraid they would call us Jew-friends and would also attack and demolish our house. My father got me out of bed—I was 13 years old at the time. He took me to the window so that I should witness it. He was crying. None of us had imagined anything so inhuman; and I think it was supposed to be a warning for all Germans who were not yet Nazis, that the same thing would happen to them if they would show resistance to the system. In Beckum, nothing was undertaken against these acts of violence; everybody feared for his own life and his property, and we all could not guess where all this would lead to.

I remember the day when Mrs. Terboch, another Jewish neighbor, came to say goodbye to us; she cried terribly. My father and grandfather were standing next to her, and she said, "You were our best neighbors; but don't forget, now it

133

is the garlic and next comes the incense." I did not understand
what she meant, and my father had to explain it to me. Mrs. T.
meant that it was the Jews who suffered now, and then the
Nazis would begin with the Catholics.

On the other side of Novd Street, and we could hear
it–they had begun to demolish the synagogue. Books and
religious objects were thrown into the street. The next morning on my way to school, I saw Erich Stein and a stepladder
in front of the synagogue; with hammer and chisel he had to
remove the Hebrew letters over the entrance which said, "This
house is a sanctuary for all peoples." I still see in my mind
Mr. Stein standing up there; he had a rag wrapped around
his hand, probably because he had wounded himself; an S.A.
man in uniform stood watch over him.

At this time the last remaining Jews in Beckum suffered
from terrible persecution.They had to wear a yellow star on
their clothing–the Star of David. They were allotted only a
few food items and had to turn over all their valuables. They
were not allowed to walk on sidewalks, only on the street,
and had to greet every passing-by Nazi party member.

I remember very well the old gentleman, Louis Rose, who
had stayed in Beckum, because like many others he just could
not believe that the Germans could do such things. He also
relied on the coveted military award which he had received
when he had joined the army as a volunteer in the Chinese
revolt in 1902; it was the Iron Cross 1st Class, the highest
military award at that time, an award which Hitler had also
received. He wore the Iron Cross next to the yellow star, but it
did not help him. His house was also completely demolished,
and he and his wife perished in the concentration camp of
Theresienstadt.

The worst things happened on Novd Street in the house of
Alex Falk, an old gentleman who lived alone. Part of the
building was used by a grocery store, and the manager of the
store, a young lady, lived upstairs. When this terrible destruction began, the 80-year-old man fled upstairs to call the lady
for help. He found the door of her apartment locked, and it
was there that the S.S. and S.A. found him. It was declared
that he had tried to enter her bedroom to rape her–the insanity of it!

Right there and then he was beaten to death.

Three well-known Beckum men were responsible for the
death of Mr. Falk, one of them, a neighbor. It is known that
all three of them took their own life at the end of the war.
The young woman was led through the city the next day with

a sign hanging around her neck in front and in back reading: "I, a German woman, had relationship with a Jew." Following this march she had to stand for some hours on a flat truck, and was insulted by the Nazis. It is said that she later suffered from a nervous disease and left Germany.

The next day my father walked with me through the city to see the destruction. Everywhere we met people who were shocked and who told my father so—because they knew him. The streets were littered with splintered glass of all the many shattered windows. It glittered everywhere, and for that reason has come the name "Kristallnacht."

After this night the last remaining Jewish citizens disappeared from the streets. They stayed in their ruined houses. I am puzzled how they got something to eat and continued to exist. Shortly after that they must have been picked up secretly at night, because suddenly they were not there any more.

The Loehnberg house was standing as a ruin for several months or years. Then suddenly it was pulled down, because the "Altegarde," the party members who had joined the Nazi Party before 1933, was expected on a visit to the city. They came riding through town in open trucks, flags were cut, and the school children had to stand by and shout "Heil." Most of these men were terribly drunk, and it was more of a disgrace than a joy to have to watch something like that.

My father had been approached several times and was offered the purchase of Jewish houses. But he declined. I don't believe that he could ever think of it. His motto was always: "Unrecht gut gedeiht nicht"—There is no blessing in something gained dishonestly.

But now back to the Kristallnacht: the events which preceded it. You will ask now, and rightly so: What did the citizens of Beckum and the people in general, who were not Nazis, do to prevent the happenings and to protect the Jewish citizens?

I'll try to be open in giving you an answer.

Unfortunately, Hitler had found an existent anti-Semitism among the German people, stemming from the disastrous mistake in the thinking of the Christian religion. He took advantage of this and developed it up to the fatal culmination. For years he had spread the message: "The Jews are our misfortune!"—the Jews were made responsible for everything that was bad: the disastrous First World War, the inflation of the 20's, etc. Added to that came the insane race politics! In the schools the children were indoctrinated with Nazi ideas by otherwise good teachers.

For instance, I had a professor in college, an avid Nazi who always came to class in his uniform. He judged the students by their service in the Hitler youth organization. As soon as he heard that a student was not enthusiastic about that, the student could expect a bad report card. It was practically the same for adults. City or government officials, for instance, had to be party members. Otherwise, they could not be promoted or were transferred to different places and inferior positions.

And so, slowly, everybody adjusted partly from conviction, more likely out of fear and personal considerations.

I remember that my father withdrew from all his posts of honor. He was head of his trade guild. He left the voluntary fire department because he had to use the "German Salute." My mother with, her timid nature, was fearful because he continued expressing his opinion, and had already the reputation of a grumbler.

And—not to forget—and unfortunately this will be the case with all peoples—one could trust almost nobody. Many people became traitors and sold their fellowmen to the party organizations to gain advantages for themselves.

Only in this way can it be understood why the people remained silent in face of the devastations and the inhuman acts. One simply feared for one's own life, for one's family, and for one's position; or, and that is worse, through these years of propaganda one was already so brainwashed and indoctrinated that one really believed to do his fatherland a service by remaining silent.

Humans are simply no heroes—that proves true especially in such critical situations. So it was in the Kristallnacht in Beckum; the people who had to watch stood by, deep down shuddering, but silent: no one trusted the other, and each one thought only of his own safety.

But I give you my word of honor that at that time neither my parents nor anyone around us knew that there were already concentration camps in which death awaited these poor people.

One wanted, by all means, to expel the Jewish people from Germany and wanted to slam the door between them and themselves, not realizing that one had slammed the door suddenly between themselves and all humanity and that one stood alone outside.

CHRONICLE OF THE LODZ GHETTO

The Chronicle of the Lodz Ghetto, 941-1944. Lucjan Dobroszycki, ed.
Yale University Press, 1984. 551pp. $35.

Reviewed by PROF. NORA LEVIN

When Dr. Dobroszycki spoke at the Third Conference on
the Holocaust in Philadelphia in 1977, he remarked on the
absence of any comments by the German perpetrators of murderous crimes against Jews, of the feelings and attitudes of
the victims before they were destroyed. In the vast quantity
of their documentation, the Nazis mechanized their reporting
as well as their machinery of death. The Jewish victims, however, were impelled by a bursting urge to write on any and
every scrap at hand, and we now have an immense literature
of personal testimony. We have the Ringelblum archives of
the Warsaw Ghetto, the archives of Sutzkever and Katcher-
ginski from the Vilna Ghetto, and the Tenenbaum archive
from the Bialystok Ghetto. Now, thirty years after he first
became acquainted with *The Chronicle of the Lodz Ghetto*,
Dr. Dobroszycki has given us a one-volume abridgement in
English of this remarkable archive, about one-fourth of the
original, carefully retaining the authenticity and integrity of
the Chronicle as a historical record.

Dr. Dobroszycki himself was confined to the Lodz Ghetto
from September, 1939, until August, 1944, when he and his
family were deported to Auschwitz, where his parents and two
younger brothers perished. He was sent to other concentration
camps to do forced labor and was liberated in May, 1945. A
trained historian who received his Ph.D. at the Polish Academy of Sciences in Warsaw, Dr. Dobroszycki published two
volumes of a planned five-volume edition of the Chronicle in
Poland in 1965-66 and, as a research assistant at YIVO, has
published many studies of Polish Jewry and the well-known
Image Before My Eyes (Poland refused to allow further publication after the Six-Day War).

The Lodz Ghetto was the first ghetto in Poland to be en-
closed and it became the one most hermetically sealed from
the rest of the world. By May, 1940, over 160,000 Jews were
pushed into the slum quarter of the city, the Baluty area, and
all Poles and ethnic Germans were forced to leave. The ghettoization process, outlined in Heydrich's Order of September

137

21, 1939, was followed remorselessly: the marking of Jews with a yellow star, confiscation of property, conscription into forced labor and the setting up of a Jewish Council. Periodically, Jews from other towns in Poland and Jews from Germany, Austria, and Czechoslovakia were brutally thrust into the Lodz Ghetto. The *Chronicle* was composed in the Department of Archives, one of the sections in the large Ghetto Administration headed by the Eldest of the Jews, Mordecai Chaim Rumkowski. The Archives were known to the German authorities but the *Chronicle* was not, and entries were couched in language that was cautious and guarded. The authors had to be constrained for fear of discovery by the Germans who were in the Ghetto every day. They were also constrained in their references to and appraisal of the otherwise severely criticized, authoritarian Rumkowski.

The Archives were originally founded to preserve materials from both the pre-war Jewish community and the Ghetto offices that had ceased to function, but the range of work expanded greatly to the collection of materials for a detailed history of the Ghetto. In slightly less than four years, materials were gathered from both the German and Jewish Ghetto administrations, including orders, proclamations, the texts of speeches, official correspondence, statistical data, photographs, books and manuscripts, monographs and biographical data. Its most comprehensive project was the Chronicle, a well-known literary genre since Biblical times and, ironically, the name given to the periodical of the robust pre-war Lodz kehillah.

The *Chronicle* was written by a group of men of different cultural and professional backgrounds and ages, but all were drawn together by the common experience of ghettoization and the desire to record that experience—the life of a Jewish community *in extremis*. We should cherish the names of the writers, generally unknown and unrecorded, except in Dr. Dobroszycki's introduction: Julian Cukier, a gifted journalist from Lodz, who initiated the writing of the *Chronicle* and was called the Plutarch of the Ghetto; Dr. Bernard Hellig, an outstanding scholar from Prague specializing in the economic history of Moravian Jewry; Szmul Hecht, a seventeen-year-old youth sent from Wielun to Lodz in 1942; Dr. Abraham S. Kamieniecki, a Biblical scholar from Slonim and one of the chief editors of the Jewish Encyclopedia published in Russian, 1906-13, in St. Petersburg; Dr. Oskar Rosenfeld, a colleague of Herzl, editor of the Zionist weekly in Vienna, well-known writer in Prague, from which he was deported to Lodz in

1941; Dr. Oskar Singer, publicist and writer from Prague, deported to the Lodz Ghetto; Jozef Zelkowicz, a Polish Jew, ordained as a rabbi, but who worked as a writer and ethnographer of Jewish customs and contributor to the Vilna YIVO. Cukier, Hecht and Heilig died in the Ghetto; Kamieniecki, Rosenfeld, Singer, Zelkowicz and all but one of the archivist staff perished in the final liquidation of the Ghetto in August, 1944.

The first entry in the *Chronicle* was written January 12, 1941, and continued almost every day until July 30, 1944, first in longhand, then typed. Altogether about 1,000 entries or bulletins were produced, ranging from a half-page to ten or more pages. Until September 1, 1942, the *Chronicle* was written in Polish; after that time for a few months, it was written in Polish and German, and after December, 1942, in German, by deportees from the West. Certain headings such as weather, births and deaths, shootings, suicides, food supplies and rations, public health and disease matters, news of the day, resettlements, inspections of the Ghetto, incidents of smuggling, and cultural events are frequently repeated, supplemented occasionally by more discursive articles and sketches.

The tone of the entries is, in the main, straightforwardly factual, almost clinical. There is almost no interpretive analysis of the events recorded, but occasionally the dread, horror, and ghastliness of those events breaks out: "macabre lines of corpses awaiting burial"; "a horrendous rise in price of necessities"; resettlement actions causing "severe depressions in the ghetto"; "March [24, 1942] will long be remembered. . . . From morning on, for twenty hours nonstop, processions of deportees headed on foot for Marysin"; ". . . now the eye has already grown accustomed to seeing spring-carriages pass loaded with people who are more dead than alive. Wrapped in rags, barely visible, they lie motionless on the wagons. Their blank gazes fixed on the sky, their faces bloodless and pale, hold a silent but terrible reproach to those who have remained behind"; "the despair of parents and other family members who had been parted from their brothers and sisters is beyond description."

Pervading the Chronicle are the urgent exhortations of Rumkowski to work, to work at all costs, and to be prepared for the consequences—resettlement—for not working.

As is well known, Rumkowski's sole solution to Nazi demands and the only salvation for Jews in the Lodz Ghetto was a highly productive work force, and although he succeeded in sustaining a remnant of Jews in the Lodz Ghetto longer than occurred in any other ghetto, he was a much-hated man against whom vehement attacks have been leveled in many Holocaust sources—but not in the *Chronicle*. There he appears as an efficient, caring Chairman of the *Aeltestenrat*, ruling a besieged community along principles of law and order, who must obey the German overlords, and, thus, must himself be obeyed. In view of this one-dimensional description of Rumkowski, in order to obtain a full-bodied picture of the Lodz Ghetto, one must read other accounts of this complex, controversial figure. Childless and a widower, with a tumultuous past of trying to make a living, Rumkowski finally became head of a Jewish orphanage outside of Lodz, a position which gave him the authority and prestige he craved. It is still not clear whether he was appointed head of the Jewish Council, or sought the office. In any case, he took the responsibility very seriously. Undoubtedly he enjoyed the power and honor, but, as Dr. Philip Friedman has noted, "he was also impelled by a profound feeling of historical mission, which only a chosen few merit and which he was obliged to fulfill." He was convinced, as were other Jews, that proper behavior, appropriate approaches, and, above all, work, would persuade the Nazis to come to a modus operandi with the Ghetto.

The working remnant and Rumkowski himself exhausted themselves in struggling to live by his obsession, but the Nazis held to their plan for total annihilation. Rumkowski was, as a Lodz journalist put it, at the "wheel of a hell-ship." He was a vain man who wanted to be a surrogate father to orphans and deluded himself into thinking that he could be a Jewish savior. And yet . . . in the summer of 1944, just before the Ghetto was liquidated, the Red Army stopped its offensive just seventy-five miles from Lodz. Had it continued rolling forward, thousands of Jews still in the Ghetto would have survived.

Dr. Dobroszycki touches on Rumkowski's life before and after the ghettoization period in his long and immensely informative Introduction, which every reader of the *Chronicle* should read. We are greatly indebted to him and to the English translators of this unique work—Richard Lourie, Joachim Neugroschel, Jean Steinberg, and Howard Shern. It is a massive contribution to Holocaust documentation.

THE TRAINS RAN ON TIME

Kursbuch fur die Gefangenwagen. Horst-Werner Dumjahn, ed.
Horst-Werner Dumjahn Verlag, 1979. 201pp. DM36

Reviewed by PROFESSOR HENRY R. HUTTENBACH

Who would have thought of consulting a seemingly in-
nocuous train schedule for damning evidence of the extermination process? Perhaps it would be someone knowing of the
existence of a sub-category entitled *Schedule of Prisoner
Cars*, especially if one issue had been for the keen and sensi-
October 6, 1941." Yet, had it not been for the keen and sensitive eye of Horst-Werner Dumjahn this key document for the
study of the Holocaust might never have come to light. Reading over a Catalogue of German Railroad Schedules, Dumjahn
chanced upon such an entry, immediately sensing an extraordinary item. Equally extraordinary was his luck in locating
the one surviving copy; all other copies had "disappeared"
from otherwise complete collections! Prior to him, an unknown
order must have been issued to destroy this damning piece of
evidence and to remove all traces of its existence. One owes
Dumjahn, therefore, a special debt for assigning an individual
volume of his documentary series on railway history to this
reprinting, for it sheds less light on the technological past of
the German transportation system than on the less chartered
moral dimension of its otherwise brilliant past.

Prior to 1941 the German railway network had been used
to transport criminals on a regular basis; hence a special category of railway cars (Gefangenen- or Zellenwagen—Prisoner
or Cell Cars) whose itinerary was carefully integrated into
the existing flow of civilian trains. They left at appointed
times as part of regular trains, they were detached and attached at assigned locations and they were maintained at
specified locations and returned into service according to a
strict timetable. Railway stations were identified in terms of
the nearest prison to and from which prison cars were transporting their prisoners. So far there is nothing unusual.

Suddenly, in the October, 1941, *Schedule of Prisoner Cars*,
the observant reader will discover the inclusion of concentration camps. The task of the prison cars was officially no longer
the transportation of simple criminals but the deportation of
other categories of prisoners. A major destination is no longer
the conventional prison but such locations as Buchenwald,

Dachau, Mauthausen, Ravensbruck and Sachenhausen. Obviously they had been a destination for the prison cars before October, 1941, so that at the time of the issuance of the new schedule these destinations had become so commonplace that they were included as part of the regular function of this category of railway cars. The mass shipping of humans to concentration camps had become such a normal occurrence that it could be listed openly in a schedule which fell into the hands of hundreds of managers and railroad workers, none of whom could thereafter claim not to have been aware of the new use of the prisoner cars and what their specific terminal points were.

At the time of the printing of the 1941 Schedule, the German railroad system only had 64 prisoner cars at its disposal. Thus, when the order came a few months later to deport German Jewry *en masse,* these few cars were clearly insufficient. It was only natural, therefore, to resort to cattle cars, an easy transition, without disrupting the overall schedule structure which could accommodate a far greater flow of human cargo. Given the existence of the prisoner car schedule within the framework of the overall German railroad schedule, the administering of the Final Solution posed no serious problematics on a managerial level. All that had to be done was to superimpose the policy of mass deportation upon a pre-existing transportation schedule, which, if needed, could then be extended to meet future developments.

Thus, tucked away in the October, 1941, Schedule are such harmless sounding locations at Litzmannstadt, Nordhausen and Auschwitz (Auschwitz is merely identified as a location where prisoners "change trains" and Litzmannstadt as the end of the line where each car would undergo a thorough overhaul and cleaning). It would not take much organization to graft onto this schedule the task of moving tens and even hundreds of thousands of people to ghettos, concentration camps and to death factories.

Thanks to the Schedule, the railroads of the Greater Reich and those of its neighbors could be programmed and coordinated to handle enormous loads of human cargo. By October, 1941, railway functionaries on all levels were already accustomed to manage, organize and supervise transports to a variety of concentration camps. It was, therefore, simply a matter of routine to order the systematic removal of all Jews from any given location.

Seen in the context of Holocaust chronology, the Schedule acquires great significance as a carefully planned and timed instrument of genocidal policy. We have here a crucial document that stands mid-way between July 31, 1941, when Goering appointed Heydrich to oversee the total destruction of the Jews, and January 20, 1942, when the Wannsee Conference rubber-stamped a program of genocide already in progress and which was increasingly becoming dependent on the smooth running of the railroads. Thus, just before the Schedule went into effect on October 6, experimental gassing had begun on September 23 in Auschwitz. Shortly after the Schedule was operational, Theresienstadt opened on October 10. On October 14, the order came to deport all Jews from the Reich. On November 15, train transports began to leave for Riga and Minsk.

As the number of transports increased in number and in size, so did their destinations. For the trained eye, the application of the Schedule to new destinations posed no difficulties: Lodz and Auschwitz were already listed. Unlisted destinations such as Bergen-Belsen, Sobibor and Treblinka could easily be associated with neighboring rail junctions. Thus, the professional eye would have little trouble reading the Schedule in terms of unlisted camps: for example, the notation next to Danzig "prisoners change trains" translates to mean "Change here for K.Z. Stutthof" (opened in September, 1939, lying 35 kilometers east of Danzig).

Placed alongside the extant lists of deportation transports compiled by the Germans, the Schedule further fortifies the documentary arsenal of incontrovertible proof of the Holocaust. The Schedule demonstrates once again the careful, long-range planning that went into the Final Solution. Without doubt, the architects of the extermination of European Jewry depended heavily on the railroads to realize their goal. In issuing the Schedule, they could be sure the trains would run on time.

(What better example than Dusseldorf Police Captain Salitter's December 26, 1941, report that transports to Riga were hurried up because "the railroad had urged [their] departure in accordance with the schedule.")

One must conclude all over again, this time with the Schedule in hand as further evidence, that a strategic bombing of the railroads of central and eastern Europe would have slowed down considerably the wholesale slaughter of the Jews of Europe.

A LETTER TO GOD

God? How good You are, and how kind, and if we had to count all You have bestowed upon us that is good and kind, our coming would be without end. . . . God? It is You who command it. It is You who are justice. It is You who reward the good and punish the evil. God? I can, therefore, say that I will never forsake You? I will always be mindful of You, even in the last moments of my life. You can be absolutely certain of that. For me, You are something beyond words, so good are You. You may believe me.

God? It is thanks to You that I enjoyed a wonderful life before, that I was spoiled, that I had lovely things that others do not have. God? As a result, I ask just one thing of You. BRING BACK MY PARENTS, MY POOR PARENTS. PROTECT THEM (even more than myself) SO THAT I MAY SEE THEM AS SOON AS POSSIBLE. HAVE THEM COME BACK ONE MORE TIME. Oh! I can say that I have had such a good mother, and such a good father! I have such faith in You that I thank You in advance.

(*A Letter to God is reproduced from* The Children of Izieu (*Abrams, 1987*) *by Serge Klarsfeld. Izieu, in France, was the village where Jewish children had been placed by their parents, out of the reach of the Nazis.*

M&R 12:6, March-April, 1986

III. Jewish Resistance: Saying No to the Exterminators

The Final Solution was designed to extirpate all signs of Jewish existence: it was a war against Jewish bodies and souls. Nevertheless, the victims resisted: till their dying breath or the arrival of the allied forces, they refused to be destroyed and dehumanized.

They smuggled food; they prayed; they celebrated Holy Days; they loved one another; they kept records of the crime against them; they formed secret groups in ghettos; they planned escapes; they joined partisan and underground movements from the Soviet Union to France; they fought inside and outside the camps; they blew up the crematoria in Auschwitz, rose up against the German Army in Warsaw, and rebelled in Treblinka—always demonstrating that they remained a spiritual people, even though they were basically unarmed civilians facing the modern military might of a merciless conqueror.

Though six million Jews were massacred, their death is an indelibly recorded chapter in history. Their defiant, individual acts of resistance form a collective moral statement unparalleled in human chronicles of man's ability to counter inhumanity, of the victim's capacity to resist evil.

Particularly noteworthy are these articles from M & R: "Dimensions of Heroism" (Cynthia J. Haft, 6:10, Sept-Oct. 1979); "Gisela Fleischmann Uncommon Martyr" (Dorothy Fuerst 7:5 Jan.-Feb. 1981); "The Heroism of Rabbi Weissmandel" (Dorothy Fuerst 7:6 March-April 1981); "Recall Physician-Educator on 40th Anniversary (Tribute to Janusz Korczak . . . Rachmiel V. Tobesman (9:9 Nov.-Dec. 1982); "Meeting of Yitzhak Zuckerman and Elie Wiesel (Luba Gurdus 8:5 Jan.-Feb. 1982); "Legacy of Ann Frank Enhanced in New Edition" (10:13 May-June 1984).

M & R AS A GUIDE TO HISTORY
OF THE HOLOCAUST

By PROF. ROBERT MICHAEL

What does *Martyrdom and Resistance* have to say to those who want to know about the Holocaust?

For one thing, it is through the pages of *Martyrdom and Resistance* that one gets a better perspective of the problem of evil. It has been with us since the beginning of history. Radical evil, the suffering and death of human beings, highlights the problem of the existence of evil in general. And the Holocaust, the most extreme form of radical evil, brings the issue into even more focus. The Holocaust points to the fact that there is an irreducible excess of evil in the world, much more than is necessary to stimulate any compensatory goodness. Nowhere is the radical evil of the Holocaust so keenly felt as in the destruction of six million Jews. The murder of these people, the destruction of nearly a whole generation of the Jewish people, including their children, represents the clearest confrontation of helplessness and innocence with an evil that causes agony and death. And so in many ways the Holocaust represents the apparent victory of death over life, evil over goodness.

The Holocaust, therefore, is a perplexingly difficult subject to learn about. True, it must be studied, analyzed, explored, accounted for. But this process is confronted by the *mysterium tremendum,* the noumenal reality before which we tread with fear and trembling. As we begin to know, the effect is like that of the blazing sun on newborn eyes. But the risk of emotional devastation is one we must take.

Indeed, there are intellectual and emotional problems that are faced by writers, in dealing with the Holocaust although they follow the canons of rigorous scholarship. According to Emil Fackenheim, "The Holocaust . . . is a horror . . . that is indissoluble. . . . The facts *themselves* are outrageous; it is *they* that must speak through *our* language. And this is possible only if one's feelings are subject to a disciplined restraint. The language necessary, then, is one of sober restraint, but at the same time unyielding outrage."

Prof. Michael is professor of history, Southeastern Massachusetts University.

In reviewing the 20 years of *Martyrdom and Resistance,*
one can not but notice the disciplined restraint in its presentation of the historical events. The language of the publication
has been sober and restrained, and, most important, it has
been the vehicle for conveying the outrage felt because of
unparalleled atrocities.

The survivors, those who had to confront the Holocaust,
those who were there, those who directly experienced it, those
who suffered at its heart and lived—within a generation almost
all will be dead. Their anguish and their sadness, theire horror
and their revenge, their love and their courage will all be
gone. All we will have left will be their recorded memories,
photographs and films, and their words.

Historians should be grateful to *Martyrdom and Resistance* for offering the thoughts, experiences, and words of the
survivors. This is all part of a vital historical record. I can
think of no journal that has presented so much and so varied
a record as that of *Martyrdom and Resistance.*

In analyzing the Holocaust, historians speak of the historical background of anti-Semitism, the uniqueness of the
Holocaust, and the Nazi system. These historical concerns
have received intensive treatment in *Martyrdom and Resistance.*

An oft-repeated thesis in *Martyrdom and Resistance* has
been that it was the Nazis' combination of traditional Christian *Judenhass* so deeply ingrained in German culture, plus
racist and social Darwinist ideas, rationalism and scapegoat-
ing, as well as the application of technology and bureaucracy
that led to the Holocaust.

What was unique about the Holocaust? *Martyrdom and
Resistance* has the answers: 1. a *raison d'être* of the Nazi
regime and international policies was the destruction of European Jewry: 2. the significance of the enemies of the regime
was judged by the degree of their friendly relationship to the
Jews—just as the friends of the regime were determined by
their anti-Semitism; 3. Jews were the only group whose members' very birth the Nazis considered a crime against the state
and against humanity to be punished by death; 4. Jews were
the only people seen as demonical enough totally to be destroyed in work and death camps, and in *Aktions,* even at the
cost of a Nazi victory on the battlefield.

The Nazis were out to annihilate the Jews, after first
punishing them. They meant to degrade them, to dehumanize
and to inhumanize (diabolize) them, to exterminate them
like vermin, and then to remove all traces of them from the

face of the earth—totally to destroy their history, their culture, their religion, their children, their God, their lives. Jewish bones were meant to be fertilizer; their fat, soap; their skin, lampshades; their hair, cloth; their gold teeth, bullion; their labor unto death, the victory of the Third Reich.

Heinrich Himmler himself made the distinction between genocide and Holocaust. In a speech on October 4, 1943, at Posnan to SS leaders, the head of the SS pointed out that it was no secret that the Third Reich sought to exploit the Slavs, even unto death if necessary, for the economic and political goals of the Nazi government. So if it took the lives of 10,000 Russian or Czech women to dig tank traps for the Nazis, he did not care. So long as the work was done. Later in the speech, however, he noted that the "annihilation of the Jewish people" must be accomplished at all costs even while it was kept secret. He implied that were 10,000 Jews to dig tank traps for the Third Reich, it would be for the express purpose of murdering them.

The above facts are what made the Holocaust unique. If one had been reading *Martyrdom and Resistance* during the past 20 years, one would have learned of these historical considerations.

What the reader would also have found would be seemingly endless details of the Nazi system, with its ghettos, aktions, work and death camps.

Once the Nazis invaded Western and especially Eastern Europe, the largely theological and theoretical Jewish problem demanded a practical solution, for now nearly 10 million Jews were in Nazi hands. Jews had been ghettoized in Europe for more than 1,000 years. The major purpose of these ghettos had always been to segregate the "evil" Jews from the rest of the population of Christendom. Although the Nazis saw this as a valid reason for the ghettos of their creation, they took the next "logical" step when they used the ghettos both indirectly to murder the Jews, through starvation and disease, and as huge reservoirs from which to select Jews directly to murder in *Aktions* or at the death camps. And so it was at Lodz, at Vilna, at Minsk, at Kovno, at Theresienstadt, at Warsaw.

The Nazi decision to murder the Jews, all the Jews everywhere in Europe, probably came in May 1941. At this time 4 *Einsatzgruppen* were organized to murder the Jews in *Aktions* wherever they were found in Eastern Europe. The *Einsatzgruppen* worked under the cover of the invasion of the Soviet Union. They slaughtered in cooperation with units of the regular German Army. They killed under the command of German Ph.D.'s and other professionals–lawyers, teachers, even a former pastor. They murdered in collaboration with native people, Latvians, Lithuanians, Ukrainians. They slaughtered Jews because of their birth, because of their existence, and because of the myths so deeply ingrained in their hearts and minds. And they killed, alas, with the silent collaboration of the Allies and the Churches.

At Auschwitz and other death camps, a new moral universe was created: a world in which the old categories and language of right and wrong were superseded by the Nazi system. In the words of Lawrence Langer, a system "where different and unorganized values prevailed, inspired by a constant death threat that is totally alien to our world and resembles nothing we can imagine."

The Nazis created a system that was contemptuous of all that was Jewish and all that was truly human. All this has been recorded on the pages of *Martyrdom and Resistance*, which thus seem to burst into flame or into tears. The reader must somehow cast off the shadow of the wings of evil by trying to learn from the Holocaust without neglecting its horror and sadness.

What does *Martyrdom and Resistance* tell those seeking to know more of the Holocaust? The stark truth! The terrible facts have always been in the pages of this periodical. Those who have come to learn have been taught well by *Martyrdom and Resistance*.

TRIBUTE TO JEWISH HEROISM

Today we pay tribute to Jewish heroism. We survivors embody this heroism. Indeed, the concept of Jewish heroism is markedly different from those of other peoples.

Throughout the ages those nations who lived by the sword did not survive. However, the strength of the Jewish people is entwined with spirituality. That is why Jewish heroism is eternal. We recall the religious youth who refused to eat soup in Auschwitz because it was not kosher, or the partisans who lit Chanukah candles under the most trying conditions. This is heroism of the highest order. . . .

How fated for our generation that in keeping with the vision of Ezekiel, our skeletons took on flesh, as we arrived in Eretz Israel. We survivors embody the eternity of the Jewish people. We burn, but we are not consumed because spirit can not be extinguished. The spirit that lit up the bunkers has continued in the Galil and has reappeared in the mountains of Judea. . . .

I love my generation. It is a generation of idealism. And until the last days, its light will continue to fall on us. I love my generation that kept the faith, despite being bloodied and persecuted; truly, until the last day, its faith was unshaken.

SOLOMON ZYNSTEIN

●

Our heroism lies in our sanctity. And in our sanctity lies our heroism. With these two elements is created the magnificent synthesis of our being and of our eternal existence. . . .

No self-respecting human being in this world can now claim ignorance of how European Jewry was humiliated, tortured, confined in ghettoes, and finally consigned to death by disease, starvation and gas chambers. . . . However, in the midst of this horror, brave men were determined to survive and also to fight back and save other tortured Jews.

Until now, the story of Jewish resistance has been the best kept secret of the Second World War. That's why the gathering is playing a historic role in showing the world that Jews did not go like sheep to the slaughter.

To succeed in escaping from the Nazis, to survive in the hostile environment of the forest, with roving bands bent on killing Jews, and to secure weapons as well as food and clothing, required luck as well as courage. . . .

The Jews in Europe formed a very significant segment of the resistant movement. Despite . . . anti-Semitism, they fought back and hit the Nazis hard. All over Poland, the Jews . . . started to organize and fight back, just to mention a few ghettoes: Warsaw, Wilno, Grodno, Bialystok. There were revolts in concentration camps like Sobibor and Treblinka.

Around Wilno, Lublin, Lida and Naroch, Jewish partisans fought back the hated Hitlerites. Among them were groups of 1,200 men and women in the brigade led by Tuvia Bielski and a group led by Chill Grynspan and myself. In every unit of Polish or Russian partisans, Jewish fighters played a big role. It is estimated that 50,000 Jews fought as partisans against the Nazis, and over 1 million fought in the Allied Armies. . . .

SAMUEL GRUBER

M&R 10:9, Jan.-Feb., 1984

(Presented above are excerpts from remarks at the 1983 World Assembly in Jerusalem to Commemorate Jewish Resistance and Combat during World War II. Solomon Zynstein is a former president of the American Federation of Jewish Fighters, Camp Inmates, and Nazi Victims, while Samuel Gruber, a former partisan commander, is a leader in the Federation of Former Jewish Underground Fighters.)

LESSONS OF THE DEATH CAMPS

The Survivor: An Anatomy of Life in the Death Camps. Terrence des Pres. Oxford University Press. 1976, 218 pp., $10.

Reviewed by BARBARA KESSEL

There is a singular appropriateness to the circumstances in which I read *The Survivor*. It was on a Friday night during the interim days of Passover that I sat next to my father-in-law, himself a survivor—who was engrossed in *O, Jerusalem*. On this, the festival of "retelling," he was learning the details about the birth of the State of Israel, which followed suggestively close upon the footsteps of the Holocaust and I was learning the lessons of the death camps whose cessation immediately preceded my birth. Thus, he was reading of a development particularly enriching to him and I was likewise gaining insight into a period I had not personally experienced.

The Survivor presupposes an acquaintance with the Holocaust experience and, especially, with its literature. On the assumption that the reader is familiar with the phenomenon, des Pres proceeds to analyze survival and survivors. He gleans from the literature some valuable lessons, and dispels in an objective but compassionate sweep some prevailing notions, among them those fostered by Bruno Bettelheim.

Des Pres begins his analysis with a brief, representative survey of survivor literature with examples from Holocaust and Soviet literature. He concluded from his own research that the Jewish experience was the more massive and the more painful (because Soviet labor camps consisted of drudgery, cold, and hunger, whereas Nazi concentration camps were characterized by unspeakable cruelty, medical experiments, stark terror and a constant life-or-death struggle). Yet, the two aspects confirm the same lessons about survival.

Lesson number one is that men living under extreme conditions must act as social beings. No one may live for himself, much less live in opposition to his peers. Selfishness is the beginning of the disintegration process, which des Pres documents in several personal testimonies of survivors. The testimonies are many but not various, which is to say that the external circumstances may vary from camp to camp or individual to individuals, but the reactions and attitudes are strikingly similar. The survivors seemed to share an instinct to live through their ordeal partly in order to bear witness, and there is a surprising uniformity to their stories.

Lesson number two incorporates the first. Des Pres very logically and firmly disputes the notion that Jews went "like sheep" to their death. (One cannot even say "to their graves" because this was not often the case.) First of all, he argues, where were they going to procure the weaponry with which to launch a defense? In those cases like the Warsaw Ghetto uprising where victims did defend themselves, it took years to assemble the parts with which to put together guns and ammunition.

Second and more fundamental is the fact that circumstances often did not permit open rebellion, at times because that would endanger more lives than it would save, but rather made covert resistance the wisest—and only available—option.

Resistance took many forms. Sometimes it was in the form of smuggling. Food was never good or enough, and those who worked in storage areas or kitchens would bring back to their barracks, always, of course, at the risk of losing their lives, whatever extras they could muster and hide on their persons. The same went for spare articles of clothing or medicine. Whenever possible, hospital staff would hide condemned inmates in the typhus ward, where the S.S. was afraid to venture for fear of contagion, until the victim could be supplied with a new identity, often of someone who had died. In this way, they frequently saved sick prisoners from assignment to the labor force. Sabotage was another covert means to obstruct the persecutor's progress. This was a particularly dangerous method, for apprehension could bring a punishnent on hundreds of innocents. And, des Pres earnestly argues, survival alone—defying the death machine—was resistance in itself. It deprived the enemy of one more victory, and this is no small rebellion.

The seven chapters which make up this slim volume are written in exemplary English. If they were describing a different subject, one would not hesitate to describe them as a pleasure to read. At the very least, this is a punctiliously articulate book. It is dispassionate enough to distill from a horrifying era universal lessons which speak to all men in all times, though one hopes the lessons need never be practiced. Its analysis of human reaction to extremity, cruelty and physical adversity is lucid and incisive. Above all, there is a warm compassion to every word. There could be no more apt ending to *The Survivor* than the quotation the author has chosen, himself quoting a Jewish guard who would greet new arrivals to the camps with tales of what to expect: "I have not told you of our experiences to harrow you, but to strengthen you. . . . Now you may decide if you are justified in despairing."

In sum, this is an excellent volume. It differs from most post-Holocaust literature in its focus. Rather than provide lengthy extracts of survivor accounts, it culls the essence of the experience and its meaning for those of us who live among and after the survivors themselves. It is an important book and deserves a wide audience.

BREAKING THE SILENCE

By Roger S. Gottlieb

"They went like sheep to the slaughter . . . sheep to the slaughter . . . like sheep . . ."

Too often have these painful words echoed in our minds when we think about the Jewish victims of the Holocaust. Too often have they aroused anger, resentment and shame in us. Too often have we sworn 'never again,' yet wondered if we would have the courage which we sometimes feel the six million lacked.

Too often.

And that is why the study of Jewish resistance during the Holocaust is of crucial importance for Jews. The haunting spectre of six million passive victims of genocide has had a devastating effect on our consciousness of ourselves as Jews—weakening our capacity for Jewish pride, forcing us to seek models of heroism mainly in other peoples, leading to shame of ourselves and contempt for other Jews.

But it is not easy to study Jewish resistance. Outside of occasional accounts of the Warsaw Ghetto uprising, Jewish education tends to focus on 'victimology' when the Holocaust is discussed. Images of Jewish heroism often come to us through a mythology in which Jewish bravery is possessed solely by those who fought to establish and defend the State of Israel. Progressive groups in general rightly celebrate the heroism of black slaves, Puerto Rican women and Vietnamese guerilas, but they omit mention of Jewish freedom fighters.

There has been an unconscious conspiracy of silence surrounding Jewish resistance. Perhaps the conspiracy derives from an anti-Semitism in which Jews cannot be heroes, no matter what. For the anti-Semite, everything the Jews do is wrong—we even died the wrong way in concentration camps. And Jews, like other oppressed peoples, are never presented as fighting back.

Perhaps this silence is partly caused by a curious twist of Jewish consciousness in which it is easier to believe that we didn't fight back than that we did. After all what kind of world is it if the slaughter of the six million is *in no way our fault?* If we did everything we could and were still destroyed?

154

Professional historians have contributed to this silence. Raul Hilberg in his influential book *The Destruction of the European Jews* claims that Jewish resistance was minimal. Fortunately, Hilberg's claim is based almost completely on Nazi sources. It would indeed be strange for the murderers of the Jews to admit to Jewish heroism.

Whatever the cause of the conspiracy, it must be broken. This is beginning to happen and we are involved in one of the efforts. A group of members of BCCAS, an organization of Jews and non-Jews dedicated to fighting anti-Semitism and sharing Jewish culture, have joined together to create a multi-media presentation commemorating Jewish resistance during the Holocaust.

From the beginning, however, we faced a conceptual problem: how to define 'resistance' itself.

Of course, many cases were absolutely clear: the Jewish Fighting Organization of the Warsaw Ghetto attacked German soldiers with rifle-fire and molotov cocktails; the Jews of Lackwa (in Pinsk) resisted deportation to the death camps with knives, axes, and sulphuric acid, setting the ghetto on fire and fleeing to the forest; the Jewish underground *inside* Auschwitz blew up a crematorium; thirty settlers, Hannah Senesh among them, left Palestine to be parachuted behind German lines in Eastern Europe in order to organize resistance; tens of thousands of Jews fought in partisan groups in France, Poland, Russia and the Balkans. This resistance was the work of women and men alike. Of the 300-member 'Death to the Invader' unit, one-third were women.

The fighting spirit of these Jews is recorded in their actions, songs and leaflets.

Yet in some cases the nature of resistance remains problematic and confusing. Consider the following story. The Jewish community of Kelme was about to be machine-gunned. The local Rabbi managed to receive permission from the Nazi officer to bid farewell to his people. He spoke about Kiddush Hashem—sanctification of the name—the command that Jews who are martyred for their faith die in such a way as to glorify God's name.

You see, if it is only one's body that is under attack, then 'resistance' means simply defending that body. But the Nazi attack on the Jewish people was not simply an attack on our bodies. No, it was an attack on everything that made us human, made us a people, made us ourselves. The goal of the Nazis was to destroy us as a *people*. They sought to exterminate not only individuals, but our ties to each other, our families and our communal values.

And some of us working in the memorial to Jewish resistance have come to see 'resistance' in a broader light, no longer confining it to armed uprisings and sabotage. We have come to believe that in a world dedicated to dehumanization, remaining human was an act of resistance. To stay alive, to maintain one's self respect, to help other Jews: these were acts of resistance against a Nazi machine which sought to obliterate the human image among us.

Therefore, some of us have come to believe that for an Orthodox Jews to cling, with pride and dignity, to the commandment of *Kiddush Hashem* may well be an act of resistance. For that Jew is protecting what is for her or him the most sacred and important aspect of Jewishness: a religious tradition. That Jew is defending what is crucial in his or her vision of Judaism.

In Auschwitz, people made birthday cakes from crumbs. Throughout the camps, people would sacrifice themselves rather than be separated from their families. On trains to gas chambers people sang partisan songs. In Vilna, in Cracow, in Warsaw and in many other crowded ghettoes amidst a daily life of starvation, disease and death, Jews created schools, orchestras and newspapers. They wrote poems and songs and they celebrated Jewish traditions.

Not only did the Jews of Europe resist the Nazis, but they did so in a context in which everything worked against resistance. The Jewish communities of Europe were a series of islands in a sea of mainly (though, of course, not entirely) hostile or indifferent Gentiles. Jewish underground groups were frequently denied aid by non-Jewish partisans. Jews who escaped to the forests might well be betrayed by Gentiles.

Also, the Nazis responded to acts of Jewish resistance by 'collective reprisal.' An act of resistance by one person or by a small group thus threatened the lives of entire communities.

Perhaps, most importantly, we must remember that in their confrontation with a genocidal world, the Jews lacked both weapons and military training. A constant theme in all accounts of the Warsaw Ghetto uprising is the lack of real arms, the fact that the Jews faced the conquerors of Europe with ancient pistols and worn-out rifles. In uprisings in other ghettos and camps, resistance-fighters were forced to use knives against machine-guns, or bottles of acid thrown by children against the power of well-equipped soldiers. The lack of arms and training often made armed resistance a form of suicide, an action which demanded almost superhuman courage and dedication.

Finally, we must remember that the ultimate meaning of the Nazi activities were, for a long time, simply incomprehensible. The Final Solution was kept secret. Jews being deported to death camps were sometimes made to buy return-trip train tickets. On their way to extermination at Auschwitz or Treblinka, they would be told that they were simply going to labor camps. The ruse of masking the gas chambers as showers is well known.

And the Jews themselves had no concepts by which to understand the utter savagery of the Nazi program. Why risk death, many Jews thought, when the Nazi rule will blow over, like so many other persecutions, pogroms or expulsions? To believe that the Nazis actually sought to destroy every living Jew required an act of mind by which Jews wrenched themselves from a world of traditional European anti-Semitism into a universe shaped by genocide.

Those of us who have grown up since that time have always lived in a world in which genocide was possible. For the Jews of Europe at that time, it had not been so. They were the victims of a campaign of death which violated even the elemental rules of human rationality. In the final years the mass murder of the Jews cost the Germans money, time and energy, and led to the destruction of skilled labor which might have helped the war effort. Never before had the Jews witnessed destruction on such a scale, in which their death was the goal of a huge war machine.

The facts of Jewish resistance during the Holocaust are a cause for celebration. And thus, our first duty to the memory of the courage of Jewish resisters is to inform ourselves about them. This is not easy. The atmosphere of terror which surrounds everything that has to do with the Holocaust makes reading difficult. Books are started and abandoned. Material read is quickly forgotten. The emotional impact leads to mental avoidance.

This struggle can, for many people, only be waged collectively. In our experience, reading and study groups, in which knowledge and feelings can be shared and mutual support provided, can make possible a learning which is often too painful and difficult by oneself. For some of us, it has been easier to approach the Holocaust by studying Jewish resistance against it.

Once this knowledge is acquired, it must be spread. We must alter the present content of Jewish education. Jewish calendars and catalogs, of memorials to the Holocaust and of celebrations of human heroism and nobility in general. We must alter all these until both the Jewish community and the whole world know that Jews were not sheep—they were brave human beings who can be an inspiration to all of us.

Finally, we can celebrate Jewish resistance in our own lives by the most difficult task of all: that is, to seek, each in our own way, to resist all the forces in the world that would make us—or anyone else—less than fully human.

M&R 7:4, Nov.-Dec., 1980
Reprinted by permission of *Genesis*, © 1979

EMMANUEL RINGELBLUM: HERO AS TEACHER

By HANNA HIRSHAUT

When I think of Dr. Ringelblum I can't help reminiscing about a man and an era of greatness, of dreams and hopes, of ideas and accomplishments.

Those were the years from the 20's through the 30's, when Jewish cultural and spiritual life blossomed in Poland in spite of anti-Semitism and economic hardships. The young generation was involved in new idealistic movements, many in various factions of the Zionist organizations.

The Jews, who until the beginning of the twentieth century put more emphasis on religious rather than secular education, began now to strive for the higher and better education for their sons and daughters.

I was a student in a high school known under the name "Jehudia." It was an all girls school, most of whose students were daughters of middle-class parents. Most of the time they struggled for survival in the times of depression, but yet they made the effort to send the girls to our school for the good education, the Zionist foundation and a second major language —Hebrew.

Among my friends were daughters of famous Zionist leaders, educators and writers. Many of the teachers were outstanding, enriching our lives. This is why I remember Professor Ringelblum with warmth and affection. His subject was history, and he made special efforts to make us understand why it is so important to learn about the past in order to shape the present and plan for the future. I remember that even then, when "women's lib" was not preached, he would encourage us to go further and become whatever we wanted to be in our lives.

He was a pleasant man, rather shy, and I had a feeling that he felt somewhat awkward facing a class of some 40 teenage girls, who saw in each male teacher either an idol or a failure. We were a group of mischief makers, and many times we played unpleasant tricks on our poor teachers.

Dr. Ringelblum had a habit of coming into the classroom at the last moment a little perspired, his clothes kind of rumpled. He would always pick up a pencilholder from the nearest student desk and play with it and gesture with it.

One day he came in and picked up the pencil holder and found a smelly herring inside. He dropped the whole thing to the floor and ran out of the classroom. I felt sorry for him, realizing how upset he was. He returned after a while without mentioning the incident to the principal or discussing the matter with us.

He conducted his lessons always standing or walking back and forth. I don't remember him ever sitting down. His cheeks were sometimes very pale, but most of the time they had a dark feverish blush. He used to cough a lot and spit into a handkerchief. The rumor was that he suffered from the remains of an old bout with tuberculosis.

His lessons were exciting and challenging. History became filled with life again, instead of a dull subject. When we were "good," he would tell us special stories pertaining to the period we were studying at the time.

I knew that he was an ardent Zionist, member of the Poalei Zion party, with leftist orientation. But he never talked to us about his personal beliefs or tried to influence us politically.

I can only guess that the board of our school set a firm policy of non-interference in our political choices, as long as they were not Communist-related.

Although the school didn't preach religion, traditional holidays were observed with great joy. Dr. Ringelblum participated with us in every festival: Purim, Hanukkah, Lag B'Omer, and others. I can see him so vividly as if it were yesterday, his shirt collar spread out, his hair blowing in the wind, striding with us for an outing in the woods. He looked

young and quite handsome. While marching through the
streets of Warsaw, he sang Hebrew songs with us.

His greatest weakness was his son Uri (Urus). If we
wanted to distract him from an impending test, we would ask
how his little Uri was doing. A smile would brighten up his
face and he would rave about how smart Uri was and how
quickly he was learning.

I had an especially good rapport with Dr. Ringelblum.
History was one of my favorite subjects, and because I liked
my teacher, I devoted more time to my homework in history.
I was an "A" student in this subject, and for one of my bigger
essays he presented me with an award—his own book, under
the title "The Jews In Warsaw" (Zydzi w Warszawie). On
the first page of that book was an inscription: "To Hanele:
for an outstanding work," signed Emmanuel Ringelblum. I
was very proud of this gift. Some time later he invited me to
visit him at home.

I vaguely recall the meeting, in a building called Passage
Simonsa. The apartment, for some reason, seemed dark.
Everywhere I looked there were walls of books. I met Uri, who
was adorable. I did not see the wife of my teacher during my
visit. He showed me a collection of books and photographs
of Zionist leaders, letters from his students from Kibbutzim
in Israel. I was very happy and flattered to have been able to
spend a little time with him. In retrospect, I guess, there was
a mild and innocent "crush" between us.

After I was out of school, I lost touch with Dr. Ringelblum.

In 1942, we were living in the Warsaw Ghetto under
dismal conditions, trying to survive each day. Yet my father
took upon himself the responsibility of caring for many refugees who were deported from towns and villages and then
dumped in the cellars of apartment buildings. A group of
about 150 in our building had to be fed and cared for. One day
I overheard Father telling Mother how much help he had
been getting from Dr. Ringelblum. At that time, Dr. Ringelblum was the head of the Self-Help organization in the
Ghetto and was doing a "tremendous job." I was thrilled to
hear about my teacher and I asked my father to say hello
from me.

The following week my father met again with Dr. Ringelblum and mentioned that I was his student not long ago. My
father told me that he was very happy to hear my name and
sent his regards. He also mentioned that he would be delighted
if I could come to see him in the office. For reasons beyond

my control I never visited my teacher and my friend. After the Holocaust ended, I learned about the horrible death he met at the hands of the Nazis. I also learned how much heroism and vision this man possessed and how invaluable his memoirs became to history and study of the Holocaust. In his book *Jewish Martyrs of Pawiak*, my late husband, Julien Hirshaut, describes the last moments of Dr. Ringelblum and Uri in the Pawiak prison, where my husband was incarcerated. He managed to see Ringelblum for a few minutes, and told him that there may be a slim chance for him to get out from the death cell. Ringelblum then asked, "What about my son? I will never leave him." The next day they were executed in the ruins of the ghetto.

M&R 7:7, Nov.-Dec., 1980

PARTISANS

A gun on my shoulder, with bullet-belt girt,
With eyes full of fury, with hate in one's heart,
Thus against 'brown ones'[1] did we sally forth,
Thus against 'black ones'[2] to fight did we part.
Though as railway men, bricklayers,
    miners we came.

Partisans all in the war we became—
In bunkers, in caves, in dense forests that lower;
Our blows unexpected on the foe did we shower,
To sow turmoil, the foe from behind to attack,
Our thirst for vengeance on him to slake—
Exploding his trains! his bridges we'd rend:
The "Fritzes"—and them to the
    other world send . . .

Thus against 'brown ones' did we sally forth,
Thus against 'black ones' to fight did we part;
A gun on one's shoulder, with bullet-belt girt,
With eyes full of fury, with hate in one's heart.

[1]This refers to the brown shift uniform worn by Nazis or Fascists.
[2]The reference is to the uniforms of the Baltic auxiliary police who helped the Nazis.

Yitshok Papirnikov, Tr. Prof. Percy Matenko

M&R 6:11, March-April, 1980

IV. The Failure to Rescue

While the direct legal responsibility for the murder of six million Jews falls squarely on the Nazi regime and its collaborating allies, a far more damaging *moral* guilt has settled permanently and unevenly upon those with some power to effect the rescue of the victim and otherwise frustrate the execution of the Final Solution.

Between 1933 and 1941 when millions might have been saved via immigration, U.S. quota policies remained fixed and the British White Paper closed off Palestine. Between 1939 and 1945, the plight of the Jews never became part of the allied war effort: underground movements in France or Yugoslavia or Poland, for example, were not instructed to derail trains of deportees headed for extermination camps; the railroads lines to Auschwitz were deliberately not bombed; supply ships crossed the Atlantic ocean westward empty; newspapers informed unsystematically and editorialized not at all; Stalin failed to warn Soviet Jews so they could evacuate in time; Roosevelt was aware but refused to act; the Papacy remained significantly silent; and Polish clerics preached the sole "mysterious" virtue of the terrible German occupation, namely, the removal of Jews from Polish soil.

The slaughter of European Jewry took place in full knowledge of those with the power to act. Unfortunately for the victims, the Holocaust took place at a time when moral fortitude and commitment to principle was at an all time low.

A very informative series in *M & R* was that of Monty Penkower: "Response of the Free World" (9:13, Jan.-Feb. 1983, 9:10, March-April 1983). Also very commendable is his book *The Jews Were Expendable: Free World Diplomacy and the Holocaust* (10:2 May-June 1984, Review, Henry R. Huttenbach). Other noteworthy articles and reviews: "The Role of American Jews in the Death of Their Brethren" (Gerhard Falk, 4:11 May-June 1978); "Why Photographers Failed to Identify Auschwitz-Birkenau, Dino A. Brugioni, 10:5 Sept.-Oct. 1983); *None Is Too Many: Canada and the Jews of Europe, 1933-1948* (Irving Abella and Harold Tropper, 9:3 Nov.-Dec. 1982); *Haven: The Unknown Story of 1,000 World War II Refugees* (Ruth Gruber, 10:2 Jan.-Feb. 1984, Review, Herbert Druks).

CONGRESSIONAL RESPONSES
TO THE HOLOCAUST

By Dr. Herbert Druks

In the past few years several works have emerged on America's response to the Holocaust, but most have failed to seriously consider Congressional responses to the Holocaust. This is an unfortunate omission. Members of Congress (MCs) were aware and informed of the Nazi bestialities, and they made their views public, particularly from 1942 to 1945. Their representations were detailed, and, for the most part, accurate. Their views provide evidence that Americans and their government were informed about the Nazi German atrocities against the Jews.

But what did the Congressmen do with this information? At times they denounced the atrocities—individually or by means of resolutions. They voiced their sympathy. In 1943 a number of MCs asked the President to establish a special executive commission to help rescue the Jews of Europe. President Roosevelt established such an agency in 1944. It was called the War Refugee Board, and it helped rescue Jews and other enemies of the Reich who could escape the Nazis, but few were given refuge.

What did they fail to do? While some Congressmen asked for the admission of those who could escape Nazi entrapments, there were no resolutions or laws passed or introduced that advocated the admission of the persecuted to America. When FDR admitted 982 people, outside U.S. quotas, and encamped them at Fort Ontario, New York, from August, 1944, there were some Congressmen like Ellis of West Virginia who demanded their return to Europe. Ellis felt that America had "enough" people.

During 1943 the Nazis continued to murder Jews. But even in the midst of the Nazi hell there were possibilities to rescue the hunted Jews, and yet the free world failed to take advantage of these possibilities.

As more facts about the Nazi atrocities became known to the American people, Congressmen became more demanding and called on FDR to help. While most of these views and demands were expressed by Congressmen from states with significant Jewish populations, the call for help also came from Congressmen with little or no Jewish constituencies. Members of Congress like Emanuel Celler urged FDR to do more than just condemn the Nazis. The slaughter of millions could not be stopped merely through condemnations. It was necessary to declare Allied intentions to punish the guilty with widespread reprisals. In January Celler asked the President to warn the Germans that "hell and fire" would befall them, that in reprisal "the German countryside would be systematically razed" and that German cities, one by one, would be block bombed and pulverized unless the killings stopped. There was no more time. If the free men of this world waited any longer, "all Europe would be Judenlos."

Over thirty thousand people gathered at New York's Madison Square Garden on February 28, 1943, to protest the murder of European Jews. Congressman Celler gave the Congress a detailed report of that gathering and its resolve that neutral states have Germany release its Jews and permit them emigration to safe havens; and places of refuge be established in the U.S., Eretz Israel, the British Empire, and Latin America. They also asked that the U.S. help feed victims of Nazi persecution and bring the Nazis to justice. Celler reminded his fellow Congressmen that two million Jews had already been "liquidated through hangings, shootings, lethal gases, starvation and all manner of mass execution and pogroms." He called on the U.S. to save the rest.

Congressman Samuel Dickstein of New York was much more critical of the U.S. "Every nation has protested except the USA,'" and the USA took "no steps to join the other Allied nations to save as many as we can." He found a great contrast between "the silence shown by the American people at large and the energetic expressions of the British people." America's "virtual silence" could only serve to "injure and retard" the efforts of others who would act but looked to America to take the first step. We must not fail to act. "It must never be said that we failed to attempt every possible method of rescue." He asked his fellow Congressmen to consider what the Germans were doing: "Can you imagine a bunch of mad sadists forcing people to dig their own graves and then shooting them in cold blood? Heavenly Father! Where is the Christian world? Where are all the fine Christian people? Where is America, which is supposed to be the champion of liberty? Why has not our voice been raised in protest against the inhuman treatment of millions of innocent victims of Nazism?" Dickstein concluded by pleading for some sort of immediate action to help save the Jews, and he warned all the non-Jews that they were next: "... the Jew was the first target of Nazi propaganda, but you Catholics, you Protestants are next."

MC Louis J. Capozzoli of New York joined Dickstein in protesting America's indifference. The Jewish people, reported Capozzoli, were "scheduled for extermination." It was unbelievable, but true. This was "confirmed," by the State Department "on the basis of confidential reports received by it." Those reports indicated that the Nazis used diabolical ways to destroy the Jewish people. Nazi doctors injected air bubbles into their victims and in this way killed 100 people an hour. They led their victims to barracks with metal floors after forcing them to strip. The doors were locked and an electric current was turned on. All the victims were killed. Nothing could be done to bring back the dead, said Capozzoli, but something had to be done to save the living. Capozzoli asserted that no time should be lost "in initiating whatever steps might be productive of this result." All "decent" Americans will "stand four-square behind the Government in this effort."

The following concurrent resolution condemning the atrocities was presented by Senator Alvin Barkley of Kentucky on March 5, 1943, and approved on March 10, 1943:

"Condemnation of Outrages Inflicted Upon Civillians in Nazi-Occupied Countries and Punishment of Persons Responsible Therefore—

The concurrent resolution (S. Con. 9) was ordered to lie on the table, as follows:

"Whereas the American people view with indignation the atrocities inflicted upon the civilian population in the Nazi-occupied countries, and especially the mass murder of Jewish men, women, and children; and

"Whereas this policy of the Nazis has created a reign of terror, brutality, and extermination in Poland and other countries in eastern and central Europe: Now, therefore, be it

"Resolved by the Senate (the House of Representatives concurring). That these brutal and indefensible outrages against millions of helpless men, women, and children should be and they are hereby condemned as unworthy of any nation or any regime which pretends to be civilized:

"Resolved further, That the dictates of humanity and honorable conduct in war demand that the inexcusable slaughter and mistreatment shall cease and that it is the sense of this Congress that those guilty, directly or indirectly, of these criminal acts shall be held accountable and punished in a manner commensurate with the offenses for which they are responsible."

The cry could be heard again and again in the halls of Congress: "something must be done." When Winston Churchill was in Washington visiting FDR, MC George G. Sadowski of Michigan urged Congress to "appeal" to both leaders. Throughout Europe Jews were "shot in the streets, or in their homes, or in huge gas chambers." Nothing was being done to stop the Nazi campaign to annihilate the entire Jewish people ". . . something must be done to try and help these unfortunate and defenseless people." Palestine was the most logical haven for the displaced persons since it could easily be reached by train from Turkey and the people could easily receive assistance "from the Hebrew people of the Colony." Every liberty-loving person cried out to Churchill and Roosevelt: "Do something—and please hurry!" There was no resolution forthcoming from Congress in support of Sadowski's appeal.

The reports of Nazi atrocities and some public protests seemed to have embarrassed British and American officials into calling for another conference of refugees. But neither British nor American spokesmen wanted the conference held in their own backyards. When they finally agreed to meet in British Bermuda, Assistant Secretary of State Long breathed a sigh of relief as he declared, "they have the baby now." But while the Allies agreed to meet in Bermuda, they also agreed not to admit the refugees unless they fulfilled rigid quota requirements. And they refused to consider Palestine despite Dr. Weizmann's urgings that it be a place of refuge because of its proximity to Europe and because there was plenty of room as well as a Jewish population eager to welcome them. From the very start of their conference, the Allies made sure that it would not succeed. The one gesture of rescue they performed was to call for the transfer of a few hundred people from Spain and Portugal to North Africa.

While British and American officials tried to keep the Bermuda failures secret, some MCs attacked FDR's administration for its hypocrisy and for its unwillingness to help rescue the persecuted Jews of Europe.

When the Bermuda conference ended, and it was readily apparent that it had not made any real effort to rescue the Jews of Europe, various members of Congress let FDR know what they thought of the entire fiasco. Congressman Arthur G. Klein of New York recalled that Germany had declared war against the Jewish people back in 1933. Jews had been degraded and thrown into concentration camps while the

democratic governments of the world, which could have
stopped this cruel and sadistic conduct, remained silent. No
one helped the Jews then. No one helped "millions of men,
women and children, who by accident of birth or the will of
God were born Jews." An entire people was being systematically slaughtered and the Bermuda conferees—the U.S. and
Britain—still refused to use the word "Jew" in their com-
munique.

Klein called upon FDR and Churchill to publicly condemn the atrocities and promise that the Allies would take
some action. Such a declaration would at least "revive the hope
and faith of those poor suffering people who are so hopeless
at present," and it would serve notice to the Nazis that the
world would not "condone or forgive their brutal action toward
an innocent minority and that retribution would surely
follow." The declaration which Klein and others asked for was
was not forthcoming until March, 1944. Only then were Jews
specifically referred to as the people being persecuted, only
then were the Nazi atrocities referred to as the blackest
crimes of all time, and only then were they warned that "none
who participate in these acts of savagery shall go unpunished."

Congress waited for the Bermuda report, but there was
no report. Sen. Langer proposed that a special intergovern-
mental agency be established to help save Jews, and that
neutral states like Sweden, Switzerland, Spain, Portugal,
Ireland, and Turkey be provided full compensation for any aid
they might provide. Moreover, England should be advised that
Americans were perplexed by their discriminatory policies
in Palestine. While Polish, Yugoslav, Greek, and others were
permitted into Palestine, ships that carried Jews were "allowed
to sink rather than to discharge their human cargo in their
land of destination." When a government failed to perform
its duty, said Langer, then it needed to be reminded of that
duty.

But the duty was not performed. The facts concerning
U.S. quota restrictions were easily available .They were cited
in the Congressional Record. Any one could have read that
merely 6.4 percent of the total yearly quota had been used in
the fiscal year 1943. In contrast to the 1920's when 98 percent
of the total quota had been invariably used, in 1943 no state,
except Spain, had used its quotas. Some 5.6 percent of Germany's quota was used, and only 27.2 percent of Poland's. The
facts were there for all to see. But Assistant Secretary of
State Breckinridge Long testified before the House Foreign
Affairs Committee in December, 1943, that America had done

all it could to admit the refugees. He said 580,000 refugees had been admitted in the ten-year period since the Nazis began their persecutions. As it turned out only 568,000 visas had been authorized, and of those only 545,000 were issued. Moreover, few Jews ever had a chance to use them because of the regulations strictly enforced by American consuls in Europe.

After Long finished testifying, he became worried and asked his people in the State Department to justify his misrepresentations: "They asked the question where we got the 580,000. We ought to be able to answer that." Later he explained to Member of Congress Sol Bloom that he had made a tiny error in wording. Instead of "We have taken into this country since the beginning of the Hitler regime . . . approximately 580,000 refugees," he should have said that only such a number of visas had been authorized. But he still held on to the false claim that the Roosevelt administration had "tried to be helpful to a large number of people and that we gave them an opportunity to escape from their oppressors and come to the United States." But it was no minor error. The figures he used before the Foreign Affairs Committee were the very same figures he had used in briefing sessions with other State Department officials and with FDR.

Emanuel Celler, among other MCs, would not allow Long to continue his misrepresentations and distortions. Cellar quoted Earl G. Harrison, U.S. Commissioner of Immigration Services, who said that not since 1862 had there been fewer aliens admitted to the United States. And this, said Celler, was due to such individuals as Long, who was one of the "least sympathetic to refugees in all the State Department" and was responsible for "the tragic bottleneck in the granting of visas." Because of individuals like Long it took "months and months to grant the visas and then it usually applied to a corpse." State Department officialdom had complained that there was a lack of shipping space and therefore the refugees could not be brought here. This may have been a problem years ago, said Celler, but it was not a problem in 1943. There were "bridges of ships reaching to all parts of the world," and while they came back empty they could have brought people. Celler concluded that while people like Long continued to work in the State Department, the U.S. could just as well "take down that plaque from the Statue of Liberty and block out the words 'lamp beside the golden door.'"

The Nazi slaughter of 100,000 Jewish civilians each month moved Samuel Dickstein to introduce a resolution which called

upon Roosevelt to admit those Jews who could escape. Dickstein's proposal failed to win Congressional approval. On
March 10, 1943, Congress had passed a resolution condemning
the Nazi atrocities and later it called upon FDR to create a
special rescue commission, but there was no resolution which
called for the admission of those who could be rescued.

At Christmas time Congress still talked about a special
agency to be created on behalf of the Jewish people of Europe.
Congressman Somers wondered how long it would take for
such a commission to be established. A special American commission for the protection and salvage of artistic and historical monuments in Europe, under the chairmanship of Justice
Owen J. Roberts, had been established, but there was, as yet,
nothing for the rescue of human beings. Somers wondered
when Congress and the American government would consider
it is important to save human beings as it was to save art.
Since it was the Christmas season Somers suggested that it
would give "the Jews of the world an assurance of our sympathy and our willingness to act in their behalf" if a rescue
commission were established.

On December 20, Celler spoke on behalf of the House
Baldwin-Rogers resolution, which recommended "the creation
by the President of a commission of diplomatic, economic,
and military experts to formulate and effectuate a plan of
immediate action designed to save the surviving Jewish people
of Europe from extinction at the hands of Nazi Germany."
He felt that the resolution had not gone far enough, but it
was a step in the right direction because it called for special
rescue measures. Over and over honorable people had spoken
of the two million Jews killed, and it "lost all meaning in the
repetition," complained Celler. But Celler insisted that America could not forget its responsibility to the four million European Jews still alive." The shame was America's if we Americans did not "strain every fiber of our being to bring to
safety the imperiled Jews." The Bermuda conferees felt that
they could not send food to the Jews starving in Europe, and
the President seemed to feel that any food sent to the Jews
would be taken over by the Germans and used by them to
fight the war. But this was not the case. Celler reported that
Spyros P. Skouras, the head of the Greek War Relief Association, had told him that when food was sent to Greece the
Germans had permitted it to be used by the people that
needed it. Let us at least try to get the food to the starving,
pleaded Celler. If the Germans would, in any way, interfere,
the shipments could be stopped, but let us try.

In 1944 FDR established the War Refugee Board, whose primary function it was to help rescue Jews and other persecuted peoples of Europe. But American doors remained closed. Even if some people were rescued, where could they go? Who would let the Jews in? FDR symbolically opened a port of refuge at Fort Ontario, Oswego, New York. He opened that former army base to 982 displaced persons. No other country followed his example. Nor for that matter did the U.S. open up any other 'port' to the Jews. Above all, Palestine was still kept closed to the Jews.

Some Members of Congress continued to express their concern for the plight of European Jewry; some even made speeches on behalf of the Jewish Homeland idea. But, for the most part, all the concerned MCs did was make speeches and introduce a few resolutions that never got off the ground. When FDR and his men flashed the sign to stop, they stopped.

M&R 7:4, March-April, 1981; 7:4, May-June, 1981

WHERE WAS MAN?

You know I hated you O Lord.
I cursed your blessed name.
I needed help: a signal, a word.
And there was no one else to blame.

Because your silence drove me mad,
I climbed the walls and tore my hair.
My lungs were spitting blood and yet
You wouldn't listen to my prayer.

I called on you in torment wild
And desparately cursed your name.
Then I was nothing but a child
And there was no one else to blame.

But now I feel God wasn't dead
And where was man, I ask instead.

SONIA WEITZ

M&R 9:6, May-June, 1981

V. The Commonwealth of Concentration Camps

A network of camps inside and outside Nazi Germany, before and after World War II, incarcerated the unwanted Jewish masses. The process began with the Dachau concentration camp, opened in 1933, and ended in 1948 with the closing of the detention camps in Cyprus. Dachau was designed, in part, to encourage Jews to leave Germany; the Cyprus camps were designed exclusively to prevent Jews from entering Palestine. During those fifteen years of turmoil, Jews experienced the gamut of camps erected to keep them from the rest of mankind. These ranged from the British internment camps (where they found themselves suspected of being part of a Nazi Fifth Column), to Stalin's Gulag in Siberia (for being bourgeois agents of Zionism) to the SS Death Camps (to which they were sent for being implacable enemies of the human race), not to mention the post-war Displaced Persons (D.P.) camps, from which Nazi war criminals found it easier to leave for the United States than their Jewish victims seeking to enter Palestine.

Central to the Jewish Holocaust experience during the era of international rejection is the camp and ability of individuals to maintain their humanity and Jewishness despite conditions designed to humiliate, demoralize, and, ultimately, to dehumanize. The following short set of selections focuses on that unparalleled ability and will to survive as a person and as a Jew.

Insights on life in the death camps can be found in "Lessons of Treblinka (Terence des Pres, 6:4 March-April 1980). An overview of the death camps is presented in *Hitler's Death Camps: The Sanity of Madness* (Konnilyn G. Feig, 9:1 Sept.-Oct. 1982. Review, Professor Henry R. Huttenbach). Another perspective is offered in *Deliverance Day: The Last Hours at Dachau* (Michael Selzer, 5:2 Jan.-Feb. 1979, Review, Werner J. Cahnman).

BELZEC, SOBIBOR, TREBLINKA

Belzec, Sobibor, Treblinka: The Operation Reinhard Death Camps.
Yitzhak Arad. Indiana University Press, 1987. 437 pp. $29.95.

Reviewed by DR. CHARLES PATTERSON

By drawing on all the existing primary sources—survivor testimonies, German and Polish records and eyewitness accounts, and evidence from trials of SS camp personnel in West Germany in the 1960's—Yitzhak Arad, Chairman of Yad Vashem, whose own parents perished in Treblinka, tells the story of the three death camps of "Operation Reinhard" as it has never been told before. (The operation was named after Reinhard Heydrich, whom Göring had put in charge of the "final solution of the Jewish question," after Heydrich was killed by members of the Czech Underground in late May, 1942.) One and a half million Jews were gassed in Belzec, Sobibor, and Treblinka in 1942 and 1943; fewer than 200 survived.

Arad begins by describing the organization and personnel of the camps. Himmler put Odilo Globocnik, the SS and Police Leader of the Lublin district, in charge of the extermination of the Jews of the General Government, but the most important personnel for the planning and construction of the camps and their gassing facilities were the "euthanasia experts" from Hitler's Chancellery, who had already gassed over 70,000 mentally or otherwise "hopelessly" ill Germans from September 1939, to late summer 1941. The SS operated the camps, and they, in turn, were backed up by specially trained Ukrainian guards.

In the first half of the book, Arad discusses the construction and physical layout of the camps (detailed maps are provided); the machinery of extermination; the transportation of Jews to the camps from Polish ghettos (as well as from Holland, France, Greece, Germany, Austria, Yugoslavia, Czechoslovakia, and the Soviet Union); the systematic economic plunder of the victims; and the work done by the Jewish prisoners. He also treats the extermination of Gypsies, Himmler's visits to Sobibor and Treblinka, and the Nazi attempt to erase their crimes by burning hundreds of thousands of corpses originally buried in huge pits.

In the second half of the book the focus is on camp life and the numerous attempts at escape and resistance. After presenting portraits of the various SS commandants and guards (with an appendix at the end of the book that describes their fate after the war—"The majority of the SS men and Ukrainians who served in the death camps of Operation Reinhard were never brought to trial."), Arad describes what it was like for the prisoners—roll calls, food, diseases, suicide, the role of religion, and even "social life."

Finally, more than a hundred pages are devoted to the many spontaneous acts of resistance and escape from the trains and camps. The two major uprisings late in the life of both Treblinka and Sobibor are described in the greatest detail: the undergrounds at both camps, the escape plans, the obstacles and delays, and finally the revolts themselves—at Treblinka on August 2, 1943, and at Sobibor on October 14, 1943. In all these accounts of resistance, the reader is struck by the fierce desire of the victims to outlive their Nazi oppressors, making their tragic fate all the more poignant and unbearable.

In a chapter on "Reports about Death Camps in Polish Wartime Publications," Arad shows that the Polish Underground knew about the work of the death camps and the fate of the Jews of Poland and passed this information on to the Polish Government-in-Exile in London and the British Government. However, their reports met with disbelief, doubt, and distrust, so that "they did not receive the proper sort of publicity, and certainly no practical or direct action was forthcoming to stop the deportations to the death camps."

Alarmed by the uprisings at Treblinka and Sobibor, the German authorities murdered all the remaining Jewish slave laborer in the General Government still working in German industrial enterprises at Trawniki, Poniatowa, and other labor camps in the Lublin district—approximately 42,000. Arad concludes with a chapter on the liquidation of the camps and the termination of Operation Reinhard, complete with Himmler's final letter to Globocnik, thanking him "for the great and unique services which you performed for the entire German people by carrying out Operation Reinhard."

For anyone interested in understanding the Holocaust this book is essential reading. More than a formidable and impressive piece of scholarship, this compelling work is an indictment, a warning, and, most of all, a dedicated work of remembrance—and of mourning.

SURVIVOR FINDS HERSELF
ONCE AGAIN IN TREBLINKA

By Haika Grossman

Once again my feet are planted on this land which has mixed in it the ashes of 800,000 Jews who were brought here from Bialystok and Warsaw, from cities and towns in which a thousand years of history of Jews and Poles together has been woven: layer upon layer of Jewish productivity in literature, art, theatre; generations of intelligentsia and of tradespeople, of freedom fighters and simply folk who labored for their livelihood. A tapestry of life with both the good and the bad was turned into ashes and dust by the barbaric Nazis.

Treblinka—a name associated with horror. Forty-five years has passed, yet every detail of the railway station, Malkenia, not far from here, is engraved in my memory. It is halfway between Bialystok and Warsaw on the border of the area of the general government, the crossroads of the ghettos which were isolated from one another, the crossroads of the fighting Jewish underground. How many moments of fear and trepidation did my soul suffer at this border! Many of my comrades were arrested here by the Gestapo. And the terror in my heart remains, and I will feel it to the end of my days.

Fifty million souls were sacrificed to the Nazi madness. The truth of that history must be told. There was neither symmetry nor equality in the covenant between the various fighters against the Nazis. The Nazis couldn't destroy the ultimate hope of any nation, because despite the terrible human cost, after the victory, the nation would survive. My nation was deprived even of that hope. The battle of the Ghetto fighters was lost before it began.

There was some cooperation on the part of some brave Poles and other people, but they didn't share the same destiny. The awful isolation that existed then follows us to this very day, and it is impossible to change this fact. The final solution was planned and executed with Nazi-German precision for the Jewish people exclusively. Its purpose was the extermination of the Jews. I saw mothers defend their children with their bodies. My nation was destroyed before my eyes and I was helpless. Neither I nor Anielewicz, the Hashomer Hatzair leader, nor Levartovsky, the Communist leader in Warsaw, nor Tannenbaum in Bialystok, nor Kovner and Wittenberg in Vilna could save them. . . .

The transports to Treblinka were stopped at the beginning of August, 1943. The Jewish prisoners who worked in the camps rebelled. Most of them fell in battle, or during their attempt to escape. The ashes were covered over, the earth was smoothed, the sun went down and rose again, and the sympathy ended. How easy it is to respond with hatred to a world which stood by and watched. How much strength of character is needed simply to remain stable. We couldn't forgive the criminals, yet at the same time we had to build a new life, to keep the account and yet to remain a part of enlightened humanity. We had to gather all our spiritual strength in order to survive and continue to believe in the human race.

Today I don't carry feelings of hatred except hatred of war, revulsion for racism, anti-Semitism and insane nationalism. Those who minimize the Holocaust, the historical revisionists who would rehabilitate the Nazis, those who argue that the Holocaust wasn't unusual in the course of human history: their place is among those who would continue with Nazism. . . .

No miracle or benefit came to us as a result of the Holocaust. By the sweat of our brow, with great sacrifice and with the support of the enlightened world, we built a state for the Jewish people over the abyss of their despair. Yet, we are still a long way from comfort and peace. . . .

Peace to your remains, my slaughtered brothers and sisters. In the memory of your sacrifice may our nation and other nations live.

M&R 15:4, Sept.-Oct. 1988

I NEVER WALKED
ON JANOWSKA STREET

By JACOB FELBERBAUM

I never was in Janowska Camp.

It seems, therefore, most peculiar that this camp should bring to my mind memories, the most horrible memories of the past I never lived through, memories that haunt me during many sleepless nights with visions of real facts I never witnessed. However, being a survivor of different events and a bearer of different stories, I do claim the full right to be a survivor of the Janowska Camp.

Separated forcefully from my parents and my sister on one fateful afternoon, I was taken out of Lwow, where the rest remained in the claws of the German death machine. A short hiding experience of my family ended with a denunciation by Ukrainian peasants. The captors did not finish them immediately but transferred them into the Lwow Ghetto to work for the Reich. And what kind of work it was! Regimented into special brigades, always hungry, degraded with pedantic, sadistic details, with every step they took, humiliated in the eyes of others and in their own inner world, beaten physically, slowly they were brought into a condition where death was not only awaited, but asked for as the only salvation. In order to break the will to resist, first the will to live had to be broken.

But while my parents, because of advanced age, were slowly succumbing to the overpowering forces, the young ones found inhuman strength to endure, revolt and, finally break out. Shortly before the final action in the Ghetto (June, 1943) a group of young ones successfully broke out. Among the survivors was a young man who after the war vividly pictured the last moments of my parents' life: my father, sick, beaten up by the Germans, and my mother next to him completely devastated. My sister was gone to the "sands" long since.

Final action in the Ghetto ended in "resettlement" to the East, naturally through the Janowska Camp. They all came in waves of hundreds and were marched straight into so-called "sands," where the most horrible "death brigade" was already waiting for its victims. First the helpless victims were mowed down by the German machine-guns. Then they were expertly burned in tremendous pyres built from wooden logs, crisscrossed with corpses. The unburned bones were then ground and sifted for remaining gold. The complete job was finished by September, 1943, in order not to leave any traces. The crime was almost perfect.

My dearest did not survive. Only some German perpetrators were punished after the war.

But in my memory Janowska Street remains with the ear-shattering moanings of my father, with the tears of my mother, with the crackling of the German guns, and with the flames consuming my loved ones.

And that is why they are so vivid—those memories of a liquidation camp where I never was.

M&R 5:5, May-June, 1979

KOL NIDREI IN SIBERIA

By JACK LAITMAN

During World War II, I spent 18 months in a Russian slave camp in Siberia. It began in September, 1939, when the Germans started to bomb Warsaw. We were among the thousands of Jews leaving their homes and families for temporary refuge in Lvov. Unknown to us, Stalin's infamous pact with Hitler had opened the way for the partition of Poland. And when we arrived in Lvov after a lengthy and difficult journey, mostly on foot, the Russians had just entered.

The knock of doom came for us one morning at 3 a.m. There was a KGB officer with two armed soldiers telling us to dress quickly. The train that would take us was waiting. At the station, soldiers with drawn bayonets herded us onto the cattle cars. There was no escape. We soon realized that we were going East, not homeward.

After a seemingly endless journey—more than 12 days with little food and no sanitation—we were unloaded in the

Novosibirsk region. In the morning we were loaded onto a
ferry for a 10-hour trip deep into the Siberian woods.
Without proper clothing and with a minimum of food,
we had to work hard to stay alive. My work brigade had to
chop down and cut giant trees with handhacks and saws.
The summer passed. As the High Holidays neared, it
started getting colder. Because someone had salvaged a Jewish
calendar, we knew when Yom Kippur would be celebrated.
Snow was already covering the ground. Life was very hard
in our poor huts.

Our mood was gloomy on Yom Kippur eve. Our thoughts
went back to our loved ones left behind and to the last holidays
we spent with them.

We tried to find a way to celebrate the holiest of all days
—even here in the slave camp. One of our fellow prisoners
was Zalman, a strong middle-aged pious man who had been
deported with his three sons and wife. Although he hardly
knew how to pray in Hebrew, he would speak to God directly
in his own language. No matter how great the risk, he decided
that we say Kol Nidrei with a *minyan* (quorum of 10). He
offered his own hut as a meeting place.

We must show God, he said, that we had not given up
and, therefore, we would follow the traditional prayers with
the proper chants. I promised Zalman that I would find one
who could chant the prayers.

Zalman made all the preparations. He cleaned the room,
prepared wood for the oven, and covered the table with a
white cloth. Zalman even sent one of his sons to the village to
exchange a shirt—an irreplaceable treasure—for two candles.

After a day's hard work, we returned in the evening to
Zalman's hut. There were 12 men, 3 women, but only 3 prayer-
books and 4 *taleitim* or prayershawls. When I entered, Zalman
asked, "Well, you promised to bring someone to chant the
prayers?" "A promise is a promise," I answered. "Here I
am."

As I put on the Talit, I trembled. I felt like saying "Hineni
Heani Mimaas" (said before the Additional Service) : "In
deep humility I stand before you." Who was I to chant Kol
Nidrei? But I pulled myself together and began saying Kol
Nidrei in a low voice. I thought of myself as if I were hidden
in a cellar like the Marranos of the days of the Spanish
Inquisition.

It is hard to describe the spirit pervading the room. Each
of us must have thought back to the not-so-long past when we
were free to celebrate in our own homes. With my back to the

door, we continued the services, I sang the traditional melodies, keeping the tunes just audible to my congregation and could hear them whispering the prayers along with me. We tried to be as quiet and inconspicuous as possible, but it is said that a Jew can scream in utter silence. I hesitated a moment before saying *Shechecheyanu,* thinking. "Can I really give thanks to the Lord for enabling us to reach this season?" But we warmed to the task. As I was singing *Solachti* (I forgive) I could hear the assembled people murmuring right along. Suddenly it became very quiet. Somewhere in the distance I heard a door open. "A latecomer must be joining us," I thought. The door opened and closed again. Voices began buzzing all around me. Our commandant had paid us a visit, I was told. He had looked around, listened, and left without a word.

We were all afraid of reprisal. After a worried, sleepless night, we went to work as usual the next morning. Fasting was nothing unusual. Even on the best days we had little to eat. Only Zalman stayed in the hut. Without a doctor's note, he was taking a big risk. The commandant did not appear that day—or the next day.

A rumor circulated in the camp that the visitor on Kol Nidrei had not been the commander, but Elijah the Prophet. He is known to appear in different disguises. Perhaps a miracle was near. Perhaps we would survive; we would be free after all.

However, few survived the harsh conditions in the Gulag. Only a handful of us can recall Kol Nidrei in Siberia.

M&R 13:6, Sept.-Oct., 1986

A SPECIAL LOVE AFFAIR

By MARIE KNOWLES ELLIFRITZ, R.N.

In 1945 the 130th Evacuation Hospital was a huddle of tents where a handful of doctors, nurses, and GI's tried to hold back the escaping blood of life. Our evacuation hospital was a series of cots and air mattresses under tents and sky where God gave superhuman endurance to His helpers and the victims of the Devil; it was the place where swollen-bellied children ate a piece of bread and vomited; it was a place where women and men forever closed their eyes in escape. Our 400-bed hospital cared for the liberated victims of Nazism's Mauthausen Concentration Camp and had to be elasticized to accommodate the 1500 half-starved Jewish men, women and children who became our patients.

Few American women had ever before been called upon to undertake the gigantic task. I became concerned as to the impact this work would have upon me. A year before I had never been away from a comfortable home in Virginia. The sight before me was one of horror—and I was part of it. I looked at myself, a twenty-three-year-old Second Lieutenant in the U.S. Army Nurse Corps. Where was the smart white of a nurses uniform? My hands were dirty. My body ached for the luxury of a bath. My teeth felt thick and my mouth was filled with grit. We had arrived by open truck and the dust from the vehicles ahead had provided a shroud; but we had arrived.

It was a large wheat field—somewhere in once beautiful Austria; it had no name. In sharp contrast to the gently waving wheat, my stringy hair poked out from beneath a combat helmet. Even my once-tailored khaki overalls drooped like my spirit, but my appearance soon became secondary to my professional duties.

The first couple of days were short of hours as nurses prepared the equipment to receive patients. The men were busy too—sorting the dead from the living. And then they came—stinking, bewildered, staggering, naked human beings—they were almost like animals, without fur. I had to tell myself over and over again that these were human beings encased in what was left of a human body, bringing with them only their faith in God and the storehouse of their brains. They had survived four and five years in the concentration camp. For some it was survival of the fittest; for others it was the desperate need to die in freedom. For others? Who knows but God? For us, there was a tremendous, overwhelming, never-before-job to be done.

It is said that nurses, though born with a heart, lose it in training or they don't stay nurses. You cannot take everyone's troubles into your heart or it will soon be so full it will burst; but in the heart of the nurse there is a special place for love.

I cannot say exactly when he came into my life—I do not remember. It was not "love at first sight." I only remember that he came, and because he came there is special understanding and tenderness in me for others.

There is a special love in my heart for a 10 or 12-year-old waif, a boy whose name I have never known. He called me "Sistra" (nurse) and I called him "Junior"—a "GI" name used for the lack of something better.

He brought me tender bouquets of blue summer flowers gathered from the yellow wheat fields which bordered the 130th Evacuation Hospital set up near the concentration camp at Mauthausen. He placed them in a huge plasma can that sat on the corner of the rough packing box which was my desk. The fragile simplicity of the flowers seemed like a symbol of truth against the ravages of war. As I sniffed the blue cornflowers, tears came to my eyes. Instantly he wrapped his arms about my waist with such force that he almost knocked me over. It is only now as a mother of two that I realize his impulsive act was the natural love of a child for a mother image.

The flowers were his words, for he spoke Yiddish, Polish, and German, and I spoke none of these tongues. Language can be a barrier, but the looks and deeds of a child are universally understood. His gentle offerings were a response to a casual American friendliness. He never knew the years of stirring memory those small deeds would cause. His goodness, his kindness, his gentleness, reflected not the five years in concentration camp, but rather his mother's love and native teachings before she was put to death in the gas chamber.

Junior looked hungry. He was not lean; he was skinny, and his eyes stared from dark, sunken pits. Sometimes he appeared sightless, staring through and beyond whatever, whoever, was in front of him. Seeing could only reinforce the horror of reality.

There were few diversions for the hospital staff. One small pleasure was the evening movie held out in the open, and on a damp, chilly night I invited Junior to go with me. The name of the movie is unimportant, but as I shook with a chill from the dampness, Junior asked, "Sistra, cold?" In a flash he was gone. Returning with his one blanket from his air mattress bed, he put it around my hunched body. His funny little nose wrinkled in pride and poorly developed teeth showed too white against the too red of his lips. He tilted his head sidewise and a little toward me, nodded like a little old man and sat down beside me. We sat for a long while. He provided a strange comfort to me.

Even when I was sent to work in the larger hospital, it was his practice to see me off each morning and to wait for my return to our tent city each evening. I knew Junior waited;

I did not know why. But I liked him to be there, and I enjoyed running my hands over his shaven head where once there had been a crop of childish hair.

One day when I returned, Junior was not waiting. Somehow the hospital seemed empty—empty because Junior was not there, empty because a number of the patients including Junior had been transferred. In the big empty tent I could hear his words, "Sistra, cold?"

Later that week our unit Chaplain sent word to me that Junior had asked that I come to see him in the new camp a few miles away. I promised myself I would visit Junior—tomorrow. My tomorrows somehow became the hurried yesterdays of life.

The whiplash of an unkept promise still stirs within me. Was I too tired, too busy, or too young and immature, that I did not go? I will never know. However, the burden of regret and recrimination carried for thirty years becomes too heavy. With God's forgiveness I must leave it here.

M&R 7:14, May-June, 1981

Reprinted by permission of *Newsletter*, Peninsula Jewish Federation, © May 28, 1976

OPENING THE GATES

As we rolled over
the bridge, I looked
at the water going
underneath and I
thought to myself,
*I don't understand
why we should
continue living
if the human race
does not consider
itself above the
animals.*

●

A shock wave ran through
everyone and the ones who
hit it first passed the word
to the others coming up
in back. *You know:*

what you're going to see,
you're not going to believe.

●

I rode into Dachau
on a jeep, over a
very narrow bridge.
It was a clear day,
a very clear day,
the kind of weather
where you'd need a
jacket. We'd just
finished a winter of
sleeping in encampments,
so any sunshine was
welcome. We crossed a
bridge and the first
thing I saw were piles
of shoes, all kinds of
shoes, a pyramid of shoes.

BARBARA HELFGOTT HYETT

M&R 3:11, March-April, 1987

Reprinted by permission of University of Pittsburgh Press from *In Evidence: Poems of the Liberation of Nazi Concentration Camps* © 1986 Barbara Helfgott Hvett

---

SUMMER IN AUSCHWITZ

By DOROTHY FUERST

Summer in the Polish countryside is beautiful. Fields stretch on either side of the road, undisturbed by man or machine. Was it like this when they were transported? It was impossible to imagine the death trains moving through with their human cargo in this bucolic scene. The ride continued, the driver's chatter oblivious to our silence. We passed a village, the village of Oswiecim, and then passed over railroad tracks; a right turn and we were in the parking lot. That day must have been a busy day, for the parking lot was crowded with buses; or perhaps every day was a busy day in Oswiecim.

A long, low, red brick building blocked off the head of the parking lot. A sign above the door read: Musée d'Auschwitz. Somehow it seemed a commercialization of what happened here and we felt distaste, a desecration, a dishonor to the memories of those murdered here. Also disturbing was the fact that the administrative building serves as the starting point for tours and the place where guides can be hired. Perhaps it was the sign which disturbed, saying that for 1,600 zlotys we could have a private guide escort us and explain.

We walked where the prisoners had been herded, forty years ago. We entered under the arch, under the sign "Arbeit Macht Frei." The guide explained as we walked. "Here is the hut in front of which the orchestra played as the prisoners returned from forced labor, carrying their dying."

We walked through the doors of the barracks. Suitcases were piled to the ceiling behind a glass wall, stenciled with prisoners' names, towns they came from, dates of birth, last remnants of an earthly existence. The guide walked on, downstairs and out of the building. There was so much to show us: the gallows where innocent beings were hanged because they somehow fell afoul of some German officer or capo; the platform on which prisoners who had escaped but were captured were executed and hanged.

We entered the next barracks. A glass case running along the length and height of the room held human hair. "Two thousand kilos of hair taken from the women prisoners," the guide told us. The next barracks displayed the children's clothing, baby clothing removed before their young pure lives were snuffed out. In two corners of the room, I noticed a wreath of flowers and memorial candles. The guide explained: "Relatives have come and lit a candle. Poles died here too, you know." Downstairs we passed a capo's room. A small bed, iron locker, table, chairs; comfort within the fair-sized room, while above there was unbearable anguish, unspeakable suffering.

We moved on. Our guide showed us where roll call was held in front of the barracks, up to 19 hours at a time. He pointed to the little hut placed in front of the prisoners to keep the German official or capo warm, while he kept the prisoners standing in front of him, according to his whim—in snow, in rain, in bitter winter weather.

The guide led us between the barracks. We passed groups of visitors on tours, although the word "tourists" seems inappropriate. Some had group leaders and others did not; many were of school age. Whatever their diverse characteristics, they were all Slavic speaking. The visitors were generally subdued, but one Polish girl, her blonde hair blowing in the wind, laughed and flirted with her boyfriend. Our guide rebuked her at length in stern Polish and she fell silent. "Is it a problem?" I asked, "this disrespect for Auschwitz?" "It is," he said, "especially among the youth."

We continued down the line of barracks. "The largest of the crematoria," the guide said, "were blown up by the Germans before the Russians came, but the smaller ones are in the last building." The guide led us to the concrete room in which the prisoners were gassed. It was not a large room, perhaps enough for one hundred to be gassed at one time, pressed tightly together, but, of course, the larger rooms at Auschwitz and Birkenau were gassing simultaneously. The guide pointed out the hole, open now, where the gas came in: "It took fifteen minutes for every one to die, sometimes twenty. Then the room was emptied of corpses and they were ready for the next group." He led us to the ovens next door. I touched the black iron. How had modern man devised such evil?

There was more to see, to know. The guide took us to the special barracks reserved for political prisoners; those victims were subjected to torture before or as a means of causing death. Yet, they were a systematic, orderly people, these Nazis. The books are there, available, open to inspection. On each blue line of each notebook each prisoner's name appears, his number, date of entry, date of death.

Our time was up. We thanked the guide and walked back to the taxi. Our driver, temporarily subdued, started the drive back to Katowice. I think back on our pilgrimage, not visit, because ordinary words do not apply. I am glad that I have been to Auschwitz, sanitized though it now is. I am glad that we have been able to honor those who have no grave and have no stone. I am glad because an English-speaking presence was there. I am glad because Auschwitz cannot be dead, but must always be part of our lives.

Hours later, on the train back to Czechoslovakia, I asked Dafna, our eighteen-year-old, who had previously been so reluctant to come with us to Auschwitz, mostly out of apprehension and partly because Auschwitz was not on her itinerary of the Grand European Tour, if she were glad she had come. "Yes, very," she said. "This is where it happened. Now it is real."

VI. The Righteous Gentile

Were it not for the brave few, the exceptional non-Jews who risked their lives to save Jews targeted for extermination, post-Holocaust Jewry would have every reason to court total despair and behave with absolute cynicism. Instead, thanks to these kind souls, faith in human decency can be maintained. They were Catholics, Protestants, Christian Orthodox, atheists, Communists, aristocrats and simple workers and peasants; they came from all walks of life. They could have cooperated with the enemies of the Jews, they could have shown disinterest in the plight of their fellow humans; but, miraculously, they did not. Their sense of humane values rose above the temptations of collaboration and self-preservation.

Most of these men and women will remain nameless, like the bulk of the millions of Jews who died during the catastrophe. But a precious few are given their proper recognition and rewarded with the undying gratitude of the Jewish people. There is no medal of valor for them; only a tree planted in Jerusalem's Yad Vashem to symbolize their love for the lives of others, and the commitment they will never be forgotten.

But if the Righteous Gentile is a beacon of hope for Jews striving to live in peace with non-Jews, then the example of these good people stands as a living warning to the vast majority of those "Christians," or those "Socialists," to all those who failed to act in the name of the humanitarian values they claim to represent. But that is another subject.

For further reading in this area, the readers are directed to these articles in *M & R*: "Nobility of a Nation" (Frode Jakobsen, 8:8 Nov.-Dec. 1981); "Righteous Gentiles: Praise for the Just; Laments That There Were So Few" (Franklin H. Littell, 10:7 Jan.-Feb. 1984); "A Study of the Altruistic Personality" (Janyce Neiman and Joanne Sullivan, 10:14 March-April 1984).

GERMAN WHO RESCUED 1,200 JEWS BURIED IN JERUSALEM

Oscar Schindler, a German Catholic who saved more than 1,200 Jews from the gas chambers in World War II, was buried in Jerusalem's Latin Cemetery on Mt. Zion, in accordance with his last wish. Schindler had died at 66 in Buenos Aires following an operation.

During the Nazi occupation of Poland, Schindler was manager of a small factory in Cracow making kitchen utensils He persuaded the SS to send him Jewish forced labor from the Auschwitz concentration camp on the grounds that it was vital to the war effort. By padding out his work force from 25 to over 1,000, and hiding many other Jews, he saved them from death. He was arrested twice by the Gestapo and was freed through the intervention of his friends in the army. After the war when the Soviet army entered Germany and expropriated his factory, Jewish organizations helped him settle in Argentina, where he operated a small farm outside Buenos Aires.

He devoted the last years of his life to working as secretary of the Society of Friends of Hebrew University and was a frequent visitor to Israel.

Schindler's story is related in a book by Kurt R. Grossman, *Die Unbesungenen Helden* (*The Unsung Heroes*). The following are excerpts:

"In 1942, when the Germans started dissolving the ghettos sending Jews to extermination camps, I had to decide whether to abandon my workers to their fate or have them declared prisoners working and housed at my factory. I could not disappoint the absolute confidence they placed in me and so I set up a camp for them and their families on the factory premises. Since the managers of three neighboring factories were about to hand over their 450 workers to the nearby Plaszow concentration camp, I volunteered to take in their men too.

"I was only able to raise the enormous sums needed for the upkeep of so many people by selling part of my production on the black market. Similarly, I had to acquire up to 80 per cent of my food supplies on the black market or through barter. The factory kitchen alone cost me 50,000 zlotys a month.

"In many cases I took the aged parents and other relatives of my men on my payroll, although I had no real work for them. Refusal would have meant concentration camp for these people. For every name on my work list I had to pay the SS five zlotys a day.

"The motive for my actions was the daily sight of the unspeakable suffering inflicted on Jewish persons and the brutal conduct of the Prussian supermen. This group of lying hypocrites and sadistic murderers promised to liberate my homeland, the Sudetenland, only to turn it into a colony, to be plundered at will. The memory of a happy childhood, spent with many Jewish friends and schoolmates, was for me a moral obligation that drove me on."

M&R 1:6, Nov.-Dec., 1974

RIGHTEOUS LIST GROWS; CHANCES TO HONOR HEROES DECLINING

In 1976, less than 2,300 individuals had been honored by Yad Vashem as Righteous Gentiles. In a little more than a decade, the total has more than tripled to nearly 7,000.

However, as the numbers dwindle in the ranks of survivors, the chances to honor these heroic individuals decrease. And with the passing of time, the intended honorees have in many cases passed from the scene. In some 25 percent of the cases, the honor is accepted by a close relative of the deceased Righteous Gentile.

Israel's duty towards the Righteous Gentiles is detailed in the 1953 Yad Vashem law. Yad Vashem is charged with commemorating "the *hasidei umot ha'olam* who risked their lives to save Jews." The term "The Righteous Among the Nations" has found greater favor among Yad Vashem officials.

In 1985 the Yad Vashem law was amended to offer honorary Israeli citizenship to the Righteous Gentiles.

A lengthy article on the Righteous Gentiles was recently written by Ernie Meyer for the *Jerusalem Post*.

Although the designation of Righteous Gentile was intended for those who risked their lives to save Jews, Meyer points out how flexibility has functioned. Diplomats Aristides

de Sousa of Portugal and Sempo Sugihara of Japan did not
risk their lives, but their careers were ruined.

"We must be generous in interpreting the law," said Is-
raeli Supreme Court Justice Moshe Bejski, chairman of the
Yad Vashem committee dealing with applications for the
Righteous Gentiles.

"'Thus, the committee gradually established precedents,"
writes Meyer, "and developed its own criteria. Two conditions
were established: that a beneficiary of the rescue action must
present his or her testimony in writing; that the rescuer must
not have received any financial benefit." The latter has been
a tough clause, for individuals, in many countries, especially
Poland, had great difficulties in feeding and providing for
their own families. "Accepting payment in return for supply-
ing food to a Jew in hiding was entirely justified," according
to Meyer. "But on occasion the committee faced the question
whether a payment of, say 25,000 zlotys constituted a financial
inducement, or was merely intended to defray the cost of
feeding four hidden Jews for several months."

Dr. Mordechai Paldiel, Director for the Designation of
the Righteous Among the Nations at Yad Vashem, clarified the
matter: "As a rule, the committee takes the liberal view, without looking too closely at the actual sums of money that
changed hands. The idea is to weed out cases of people who
made a financial killing out of the business of hiding Jews—
although even that was risky enough."

While the heroic Christians receive their due honors, concerned individuals and organizations have maintained that not
enough has been done for these exceptional people, many of
whom live in dire economic circumstances. "We should raise
about $500,000 to support those in need," Dr. Bejski maintains.
"I regret that the Claims Conference budgets only about
$100,000 a year to dole out monthly pensions, which are only
$20 for those in Poland, $135 for those in Germany and $100
for some cases in the U.S."

Holland and Poland account for some 70 percent of the
Righteous Gentiles. Poland is catching up, according to Meyer,
because of the involvement of the country's Commission for
the Investigation of Nazi War Crimes and the Jewish Historical Institute. "The fact that the honorees become part of other
veterans' organizations and enjoy certain financial advantages
may also be a factor," Meyer added.

The underrepresentation of certain countries often comes
to the attention of Yad Vashem officials. There are less than
500 Righteous Gentiles from France, a country where some

50 percent of the Jewish population survived, often through the help of rescuers. "This may be due," Paldiel said, "to the absence of an official body promoting the matter or simply to a general ignorance of the existence of the award."

There have also been few honorees from Yugoslavia and Greece. "When I tell knowledgeable people that we've had only 39 cases from Greece in 24 years (60 Righteous Gentiles), they are stupified," Paldiel said. "Apparently, there is nobody there to tell us, although the Jewish community in Athens is now beginning to gather material."

Germany/Austria, Italy, and Romania are among other countries not adequately represented in the chart of Righteous Gentiles. "'In Berlin alone," Paldiel said, "a few hundred Jews survived in hiding. There must be more cases of rescuers than we have on record so far."

Is heroism only reserved for Christians? Meyer posed a question to Paldiel about recognition for Jews who saved their brethren. "I get letters," answered Paldiel, "asking for such recognition about once a month. Perhaps something should be done on this matter, but the feeling at Yad Vashem is that a helpful Jew only did his duty."

M&R 14:9, Sept.-Oct. 1987

IN SEARCH OF THE SWEDISH ANGEL OF RESCUE

The Swedish Angel of Rescue: The Heroism and Torment of Raoul Wallenberg. Harvey Rosenfeld. Foreword by Congressman Jack Kemp. Afterword by Ambassador Per Anger, Prometheus, 1982. 262 pp. $19.95.

Reviewed by Prof. Henry R. Huttenbach

In recent months, a spate of books on Wallenberg have made the run through the popular market. Most of them smacked of exploitation, too many lapsed into iconography, lavishing praise on a heroic man about whom very little personal information is known. Others were examples of undisciplined speculation about the tragic and still unresolved fate of a man who single-handedly saved thousands of Jewish lives.

Yet, even his achievements were inflated into tens and hundreds of thousands, stretching credibility and undermining faith in the actual successes of the self-effacing Swede.

It is with considerable relief that one can finally turn to a sober study of Wallenberg which calmly exposes the reader to the Wallenberg case without straying from the facts and wandering off into endless hypotheses. Thirty-seven years after his disappearance the whereabouts of Wallenberg remain essentially unknown despite a frail chain of reports. Twenty-five years after the Soviet government officially admitted to Wallenberg's death in 1947, deep suspicions to the contrary feed off the scattered rumors that he is still alive. A generation of speculation, misinformation, and political rivalry has enmeshed the Wallenberg case in a tangled web of confusion from which Rosenfeld manages to extricate the reader, reducing the story to its essential issues.

In brief the Wallenberg story breaks into three distinct components: 1) his role as a rescuer of Hungarian Jews in 1944, 2) the action or inaction of the international community on behalf of Wallenberg, and 3) his fate at the hands of the Soviet abductors since 1945. It is to Rosenfeld's credit that he devotes his book equally to all three, without pretending to know answers when the evidentiary trail runs out.

In his review of Wallenberg's frantic work in war-torn Hungary, Rosenfeld does not fall into the numbers trap. Instead he evaluates his rescue mission in terms of the obstacles confronting Wallenberg, including the crucial element of time. Leaving it to others to count the number of Jews who escaped the Holocaust thanks to Wallenberg's interventions, Rosenfeld concentrates on the man's daily and nightly crusade. The impression is of a man obsessed with his task, driven by the total evil of the enemy but never distracted by the goodness of his own mission.

As Rosenfeld shows, the ranks of those devoted to Wallenberg are still distressingly slim. The stance of the Swedish government is a permanent disgrace, an indelible stain on its history of neutralism. Post-World War II Swedish neutrality seems, according to Rosenfeld, to be predicated on an admitted fear of the Soviet Union, a paralysis of will that has emasculated this nation's ability to pursue the interests of its own citizens, even those with diplomatic status. In this sense, Wallenberg is a victim of Swedish impotence, which has a far longer history than Rosenfeld and others suspect, and, in this case, would make a fruitful study for socio-psychologists interested in the politics of the amoral. Sweden was Finlandized long before its more vulnerable and less powerful neighbor had to adjust to the threat of Soviet intervention: Sweden did so not out of necessity but as a result of voluntary, cynical calculation—its leaders know that non-involvement can be profitable. Wallenberg is the victim of a century-old Swedish formula of disinterest, the noble efforts of private citizens notwithstanding.

Is Wallenberg still alive? Rosenfeld leaves no clue untested. He surveys all the bits of evidence and analyses carefully all the fabricated theories, both the tenable and the poignant expressions of hope held by Wallenberg's family. But he can come up with no satisfactory answer, admitting that this is the great unknown of the Wallenberg saga. He wonders aloud whether a man such as Wallenberg could have withstood the cruel rigours of the Soviet camp system but realizes that any answer is pure speculation. The real issue is the motivation of Wallenberg's abductors: why did they arrest him? why did they imprison him? and why have they bungled in their public handling of the Wallenberg case?

Was it sheer cruelty or calculated decision which dragged the Wallenberg case on for over three decades? Rosenfeld devotes considerable attention to this insoluble question. Putting the Wallenberg affair into perspective, Rosenfeld attempts to find reason for his arrest by the Russians in terms of the prevailing Soviet attitudes: Wallenberg was a Swedish spy with connections to the Germans, with family ties to the United States, with Jewish sympathies, of capitalist background, aristocrat, etc. All of these possibilities are examined, but there simply is no proof to turn them into probabilities. What happened to Wallenberg?

In the end, when the stream of books comes to an end, he will probably be forgotten unless those thousands who owe their lives to his martyrdom raise their voices in a persistent chorus of protest. Hungarian Jewish survivors and their children have a permanent moral obligation not to let the matter of Wallenberg die. They could not do better to inform themselves of the heroic, tragic and sordid episodes of the Wallenberg story than to read Rosenfeld's admirably objective book.

A JOURNEY BEYOND HATE

By The Rev. Robert McAfee Brown

It happened in Eastern Europe. It doesn't matter much where it happened, although it happened to be a town in Poland. Let us call the town Z-. Before World War II, Z- was a small town of craftsmen and farmers, with about 1,500 Jewish families. The Jews had their own cultural life centered around their learned people, the rabbis in the various small prayer houses, along with one main synagogue. When the Nazis arrived, the Jews were forced to live in a ghetto. By the time the Nazis left, the town of Z- had become a small town of craftsmen and farmers, with no Jewish families, no ghetto, and no synagogue. For according to plan, the Jews had been rounded up and sent to the death camp of Treblinka, and the main synagogue had become a social club.

The "final solution" had worked in the town of Z-. There were no Jews left. Or so the Nazis thought. But their count was off by four. A Jewish mother and her children, two sons and a daughter, survived months of Nazi occupation in the town of Z-, hidden by a Catholic family in the garret and basement of their home.

We heard the tale, and then re-lived the tale, through the eyes and ears of Eli Zborowski, one of the two sons who survived. This, his story, now becomes two stories: the story of the grandeur and the terror of being a Jew back then, but also the story of the grandeur and terror of being a Jew right now.

Let us flesh out the earlier story. Eli's father, a merchant, contracted with a builder to construct a house for his family. One of the builder's employees was a young Catholic brick layer. Every noon, the young brick layer remembered, Eli's father would come by during the lunch hour with a bottle of vodka, and the group of them would eat and drink and converse together. To the Jewish merchant, the workers were not just workers doing a job for him. They were persons with whom he liked to associate. And they all became fast friends.

But they did not all live happily ever after. When the Germans came, the Jewish merchant had to jump out of the second floor window of the synagogue into the river. Two

193

miles upstream he was apprehended by fellow Poles. Rather than hiding him, they shot him. After all, he was a Jew. That was the last Eli Zborowski ever heard about his father.

But before his death, the father had made a very heavy request of the young Catholic brick layer and his family: In the event of trouble, would they be willing to shelter a Jewish family? In all the other occupied countries of Europe, such an action meant arrest or deportation. In Poland, however, it meant death. The brick layer, not surprisingly, asked for a little time to talk it over with his family. Two days later he agreed to the request. One dark night some months later a Jewish mother and her three children were spirited up into a garret. Since garrets were already notorious as places to hide Jews, the brick layer also constructed a bunker in the basement of the house, with a false brick wall that fit into place so cleverly that it could not be detected. The bunker was very small, not large enough to stand in, but large enough to hide four people for a few hours when the Germans were conducting one of their periodic sweeps of the neighborhood on the lookout for hidden Jews.

Eighteen months passed this way, with about 10 emergency transfers to the basement bunker. Food was passed up each day, and wastes were passed down each night. And every hour of every day and night, a sentence of death hung over the entire household.

One night a friend came over to have a drink with the Catholic family; the father made a splendid brand of gooseberry wine. After several glasses, the friend said in an unguarded moment, "You are hiding Jews." The moment he left a tense assessment took place. Had the comment been a threat of disclosure, or a hint that word was getting around? Was it a taunt or a warning? No time to investigate. Mother and children left the next night for another place of hiding. Six days later the Nazis broke into the house, demanding not "Jews" but "Zborowskis." Someone, never identified, had informed.

But thanks to the chance warning of a friend (if it was a warning), four Jewish lives were saved, and because there was not enough circumstantial evidence to bring charges against the Catholic family, three Catholic lives were saved as well.

Now, 35 years later, Eli Zborowski, one of the sons, was returning to the town of Z-. The mother and daughter of the Catholic family were still alive, and there was a reunion. A television director from NBC was along to film the story of the return. So was Eli's wife, Diana. Diana had lost her entire family in World War II and was understandably apprehensive. And with them all were three of us, Protestants as it happened, to share in the joy. A truly ecumenical situation: a Jew, whose life was saved by Catholics, returning to his home town in company with Protestants. Why did he ask us? Since Christians had saved his life, Eli told us, he wanted Christians to share in his celebration of that fact.

Tony, the television director and a real pro, recorded Eli's entrance into the town of Z-. Eli showed us the house in which he was born, and then the house in which he grew up. The camera recorded all, before a crowd of youngsters both excited and appreciative, who followed from street to street. There was one adult in the crowd, who was also excited but definitely not appreciative. We learned in a few moments why he had left so abruptly. When we arrived at our next filming site, the local police were waiting for us.

"What are you doing here?" they asked Tony, not kindly. "Why are you filming the houses of former Jews?" And then, "You must come to the police station for interrogation."

The television director tried to pass it off. "Later," he responded, "the light is fading."

"Right now," was their only response, and off they went into a labyrinth of side streets, the television director in tow. He played it cool, assuring us that after the proper explanations he would be back in a couple of minutes.

When 20 minutes had passed, Eli told us that he was going to go to the police station himself to investigate. We stayed in the car with his wife, who was, understandably, increasingly apprehensive. "I want to get out of this town," she said. "This is just like 35 years ago. The police take people off for 'questioning' and they never return."

Eli and Tony didn't come back, and so finally we too made our way toward the police station. At the station, as we learned later, the television director had continued to play it cool.

The civilian official who had lodged the complaint then saw Eli walk into the police station. He turned on the television director and asked, "What are you doing to us, bringing these Jews back here?"

Eli started to protest: "I was born here. I have a passport, a visa. I have come to see friends." He was abruptly cut off by the official: "You are not wanted here."

Diana Zborowski was right. Anti-Semitism was alive and well after 35 years.

Phone calls had already been placed to Warsaw, seeking

an answer. Eli, adrenalin flowing, pursued his questions.
What were the charges against them? The police chief did not
like the word "charges." Patiently he explained they had not
been "arrested," so there were no "charges." They were only
being "detained" until some "clarification" could be attained
from Warsaw. Eli pressed his point: "There are no charges?
Then that means we can leave?"

So we filmed the synagogue-now-a-social-club, from which
Eli's father had jumped. And then, in grace-filled climax, we
went to the Catholic home where the wife, though ill and very
feeble, and her daughter were waiting for us.

Although the home was small and simple, this was clearly
an occasion. There was special tea, homemade Polish dough-
nuts—and there was a bottle of gooseberry wine which the
daughter produced, tearfully telling us, "We have saved this
bottle for a special time. It is wine my father made immediately after the Germans left, 35 years ago." We drank to
the father, to the reunion, to the health of the ill mother, and
to the future happiness of the hearty daughter.

Even the joy of that reunion table, however, was not
without its shadows. A woman from the other side of town,
obviously a party functionary, burst in without knocking.
She had heard about some "commotion" and she wanted,
curtly, to know just who these strangers were.

But when the curt woman had left, and the television
director had returned, the old mother, breast heaving from
the emotion of the entire experience, told us not to worry, and
explained that some people in town still hated them, for having harbored Jews.

"I do not understand," she said, very lucidly. "We are all
Catholics here. Why should they object to what we did, when
our Lord told us that we should help those in need. When
I ask them, they have no answer. So do not worry."

We asked her how, in the face of this, she had borne up
under years of hostility from people who had once been her
friends. Her eyes moved to a simply holy picture on the wall,
of the Virgin suckling the child Jesus. "She feeds us all,"
was her complete and totally adequate response.

We went down to the basement and saw the bunker, and
how the fake brick wall worked, and remarked on how claustrophobic a place it must have been. Well, yes, Eli gently
reminded us, but not as claustrophobic as a gas chamber.

As we came up the tiny stairs and prepared to leave, the
old woman, having gathered in the course of the translated

conversation that two of us were Christian ministers, asked for a "blessing" and for prayers for her health.

And then there was a beautiful moment. For her, I prayed a very "Catholic prayer," using imagery she could understand, invoking the intercession of the saints and the healing power of Jesus, the Great Physician. The two of us then laid our hands upon the venerable head and blessed her. And those Catholic words, on the lips of Protestants, were translated for her in Polish by a Jew.

The kingdom of God is alive and well in the town of Z-.

M&R 6:7, May-June, 1980
Reprinted by permission of A.D. © 1980

VII. War Criminals: In Pursuit of Justice

In all "B" Western films, the audience is assured that crime does not pay, and, in the end, after 90 minutes of cheap thrills, is rewarded with a scene in which the villain must pay his dues to society, no matter how old his transgression. The moral that justice triumphs in the end pervades most great 19th century novels. In 20th century life, however, this ideal is often contradicted by the real world where politics interferes with the execution of justice, often criminally. The efforts to bring suspected Nazi criminals to court are a sad case in point.

Since the end of World War II and the closing of the Death Camps, more of these have evaded the law than faced it. For every SS murderer brought to trial at Nuremberg and afterward, a half dozen equally guilty have managed to escape. The ranks of the Mengeles who died untried and free are greater than those few who served a prison sentence, or the handful who suffered the death sentence, such as Eichmann.

And Eichmann embodies the problem of post-Holocaust international efforts to punish the crime of genocide. Thousands of the criminals went underground with the help of government officials ranging from the Vatican, through the CIA (U.S.), all the way to the United Nations. Only decades after the Final Solution are a small fragment of these soldiers of extermination, the murderers of countless Jews, being brought singly to the surface and into court. Their names are briefly capturing headlines: Barbie, Demjanjuk, Linnas.

The files of tens of thousands of suspected Nazi criminals have recently been made available by the United Nations, among them the file of former U.N. Secretary General Kurt Waldheim, now President of Austria. How many other "distinguished" persons will emerge from these names hidden from public view for almost half a century?

The reader will profit by reading these articles: "Nazis on Campus: Ivy League Style" (Bob Lamm, 5:7 March-April 1979); "Klarsfeld Family Brings Ex-Nazis to Trial" (Janet Mendelsohn, 6:12 Jan.-Feb. 1980); "Operation Haystack: Capture of Rudolf Hess" (Francizek Palowski, 7:12 March-April 1981)"; "Karl Linnas: An Ex-Nazi Almost Escaped Justice" (Menachem Z. Rosensaft, 13:8 May-June 1987).

MURDER TRIAL GERMAN-STYLE

By Ernest J. Goodman

The trial in Duesseldorf, W. Germany, of 14 guards and other personnel from the Lublin-Majdanek extermination camp is progressing slowly. It is generally believed that at least another two years will pass before a verdict is handed down. The trial, in which 5 women and 9 men (average age 59) are accused of murder and excesses in the treatment of inmates, began on November 26, 1975, and one of the defendants, Alice Elisabeth Minna Orlowski ("Slonecznik"), has since died. This, by the way, is the first trial that includes women guards.

At least 250,000 victims are believed to have died at Majdanek though some estimates speak of as many as one million or more. Yet all the accused are free to come and go as they please and even Mrs. Braunsteiner-Ryan is free on $17,500 bail paid by her American husband and his family of Queens, N.Y. Mr. Ryan sits in the back of Room 111 of the Nordrheim-Westphalian Land Courthouse, where his wife together with her colleagues of about 33 years ago must appear every Tuesday, Wednesday, and Thursday to hear the case against Hackmann and others, as the proceedings are officially called. Hackmann is SS-Hauptsturmfuehrer Herman Hackmann (63), nicknamed "Jonny," one of the most cruel and cynical of the accused, who was already sentenced to death by a U.S. court after the war, a sentence that was later commuted to life imprisonment. He was released from prison in 1955 and has been a furniture salesman in W. Germany for a number of years. Another of the accused is 56-year-old Hildegard Laechert, (called Bloody Brygyda by the inmates) who recently told the court that she has a Jewish boyfriend who wants to marry her.

German authorities claim that it took until now to gather all the necessary evidence, and the 70 volumes of 15,000 pages that are before the panel of five judges, two of them laymen, would tend to back up the claim. The detailed accusations are there, too, in two folders amounting to 322 pages. Three hundred witnesses will be called to testify. So far, however, most of the witnesses have been former colleagues of the accused, guard personnel of various work details, and the court did not begin to call former inmates until last fall. Defense strategy soon becomes obvious to the observer. Thirty years

199

is simply too long a time to remember facts and events and the testimony of witnesses will be challenged for that reason. As in previous Nazi atrocity trials, the accused claim to have seen nothing, to have heard nothing, to know nothing. Yet, most of them are confronted by the presiding judge, Guenther Bogen, with earlier testimony in which they frequently admitted having seen and heard what went on.

On the benches at the back of the courtroom sits one lonely, grey haired Jewish camp survivor, Mr. S. Weisbeker. He comes faithfully day after day and intends to be in that courtroom until the end of the trial. Only rarely is he joined by other spectators sympathetic with the Jewish victims.

Questioned about the date of November 3, 1943, when 18,000 Jews were shot in one day while loud music blared over the camp loudspeakers, a woman witness who guarded Jewish women in the camp laundry has stated that there was always music in the camp but that she heard and saw nothing unusual on that day at all. Typically also, witnesses deny that they carried weapons, though several have stated that their boyfriends sometimes allowed them to look at their pistols or even to handle them. One witness added that they all had boyfriends and that "things are far worse today when girls have boyfriends at the age of 15." She also instructed the presiding judge, that in those days there was order, that more crimes are committed today than in those days and that lenient judges are to be blamed for that situation. The court listens patiently and the presiding judge continues the examination. (In German courts, judges are more than umpires. It is they who examine witnesses.) Insults and impudent conduct are not apparently considered grounds for contempt citations. It is obvious that witnesses and defendants are practiced hands in the art of testimony. All of them have spent varying lengths of time in Polish, Russian, or German jails.

Defense strategy has also involved attacks on the court-appointed historian, Dr. Wolfgang Scheffler, whose credibility is said to be impaired because he is alleged to have a number of Jewish friends and one of his professors was also said to have been Jewish. Dr. Scheffler was suddenly "excused" last summer from further appearances in court, though he is now back in the courtroom again.

The German press ignores the trial almost without exception though it is certainly no less important than all the previous Nazi atrocity trials. Not one German I questioned last summer had heard of the trial. And apart from the neo-Nazi underworld, that is always represented on the press and public benches in the courtroom, to give inspiration and support and occasionally also instructions to the 30-odd defense lawyers, some of whom already served the Nazi judiciary, the public remains remarkably conspicuous by its absence. The Westdeutsche Rundfunk of Cologne is alone in commenting regularly on the trial through its young and committed correspondent, Carl Heinrich Lichtenstein. He was instrumental in my presence last summer, in bringing to the trial a class of 18-year-old students from a Dusseldorf School.

The students noted the contrast between the battery of more than thirty thoroughly experienced defense lawyers, experience that in some cases goes back as far as the Nuremberg trials, and the two prosecutors, Grassnick, in his mid-forties, and Weber, mid-thirty. The students were told about the difficulty of finding credible witnesses after so many years, a search that took Mr. Weber to Israel and other places and about the court's trip last Easter to Majdanek. The public prosecutors advised the students to take the trip to Lublin/ Majdanek at their earliest convenience. The students noticed the comfortable seating arrangements, especially for the accused and their attorneys, not at all what they expected in the case of a trial involving mass murder. They left the courtroom as astonished and confused as other observers too.

M&R 3:5, May-June, 1977

SURVIVOR READY TO TESTIFY
SO THAT PEOPLE KNOW

The last time the concentration camp survivor testified, the two defendants, former SS officers who had become successful Austrian businessmen with a bank of lawyers, laughed at her. And then they were exonerated of participating in the murder of six million Jews.

That was 14 years ago. Now, Linda Breder is ready to go back to Germany again—to testify once more at the murder trial of a Niza war criminal, Gottfried Weise. . . .

Sifting through 200 pictures of SS officers supplied by the Simon Wiesenthal Center in Los Angeles, Breder said she was able to identify Weise as one of the SS officers at Ausch-

witz who beat, tortured, and killed Jews, and who warned the
few who were allowed to live that they'd never survive to tell
anyone about life in the death camps.

"Even if it does no good," the Bay Area resident said in
an interview in San Francisco, "I still have to go. It is important that the story is told, that people know what went on.
I'm a chronicler, and I'll tell about it until I get senile."

At the 1972 trial in Austria of Franz Wunsch and Otto
Graf, Breder recalled, the judge asked her if it was day or
night that she saw them walk through Auschwitz killing every
fifth Jew.

She told the judge, "Day or night? It was 40 years ago.
How can I remember if it was day or night? There was no
daylight at Auschwitz. It was always night. The chimneys
were always going night and day. It was like a fog over the
camp. It smelled like a barbecue—flesh burning."

Breder added, "The judge let them free. They were laughing in my face. They recognized me."

The witness . . . was born in Slovakia sixty years ago.
In 1942, with 1,000 Jewish girls and women from her area,
and one Jewish male doctor, she was transported by train to
Auschwitz. The doctor never made it there. He was beaten
to death by Nazis on a field outside the camp.

For the next three years, Breder lived in Auschwitz, right
next to the gas chamber and right in front of the wall where
Jews routinely stood and were shot.

Breder lived at the camp so long that the time the Russ-
sians liberated that part of Poland in 1945 she almost looked
like a normal citizen of the world. Her hair, shorn when she
entered the camp, had grown out. The stiff, blood-covered
uniform of a Nazi-murdered Russian, issued to Breder when
she entered Auschwitz, had been replaced with clean work
clothes.

She remembered that earlier, as soon as the SS officers
had the gas chambers in operation, her job was to sort through
the clothes and the bowls of possessions taken from Jews
before they were murdered. In addition, she said, she witnessed
daily thefts by SS officers, as they routinely stole the most
valuable items Jews took with them to the camps.

As Breder, young and strong, kept quiet, she was permitted to live and work, she recalled.

The witness noted that she has survived three years in
the death camps, the death march out of the camps, post-war
Slovakia (which, she said, reeked of anti-Semitism), and the
Jewish community of the United States (with all its fear and

guilt) over the Holocaust. And she said she will survive the ridicule of former SS guards who grew rich and began their fortunes with the possession of dead Jews.

As a survivor, she asserted, "I am the Jewish nation." As long as the Federal Republic of Germany, and other countries continue to try war criminals, and as long as they ask her to testify, she added, she will be there. Her entire family died in the Holocaust, but "in me," she said, "is the history of my nation."

M&R 12:5, May-June, 1986
Reprinted by permission of *Northern California Jewish Voice.*

BARBIE: PROTECTORS, EMPLOYERS

By CHARLES R. ALLEN, JR.

Klaus Barbie . . . was aided in his escape from Europe in late 1949 and early 1950 by the Vatican, the U.S. Army's Counter Intelligence Corps (CIC) and the International Red Cross. . . .

Barbie took the so-called "monastery-route," an underground railroad so to speak, for scores of wanted Nazi war criminals. The route was known to the U.S. Embassy in Rome, which did nothing to stem the flow of wanted war criminals from Europe, most of them originating in the American-occupied zone of Germany.

The northern starting point of the "monastery route" was in Bavaria and the Austrian frontier, then dipped south to the Italian Alps, dropping further south to way stations leading to exits from the ports of Genoa and Naples.

. . . Barbie disguised as a monk was secreted from monastery to monastery along the route. He went to Milan and then to Genoa, from there to Franco Spain, then to Portugal, ruled by fascist Premier Antonio de Oliveria Salazar, and then by boat to Latin America, where his first country of call was Peru, not Bolivia. . . .

Confirmation of the knowing role of the Vatican in the escape of Barbie—as well as scores if not hundreds of other SS genocidists—came in a hitherto "Top Secret" 35-page set of State Department documents which have come into my possession largely by way of Freedom of Information requests over the past five years. . . .

The "La Vista Report" also noted in detail the names and political backgrounds of the high-ranking members of the Roman Catholic hierarchy who masterminded the war criminals' escape routes along which Barbie successfully fled.

The State Department report stated: "The Vatican, of course, is the largest single organization involved in the illegal movement . . . the Vatican's justification for this illegal traffic is simply the propagation of the Faith. The Vatican ('s) desire to infiltrate not only European countries but Latin American countries as well . . . with people of all political beliefs as long as they are anti-Communist and are pro-Catholic Church."

. . . This "Top Secret" document went on to state that the "Vatican at various times and under certain conditions utilizes the International Red Cross" in order to obtain "Red Cross Documents" (for passports) for Nazi escapees. . . .

Barbie, who bragged to his American intelligence case officer after World War II how he had filled "my mass graves" with French Jews and heroes of the Resistance, operated for three decades under orders of a secret underground headed by the Nazi terrorist Otto Skorzeny.

Skorzeny was, amazingly, acquitted of war crimes charges by an American war crimes tribunal, held at the Dachau KZ. He escaped in 1948.

At the same time, Klaus Barbie, from the same SS detention pens at Darmstadt, was released for secret utilization by the American Counter Intelligence Corps. . . .

Before leaving for South America, Barbie was given his orders, a list of key Nazi war criminals to contact in both low and high places. . . .

He quickly established a working relationship with some of the prominent killers of the Holocaust, alive and well in South America.

Barbie was picked up from the U.S. Army Intelligence (CIC) in 1948 and used by the CIA as a "contract agent" for nearly three decades. . . .

Arriving in Bolivia in May 1951, Barbie found a most accommodating atmosphere in which to carry out his work. For years the Bolivian economy had been dominated by German investment interests and the large Germany colony there. As far back as the 1920's, officers of the German General Staff trained Bolivian armies.

Barbie, according to my own sources, quickly organized "coordinated" activities with the large Nazi concentrations in Argentina, Brazil, Chile and Paraguay, where fascist military dictatorships reigned.

In Bolivia, Barbie trained a secret police and national police along the lines of the Gestapo he ran in France during the Holocaust.

He was granted Bolivian citizenship in 1957. His name was linked to several notorious political killings in 1964, 1972 and 1976.

Barbie enjoyed the full backing of the government of Colonel Hugo Banzer Suarez, which in the 1970's blocked all attempts to extradite Barbie for his war crimes in Europe.

M&R 9:16, March-April, 1983
© Charles Allen and Jewish Telegraphic Agency

VIII.
Holocaust and Christianity

It has been forcefully argued, though never fully examined, that the annihilation of six million Jews is as much a Christian trauma as it is a Jewish tragedy. By the time racist anti-Semitism struck full force, it had been preceeded by nearly two millennia of unremitting Christian (Catholic and Protestant) theological anti-Judaism and anti-Jewish Church policies. In Auschwitz, the belief in the Jew as the Christ-killer found its logical final expression.

Christian Judophobia energized the Final Solution. Church-attending Christians found their way to the upper echelons of the Nazi Party and government, as well as into the ranks of the SS units that administered the ghettos and death camps. Baptized genocidists were never excommunicated; pro-Nazi pastors kept their post-war pulpits; after the war unrepentant Nazis found haven in Latin America thanks to the Vatican; during the war church hierarchies remained unmoved by the assault on the Jews; on the Sunday following the November 9/10, 1938, burning of hundreds of synagogues and scrolls containing the Five Books of Moses, churches conducted Christianity-as-usual services as if no un-Christian event had taken place. It is a terrible legacy.

Luckily, a few courageous men and women have pioneered the way: raising agonizing questions and attempting equally painful answers. Unfortunately, their voices remain exceptions. The mainstream seminaries and church chancelleries operate as if there had been no Holocaust, as if the Christianity-Holocaust connection did not exist. To date, the tensions accruing within Christendom are like a time-bomb, ever-threatening to explode. The most recent was the Pope's public embrace of Austria's President Kurt Waldheim, despite the latter's Nazi past. The last act of the Holocaust drama as it concerns Christians has not yet been played.

206

HOLOCAUST WAS "SHAME" FOR CHRISTIANS

By The Rev. John Whiteford

There are times when someone or some group assaults us with an urgency for a cause which we do not share. They're all excited and we find no shared sense of urgency within ourselves. It happens with some regularity—the emergence of a new explanation of the world's woes and an accompanying solution offered.

The Holocaust is not a new cause to be urgent about. It is not a new explanation for our problems' existence or their solution. Our setting aside a Sunday to remember the Holocaust is an acknowledgement, a penitent time and an awareness time. It is looking at the reality of the cost of hatred and bigotry in and purveyed by the Church.

The burnt offering of 15 million people, Jews, Gypsies, mentally and physically handicapped people and 250,000 Christians who objected to the "final solution,"—that is the Holocaust. It is a unique horror in all of human history and it was envisioned and carried out by Christians.

Emotions rise when that is said. The doers of the Holocaust could not have been real Christians. Real Christians do not create horror.

That is a deception. For centuries the Church taught anti-Semitism ("His blood be upon us and upon our children"). The Jews were persecuted as Christ killers. It took a very long time for the Church to say and teach that Jesus is crucified by humanity. It takes a long time, too, to understand that the Holocaust was not German.

There was a time during the late '30's when the Nazis offered to allow, at a price, the Jews to go to other countries and there was no country that accepted the offer. Norway, Sweden and Holland did give haven to many, but the doors of the nations were closed.

In my own remembrance of pre-WWII days there is a large place given to anti-Semitism. It was an assumed part of Church attitudes, mostly unspoken but sometimes spoken with zeal—anti-Semitism. Father Coughlin spoke of the Jews as anti-Christ. He thought of them as the secret plotters for world power and he thought out loud to millions of listeners of his radio programs and millions of readers of his paper "Social Justice."

He taught that the Jews in their cabalistic gatherings were making plans to subdue this Republic and that Hitler was about the business of preventing Germany from becoming a Jewish resource. Fr. Coughlin was an unwitting ecumenist. The anti-Semitism he taught and passed on was comfortable in all parts of the Church.

Scapegoats were sought at the time; a world depression and a red revolution made scapegoats necessary, and the Jews had been used before. The "final solution" of Hitler had both hidden and open assent in this country, in the Western hemisphere. Beyond that there was, as Rabbi Joachim Prinz has said, "a ghastly silence. . . ."

After the war the scope of the Holocaust was too enormous to absorb. Neither Jew nor Christian was able to look very long at the Holocaust.

Pictures of Auschwitz, Treblinka and on and on called for skills in turning away from such horror. There was no great surge to "understand." There was, in some, an awareness that we had better understand.

Just now there is a beginning of understanding amongst Jews and Christians of the Holocaust. There is both shame for us, a chance for penitence, a thanksgiving for our brothers and sisters who were martyred. There is too for us an awareness that Christlessness in the Church has a great cost.

In the resolution passed at the last Diocesan convention we said that we would set aside the Sunday after Easter (Low Sunday) as the time for Holocaust observance and that we would teach the meaning of the Holocaust, that we would make efforts to share with the Jewish community their observance of the Holocaust.

Finally, what we began with is an accusation and the desire to deny. The observance of the Holocaust is not an overdue flagellation. That is much too easy and ends in appreciating my own pain. It is not easy to grasp the meaning of Holocaust—the burnt offering that took centuries to prepare, centuries of Eucharists and preaching and reaching for the Word of God.

Wars and Inquisitions and Crusades; earth soaked with the lies of sacrifice. We have been marked by all of that and the Holocaust and we in our resolution say that we want to know why we, in our forefathers and foremothers, did that.

IMPACT OF THE HOLOCAUST ON CHRISTIAN THEOLOGY

By THE REV. ROBERT A. EVERETT

... The Jews of Europe were murdered in a cold-blooded, systematic reign of death which established itself in the heart of civilized Western Christian society. What our imaginations deny and our words fail to comprehend, reality forces us to believe.

The Holocaust marks a new epoch in human history. Theology has for ages talked about the Ultimate Evil, but always in the abstract sense of the idea. ... We know of evil in the world, and it is proper to speak of the evil of Hiroshima, Cambodia, and Biafra. The Holocaust, however, is more than simply another manifestation of evil in the world. It was the revelation of Ultimate Evil's presence in the world. "The Holocaust was . . . murder simply for the sake of murder on a scale never seen in human history. It was the total rebellion of man against morality and life in the name of death. It was the total restructuring of the universe dedicated to the demonic, to Ultimate Evil. This is why one cannot scan the landscape of human history and human endeavor today without always seeing somewhere in the distance the chimneys and ovens of the death camps where Jews were murdered.

Those who would universalize the Holocaust also work under a false consciousness. I am not denying the sufferings of so many others during the war. But it was the Jew who was singled out for murder. It was the Jew who was killed simply for being *who* he or she was, not *what* he or she was. ...

I say all this with a good deal of fear and trembling. Any Christian who speaks to a Jew today must do so fully aware that it was his or her tradition which helped to create the Holocaust. In speaking of the Holocaust, I fear making it sensible, or worse, romanticizing the suffering. Yet, the Holocaust was an event which cannot be forgotten, and Christians as well as Jews must struggle to come to grips with the reality. Nor can I allow the irrationality of the Holocaust to serve as an excuse for its happening. The soldiers of Ultimate Evil, the Nazis and their supporters, were shockingly rational and reasonable.

Such is the perversity of Ultimate Evil. They built death

camps from blueprints, they created a philosophy with the
support of some of the most well-educated people in Europe;
the SS and its death squads were headed by educated men,
some of whom had their Ph.D's. . . . Ultimate Evil cannot go
unheeded. I say all this because I believe that the Holocaust
was an event in Christian history as well as Jewish history.
It was the church which created a caricature of the Jews
which was monstrous: a theological abstraction. It was the
church that created the idea that Jews were rejected by God,
that they were the children of the devil, and that they were
evil. The theological anti-Semitism of the church helped to
prepare the foundation of Holocaust. Even the racial anti-
Semites who were often anti-Christian were most successful
when they were able to link their racist ideology with Christian
symbols and prejudices. Hitler was able to tell two Catholic
bishops that he was just doing to the Jews what the church
had been trying to do for nearly 2,000 years. More than one
Nazi war criminal appealed to Luther as justification for
their actions. The Anglican theologian and historian James
Parkes is correct when he says that "there is no break in
the line from the charge of Jewish deicide and punishment to
Hitler's death camps, and the line is still unbroken by any
adequate recognition of the sin, by any corporate act of amendment or repentance on the part of the Church."

In the face of this indictment against Christianity, the
Christian is forced to ask, "Do we still have the right to
continue to exist after such a history? Can we redeem ourselves from such complicity with Ultimate Evil? Can we ever
be a force for life again or is it too late?"

I believe these are questions which can be answered in
the affirmative, but only at a high price. Christians must
experience a *metanoia*, a radical changing of the mind concerning the way they view Jews and Judaism. We must stop
telling lies about Jews.

. . . We must now enter into solidarity with the Jewish
people so that their pains and sufferings and joys are ours
as well. The fate of the Jew must become the fate of the
Christian.

Repentance is the key to Christian theology after the
Holocaust. There should be a feeling of guilt and contrition.
This need not be a psychological handicap, but simply the
first step toward repentance. Nor is it simply done in order
to ask forgiveness from the Jews for the crimes we have
committed against them, although that, too, is to be sought.
It is something done to redeem Christianity from its past in

order that it may find a future after the Holocaust. But any Jewish response to Christian contrition needs to be based on only one criterion: Are Christians concerned about Jewish life? Here I think Jews need to weigh the support Christians give to the State of Israel.... Let me close with a statement from a leading Christian theologian and my friend, A. Roy Eckardt: "Does the affirmation that the task of the Christian Church to bring the world into covenant through Jesus the Jew, contribute in and through itself to the perpetuation of anti-Semitism. In the measure that the answer is yes, the Christian gospel cannot be preached." To many this will sound extreme. But is not the time after the Holocaust a time for radical statements and change? I think it is.

M&R 9:6, Nov.-Dec., 1982

WORK OF LITTELL
A CONDEMNATION OF CHRISTIANITY

By CHARLES R. ALLEN, JR.

Franklin H. Littell is a very wise person, perhaps one of the wisest among us. Dr. Littell, an ordained Protestant clergyman, may seem somewhat of an anomalous choice as the director of a center of learning whose concern is the decimation of the Jews of Europe. Yet, no finer character, no better scholar, no more sensitive thinker can probably be found to pursue such a solemn, moral obligation coupled with the highest intellectual and scholarly demands in seeking out the truth(s) of the Holocaust.

A high amalgam of Dr. Littell's extraordinary insights is to be found in a series of integrated essays published five years ago under the collective title *The Crucifixion of the Jews*. He stated that the prestigious and, nominally liberal, *The Christian Century* had refused to review the book as it carried the "very bad record" of this publication during the Holocaust. Furthermore, the religious thinker said, "a leading Jewish defense agency" had barred its inclusion in a bibliographical listing because the book was "too hard on the Christians."

After having read (studied, actually) *The Crucifixion of*

the Jews, I readily see why any timid Establishment—Jewish or non-Jewish—wants no part of such a work. *Crucifixion* is a strong, often overwhelming indictment of Christendom as the world's oldest, most effective fount of anti-Semitism. Dr. Littell does not presume to define the meaning of the Holocaust for Jews but rather from his own perspective as a Christian of deep conviction. In this respect, he writes, "I will exercise my liberty to speak."

He points up the often conveniently overlooked fact that "[t]he Jewish people have in our time experienced crucifixion and resurrection (i.e. the Holocaust and the establishment of Israel). The Christians who fled the time of testing, who have refused as yet to face the truth of their apostasy, who are still flying high with abstract resolutions and generalizations, must be brought to book."

Professor Littell brings Christianity to book, perhaps as it has not yet been done. He does not simply draw up an unanswerable bill of particulars (others have also done so); his scouring self-critical analyses constitute, in effect, a Nuremberg judgment on Christendom.

By chapter and verse, by scripture and ecclesiastical decree, Professor Littell argues persuasively that up through the post-Holocaust world, Christianity has created an institutionalized anti-Semitism which step-by-step led to the gas chambers.

He sees this anti-Semitism in three stages. Theological anti-Semitism began immediately upon Christianity's successes when it became an Establishment religion, when it forsook its mission in behalf of the oppressed, the despised, when its demographics went from Jewish to gentile. There followed centuries of what he calls "cultural anti-Semitism," which were the distinct working out of peculiar social processes and manifestations whether Catholic, Protestant or Orthodox; in turn, an activist or political anti-Semitism led to genocide, the Holocaust "in the heart of Christendom."

A summary review can not possibly do justice to Dr. Littell's admirable analyses, wedded to a classic style of expression.

When Christianity abandoned its essential Jewishness, it slipped over into "mass apostasy" (the conscious denials of its most precious truths, its own best self and Faith). The author does not let the reader forget for one moment that millions of "baptized gentiles"—frocked and simple members of the flock—approved and participated, directly or complicitly, in the Holocaust.

"The worst set of crimes in the history of mankind were engineered by Ph.D.'s and committed by baptized Christians ... [their] apostasy is the most significant religious factor in the present crisis of Christendom. It did not end with the Holocaust. It will not be cured until the churches face with utterly ruthless self-appraisal the meaning of that mass apostasy and trace it to its source." Otherwise, he concludes, nothing will save the churches from "damnation."

Dr. Littell is not preaching in any overwrought revivalistic sense. His is a broad and cultivated mind, noting that religious institutions play a vital (in his own view, of course, central)—not exclusive—role in humankind's prospects for survival and the realization of true brotherhood here on temporal earth. But he warns, twice, of his misgivings upon our entrance into "the Spirit of the Space Age": "[The believing Jew or Christian] will think of six million who died in scientifically designed Death Camps. He will remember three million lovely ... simple Vietnamese slaughtered by ruthless machines controlled by men who think in abstractions. There is a line connecting Auschwitz and My Lai but ... not in abstractions; it is defined by the truth that a 'Christian' civilization's attitude to Jewish history and treatment of the Jewish people afford the litmus test as to how it will act on all critical decisions involving the resistance of helpless or weaker peoples."

Reading (studying) *The Crucifixion of the Jews* is an intensely rewarding experience. One is constantly being challenged to think and re-examine long-held assumptions. I for one would look forward to an exchange with Dr. Littell concerning his observation that while Christian Establishments can be fairly charged with theological and cultural anti-Semitism, they "are not directly guilty of political anti-Semitism." Such a sphere is peopled by "marginal men and movements." I do not consider the Vatican Concordat of 1933 with Hitler and the behaviour of the Cardinal of Nazi-occupied Paris (Beaudrillant) as anything except political. Nor that a disproportionate percentage of the field command of the Einsatzgruppen and, by my own research, that 28% of the more than 300 Nazi war criminals and collaborators who found post-Holocaust refuge in the United States were clerics, are something "marginal."

In such a dialogue, I know that I will learn much from the enriching teaching and ennobling thought of the author of *The Crucifixion of the Jews.*

NOBELISTS LOOK AHEAD
TO THE 21ST CENTURY

By Robert McAfee Brown

The novelist Elie Wiesel has written that "Words can sometimes, in moments of grace, attain the quality of deeds," a luminous reminder I keep posted above my desk for those moments when writing an article seems like a cop-out in a world where direct "action" is called for.

Wiesel himself is a supreme instance of the melding of word and deed. His writings on the Holocaust have been the single most important reminder to our generation that if we forget what happened in the death camps in the past we will generate the seeds of a repetition of such events in the future.

But Wiesel does not simply sit at a desk and write. He is also an increasingly active "doer. . . ."

In 1986, Wiesel received the Nobel Prize for Peace, another interesting confirmation of the way that "words can . . . attain the quality of deeds," since one who could well have been the Nobel laureate in literature was chosen Nobel laureate for peace. The Noble Prize Committee saw clearly that to write about such things as the human need to transcend hatred was in itself direct action on behalf of peace.

With his prize money, Wiesel established The Elie Wiesel Foundation for Humanity, the first activity of which was to sponsor (in conjunction with President Francois Mitterand and the French government) a conference for all Nobel laureates to deal with the theme, "Facing the 21st Century: Threats and Promises." Wiesel had been hopeful that as many as 30 laureates might accept the invitation; 76 attended when the group finally assembled in Paris for a meeting January 18-21, 1988.

Wiesel's concern in initiating the conference—the first time Nobel laureates have ever met in such fashion—was to invite this highly gifted group of intellectuals to reflect on ways in which the barbarism of the 20th century could be avoided in the 21st century. . . .

Although the conference formally convened . . . at the Elysee Palace, an extremely important pre-conference event took place one day earlier, participated in by a few of the laureates and about 30 of the nonlaureates attending the con-

214

ference. Since January 17 was the anniversary of the liberation of Auschwitz, it seemed appropriate to Wiesel, who was
an inmate of Auschwitz during World War II, that conference
participants make a pilgrimage to the concentration camp as
a solemn beginning of their deliberations. He felt, rightly,
that to visit Auschwitz—which will be the enduring symbol of
the 20th century as an age of barbarism—would provide an
appropriate context for reflecting on the imperative need not
to repeat such barbarism in the 21st century. A charter flight
was arranged to Cracow, and the group then visited Auschwitz and also Birkenau, the death camp for Auschwitz.

The trip had added meaning. Lech Walesa, another Nobel
Peace Prize winner, had to decline the Paris invitation, fearing
that if he left Poland he would not be allowed to return. And
since Walesa could not come to the conference, members of
the conference went to Walesa, who met the plane and was
with us for the entire day. (He said several times during the
day that the Nobel Prize had saved his life.) The symbolic
power of Wiesel and Walesa, Nobel Peace laureates, one a
Jew, the other a Pole, standing on a cold January morning in
front of the monument at Birkenau, and making mutual
pledges to one another to create hope for the children of the
future, in the place where a million children were murdered,
was a powerful symbol indeed.

Another symbol, devastating to me as a Christian, was
created during this visit. Although I do not know how many
other members of the group sensed it, its impact will never
leave me. We concluded our visit to Auschwitz close to the noon
hour by entering one of the crematoria, and standing silently
in front of some of the furnaces, with their tracks for the
more "efficient" disposal of corpses. A rabbi led some prayers.
A Polish priest then read Scripture—Psalm 130, the De pro-
fundis ("Out of the depths"), I think—after which, in the
presence of these instruments of death, the Jews quite appropriately began to recite the Kaddish, the prayer for the dead.

And then it happened: Interrupting the Kaddish and
continuing in competition with its high solemnity at that
special moment, the church bells from just outside the camp
began to peal, celebrating the consecration of the host at the
mass in the parish church. My mind involuntarily and instantaneously took a leap back 45 years. I reflected that at that
time real guards would have been in the room in which we
were now standing, thrusting real corpses into real ovens
heated to temperatures extreme enough to dispose of the
corpses quickly, and that those same guards who were burning

those same bodies would have gone out of that same camp, traversed the few hundred yards to that same church, gone to mass, received communion, and returned that afternoon or the next day to continue that same grisly occupation. . . . The episode remains highly disquieting, for it symbolizes so much of the attitude of the church in the presence of massive evil, and suggests that if the church in the 21st century (not a high agenda item for most Nobelists) is going to help stem the tide of barbarism it will first of all deal a mortal blow to its own greatest institutional sin: indifference.

M&R 15:7, Sept.-Oct. 1988

CAMP SURVIVORS RESPOND TO POPE PAUL JOHN

By ALFRED LIPSON and SAMUEL LIPSON

During his visit to the former concentration camp at Mauthausen, in Austria, Pope Paul John II addressed the victims of the infamous death camp: "Speak, for you have the right to do so, you who have suffered and lost your lives, and we shall listen to your testimony." As survivors of Mauthausen, Auschwitz and Dachau, we respond to this public mandate.

Your Holiness, in 1944 our brother Moshe, age 30, a master tanner and a gifted artist, was killed in Mauthausen by Austrian guards. Also, in the summer of that year, Adolf Eichmann, ordered the liquidation of the remnants of the Jewish community of Radom, Poland, our birthplace.

Following a forced death march that lasted four days, 3,000 men, women and children were packed into cattle cars provided by Eichmann. On arrival in Auschwitz on Aug. 6, most of the people were led into gas chambers and their bodies were later pushed into fiery furnaces.

Among those to meet this horrible death on that day were many members of our family, all selected by Dr. Joseph Mengele, the "Angel of Death." They included our mother, Sarah, age 50; our 11-year-old sister, Bella, and Helen Frenkel, a close relative. (The image of their walking hand-in-hand to trucks that took them to the gas chamber haunts us to this day.) We survived—to be tortured later. This, then, is our personal testimony.

Our family was among the six million who were killed because they were Jews. Yet, at Mauthausen and Auschwitz, at Treblinka and Sobibor, at Maidanek and Babi Yar, they are memorialized and referred to as Poles and Austrians, as Russians and Hungarians, as Germans and Ukrainians.

Your Holiness, hours after cordially greeting President Kurt Waldheim and giving him holy communion, you couldn't find it in your heart to mention the Jews as the principal victims of Waldheim's generation. Why? By failing to do so, you seem to have embraced the long-established policy in Eastern Europe of robbing the Jewish victims of the Holocaust of their Jewish identity.

At Mauthausen, Your Holiness asked a rhetorical question, "Do we not delete from our memories and from our consciousness the traces of past misdeeds?" The answer is obvious. Waldheim is a prime example of deleting "past misdeeds" from one's memory, but it is the Austrian nation, which clings to the myth of having been "the first victim" of Nazi Germany. But doesn't your silence on the Jewish victims help to delete the memory of our brother Moshe, one of the 60,000 Jews murdered in Mauthausen?

Your Holiness, during your visit you stated, "It would be unjust and not truthful to charge Christianity with these unspeakable crimes." But weren't the perpetrators and their helpers faithful Christians? What about the Arrow Cross, the rabidly anti-Semitic Nazi units in Hungary, the Rumanian Iron Guard killers, the murderous Croatian Ustashis, the Ukrainian and Latvian SS units that functioned as Jewish executioners? They were all Christians, but had never been restrained in their "work" by church officials. . . .

After the collapse of Germany, many war criminals and murderers of the Jewish people were aided in their flight from justice and punishment by the Vatican and groups associated with the church. In South American countries, some top Nazis found shelter and protection among church leaders. They prospered in Christian communities sympathetic to their anti-Semitic ideology.

Your Holiness, you ask us, the victims, "Tell us which direction Europe and mankind should take 'after Auschwitz,' 'after Mauthausen'?"

To begin with, as head of millions of Christians you could,

henceforth, exert your moral authority to strongly condemn anti-Semitism and neo-Nazism at every opportunity. Failure to do so would be reminiscent of the silence of the wartime Pope, Pius XII, in the face of the Holocaust, in which much of Christian Europe participated. Furthermore, your refusal to recognize the only Jewish state—born from the ashes of the Holocaust—sends an ominous signal to those bent on Israel's destruction.

A firm unambiguous stand on your part, your Holiness, would go a long way toward ending anti-Semitism as the scourge of humanity and toward peace in the Middle East.

M&R 15:6, Sept.-Oct. 1988.
Reprinted by permission of *New York Times* © 1987.

IX. Teaching the Holocaust Lessons

What does the Holocaust teach us? Why should educators expose their students to this historical event? Is there a hidden moral lesson contained in the fact of the Final Solution and in the messages of the survivors? Can the significance of Auschwitz be conveyed in a brief classroom encounter? How should young people be introduced to the stark realities of genocide: through the medium of tempered fiction or raw photography, or a combination of both?

Should the implications of the Holocaust be discussed in theological seminaries, in medical schools, in law schools, in business schools, in schools of journalism, etc.? Ought politicians to be required to study the role of their counterparts during the international crisis of the Holocaust era?

These are but a sample of the range of questions troubling educators as they debate pedagogical issues associated with the inclusion of the Holocaust into the curricula of grade schools, secondary schools, colleges, graduate programs, of Sunday schools, of adult education, and other forms of specialized learning. Their tentative answers reflect common concerns of devoted amateurs and specialists confronted by an enormous intellectual challenge—the meaning and significance of the extermination of the Jews of Europe in the midst of World War II by a modern state in the full view of the international community. The problem will trouble future teachers for many years, thereby insuring some degree of involvement with the Holocaust.

Insights into the teaching of the Holocaust will be found in: "Repeating the Holocaust to the Young Generation" (Henry Bulanko, 6:13 May-June 1980) ; "Teaching the Holocaust" (Arye Carmon, 6:12 May-June 1980; "A Priest Teaches the Holocaust" (Rev. Peter Holroyd, 12:10 March-April 1986).

M & R: THE EDUCATIONAL TOOL

By Dr. Eva Pallay

There is no revelation in the fact that Yom Hashoa V'Hagvurah, the English calendar date corresponding to 27 Nissan, has become a growing observance in the United States —in terms of the number of communities involved and in the scope of the programs.

But what is not well known is that much of this credit belongs to *Martyrdom and Resistance,* the medium of communication of the American Federation of Jewish Fighters, Camp Inmates, and Nazi Victims. The accomplishments of the Federation are detailed elsewhere in this anthology. What should be recorded here is *Martyrdom and Resistance's* role as an ongoing tool for teaching the lessons of the Holocaust.

In terms of Yom Hashoa observances, the periodical has been invaluable. On one level, there have been articles and programming techniques and suggestions for these observances. Then, there has been the free distribution of the periodical itself at the observances, with the wealth of news and features opening new vistas of thought to the readers.

But the most impressive contribution is the "education" that teachers of the Holocaust, from elementary school through college, receive in reading the periodical. Those who teach the Holocaust have come to realize that there is a need for an in-depth study of the Holocaust—not just in the Yom Hashoa season.

As a professional educator, I can attest to the improvement of my skills through careful reading of the periodical. It is a veritable eye of the Holocaust, with a fascinating blend of material: dreams of the martyred who did not live to realize them, details of demons and sadists from the Third Reich, reviews of the latest cinema, and poignant recollections from the liberators and the liberated.

One must single out for praise the *Index* of *Martyrdom and Resistance,* painstakingly compiled by Dr. Harvey Rosenfeld. In tandem with the microfiche, this resource opens a wealth of information for educators. There are more than 350 articles on every type of community programming, Holocaust studies

---

Dr. Pallay is an educational consultant with an expertise in Holocaust curricula.

in schools, and discussions of curricula in Israel, Canada, Sweden, and West Germany, to name a few countries.

There is news about the programs at the Center for Holocaust teaching at Yad Vashem, in Jerusalem, the acclaimed international teacher of our dark days.

In particular, the educator should consult the following in the Index for direction to valuable articles: Education, pages 7-14, covering these areas—Attitudes, Responses, Curricula, Methodology, College-Holocaust Studies, Worldwide Programs; Judaism-Religious Observances, on pages 19-20; Remembrance, on page 35; Resistance and Heroism, on pages 36-37; Media, on page 23.

I dedicated *I Can Cook for my Jewish Holidays*, an innovative videocassette, to the more than 1 million Jewish children killed in the Holocaust. As an educator, I am deeply concerned about the education of children.

Today, we are being flooded with literature that would deny the Holocaust, or we are continually being asked to forget the past. It is imperative that the youth be taught properly and that their teachers be fully qualified and professionally prepared.

In November, 1979, I was privileged to be Executive Director of an educational program in conjunction with the International Year of the Child. The program was chaired by Eli Zborowski, editor-in-chief of *Martyrdom and Resistance*, and cosponsored by many prestigious dignitaries, organizations, and schools. A memorial was erected at Eisenhower Park, East Meadow, N.Y., and a program was arranged for 2,000 children *Martyrdom and Resistance* fully recorded the program for all to adopt and teach.

Martyrdom and Resistance, whose readers include several thousand teachers, scholars, and others concerned with the pedagogical aspects of the Holocaust, has developed into a treasured resource in the ongoing process of learning. By recording the Holocaust, it ensures that there will be no gap, no denial of the martyrdom and resistance of our *kedoshim*. *Martyrdom and Resistance* has become a witness as it were to the testimony of the Holocaust, the survivors and the perished innocent.

To conclude, *Martyrdom and Resistance* will teach young and old—zachor, gedenk, remember.

WHY WE TEACH THE HOLOCAUST

By Dr. Franklin H. Littell

As a Christian, I am often asked why I am concerned about the Holocaust—a "Jewish issue." As a teacher, I am often asked whether teaching the Holocaust serves any useful purpose. Both questions are misguided.

In the first place, the Holocaust is not solely a "Jewish" issue—although it is obviously that, too. Like the Exodus, the Holocaust is at one level distinctly particular and limited in time and place. But the Exodus now carries a message to many tribes and peoples far from the Sinai and the Red Sea. And the Holocaust is reaching into the conscience of many peoples outside Jewish circles.

A Christian has special reasons for confronting the implications of the Holocaust, for the monstrous crimes were committed by baptized Christians. With few exceptions, like the Orthodox Patriarch of Bulgaria and the Lutheran Archbishop of Denmark, church leaders betrayed the trust imposed on them. The so-called "Christian nations," whether by complicity or by indifference, disgraced their professed religion. In sum, just as the rabbis of old used to say that if the gentiles had understood the meaning of the destruction of the Temple, they would have mourned it more than the Jews, today the Christian teacher must declare that when the Christians understand the meaning of the Holocaust, they will mourn it more than the Jews. . . .

We do not teach the Holocaust because it "serves a useful purpose." We hope, of course, that there will be benefits from telling the truth. As with all formative or "epoch-making" events in human history, "40 years in the wilderness" must pass before many can stand it to confront the epoch proportions of event. And then some years must pass before words are found—in songs, liturgies, psalms, and prayers—that heal rather than burn the soul.

We teach the Holocaust because no society, just as no single person, can afford to allow unexploded mines and shells to lie beneath the surface of daily existence. We tell the story of the Holocaust because when we say we will keep still, there is a consuming fire shut up in our bones and we are weary with containing it. The story forces itself to be told. We teach the lessons of the Holocaust because more than any other event in European history, it is predictive of total destruction if the lessons are not learned in time. Genocide, once explored, is becoming a habit of governmental policy. Terrorism, once successful, had become a model politic insurgency.

We teach the Holocaust because teachers, whether in the schools or in the congregations, are products of the modern university. And it was the modern university, with all of its technical proficiencies and all of its indifference to religious truth and ethical restraints, that made the Holocaust possible. The evil thing was planned, supervised, and carried out by professors and Ph.D.'s and doctors. And they were graduates, not of Nazi universities, but some of the best universities in the world, before the Nazis took over. As educated people, teachers whose consciences have been smitten by the Holocaust know very well that universities have yet to face the implications of the Holocaust.

Many gentiles still don't want to face the implications of the Holocaust. Many Jews don't want to share its message and its lessons with the outside world. They would rather nurse it as a private Jewish sore, the scab to be picked out again and again. But the Holocaust, for all its unique points, is an event like the Exodus. In generations to come, men and women will speak of the years "before the Holocaust" and the time "after the Holocaust."

In the United States, we face each other in strength—as Jews, Roman Catholics, and Protestants. And in the establishment of a solid foundation of discussion, understanding, and cooperation, nothing is so important as the teaching of the Holocaust and its lessons.

M&R 12:8, Sept.-Oct., 1985
© Jewish Exponent, Philadelphia

HOLOCAUST METHODOLOGY GAINS

By Dr. Luba K. Gurdus

We have come a long way from the vehement ideas about the usefulness of Holocaust studies in American learning institutions to the present availability of comprehensive curricula for colleges and universities. After a prolonged period of initial apathy and indifference and subsequent controversy

and polemic, Holocaust studies have surfaced as an important
learning experience and are an integral part of American
socio-historic education. The reservations and doubts questioning its effectiveness are rarely voiced, though some Jewish
educators still caution against its interference in inter-reli-
gious group relations and tensions between Jews and other
ethnic groups. But even these fears proved unjustified.

Among the earliest manuals on Holocaust methodology is
a Unit Outline, prepared for the Jewish Educators Workshop
by the Jewish Community Council in Perth Amboy, New
Jersey, in April, 1972. It contains practical guidelines for
teachers programming Holocaust curricula. During the course
of the 1970's their number increased considerably for a growing number of teachers. On November 6, 1979, two hundred
teachers participated in the first citywide conference on Holocaust education, held by City University of New York. The
Conference, co-sponsored by the Federation of Teachers, the
Anti-Defamation League of B'nai B'rith, the Eisner Institute
for Holocaust Studies, and the Jewish Labor Committee, was
addressed by the Chancellor of New York City Schools, Frank
J. Macchiarola, who urged the teachers "to confront reality
by using the universal lesson of the Holocaust as a tool in
the classroom."

Recent statistics show that there are more than ten accepted Resource Centers preparing Holocaust studies curricula
for colleges and universities and "lesson plans" for elementary
and secondary schools. The curricula and plans are used
throughout the United States after being reworked and adjusted in state curricula centers in accordance with the
pedagogical requirements of the respective school system. Most
popular are the curricula prepared in four known resource
centers, in New York, Philadelphia, Great Neck, N.Y., and
Brookline, Mass. They are used on both graduate and undergraduate levels but aimed primarily at working with prospective teachers. Most of the educators subsequently prepare their
own "modules" for high schools or elementary schools, including detailed "lesson plans" of activities and objectives, supported by bibliographies and audio-visual material.

Extensive research is still going on and new curricula are
introduced. In November, 1982, a gathering of 70 New York
State Teachers took place in Albany, N.Y., where a new curriculum was proposed for upstate schools. After being field-
tested this curriculum is being introduced, following the example of New York City, where Holocaust education is man-
dated by the City Board of Education. In the ten American

states with substantial Jewish presence, there is a built-in
source of support and encouragement for teaching the Holocaust. In states with mixed population and only a small percentage of Jews, educators of all creeds and persuasion are
encouraged to establish departments of Holocaust studies in
their colleges and universities.

Drawn into the process are primarily professors of history, psychology and religion, often joined by clergymen and
civic leaders. In order to introduce them to the methodology of
the difficult subject, experienced educators from resource
centers are invited to set up training seminars and workshops.
After a forseen period of study, the teachers are encouraged
to call a conference where each presents a particular aspect
of the Holocaust in which he possesses some expertise. Guest
lecturers and keynote speakers often participate in the event,
which is usually covered by the local media and prepared in
preconference activities. The aim is to draw the interest of
educators from their entire state.

This method represents the Holocaust against the political,
social and ideological background of Nazism in the areas of
the Weimar Republic and the Third Reich. It outlines the
spread of anti-Semitism in Europe before and during the Nazi
occupation and demonstrates the Nazi strategy of first singling
out and then annihilating the Jews. It clearly stresses the
point that the problems involved in recording the history of
the Jews during World War II differ considerably from the
problems concerning the overall history of that war.

This type of curriculum was also devised by the Great Neck
Resource Center with additional emphasis on social study.
The program stresses the impact of Nazi persecution on Jews
and their reaction and attitudes in the face of the disaster
as well as the reactions of various peoples and social milieus
to the acts of violence applied to the Jews. The students are
made to realize that man's inhumanity to man can surface
at any period in history when moral and ethical standards are
allowed to deteriorate. They are confronted with the fact that
genocide is a threat to all humanity and invariably results in
the destruction of heritage, tradition, and culture of a people.
In conclusion, the student is introduced to the meaning of active citizenship and made aware of the implication of modern
technology and the need to control it for the benefit of mankind. It seems that the Great Neck method tries to adapt
Holocaust studies to the developmental needs of adolescents,
thereby making it an integral part of overall social studies.
Another type of curriculum has been introduced in Brook-

line, linking Holocaust studies with human behavior. It focuses on the history of anti-Semitism, simultaneously drawing the student's attention to the damaging effects of any kind of discrimination. The student is encouraged to place himself in the position and situation of another person in order to understand more than one perspective of a problem or dilemma. The study centers on the method of drawing from the past in order to understand the present. It actually becomes a study in ethics and morality and gives the teacher an opportunity to bring into his classroom a lesson in humanity. Each student is encouraged to keep a journal, reflecting his personal ideas and reactions to the studied material.

The preliminary results indicate that this method instills in the student a respect for human life and a sensitivity to human suffering. It also makes him reflect and analyse before judging human behavior in the face of adversity. It fosters his appreciation of a moral code which would assist him in making the right choice of the many options of a free society.

A related method, introduced in Israel by Professor Arye Carmon, senior lecturer at the Ben-Gurion University's Department of Education, has also been used in the Los Angeles Jewish day and public schools during 1977-78. This method, challenging conventional curricula and existing Holocaust studies programs, became increasingly popular in California. It is based on three elemental assumptions: "the necessity to cope with ambiguities and conflicts in today's complex world; an individual's need to assess a particular value and perceive the personal consequences involved in accepting it; and the appropriateness of teaching values using familiar and relevant subject matter."

Most educators are convinced that the universal lesson of the Holocaust makes it a valuable tool in the classroom. They believe that the harrowing inhumanity of the Holocaust sensitizes the students to human suffering and increases their awareness of the dangers and ills plaguing their own society. They realize that its unique message in ethics and morality must be brought to students of every race and creed.

The curricula mentioned do not exhaust the multitude of theories and methods used in Holocaust study programs in the United States. They only point to an evolving trend to move away from the strict adrerence to historiography in conventional curricula to free interpretation of the event for socio-moral education. This trend is also joined by a tendency to shift the emphasis from subject to student and from historical data to personal accounts.

Philip Friedman, "the dean of Holocaust methodology," has warned that dealing with the history of the Holocaust is in itself a most serious task. He tried to draw the attention of educators to the pitfalls confronting them in coming to grips with the ever-growing material including the literature of the survivors. The compilers of conventional curricula seem to remain conscious of the responsibility confronting them in dealing with the methodology of the Holocaust but neglect emphasizing its universal message. Those preoccupied with the emphasis on human values show a disregard for historical data and an attempt to resort to simplifications and omissions in molding the material for a specific need. There is no doubt that the tremendous gap between these two trends is not easy to bridge. A perfect balance between the two will not soon be achieved. There is, however, an effort to devise a comprehensive curriculum which would take into account the needs of the large number of students while sharing with them this difficult lesson of history, which may eventually also contribute to their socio-moral development.

M&R 10:10, Jan.-Feb., 1984

NEVER TO FORGET

By Dr. Edward C. McGuire

These United States has existed for a little more than 200 years, during which time it has been unfortunate enough to have engaged in nine major conflagrations. Slightly more than one million of its best youths have perished during these ventures. Because of the horrors associated with war, we as a people have learned to abhor war with just reason. Collectively we do not even believe war is a solution to the resolving international differences. We seek fair and equitable resolutions of differences in many world councils.

Imagine the magnitude of our remorse if these wars had decimated our population by forty percent. We are talking now about over 80 million people. It is beyond us! Nuclear attacks, theoretically, can produce this degree of havoc on these United States. Small wonder, we have been talking for many years to other nuclear powers to avert just such a disas-

---

Dr. McGuire is a past Commissioner of Higher Education, Commonwealth of Pennsylvania.

ter. Nobody wants a nuclear war that I know of. It could only
result in setting mankind back perhaps to a state a bit more
advanced than that of his cavemen ancestors.

Yet something akin to such a tragedy did happen in the
lifetime of many of the people reading this article, yet hardly
a voice or a finger was raised in protest. Of course I am
referring to the Holocaust—the systematic destruction of European Jewry by the Nazi hordes that engulfed Europe during
World War II. Six million souls perished by the design of a
madman and his cohorts. Think of it—six million people—forty
percent of the Jewish population of the world destroyed in
a few years. Their only crime—that of existing. It is also true
that the Nazis persecuted their political and idelogical oppo-
nents—Marxists, Liberals, Churchmen—for what they believed,
said or did; only the Jews suffered for existing.

The Holocaust is a major historical event, similar to the
Fall of Rome or the French Revolution. It is not enough to
study the event itself; we must also study the impact. This
means studying the historiography of the event, because this
illuminates the past through the concerns of the present. . . .

How to prevent such things? We must learn from history,
we must teach and learn sensitivity to another's pain.

The treatment of the Holocaust in history texts more
than thirty years after this horrendous event, the teaching
of it in the classroom, including the college classroom, are the
proper concerns of any society that espouses the dignity of
man, and the value of a single human life.

Henry Friedlander in his booklet "On the Holocaust"
states:

> "In 1961 a study of American high school textbooks
> showed that their treatment of Nazism was brief,
> bland, superficial, and misleading. It found that ra-
> cism and anti-Semitism received only perfunctory
> coverage and that the Holocaust, if mentioned at all,
> was discussed in a few lines. . . ."

There is no reason to believe that these textbooks have
improved during the last decade. Moreover, even at the universities, coverage of the Holocaust in history textbooks is
not substantially better than those used in high schools ten
years ago. Thus, a survey of Western civilization widely used
by college freshmen takes 131 lines to discuss the persecution
of the Jansenists and Huguenots by Louis XIV, but only 8 to
discuss the persecution of Jews during the Second World War.
It mentions Dunkirk and Stalingrad, but not Auschwitz and

Treblinka. Discussing "conquered and intimidated peoples," it alludes to "mass extermination" in the appalling concentration camps, but does not even mention Jews.

There is growing evidence that the subject in our schools and colleges is treated with benign neglect, in a cursory or cosmetic fashion, if indeed at all, and that too many textbooks confine the entire matter to a few lines.

I quote an American professor in 1977 who states "there was no German policy of Jewish extermination . . . Millions of European Jews were not deliberately slain in concentration camps" . . .

Yes, let these and others like them walk the mass graves of people who never existed. People like this are living testimony that time, distance, space and the viscissitudes—economic and political,—blur memory and dim the lessons of our past, no matter how brutally stark, staggering or stunning. The sobering reality is that we cannot be reminded often enough of the possibilities of human indifference and depravity and of the inexplicable potential that lurks in the depths of man's darker side. To disregard the realities of our recent history is to court the likelihood of their re-occurrence in the present or foreseeable future. . . .

Indifference is the greatest sin. Ignorance, a close second. To forget what we know would not be human. We owe it to our children and to our tradition to lead our youth to learn, to withstand the bitterness of truths however unsettling. To forget what we know would not be human. To remember it is to think of what being human means. . . .

I am deeply committed to the teaching of the significance of the Holocaust at the college level—yes, even making exposure to the subject mandatory at least once before graduation. After almost three and a half decades of traumatic amnesia, a realization is dawning that the ghosts of the Holocaust cannot and should not be exorcized. It is relevant to all people.

This shame and horror that occurred in our century is a story that must be told again and again, until it is imprinted indelibly in the minds of people like "you and me"; the central issue must never be forgotten! It is a moral issue, the issue of what the world has done and permitted to be done. To insist upon making the world uncomfortable with the memory of its guilt is a necessity for that moral reconstruction which may alone prevent a repetition of the Holocaust.

X. Holocaust and the Arts: Beauty and Evil

Artistic response to the Auschwitz world was unavoidable and inevitable. It was also controversial. Poems, novels, paintings, plays, films, statues, and music have been the media of creative artists who have felt the need to express their encounter with the world of Holocaust suffering and its inherent evil. Both the survivors and the post-Holocaust generations have attempted to express aspects of the Jewish tragedy in artistic forms. The record, not surprisingly, is mixed.

The range of achievements and failures—from the literary corpus of Elie Wiesel to the TV series "Holocaust"—has enjoyed and suffered the praises and stings of critics from all quarters. Opinions range from those who decry any effort to compress Holocaust reality into the parameters of the creative imagination to those who encourage further ventures to capture the emotions and truths of that terrible past by the best artistic talent and means available.

It is difficult to quarrel with Wiesel's eloquent claim that the Holocaust lies beyond the range of normal human expression. And, yet, its growing historical impact impels more and more to attempt to re-enter that reality once inhabited by the survivors and the dead victims. If, as has been concluded, there lurks a potential Eichmann in us all capable of contemplating the worst, then, similarly, there ought to be the stuff of empathy that can transform us momentarily into Eichmann's intended victim. It is an agonizing problem that will never be satisfactorily answered.

For further reading in the arts and the Holocaust, attention is called to: *Art of the Holocaust* (March-April 1978, Review, Irving Abrahamson); (Janet Blatter and Sybil Milton, 8:2 Jan.-Feb. 1982, Review, Luba K. Gurdus); *Indelible Shadows: Film and the Holocaust* (Annette Insdorf, 10:2 May-June 1984, Review, Lea Hamaoui); *Crisis and Covenant: The Holocaust in American Jewish Fiction* (Alan L. Berger, 12:2 May-June 1986, Review, Ilan Avisar); "Shoa: A Film Review" (Charles R. Allen, Jr., 12:2 Jan.-Feb. 1986, 12:4, March-April 1986); "A Film Review: The Partisans of Vilna (Charles Patterson, 13:4 Nov.-Dec. 1986); *To the Land of the Cattails* (Aharon Appelfeld, 13:2 March-April 1987, Review, Alan L. Berger).

ELIE WIESEL: VOICE AND VISION

Against Silence: The Voice and Vision of Elie Wiesel. Selected and edited by Irving Abrahamson. The Holocaust Library, 1985, Three Volumes. 1188pp. $85.

Reviewed by Dr. MICHAEL BERENBAUM

Elie Wiesel writes of himself as a Hasid of the Wizsnitzer rebbe–his melodies, his tales, his stories, and his silence are all of Wizsnitz–the master of his maternal grandfather. Irving Abrahamson writes as a Hasid of Wiesel, one of an increasing number of people, Jewish and Gentiles, whose lives have been uplifted, whose spirituality has been deepened by their encounter with Wiesel. Abrahamson's veneration is apparent from the first page, where he describes Wiesel's *oeuvre* in a simple, beautiful opening essay. Every statement is treated as part of a seamless whole. No greater weight is given to a story from Wiesel's fiction or to a statement in a major public address than to an aside in a public lecture. Sometimes, Abrahamson's comparisons are startling.

Those of us who regard Wiesel with affection and esteem have grown accustomed to comparisons with Jeremiah, the prophet who warned his people before the destruction, who lamented the fall of Jerusalem, and who consoled his people after the *churban.* Jeremiah, the pragmatist, told them to plant vineyards and marry wives in exile, yet he dreamed of the return and invested in the Jewish future. We have learned to regard Auschwitz as the antithesis of Sinai, the anti-revelation of both God and humanity. Thus, *Night* is the anti-exodus, the passage from God's presence to His absence, the journey from lands of promise into the darkness of pure evil.

But, characteristically, the disciple must go further. A bold master attracts a bold disciple. So Abrahamson characterized *Night* as Wiesel's "new *sefer Torah* for the Holocaust era" and wrote that "as his *oeuvre* grows, a new Talmud for our era also grows." After all, according to tradition, the *Torah's* origins are divine, and the Talmud is the collective enterprise of rabbinic leadership–their shared agenda to make the Jews a holy people without Jerusalem and without the Sacred Temple. But what is a disciple to do when he searches for dramatic images of a rebbe? Abrahamson has compiled with love the random offerings of Wiesel, yet not only with love. *Against Silence* is a sensitive and aesthetic work. Of the hundreds (perhaps thousands) of speeches and lectures that Wiesel has given, the thousands of articles and statements that he has written, the countless stories he has told and the many interviews he has granted, Abrahamson has chosen wisely and gathered his material so masterfully that one envies the master a disciple of such skill, filled with such passion.

Students of American Jewry know that Wiesel has attained a unique stature within the American Jewish community. With the passing of Abraham Joshua Heschel, Wiesel represents Jewish history and values to the non-Jewish world. He is widely admired by organizational Jews and anti-establishment Jews, by *machers* and by *amcha*, by students and their parents—and yes, even their grandparents. He has more disciples and admirers than peers and friends.

The author of more than 25 books, Wiesel's stature derives from these works, but not his following. After all, most Jews have not read his books (with the exception *of Night*). Of those who have, fewer understand them. Despite our reputation as the people of the book, followers are not sustained by the written word alone.

Wiesel is also a master of the spoken word. He is the premier Jewish orator of our time, a traveling *magid* appearing in synagogues and universities, on television and at scholarly forums with a message that is compelling and a demeanor and voice that evokes tears and laughter, melancholy and nostalgia. Yet, when Wiesel speaks, his silences and his sighs often tell the story.

Wiesel is an *ohev Yisrael*, a lover of Israel. He loves the Jewish people and their state and he views Jews as central to the divine and human drama that is history. He does not see a conflict between Judaism and universalism. The more deeply Jewish a statement or a work, the more universal its implications. Nothing provokes Wiesel's ire quite as much as a Jewish writer ashamed of his Jewishness or a gentile writer who demeans Jewish history in the name of universalism. To be a Jew is a privilege; to speak and to write of the Jews, an invitation to mystery.

Wiesel once wrote that he envies Soviet Jews, for only in the Soviet Union is Israel still a dream—better yet a prayer. When Wiesel speaks of Soviet Jewry, he does not deal with *olim* and *noshrim*, with the problems of absorption, or the politics and personalities of the movement. Standing above the fray, his concern is with the mystery of Jewish survival and the tenacity of Jewish yearning. Five decades, six decades after the revolution, the desire of Russian Jews to be Jewish is not extinguished. He tells and retells tales of their joy, not their suffering—of *Simchat Torah*, of greeting Golda Meir—and he avoids the humdrum aspects of the issue. He elevates the struggle and the drama, recaptures the sacred and steers clear of the profane. He tries to shape a myth that can faithfully capture the inner truth.

So, too, with the State of Israel. The miracle of '67 is recounted. The urgency of '73 and the drama of Sadat's visit to Jerusalem are all recaptured. Wiesel will not criticize Israel outside of Israel—except on rare occasions—and thus in the entire corpus, there are striking omissions; barely a word on Lebanon or on the territories, nothing on the economy or on Kahane, no mention of religious fanaticism and the politics of messianism, no real perspective on the relationship between Israel and the diaspora—but tales, rich, poignant and moving.

Time and again, Wiesel is asked by Israelis: "Why are you not here?" Each time the answer is the same and the question more disturbing. Readers may begin to feel like the students of Rabban Yochanan Ben Zakai, who said to their master after he parried a heathen's question, *"lazeh dachita bekaneh ahad—v'lanu?"* him you dismissed with one finger—and us?

Of course, Wiesel speaks of the Holocaust—often indirectly. It lurks in the shadows, but clearly it is the central mystery of the contemporary world, a harbinger of truths unfathomable, an event so disturbing that some choose to avoid it and others to dilute it.

He speaks of God with anguish. He wrestles with God and against God. He tells of the trial of God, but he never abandons God or renounces the traditions of the God of Israel. He remains private with regard to his own religious life. He reveals those who instructed him in the traditions of the God of Israel, his teacher in Paris, Mordecai Shishani, and the revered Talmudist Saul Lieberman.

And he speaks of the world that preceded the Holocaust with tenderness and love, unwilling to disturb a child's picture of a world of depth and majesty, sanctity and beauty. Shabbat is the Shabbat of Sighet, not the seventh day observed in New York or even Jerusalem. Religious life before the war had integrity, passion and depth. We are but a pale reflection of that world. Yet, the overwhelming nostalgia for a world lost does not answer the question of how are we to live, what do we make of Shabbat in Washington and Chicago, in Boston and San Francisco? Here, too, even disciples may ask, "and us?"

For those who do not read Yiddish, Abrahamson has translated sections of original 1955 Yiddish edition of *Night* published in Argentina, entitled *When the World Was Silent*. By reducing the original 800-plus-page work to one-eighth its original, Wiesel achieved an economy of style that characterizes most of his writing. He preserved the truth and merely intensified the silence.

Abrahamson also translates several of the columns Wiesel wrote as a journalist in Yiddish. As a journalist, Wiesel is surprising. If Hannah Arendt's Eichmann is banal and boring, Wiesel stares and stares at the murderer, expecting to glean from his eyes and his comportment the essence of evil.

Abrahamson has given us a rich work, the sort of book that scholars publish of a great figure posthumously, or hasidim of their master when legend can overtake truth. Fortunately for us, Wiesel is at the peak of productivity as a writer and at the height of his influence as a public figure —and we can expect more from both master and disciple in the future. Others may provide critical assessment; Abrahamson has given us a wealth of detail and a statement of adoration.

M&R 12:2, March-April, 1986

ON COMMERCIALIZING GENOCIDE

By CHARLES R. ALLEN, JR.

I've sometimes remarked ruefully while assaying American culture that its inherent commercialization on virtually every level—especially TV—frequently has the effect of coopting otherwise serious or well-intended art, literature, even politics, of neuterizing what is manifestly human. Were the world to come to an end, I'm sure that commercial TV would bring it to us by way of all three networks on prime time sponsored by Revlon in living color.

Such comment usually prompts wry laughter. But it isn't funny. NBC-TV has, I submit, done it before our very eyes. The recent so-called mini-series, "Holocaust," seen by an estimated 120 million viewers in full or in part has, on balance, reduced the martyrdom of the Six Million—as well as the sacred memory of the additional millions of non-Jews put to Nazi death—to manipulative exploitation for the aggrandizement and profit of a few.

Let me quickly concede at the outset of these critical comments the apparent truism as summarized by a young friend and militant active in Concerned Jewish Youth: "I know it was slick 'soap,' probably inaccurate—and all those commercials. So what? That's American TV, and if that's what it takes to get across the message [of the Holocaust], I'll take it!"

I won't argue the fact of network exposure in this space. Rather, I would like to question what "message" came across; how it came across; and, finally, in what contextual setting— which raises further the question of effectiveness, educationally, and moral propriety.

The trade journals called the pretelecast reviews "the most extraordinary in the history of TV." Throughout these comments, with but a couple of exceptions, there ran the contention that—in addition to its other virtues—"Holocaust" was historically accurate," a "factually unassailable docudrama."

This is palpable nonsense. The TV film constantly referred to SS General Reinhard Heydrich, head of the RHSA, as "chief" of the Gestapo (even *The New York Times* reviewer who was an exceptional critic of the series, repeats this error) ; Heinrich Mueller was the head of the Gestapo from 1935-1945. Concentrationaries at Auschwitz were not permitted to keep family photo albums, music scores or other personal belongings; nor were male prisoners allowed to visit female inmates; the standard operating procedure at Auschwitz was that 1 person per square foot was allotted for the gassings— not the locker-room casualness as depicted in the TV film. The bodies of the death camp victims were not plump, well fed. They were the skeletons of millions deliberately starved by the Nazis before being put to death.

Such inaccuracies were not only nettlesome but cumulatively assailed the TV film's credibility and any dramatic value which otherwise might have obtained in its shallowness.

However, more to the point were the general historical fallacies which the TV film sustained throughout its installments, thereby tending to distort critically the actualities of the Holocaust and to vitiate the presumed dramatic intent to present the greater truths of the Nazi genocide. At this critical level, I believe, one perceives the possible dangers of accepting the wholly uncritical conclusions that 120 million American TV viewers saw "Holocaust" and "so what's the difference?" as one nationally syndicated columnist snapped rhetorically.

With but two exceptions (and one, the depiction of the 1943 Warsaw Ghetto Uprising, was filled with substantive inaccuracies), the Jews of Europe were depicted as having gone to slaughter like the proverbial sheep. This historically is a canard, rooted in the glib conclusions of some historians relying exclusively on Nazi sources.

A colleague of mine, one of the country's prominent journalists, called me during the series: "I'm beginning to feel ashamed of being Jewish from what I'm viewing in 'Holocaust, '" he said. You should not, I told him. There now stands an entire literature which utterly refutes such egregious nonsense. I quickly listed the armed resistance of the Jews in such ghettos as Czestochowa, Minsk, Bialystok and others where the accounts, like Warsaw, have come down to us from the fighters themselves; the extraordinary undergrounds of the death camps at Auschwitz, Treblinka, Chelmno where Titanic deeds of resistance took place; at Buchenwald, where the resistance was so powerful that it took over control of the camp in its last days.

I also pointed out to him a little appreciated fact about the Warsaw Ghetto Uprising: *it was the first armed revolt in all of fascist-occupied Europe, and it was accomplished by Jews*. An astounding event of universal significance!

Finally, one can not assess the TV film without reference to its commercialization. The mass media reviewers who prescreened "Holocaust" did not view it as it was shown to the network audience, complete and replete with commercials. (By which I mean any sales intrusion, calculated to make money for its sponsor, including "spots" for products or services, a promo for an upcoming TV show or a news "update" tied-in with a spot or institutional ad.) All told I counted 217 such instrusions amounting to more than 1½ hours of the 9½ hours given over to the mini-series.

The familiar nostrum that commercials pay for the production does not hold; the costs were more than met; the author, producers, and network made a lot of money off "Holocaust," which to me is simply repugnant. That the sacred memory of the Six Million has now become a "vehicle" for pick-up trucks and life insurance is utterly obscene.

Consider the content and inter-cutting of the commercials. From the scene depicting the burning of a synagogue jammed with Jewish victims inside by the Nazis, the viewer is suddenly slammed into no less than 9 spots among them a McDonald's hamburger pitch!

From the euthanasia murders of a busload of innocents by automotive gassing, we are thrown into a Ford Motor Co. spot loudly telling us how its vehicles are protected against rusting!

From a sequence which shows (by authentic photos) Nazi atrocities, the suicide of SS Major Dorf and a confrontation in which his war crimes are revealed by the Dorf family's uncle, we sparringly cut to a "Fannie-Shaper" pantyhose spot with a zooming close-up of two models swinging backsides!

There was no justification whatever for the interminable stream of *shlock* in behalf of dog food, tooth paste, underarm deodorants, detergents, beer, etc., ad infinitum. The orgy of commercialism was a slap in the face, counter-productive even of the sharp limits of the film itself. To insist—and accept—that this is how things are, reveals a great deal about ourselves; that we have become so inured by mindless exploitation as to submit to an insouciant desecration of something truly Holy.

How Nazism once singled out an entire people for decimation simply and solely because they were Jews is for me, a non-Jew who did not experience the Holocaust directly, the supreme lesson which has been passed along to us, the succeeding posterity, from the Martyrs—a lesson which shall never be forgotten nor the crimes it records ever forgiven. Did "Holocaust" make a positive contribution—particularly to the very young—to this instruction and its resolve?

Of one thing I am certain, however. This commercial TV film does not—can not—do honor to the ultimate legacy of the Six Million: the moral imperatives of remembering their truly incomprehensible sacrifice for humankind.

M&R 4:8, May-June, 1978

BOOK OF POLITICAL PROPHECY:
MOBY DICK POINTING TO NAZISM

By Prof. Christopher Durer

The recent interest in the political world of Melville's writings has made us more aware of Melville's stature as a liberal thinker and of the multiple political and economic influences, tensions and trends which fashioned his writings . . . Seen from this perspective, and quite legitimately so, *Moby Dick* grows out of the aftermath of the Mexican War, with its rabid political and economic expansionism, the burning issue of the treatment of the Indians, and the apparently insoluble problem of slavery. The interregional and interracial society on board the *Pequod,* the structure of power which she exhibits, and numerous political allusions establish her as the ship of state in mid-nineteenth-century America.

I want to go a step further and examine *Moby-Dick* as yet another book of political prophecy, this time pointing to the inhumanities of twentieth-century totalitarianism, especially the National Socialist regime in Germany between 1933 and 1945. This uncanny prefiguration of an "ideological" dictatorship is twofold: portrayal in *Moby-Dick* of specific propagandistic techniques, similar to those used in Nazi Germany, and a more general representation in Melville's work of the very psychology and psychosis of power in a totalitarian state, such as Nazi Germany.

The leaders' reaching out for the "folksoul" of the people, an exaggerated role allotted to the will to the exclusion of reason and higher emotions, welding of individual wills into a collective will, the leader's hypnotic effect upon his followers, and the mystique with which he surrounds himself, his appeal to deeply set urges and subconscious drives of the people leading to their psychological enslavement, the view of the state as based on folk dynamics rather than on economic factors, demanding conformity, irrationalism, emotionalism, hysteria, blind obedience, pagan rituals, hatred for those who are considered the enemies of the state, "call of the blood," "blood and soil"—these, to be sure, are the hallmarks of the Nazi era. Sadly and prophetically they are also present in *Moby Dick.* . . .

Foremost among the propagandistic techniques, referred

to earlier, is the reaching for the "folksoul" of the people, which Ahab and Hitler practiced repeatedly. A good example of it is Chapter 36 "The Quarter-Deck." With Ahab in the thick of things, showing "the same bigotry of purpose" as he showed earlier, the chapter begins in a militaristic manner, with a strong-willed commander addressing expectant and cowered troops. . . . Very soon, however, the militaristic temper degenerates into hysteria, as Ahab arouses the excitement of the crew, mesmerizes the men, makes his goals their goals, and finally brings them to submission. What has begun as a roll call and a planning session becomes in effect a Nazi Party rally, where the leader and the followers swear allegiance to the sacred common cause.

Just as Hitler and other Nazi leaders brought about a state of identification between themselves and their followers, so Ahab brings about a state of identification between himself and the crew. Ahab wants the crew to join in the chase of the White Whale and devote all their energies to this purpose, but he does not issue orders. Instead he is trying to create in them a state of mind in which they themselves will want what he wants, and hence the entire chapter is an illuminating exercise not only in whipping up hysteria in a crowd but more importantly in manipulating their minds. . . .

Hitler in the early stages of his career often did not issue orders to the German nation to perform particular tasks. He was too wily for that. Instead, he was repeatedly reaching for what he called the "folksoul" of the people, and once he had found it, he tried to mold it to his purpose. Thus, for instance, during his speech at Weimar, on July 3, 1936, marking the tenth anniversary of the *Parteitag* held in that city, Hitler tried repeatedly to reach the "folksoul" of the people. . . .

It is clear that *Moby Dick* projects not only a macabre vision of twentieth-century fascism, closely resembling National Socialism, but offers also a schema and typology of this fascism—its precarious beginnings, its growth and zenith, its death-rattle, and demise. This schema begins with Ahab and Hitler's cautious manipulative techniques at the beginning of the voyage of the *Pequod,* and in Germany in the early 1930's, both before and after Hitler's accession to power. Later it includes the total domination of the crew and of the German nation and ends in the destruction of both the *Pequod* and the Nazi regime.

Adolf Hitler, the "ideological" dictator of Germany and Captain Ahab, the "ideological" skipper of the *Pequod,* begin

their rule with limited powers, granted to them respectively
by the contract with the owners and the broad rules of Ad-
mirality Law, and the constitution of the Weimar Republic,
which are a point of departure for both of them. Gradually
through manipulation of men's minds and through fomenting
fear and hatred in the crew and the German nation they
obtain progressively greater dominion over their charges.
The *Pequod* and Germany, previously so diverse, are reduced
to uniformity, and are given one collective purpose and will.
When a great challenge presents itself, the sighting of the
White Whale and the compulsive need to expand territorially
and defeat the enemies of the state, each group rises to extraordinary heights of dedication and self-sacrifice.

Examined from this typological-historical point of view,
the corresponding stages in Ahab and Hitler's tenure of office
are roughly as follows: in *Moby Dick*, Phase 1), Chapters 16
through 98, where Ahab is still a manipulator trying to win
the crew of the *Pequod* over to his purpose, and where he
employs the propagandistic techniques—Chapter 36, "The
Quarter-Deck," and 46 "Surmises," being the best examples of
his political thinking;

Phase 2), Chapter 99 through 132, when Ahab is the unchallenged dictator, controlling the crew's mind and actions—
"They were one man, not thirty"—and displaying an extraordinary confidence in himself;

Phase 3) The time of extreme challenge, the last three
chapters, 133-35, where the collective will is translated into
frantic action and a supreme and self-sacrificing effort is made
by the entire crew to capture the White Whale—the mood best
expressed by Ahab on the third day of the chase: ". . . to the
last I grapple with thee; from hell's heart I stab at thee." This
is also the phase during which Ahab's monomania and his
claims to superhuman powers are at their highest;

Phase 4), The sinking of the *Pequod* and of the entire
crew, save Ishmael, and the destruction of Ahab's empire.

The corresponding phases in Hitler's career as National
Socialist leader are as follows:

Phase 1), beginning roughly in 1930, the year of the
Nazi Party's first major victory at the polls, and leading
until roughly 1938. Even though he became Chancellor in
1933, assumed the title of *Fuehrer* in 1934, eliminated his
dangerous opponent Ernst Roehm in the same year, and
scored another victory with the passage of the racist Nuremberg Laws, Hitler is still consolidating his dictatorial powers
and is strengthening his control over the German people

through propaganda and hypnotic speeches. Hitler's speech at the *Industrie-Klub*, in Duesseldorf, on January 27, 1932, in which he alternately coaxes and frightens the German business community, and which in some respect is similar to Ahab's speech to the crew in Chapter 36, is an excellent example of his magnetism and diplomacy in this early stage of his career;

Phase 2), the years 1938-42, when Hitler is unchallenged at home and victorious elsewhere in Europe, and no longer woos the German nation, but controls it completely, showing supreme confidence in himself.

Phase 3), years 1943-45 when Germany, under Hitler's progressively paranoid rule, is making an extraordinary effort to win the war, when the "naked will" separated from reason dominates Hitler and the German people—as is exemplified by Hitler's numerous speeches and pronouncements during that time, which are similar to Ahab's frantic pronouncements during the three-day chase;

Phase 4), May, 1945, defeat of Germany, death of Hitler and many of his lieutenants, and destruction of the Nazi ship of state.

In many respects the *Pequod* resembles a Nazi state. While the formal organization is made up of the different orders within the crew, this hardly explains the political ethos reigning there. Dominating the administrative organization and hierarchy of the *Pequod*—necessary as these are for the conduct of the day-to-day business—is the figure of the dictator, who without using expressions like "the call of the blood" and "blood and soil" seeks to evoke in the crew emotions very similar to those Hitler tried to evoke in the German nation.

The facet of *Moby Dick* briefly discussed here—one of the many this multi-faceted work offers—shows Melville in the capacity of yet another prophet, and his epic illustrates the extraordinary values of literature as political prophecy. As such Melville takes his well-deserved place alongside such writers as Frank Kafka of the short stories, or Blasco Ibanez of *The Four Horsemen of the Apocalypse*, or Emile Zola of inhumanity and war, as well as alongside the authors of dystopias, such as Aldous Huxley or George Orwell. But Melville's political prophecy is often more comprehensive, revealing, and penetrating than those of many other prophets. It is also closer to the mark.

XI. Post Auschwitz:
Neo-Nazism & Anti-Semitism

It was the hope of a naive few that the shock of Auschwitz would purge modern man of the curse of anti-Semitism. In fact, the Holocaust barely interrupted the plague of Jew hatred. No sooner had the war ended than Jews returning to Poland were welcomed by murderous pogroms. Stalinist anti-Semitism swept throughout Eastern Europe from Moscow to Prague. Then the animus towards Jews in the form of Soviet-inspired anti-Semitic tracts (including cartoons) ran amock through every Arab country where the war against Israel quickly evolved into a crusade against World Jewry.

Anti-Zionism as a form of anti-Semitism reached its "highest" low with the United Nation's declaration, by a thunderous international majority, equating Zionism with Racism. By then, the restraint against overt expressions against Jews in the West had all but disappeared. New Left support of Palestinians attracted hundreds of anti-Jewish groups who recognized a good cover. The right was not slow to follow: questions of dual loyalty, of God's ability to hear Jewish prayers popped up with increasing frequency.

There were many tense moments during the planned march of neo-Nazis in Skokie, Ill., in 1978. A well-articulated perspective on Skokie is the review by Solomon S. Simonson of *Defending My Enemy: American Nazis, the Skokie Case, and the Risks of Freedom.* (Aryeh Neier, 6:2 Sept.-Oct. 1979). For a look at the '80's the reader should consult "Anti-Semitism in the '80's Examined by Survivors" (8:4 Nov.-Dec. 1981); "Report From Academia" (Joel Bainerman, 9:3 Nov.-Dec. 1982).

By the summer of 1987, the campaign to deny the Holocaust continues unabated despite a few court victories against it. For that reason—and others—one can not argue with Irving Greenberg's call to continue speaking about the Holocaust.

M & R SCHOLARLY STANDARDS
FIGHTS REVISIONISM

By PROF. HENRY HUTTENBACH

In the past two decades, library shelves have had to make ever-increasing room for books devoted to the Holocaust. At present, the steadily growing stream of publications shows no sign of slowing down. An intriguing question comes to mind: is this quickening of research into the Holocaust past in response to public interest, or did the appearance of a wide variety of books stimulate awareness of the contemporary significance of the Holocaust? It is no idle question, for the dynamics between Holocaust literature and the reading public is essential to an understanding of its role in the psyche of the new generations of the post-Holocaust era.

Is the concern for the Holocaust rooted primarily in the minds of those who remember World War II, or is also part of the anxiety of those who were born after the event? Is Holocaust literature a passing activity, satisfying the curiosity of a dying generation, or is it integrally linked to those of the younger generation who recognize a universal problem in the Holocaust, of significance to all future generations?

Not surprisingly, *Martyrdom and Resistance,* essentially a publication originating from within the ranks of the survivors of the Holocaust, recognized the danger of the Holocaust remaining only a concern of those that experienced it first-hand. As one of its central goals, *Martyrdom and Resistance* has sought to transfer the legacy of the Holocaust to the generations to come. To that end, it has made a part of its mission the dissemination of information about publications dealing with the Holocaust. Over the course of its twenty years of existence, the journal has mentioned and reviewed hundreds of major and minor books on the subject in the hopes of educating its readers, survivors and non-survivors, on the scope of Holocaust literature.

Over the years, hundreds of short announcements and lengthier critical reviews have appeared in the pages of *Martyrdom and Resistance.* In so doing, the journal has fulfilled yet another goal: to highlight the more imaginative and

---

Professor Huttenbach is professor of history, City College of New York.

scholarly publications in the hopes of encouraging even better writing and publication efforts in the future. The reviews were honest and often severe in their criticism, constantly advocating high standards from authors and publishers and encouraging discriminating taste on the part of its readers. The process of reviewing accurately, honestly, and fairly was the collective result of a broad range of reviewers—survivors, academicians, and other experts from varying walks of life, Jewish and non-Jewish. By soliciting critical opinions from a broad range of individuals about books chosen by the journal or selected by the reviewers themselves, *Martyrdom and Resistance* accumulated an envious record of reliable reviewing upon which students, teachers, researchers, and the interested public can rely. Its individual reviews are regularly consulted where the journal is found in public and university libraries. Its tradition of unfettered reviewing has contributed to the improving standards of Holocaust scholarship and the sophistication of readers in the subject.

The urgency to raise the level of Holocaust scholarship is an unprecedented imperative for the immediate future. Parallelling Holocaust studies has been the rise of "Historical Revisionism," an insidious new form of "intellectual" anti-Semitism. One of the strategies of the "revisionists" is to find errors of fact, interprative flaws, weaknesses of sources, and methodological mistakes arising in books about the Holocaust, an event they seek both to downplay and to deny.

Given such an enemy, those seeking to promote the Holocaust as a central event not only in Jewish history but of contemporary mankind, have a special obligation to seeing that Holocaust literature be as free as possible of avoidable imperfections. Carelessness, amateurism, and the results of other kinds of non-professionalism have to be discouraged by a combination of alert reviewers and a discerning readership. *Martyrdom and Resistance* has sought to recruit the former and to cultivate the latter. If the impact of "Historical Revisionism" is to be kept at a minimum, one way is to assure and to tolerate only the highest level of Holocaust scholarship. For, simply put, unlike scholars of the French Revolution or some other facet of the past, Holocaust scholarship finds itself at war, confronted by a denial, one of whose tactics is to pinpoint every single error, however, minor, as "proof" that the Holocaust is a historical fraud.

The reviews in this anthology are samples of the many published by *Martyrdom and Resistance*. Some have been chosen because of the publication under discussion, others because of the nature of the review. They are to be seen as examples of the dual mission of the Journal: dissemination of information about worthy recent publications, and advocacy of the critical examination of their contents.

At best, book reviewing is a thankless task. It involves self-criticism and self-examination, a self-policing on the part of those engaged in Holocaust research, with a minimum of rancor and a maximum of positive suggestion and persuasion in the hope that future endeavors will maintain and surpass present standards. It is an ongoing venture as the stream of Holocaust publications continues to reach the reviewers' desks and the needs to uphold the integrity of the historicity of the Holocaust become more stringent in the face of the attacks of the "revisionists." As their fabrications of the latest anti-Semitic lie—the denial of the Holocaust—confront those involved with preserving it as a part of the collective memory of the record of human deeds, the need for reliable reviewing becomes all the more essential.

In this way, no matter how imperfect a work may be, it appears in the context of a legitimate and credible intellectual enterprise. There must, in other words, be no room for sanctioning self-serving, narrow interest, parochial or otherwise questionable publications appearing in the guise of contributions or additions to Holocaust knowledge. Reviewing Holocaust literature must separate the wheat from the chaff, quality from mediocrity, to assure the reader of coming into contact with the very best available to date. In this way, his interest will be kept alive and the scholar prompted to nourish that interest, aware of the quality demands of his reading public. In this way can reviewing energize the dynamic between author and reader and help its continuation into the post-Holocaust, post-survivor generations.

NEO-NAZISM AND ANTI-SEMITISM IN THE '70S

By Dr. Cynthia J. Haft

Within a relatively short time after the collapse of Nazi Germany, neo-Fascist and neo-Nazi movements, marked by open and aggressive anti-Semitism, once more surged to the fore. Although the German constitution outlaws both race hatred and attempts to revive the National Socialist party, as early as 1951 the Socialist Reich party had achieved 11% of the vote in Lower Saxony in local elections. In the United States, extreme rightist factions combine racist anti-Negro and anti-Jewish sentiments. In the post-war era, they once again became active as early as 1950. Elsewhere on the four continents the pattern is similar.

During the 1970's, a new form of neo-Nazi activity became discernible: the whitewashing of Hitler and his cohorts, the denial of the Nazi crimes, the rewriting of history in an attempt to show that "the extermination of six million Jews is a figment of the imagination," a "Zionist attempt to extort reparations from Germany and blackmail the world powers into agreeing to the creation of the State of Israel." Adolf Hitler has been portrayed as a "Superstar," as a banal historical figure, a popular leader who rescued Germany from a deep economic crisis—a leader who unified the German people and built a new country, adored by his fellow countrymen, with knowledge of the technique necessary to generate this adoration. He is the subject of records, films, biographies, and even a rock opera.

In addition, a new form of literature became popular and its dissemination widespread—pamphlets and larger works, in many languages, some by accepted historians, denying the Holocaust as "the big lie," "the six million swindle," and the "lie of Odysseus," stating that there were never any gas chambers, that in the normal course of the war, ten thousand or so Jews were killed, and that Hitler never ordered the annihilation of the Jewish people.

The first facet of the complex phenomenon includes desecration of cemeteries, and even more crucial, on memorials to the Holocaust erected on former concentration-camp sites, the painting of swastikas and slogans on public Jewish institutions, as well as private Jewish enterprises. Attacks on the person of individual Jews appear to be the work of disconnected, isolated individuals, without prior consultation, operating outside of an established framework. For example, in eastern France, unknown arsonists set fire to the site of the Stutthof concentration camp and museum built on the grounds, which was burnt to the ground. Jewish cemeteries in Uhlfeld, Bad Windsheim, Gelsenkirchen, and Salzkotten, among others, were desecrated. At the site of the Bergen-Belsen camp, unknown individuals desecrated some eighteen gravestones. In Caracas, Venezuela, swastikas and anti-Semitic slogans appeared on the walls of a Jewish social club. In Montevideo, Uruguay, Jewish youths were attacked. Similar events took place in Bogota and San Fernando, California.

There is certainly place for reflection, and for the posting of certain crucial questions: is this really the work of isolated, unorganized individuals, or rather is it the by-product of organized groups who have been successful in inciting more and more individuals to do its dirty work?

In late March, 1976, Gerhard Lauck, an American Nazi leader was detained in Mainz (Germany) for possession of tens of thousands of anti-Semitic stickers and slogans. These had been fabricated in the United States and brought to Germany for distribution.

The existence, then, of some link between neo-Nazi activities in Germany and the United States does clearly exist. Furthermore, on Nov. 10, 1977, the anniversary of Kristallnacht, in Frankfurt placards bearing the message: "We are here again. May the Red Front be Destroyed—don't buy from Jews" were on display. The placards were signed by the American neo-Nazi party.

In London, when similar slogans were painted on the doors of a synagogue, it was again the work of the American neo-Nazi party. While the party actually has a minimal number of followers in the United States, it has become far more daring in its tactics, holding open meetings and demonstrations. However, its leader has obviously realized that while freedom of speech, press, and life in America in general, are conducive to the production of inflammatory literature, the climate for its dissemination is ripe in Europe, and most particularly in Germany. A poll taken in West Germany, on government initiative, shows that about half of the population harbors anti-Semitic feelings, which could take on aggressive proportions under certain circumstances.

A second, non-government, poll shows that 95% of Germany would like to forget the Nazi epoch. These tendencies to date are more widespread among the elderly, it would appear, in particular those who lived through the Nazi era, while membership in neo-Nazi groups is younger. The neo-Nazi groups have evidently realized that Germany has the potential to become once again the hotbed of anti-Semitism and neo-Nazism, and while they disseminate their propaganda elsewhere as well, especially in South America, the home of many former Nazis, they have come to understand a lesson with which it is perhaps time to come to grips: what has happened once can happen again, and most likely, in the same place, the same comfortable climate. One deviates from the roots of the problem in tending to pass over the importance of the German climate.

Neo-Nazi publications denying the Holocaust have appeared in many languages, during the past years. They have continued in basically the same format, with the same ideas, over the past two years. Their distribution has increased and spread; they are now often distributed at public events. In Innsbruck, for example, spectators at the Winter Olympics were handed pamphlets which attempted to negate the blame placed upon Germany for the extermination of Jews.

In some 120 German cities, monthly meetings of former SS cronies are held in coffee houses, hotels, and restaurants, as reported by *Der Freiwillige,* the official organ of HIAG (*Hilfsgemeinschaft ehemaliger Angerhöriger der Waffen SS*).

It would also appear that there has been less of an attempt to surround these events with their traditional post-war secrecy, thus marking the fact that they now believe that they have less to fear—more to gain than to hide. In Denmark, Danish Nazis held a meeting in Jutland, at which furious demonstrators attacked them.

In Bavaria, at Sonthofen, at a meeting of former SS men, the Knight's Cross was presented to a former SS sergeant. The local command of the West German army authorized the use of a hall. In Mannheim, a meeting of right-wingers, some 800 strong, was held. The participants sported black shirts and Nazi badges glorifying former "heroes." Former SS personnel from Spain, Holland, and Belgium arrived to address the meeting. Hundreds of protestors appeared, but were dispersed by the police. In an apartment in Berlin, a nucleus of some 18 people met to establish a neo-Nazi party. When police broke in, they found a small arsenal of weapons, and signs and propaganda materials, the latter showing that they had originated in the United States.

In Munich, German war veterans held a meeting at the Munich Beer cellar where Hitler had made his abortive putsch in 1923, to demand the pardon of former Nazi criminals. Beate and Serge Klarsfeld led a demonstration of French Jews on the spot; the latter was severely wounded when the participants in the meeting attacked the demonstrators. The American National Socialist Party demonstrated in front of the White House and protested "Jewish control of State and Congress." The American Nazi party also held a conference in a Washington park, and the participants wore wrist bands with swastikas. The speeches were anti-black and anti-Jewish.

During the winter and spring, the American neo-Nazi party received a great deal of publicity in America after they petitioned to march in Skokie, Illinois, a Jewish community, many of whose members are survivors of the Holocaust. Granted the right to march by the Supreme Court, they then changed plans and marched on June 25, 1978, in Chicago, in a park. They numbered some twenty men, and were met by hundreds of enraged protesters.

In Buenos Aires, a mass prayer was scheduled to take place in the Central Church, in Hitler's memory. Due only to technicality, the service was not held. Such a prayer session did take place in Guatemala. In Salisbury, Rhodesia, a new party, the "White Party," was established. Its members sport Nazi uniforms and fly flags bearing the swastika. The purpose of the party is *to oppose Zionism.*" In Pretoria, South Africa, a new party has also sprung up: the *Afrikaner Weerstand Beweging*, advocating a new regime to replace the "British-Jewish" current one. Their meeting hall was decorated in Nazi style.

A pattern of events is clearly discernible: new publications, more meetings, new editions of traditional anti-Semitic works, a greater leniency, especially in Germany, towards the perpetrators of anti-Semitic acts, mark the current period. Greater acceptance, again especially in Germany, of previously banned music, of demonstrations and group meetings, facilitate the work of the neo-Nazis.

"WE'VE SEEN THE FACE OF THE ENEMY AND IT IS UGLY"

By PROF. IRVING ABELLA

As a community we are numbed, outraged, and still in a state of shock. The past . . . weeks has been a terrible nightmare for us all: the horrors of the Holocaust recalled daily on our television screens and in our newspapers; the obscenity of those arguing that not only were there no horrors, but that there was no Holocaust.

Our hearts went out nightly to the survivors of the death camps, and especially to those in the courtroom who were put through a new and individious torture to show that what happened to them really happened. Above all, they were compelled to prove to the world that events too horrible to be believed were not too horrible to have happened. Daily these courageous men were castigated for their very survival. They were sullied, pilloried, and insulted; but they stood fast. They kept their covenant with those who did not survive. In the end, of course, they triumphed. No, society triumphed over the forces of darkness, of bigotry, and hatred. . . .

We have seen the face of the enemy and it is ugly and menacing. People capable of lying about the Holocaust are capable of anything. People so demented, so full of hate, cannot be dismissed lightly in the hope they will go away. They won't, and we must remain vigilant and united.

Fifty years ago the world was divided into two parts—those places where Jews could not live, and those, like Canada, where they could not enter. Fifty years ago the nations of the world were put to the test of civilization and failed ignominously. The failure was not one of tactics, but of the human spirit. The Nazis planned and executed the Holocaust, but it was made possible by an indifference in the Western world to the suffering of the victims. . . .

No one nation showed generosity of heart to those doomed. Not one made the Jewish plight a national priority, and not one willingly opened its doors after the war to the surviving remnant of a once thriving Jewish community. Rescue required sanctuary and there was none. Rescue required concern, but there was only apathy. Rescue required understanding, but there was only hostility.

We live in a far different society today, yet again, in front of a largely indifferent world, Jews struggle for their very existence. Both our future and our past are questioned. There are those who would deny us our future by undermining the State of Israel and by equating Zionism with racism. And there are those who would deny us our past by denying the Holocaust. And in the Zundels of the world these two streams merge. The Jews, they say, have no future because they have no past. This is the new invidious anti-Semitism of the 1980's. And that is why we must remain united. That is why we call out to our friends in the non-Jewish community for the support, understanding, and commitment denied us a generation ago. Zundel is not only an indignity to Jews; he is an indignity to all Canadians, to all men and women of good will.

We rejoice . . . in the decision of 12 ordinary Canadians who were not swayed by the vilest sophistry and demagoguery ever heard in a Canadian court, and who saw Zundel and his henchmen for the racists and hatemongers they are. We rejoice in a country which exacts penalties from those who spread calumnies, lies, and slander. We rejoice in the message of the jury: no more free rides for the hatemongers amongst us, for those who would defame, vex, and harass, for those who would attempt to isolate a community—any community—and destroy it. We rejoice in a legal system that says there are some opinions which are so beyond the pale that they must not be allowed into the free marketplace of ideas.

The Nazi taught us one thing: that lies that go unchallenged become mistaken for truths; they become policies and ultimately they become murders.

We did not take the Holocaust deniers seriously; we did not challenge them head-on. The very obscenity and irrationality of their charges prompted us to underestimate their potential for evil. We have all been guilty of an egregious, though understandable, act of omission. The fault is in us all. We did not react to the big lie with the vigor we should have. Our silence was mistaken for acquiscence. No longer!

Of course, one decision by one jury in one courtroom does not remove the lunacy. . . .

But we must commit ourselves to the task at hand. Those who control the past, George Orwell warned us, control the future, and those who distort Jewish history and deny the Holocaust, create the conditions for the denial of Jewish existence.

M&R 12:12, Sept.-Oct., 1985

(The above are excerpts from an address in response to the Zundel trial in Canada.)

THE HOLOCAUST AND THE BIG LIE

By Dr. Fred R. Crawford

On May 8, 1945, Nazi Germany surrendered, bringing victory in Europe. We had crushed the Nazi monster, but the cost was tremendous in human suffering. Now the world would be free forever from this evil philosophical and political system.

What had been revealed to the free world during those final months as our armies fought eastward were the Nazi concentration camps. Stories flooded the pages of *Life, U.S. News and World Report, The New York Times* and British papers, along with photos taken at Bergen-Belsen; at Buchenwald; at Dachau; at Mauthausen; and at the hundreds of smaller pits of hell. These thrust the truth at Americans back home. Many of us in this room saw a concentration camp at the time of its liberation or shortly thereafter. What we saw we can never forget. Many Americans who saw the news stories and photos also have not forgotten that these were the vestiges of what is now known as The Holocaust.

A few months ago I was interviewing Curtis Mitchell about his new biography of Billy Graham, *Saint or Sinner,* when he touched off the most important effort our Witness to the Holocaust project has done. Serving as a Colonel on General Marshall's staff in charge of all media materials, Curtis had gone to Europe to see a concentration camp. He entered Bergen-Belsen on Day 2. His photographer took photos. Back in Washington he presented his evidence to Marshall, who decided that the American people must be told of the Nazi atrocities Curtis now had seen firsthand. In Curtis' testimony, he expressed the deepest shock at seeing the condition of the survivors; he was surprised that so few Jews were among them. The liberated inmates explained to him that the Jews of Europe had been killed months, even years before, in the death camps of Poland, in the ghettos, in the countryside of the Nazi-conquered nations of Eastern Europe everywhere.

General Marshall decided that the Congress of the United States was the proper body to tell the story of the concentration camps to the American public. He informed Ike, who invited the Congress to send a committee over at once. Senator Alban Barkley and Representative Eduard Izac led the group. We located a copy of the Congressional report and then found Eduard Izac—now 90 years old—who agreed to be interviewed.

He is a most unusual man, the only living member of that Congressional Committee and he wrote the report. A graduate of the U.S. Naval Academy in 1915, he won the Congressional Medal of Honor during World War I by leading an escape of Allied prisoners-of-war out of Germany. He completed his military career and then spent twenty years as U.S. Representative from San Diego. He was a close friend of President Roosevelt....

They (the Committee) saw; they felt; they brought the truth home in photographs and in their report. This evidence stands as the highest verification possible. By May 8, 1945, we knew and the free world knew, that without a doubt, the Nazis had systematically, intentionally, murdered the Jews of Europe. That was the Holocaust: The Holocaust did happen, and anyone then or now who says it didn't is a liar.

But you know and I know that there were liars in the United States then just as there are now. . . . They are also haters. The Big Lie today is any statement by anyone that the Holocaust did not happen! The other dangerous characteristic of the Big Liars is that their hatred is aimed at Jews in particular and frequently spills over to engulf Blacks and other minorities. One group of Liars, and they run together like dogs in packs, are people who hide behind the academic freedom banner by calling themselves "historical revisionists." A second group hides behind the First Amendment by calling themselves "newspapers" like *The Spotlight*. Then there are people who hide behind the flag by calling themselves "patriots" like the John Birchers. And the worst are those who hide under religion by calling themselves "The Christian Crusade" or "The Way" or some other sanctimonious name. The truth seems to be that there are very few leaders who hate so totally that they support and spawn the work of these various kinds of liars including those who not only hate, but will also kill—the Klu Klux Klan and the Nazis.

The Spotlight and media of that ilk are usually recognized for the danger they represent and the fight with them must go on. The two other sources of the lies and hate that make up the Big Lie—certain so-called Christians and the odd "patriots" are very dangerous, very present.

The major Holocaust researchers here and in Israel agree that in many ways the Holocaust did not end on May 8, 1945, and that it can occur again. Then that most terrible of questions is asked. "Why?" Since we started our "Witness to the Holocaust" project at Emory University in 1978, my students have been sifting through all the available documents of the

1930's and 40's—newspapers, magazines, church journals, everything. Our search was for evidence that the murder of Jews—The Holocaust—was being described to American readers then. Robert Ross' new book, *So It Was True*, provides an analysis of the American Protestant press and the way it did present such information on the Nazi persecution of the Jews. . . . On the whole, there was a pervasive attempt to tell the truth about the persecution of the Jews. The resultant "Silence" from the American Christian population identifies the "why's" first ingredient: apathy.

. . . Anti-Semitism was rampant and deadly with its lies and hate. I felt this hate personally on June 16, 1944. My P-51 fighter was shot down—by mistake—by an American P-38. My parachute dropped me to earth in a pasture not far from Lake Balaton in Hungary. Country people carrying axes, rakes, shovels and a few guns surrounded me, tried to communicate with me. They tried Hungarian and then German before realizing I was an American. The first words I understood were "Jews" and "Hunde." I was not a Jew and saw no dogs around. But that mob meant me and proceeded to lynch me. Eventually I was dragged to the nearest tree to be hanged. One man grabbed my collar to put the noose on, and his fingers got tangled with my dogtag chain. He pulled it out. In the morning sunlight a small gold cross on my chain sparkled. This Christian symbol snapped that bunch of Catholic Hungarians back and I was saved. The mob in its anti-Semitism and hatred gave me the identity of a Jew and dealt with me as they did with Jews; hate them and then kill them. . . .

Because I was not a Jew, I was taken up to a stalag as a P.O.W. and then down to Stalag VII near Dachau, a place we were warned to stay away from. On April 29, 1945, Gen. Patch's Seventh Army liberated Dachau and Gen. Patton's Third liberated us. On April 30, I went to Dachau with a lifetime friend from home who found me in Stalag VII. We were there the same day part of that Congressional Committee was there. What I saw, smelled and felt remains with me still.

Over the past 35 years I have told this story to many Christian groups and most of them believed me. The public's general negative response to NBC's *The Holocaust* television series prompted us to seek out American soldiers, nurses, Red Cross workers, as many witnesses who saw the camps as we could, and to get their testimonies, and give these to the public. Walter Cronkite helped by telling of our work on CBS Evening News one night. We have more than 50 names of witnesses to the Holocaust. We have interviewed 105 and just now have completed surveying the remainder by questionnaire. We have been given original documents, hundreds of still photos and even movie films taken by these witnesses. The importance of this source of evidence is now recognized. . . .

Gentlemen, we destroyed the Nazi armies; we won the war. But the free world failed to understand, possibly refused to understand, that the source of the Holocaust was anti-Semitism and that anti-Semitism had not been destroyed, but was still smoldering and vicious even among many who had fought Hitler. A case was just brought to my attention involving a World War II veteran and his efforts to obey *The Spotlight's* request to obtain the names of the American soldiers who when Dachau was liberated "shot the German guards." *The Spotlight*—great patriotic rag that it is—wants to try these men as murderers. This veteran requested these names in his Division's newsletter, also saying that the Institute of Historical Review was behind it. We began to call and check on this man only to learn that the current president of this WWII division's organization was, back during the war, and still is, an avid anti-Semite. Anti-Semitism blocked the American public's acceptance of the Holocaust in post-war years, blocked our concern for the plight of the Jewish survivors, and today is the basis of the hating and of the lying aimed at The Holocaust itself. Why? Because to any rational human being, the Holocaust in all of its tragedy proved what happens when anti-Semitism dominates. The haters must destroy the truth of the Holocaust.

The haters are having trouble doing this. So they have expanded their target and now are attacking World War II itself. Now they want the American soldier to believe he was as bad as the German or Hungarian soldier, that our bombing of enemy cities was the same kind of evil as Hitler created in the death camps; that the death of civilians in Germany and its partners that we caused is worse than the intentional murders the Nazis carried out against the Jews. The truth as seen by every American soldier during that war must be brought to light. The witnesses we have contacted tell the truth, and this we share as widely as possible. . . .

First, hate—then murder. The Holocaust will happen again unless people who treasure truth over lies actively oppose anti-Semitism; unless people who understand the power of love and reject hate actively oppose anti-Semitism; unless people who believe in this greatest of nations and its future and value its freedom above self as you have done during each time of war, also oppose anti-Semitism. Now is the time, this is our duty and obligation, this is America's golden opportunity for the majority of our people, Jews and non-Jews, to rally together and expose and contain the anti-Semitic haters and their lies. By so doing, the safety, freedom, and future of all of us will be established, because as the German Christians learned too late, anti-Semitism ultimately seeks to destroy all truth and every religious faith, to destroy everything we hold to be good. Gentlemen, as Americans under this flag, we have served as comrades-in-arms to oppose foreign enemies, and we have prevailed. Now let us march together in peace against the common enemy called "anti-Semitism" so that there will never be another Holocaust.

M&R 8:3, Jan.-Feb., 1982; 8:6, March-April, 1982
Reprinted by permission of *The Jewish Veteran* © Sept./Oct. 1981

SPECTER OF KRISTALLNACHT

By PROFESSOR HENRY R. HUTTENBACH

Almost half a century ago, on November 9-10, 1938, Nazi terrorists struck at Jewish houses of worship throughout the Third Reich; during those nightmarish twenty-four hours, hundreds of synagogues were put to the torch and their religious contents willfully desecrated. The state-orchestrated assault on the heart of the Jewish religion in which untold numbers of sacred scrolls were tragically burned was the beginning of the Hitlerian campaign to expunge violently all signs of Jewish life from the German scene.

A few years later, during the invasion of the Soviet Union, units of the mobile killing force, the Einsatzgruppen, burned Jews alive in synagogues throughout Eastern Europe, from Riga on the Baltic Sea to Odessa on the Black Sea. Soon thereafter, the vision of a Judenrein society reached its climax in Auschwitz with the burning of millions of Jewish bodies.

As Europe emerged from the smoldering ruins of World War II and came face to face with the events of the Holocaust, who would have thought then that a generation later, Jews and their synagogues would once again fall prey to similar

acts of murder and arseny? Who would have predicted that
forty years later, with the memories of the death camps still
fresh before the eyes of mankind, that a new campaign against
Jews would be in progress, fed by the same psychotic hatred
that had fuelled the flames of the crematoria? Who could have
anticipated that in the 1980's no Jew in any country could
feel safe while worshipping? Who had the foresight to predict
that Jews would fall victims to a concerted war against them
on an international scale from Western Europe to Latin
America?

And, yet, as a simple glance at the following chronological
list will suggest, the ghost of Kristallnacht seems to have
resurrected with a vengeance:

The first incident took place in 1980 when Jewish schoolchildren were attacked (3 killed and 106 wounded) on their
way to synagogue in Antwerp, Holland; other acts of terrorism followed with savage regularity;

October 3, 1980. A bomb explodes outside a synagogue
on the rue Copernic in Paris, France;

August 29, 1981: Two Arabs with hand grenades and
automatic pistols kill 2 Jews and wound 20 others during a
Bar Mitzvah ceremony in Vienna, Austria;

Rosh Hashanah, 1982: Arab terrorists attack a synagogue
during services in Brussels, Belgium;

Sukkot, 1982: A 2-year-old boy is killed and 34 wounded
in an attack on the Great Synagogue in Rome, Italy;

August 7, 1983: A mine explodes prior to a visit by a
government official to a synagogue in Johannesburg, South
Africa;

January 3, 1984: Firebombs cause severe damage to two
synagogues (though no casualties) in Rosario and Buenos
Aires, Argentina;

July 22, 1985: Over a dozen people are wounded when a
bomb explodes in the synagogue in Copenhagen, Denmark.

And, now, on September 6, 1986, the worst of the attacks
took place in Istanbul, Turkey. On that Sabbath, 22 Jews were
machinegunned to death; among them were seven rabbis. Not
content with simple murder, the Arab terrorists attempted to
burn the bodies of their innocent Jewish victims by pouring
gasoline over them. Evidently, attacking Jews in synagogues
has become part of the Arab terrorist repertoire. Credit for
the majority of the assaults was claimed by Palestinian "liberation" gangs.

What have Austrian, Belgium, and French Jews and synagogues to do with Israel? By what stretch of the imagination

does one associate the war against Israel with old men in
Istanbul and children in Antwerp? How does the destruction
of religious buildings weaken the state of Israel? The logic of
association claimed by the terrorists is too transparent to hide
their real intentions.

What falls under the false rubric of anti-Zionism is
nothing but another face of anti-Semitism. The anti-Israeli
rhetoric is but a camouflage for unadulterated hatred of Jews
and Judaism. Synagogues and their congregations are legitimate (logically speaking) targets only if the motivation is
anti-Semitism, a hatred for Jews as Jews. To equate all Jews
with Zionists is merely a deceptive ploy, a propaganda device,
to distract the rest of the world from the true aims of the
terrorists. Their goal, as that of the Nazis (their spiritual
mentors), is to eradicate Jews not only from Israel but from
the rest of the world.

Supported by a medley of states whose policy is to export
terrorism and to destabilize the international community, the
Arab terrorists are able to reach around the world, almost
with impugnity as long as the countries in whose territories
these crimes are committed do not forge a strong stand against
these blatant violations of their sovereignty. For the moment,
Jewish communities outside of Israel are constant targets of
this international Arab-sponsored crime. For the moment, it is
taking the form of the tactics reminiscent of Kristallnacht
nearly fifty years ago. Nothing demonstrates more clearly the
need for Jewish unity in the face of a common enemy. But
will the international community of host states assist them
unequivocably? Or will it stand by idle as in 1938?

Will the attack on Congregation Neve Shalom in Istanbul
be the last, or merely another in an unbroken chain of assaults
on Jews and their synagogues throughout the world? Will
the violence be suppressed or is it the prelude to even worse
crimes against the Jewish people? Has the lesson from the
past been learned, or will history repeat itself? Are we about
to reexperience the crossing of the Kristallnacht threshold?
The recent years pose the questions; the immediate future
will provide the answers. Will world Jewry remain passive or
will Israel help it to overcome the heirs of Hitler? How many
more synagogues must burn before the conscience of mankind
is stirred into action? No more? Or all of them?

M&R 13:13, Nov.-Dec. 1986.

ARE WE FOCUSING
ON HOLOCAUST TOO MUCH?

By Dr. Irving Greenberg

There has been an extraordinary rise in consciousness of the Holocaust in American life in the past 15 years. Until the late Sixties Yom HaShoa was hardly noted in United States; now its observance has spread to thousands of synagogues and communities. Since 1979, the United States Government itself annually declares Yom HaShoa a national day of commemoration and the White House and Congress participate in impressive ceremonies.

In 1963, I introduced a course on the Holocaust at Yeshiva University. It was, to my knowledge, the second such course to be taught anywhere in American universities. The course was offered under the title, "Totalitarianism and Ideology in the 20th Century" because the administration felt that the Holocaust was not yet a fully respectable academic subject. Today, such courses are given at hundreds of universities; it is believed to be the most widely offered topic in Jewish studies on American university campuses.

There has been an explosion of books dealing with the Holocaust. Media programs and films with Holocaust themes have proliferated. Holocaust Memorial Centers have been established in seven North American cities and more are in development. The United States Holocaust Memorial Council is charged with establishing a national memorial just off the mall in Washington—the central visiting spot for Americans coming to the capital.

As attention to the subject has grown, objections have been raised that this is an unhealthy trend. A distinguished Jewish scholar, Prof. Jacob Neusner, has argued that there is something ersatz in the focus on the Holocaust and the associated myth of death (Holocaust) and resurrection (re-birth of Israel) which has seized the imagination of American Jewry. Says Neusner: American Jews are adopting as their myth (e.g. guiding story) events which are the life experience of other Jewries; thus, they choose to live vicariously through others instead of pursuing their own actual Jewish ways of living.

Michael Wyschogrod charged that there is an attempt to

259

substitute the Holocaust for the central Jewish message of redemption and that "inserted at the heart of Judaism, the Holocaust will necessarily destory Judaism. . . ."

At one general assembly of the Council of Jewish Federations, Rabbi Harold Schulweis added his extraordinary eloquent voice to the warnings against excessive attention to the Holocaust. Said Schulweis: "The Holocaust is the dominant psychic reality of our generation . . . It serves us as the ultimate rationale of our philanthropy, our theology, our pedagogy, our Zionism. . . ." To which he objects: "We need another mentality, another philosophy, another morality, another way of transmitting Jewish faith to the next generation. We will not transmit a Jewish will to live through a fear of death . . . We cannot build a healthy Jewish identity of the pillars of fear and anger and guilt."

Schulweis' words are wise and right; but I believe that their tone is wrong. Judaism's fundamental message is that life will totally triumph. Substituting the Holocaust story of death triumphant for the message of redemption would be an inversion of Jewish values; it would be the posthumous victory for Hitler which Holocaust theologians have feared. However, substitution is not what is going on in Jewish life today.

Coming after two decades of traumatized numbness, with Jewry bearing a wound festering so deep that it could not be exposed, the fever of attention to the Holocaust is a fundamental part of the reassertion of the life and health on the part of the Jewish people. As in the case of fever itself, physicians now recognize that the heat is less a symptom of the disease and more the counterattack of the healthy defenses against a foreign threatening invader.

The best proof that we have not stressed the Holocaust too much is the worldwide surge in anti-Semitism. For almost two decades, the stigma of association of even mild anti-Semitism with the atrocities of the Holocaust served as a shield for the Jewish people. The waning of Holocaust consciousness as the people alive in 1945 have died out weakened the barrier and allowed a resurgence of "respectable" anti-Semitism (often disguised as anti-Zionism to make it more respectable).

The critics of all this attention to the catastrophe turned out to be "premature Messianists" who taught that the lessons of the Holocaust were already learned. Anti-Semites thought otherwise. The remarkable surge in communicating about the Holocaust came just in time.

Anti-Semitic groups see how powerful awareness of the

Holocaust undermines them and, therefore, they have generated a "revisionist" group which seeks to deny that the Holocaust occurred. While the phenomenon of denial is outrageous, Jews cannot stop anti-Semites from trying to lie their way out of the burden of the mass murder. The best response is not to argue with the revisionists and thereby give them dignity, but to bury them under a mountain of evidence, accounts, courses, portrayals of the Holocaust in every form and medium—and the more the better.

In fact, we are just in the early stage of our efforts to study the Holocaust and to teach about it. We need Holocaust memorial centers in every city to commemorate it properly and to teach Jews and non-Jews alike the central issues in confronting this tragedy. . . .

Ultimately, the real issue is that the Holocaust is one of those rare historical events that transforms the world's—and Jewry's—self-understanding. The event must be studied in all its aspects and implications so as to come to grips with it and then try to apply the understanding to various aspects of life. The implications of the Holocaust need to be incorporated into a host of areas: culture, scholarship, liturgy and observance.

Of course, there will be excesses or attempts at substitution or even the risk of a depressing "faddishness." Such phenomena should be criticized or fought, but they are inescapable parts of an historic process of development. These abuses should not be tolerated, but they should not be confused with the central development—the incorporation of a major orienting event into Jewish (and universal) self-understanding comparable to the impact of the destruction of the Second Temple on Judaism and ultimately on world culture.

One thing is clear already. The Jewish message of life and redemption is being reaffirmed by Jewry in one of the most remarkable outbursts of life and culture in our history. But without confronting the Holocaust, one cannot truly appreciate the incredible power of this message. Facing up to Treblinka, one begins to grasp the greatness of faith which, knowing all the massed power of death, is yet able to defy the odds and persist and overcome ultimate evil.

One cannot truly appreciate what an act of life and affirmation of the State of Israel represents: one cannot understand how inescapable and necessary taking power was and how much the central question of Jewish life is developing an ethic of power— unless one has wrestled with the despair of mass death and the powerlessness of Jews during the Holocaust.

Finally, one cannot grasp the heroism of the Jewish people . . . without this confrontation. The very acts of life—singing, dancing, eating, praying, loving—which the critics of Holocaust theology point to—attain depth and extraordinary dimension in the encounter with the Holocaust. This is incorporation, not substitution. . . .

M&R 10:6, Sept.-Oct., 1983

"UNKNOWN" RUSSIAN HEROINE REFLECTS ANTI-SEMITISM

A few months ago if you had mentioned the name Marsha Bruskina to a student of Holocaust, even to a bona fide scholar, you might not have received a response. However, it may not be long before that name will be sounded in varied forums and activities concerned with the Holocaust.

The newly found awareness is partially due to a front-page story in *The New York Times*. Masha Bruskina is thought to have been the first person publicly executed in the Nazi occupation. However, the 17-year-old heroine has been identified by Soviet authorities for decades as an "unknown partisan." The sequence of pictures of the hanging in Minsk on Oct. 26, 1941, is reproduced in Soviet textbooks, encyclopedias, and museums, especially the Minsk Museum of the History of the Great Patriotic War. In all these places, the girl remains "nyetzvestnaya"—"unknown."

Two male companions hanged alongside her were partisans of Byelorussian stock. A few years after the war's end, they were identified by family members and posthumously honored. However, the heroine was never "recognized" although she was identified by several, most authoritatively by her uncle, in 1968. The girl had lived with the uncle, Zahir I. Azgur, before the war. A professional sculptor, Azgur was called by the *New York Times*, "a connoisseur of faces."

The case received public attention in Minsk about 20 years ago when a Russian screenwriter Lev Arkadyev was doing a film on the war and came across the photo. The photograph was published by a local Minsk paper and led to a number of responses, one being that of the uncle.

Among those deeply interested in the case then, according to the *Times* article by Bill Keller, was a Soviet radio reporter Ada Dikhtyar. But now she sees some hope of the case's resolution: "The times are changing, and I'm convinced that in the next year, we'll finally bring this to a proper conclusion."

Why do Russian authorities continue to deny the bravery of Marsha Bruskina, and have kept the case closed since the investigation 20 years ago? Many Minsk Jews view this case one of anti-Semitism, and, on a wider scale, one of denying honor to Jewish heroism during the war.

In Byelorussia, some 80,000 Jews died during the Holocaust, alongside 2.2 million non-Jewish victims of the war. "There is a resentful feeling," writes Keller, "that Jews have tried to assert a monopoly over the pain of the war."

Mrs. Dikhtyar, however, sees discussions in magazines "condemning Russian nationalist groups that believe in a worldwide Jewish conspiracy" as a hopeful sign for the case. In any event, she is planning a book on the Minsk heroine and is considering filing a law suit with a Russian federal prosecutor.

XII. The Holocaust & Other Genocides

Like a thunderbolt, the phenomenon of the Holocaust, the state-ordered extermination of millions of Jews, has revolutionized modern political thought. The state crime of genocide, the targetting of a particular group, now lies within the practical range of political action. No group can feel completely safe in the face of the power of the state. Military, technological, and bureaucratic power have combined to form a lethal alliance when prompted by sufficient ideological or circumstantial stimulation.

Millions of Ukrainian peasants fell to the minions of Stalin's USSR; uncounted hundreds of thousands of Communists fell to the onslaughts of post-colonial Indonesia. Genocidal rage threatened to wipe out millions of Hindus in Moslem Pakistan and similar millions of Moslems in Hindu India. And three million (non-Jewish) Poles were killed in Nazi Germany's unsuccessful campaign to destroy the Polish nation and reduce its people to little more than chattel. The Age of Genocide had arrived.

How to relate the Jewish experience to the tragedy of other peoples has prompted considerable debate and ill-feeling. How to prevent the loss of particularity, of uniqueness, has been an on-going concern in the face of East European governments' co-opting Jewish victims to swell the ranks of their own national losses: 3 million Polish Jews were indiscriminately lumped alongside 3 million Christian Poles; the 30,000 Jews from Kiev who were murdered in Babi Yar became simply Soviet citizens.

Over the years, the Jewish Holocaust lost its specificity as journalists, politicians and academicians spoke of nuclear "holocaust," "genocide" against the Vietnamese, thereby obfuscating and diluting terminology and comprehension.

The struggle to define the Holocaust, establish its proper context, and defend it from those dedicated to falsifying history, continues. The outcome of this intellectual battle may, in the long run, be as important as the fact of the Holocaust itself.

A valuable examination of genocide in our era is offered in *Genocide: Its Political Uses in the Twentieth Century* (Leo Kuper, 9:1 Sept.-Oct. 1982, Review, Charles R. Allen, Jr.)

THE OTHER 'HOLOCAUSTS'

The Harvest of Sorrow: Soviet Collectivization and the Terror-Famine. Robert Conquest. Oxford University Press, 1986. 412pp. $19.96; *Forgotten Holocaust: The Poles Under German Occupation, 1939-1944.* Richard C. Lukas. Kentucky University Press, 1986. 223pp. $24; *No Time-Limit for These Crimes.* Czeslav Pilichowski. Warsaw, 1980. 143pp. No price listed.

Reviewed by PROFESSOR HENRY R. HUTTENBACH

Slowly but irrevocably, the word "Holocaust" is becoming a universal term for not only all victims of Nazism but for others not associated with World War II. Once the designated appellation for the extermination of European Jewry, "Holocaust," has become the common nomenclature for the entire Polish experience under German rule. Furthermore, according to the policies of the President's Commission on the Holocaust, "Holocaust" may include not only Gypsies (as victims of extermination policies of the Nazis) but also Armenians (whose tragic experience dates back to World War I). Thus, Holocaust has not only lost its Jewish specificity but its historical temporal particularity. It has become a convenient umbrella term to cover all horrors.

This poses a new burden on scholars entrusted with the task of writing the history of the genocide of the Jews in a genocidal era: how to preserve clarity, in the face of terminological obfuscation, and how to uphold integrity, in a highly politicized subject. Forty years after Auschwitz, the fate of the Jews and the history of their suffering must be constantly safeguarded from forces determined to equate, subsume, submerge, and even to deny.

At the same time, the scholar of the Final Solution must face the delicate question of what this reviewer calls scholarly "parochialism" with respect to the accumulated academic literature on the annihilation of 6 million Jews: namely the complete avoidance of placing the policy of ridding Europe of all its Jews in the contexts of Hitler's grand scheme to obliterate other peoples and in the broader scope of the numerous state-induced massacres that characterize the 20th century. Instead of taking the intellectual initiative and locating the crime against the Jews within the spectrum of other genocides and near-genocides, scholars have held defensively to the theory of "uniqueness," thereby bypassing the obligation to be fair and accurate, and losing the initiative to others. This intellectual timidity has not led to greater clarity or academic integrity.

Stalin's campaign in the early 1930's against the peasantry in general and against the Ukrainians in particular is a case in point. Scholars of anti-Semitism from Poliakov to Bauer and Uriel Tal have made much of the fact that the word "Jew" became an artificial term signifying the devil, a non-human creature capable of satanic deeds, having absolutely no relationship to the Jew in real life. Yet, had they turned their attention to what these historians must have known—namely to the Stalin ideological wars against the kulaks—they would have been able to show fundamental similarities in totalitarian regimes. "Kulak"—as pointed out by Vasily Grosman, himself a Jewish writer much involved with the Final Solution—is nothing but a synonym for everything that is loathsome: a parasite, a pariah, a swine, an enemy of the people, disease, etc.—in other words, everything but a human being, the very antithesis of what is human, and, therefore, subject to extermination.

As Robert Conquest calculates—conservatively—the results were literally millions of victims: every man, woman, and child in the Soviet countryside was a potential "kulak." In all, six and a half million peasants were killed for the "crime" of being "kulaks," the majority of them Ukrainian farmers. In all, 11 million peasants died, alongside another three and a half million urban people: again, most Ukrainians.

Even as he waged a war against private farming, Stalin also conducted a campaign of near-extermination against the Ukrainian people and their culture. One of his weapons was a state-initiated famine: sealing off the territory of the Ukraine, Stalin extracted its rich harvests and left its populations to die during 1932-33. The story (and photographs) of the mass deaths in the cities, towns, and villages of the Ukraine makes a terrible prelude to the starvation imposed on the Jews incarcerated in ghettos by the Nazis a few years later. The willful campaign against Ukrainian culture—language, museums, schools, libraries, archives, and intellectuals—reads like an introduction to the Jewish experience in which the Germans not only killed Jewish people but sought to extirpate all signs of Jewish culture, including cemeteries.

Conquest writes nothing that historians of 20th century Europe did not know already. The silence surrounding the Ukrainian experience which antedated the Jewish one has ominous parallels with what happened during World War II. The world press suppressed, reporters prevaricated, and the news that did get out moved no governments to action, in particular the Roosevelt administrations. It all sounds so drearily familiar except that in this instance the people involved were not Jews but Ukrainians.

The fate of the Poles—simultaneously with that of the Jews—has also been given short shrift, indeed almost ignored by those concerned with putting the Final Solution into the record books. A book about to appear by Holocaust Publications by Israel Gutman and Shmuel Krakowski entitled *Unequal Victims: Poles and Jews during World War II* focuses almost exclusively on the Jews, leaving one to guess in which way the Poles were victims though "unequally." An answer is given by a Polish scholar, Pilichowski, in his account of the toll in human and material costs of the German occupation and its racist policies.

According to Pilichowski, the Germans waged a war of national extermination against Poles even as they carried out genocide against the Jews of Poland. Devoting an entire chapter to the Jews, Pilichowski seeks to place this episode of German policy into a greater framework which included the Poles. Using well-known documents, Pilichowski makes a credible case that between 1939-42 the German forged a policy and began to execute a goal of erasing both Poland and its people from the map of Europe. In other words, he sees Poles and Jews not as unequal but as equal targets of a German policy to wipe out both groups as soon as possible.

Unfortunately, he fails to explain why the Germans retreated from annihilating the Poles but zealously continued to kill Jews; even more disturbing, in the light of his seeming accuracy, is Pilichowski's failure to recognize the Polish contribution to the Final Solution. The scholarly world awaits an objective comparison of the Jews and Poles as victims of genocidal intentions.

A recent attempt at this appears in the study by Professor Lukas. Coopting the term Holocaust to signify genocide in general, Lukas makes the same case as Pilichowski with respect to the genocidal intentions of the Nazis against the Poles with even broader documentation, though none of it unknown to scholars of the Shoa. Unfortunately, in his chapter on Poles and Jews, Lukas reveals his polemical side: he becomes increasingly apologetic about the role of Polish anti-Semitism during World War II. Instead of acknowledging it as historical fact, an active and passive ally of the Nazis, Lukas seeks to shift some of the blame on the Jews for the deep anti-Semitism that afflicted various strata of Polish society.

According to Lukas, the Jews' failure to assimilate and to become *bona fide* Poles is a major cause of Polish antipathy. The Jews' welcoming German occupation during World War I —namely siding with the enemies of the Poles—also stirred up strong feelings about their patriotic reliability. That so many Jews were socialists and even Communists also made them a political threat in the eyes of the Poles. Their part in promoting Soviet interests was seen as a betrayal of Poland.

Lukas does not mention that high members of the Polish clergy rationalized that in time some good would come out of the German occupation, namely, the removal of the Jews from Polish soil: Instead, he claims, that between 1939-42, Poles perceived themselves to be worse off than Jews, unequal victims at their expense. After all, Lukas points out, were not Poles the first to be deported en masse long before the Jews?

Historically there is some truth to this, but it is not the whole truth. We must await scholars who are willing and able to write the broader history of the fate of the six million Jews in the light of what happened to others, beginning with the Poles and the Ukrainians. For Jewish historians, this will take considerable courage. But scholarship without courage is not worth the paper it is printed on.

M&R 13:2, March-April, 1987

THE HOLOCAUST AND "HOLOCAUSTS"

By ALFRED LIPSON

There is a disturbing trend of using the Nazi Holocaust, an unparalleled event in the history of mankind, and lumping it together with other unrelated events.

John Cardinal O'Connor of New York considers abortion "another holocaust." John Cardinal Krol went even further when addressing 10,000 Jewish Holocaust survivors in Philadelphia in April, 1985, marking the 40th anniversary of liberation from the Nazi death camps. Krol stated that the Nazi Holocaust was only a part of a string of holocausts, starting

with the massacre of Armenians by the Turks in 1915, the
gulags in the Soviet Union and culminating in the "murder of
millions of unborn" by abortion.

These comparisons are unfortunate and absurd. There is
no analogy to the enormous evil—the organized slaughter of
European Jews by the Nazis and their willing collaborators.
One does not wish to enter into a dispute with cardinals,
only to wonder aloud: Where were the cardinals of Rome
while six million Jews were being exterminated in the heart
of Europe, in broad daylight, on the soil of devoutly Catholic
Poland? Thirty million Polish Christians watched with indifference, many of them with delight, at seeing the "Christ-
killers" finally eliminated. The silence of the Church was
devastating and must have been interpreted in Poland and
elsewhere as encouragement for this stand. The Vatican was
not that far from Auschwitz not to have heard the deafening
cries of its victims.

The Holocaust was a unique event with implications for
the Christian world because of its historical tradition of anti-
Semitism which led to the Final Solution. Some Christian
leaders and writers have, therefore, tried to universalize the
Holocaust by "proving" that Jews were not the only victims.
Thus, they hope to diminish or completely erase the burden of
guilt initially felt by the outside world. As a result, we now
confront a tragic irony—requests to join in memorializing the
"Armenian holocaust" and the "Ukrainian holocaust."

Ukrainian holocaust? Does this refer to the Chmielnicki
pogroms against the Jewish communities in the Ukraine and
Poland in 1648-1649? Of course not. Or was it the Babi Yar
massacre of nearly 100,000 Jewish men, women and children
of the Ukrainian city of Kiev? . . . Ukrainians were killed
by the Nazis—on the battlefield, when the Germans invaded
the Soviet Union in June 1941. The Ukrainians wore Soviet
uniforms. Many of those who surrendered to the Germans
changed allegiance, donned SS uniforms and became our executioners in the ghettos and camps.

This attempt at historical revisionism and of distorting
the Holocaust is an ongoing process. It robs the Holocaust of
its moral significance. It is a betrayal of the sacred memory
of those who perished in the gas chambers, a profanation of
the destroyed Jewish communities and their cultural values.

One despairs to see some Jewish leaders join this obscene
process of diluting and diminishing the Holocaust. Perhaps
they do it unwittingly. Or is it just an attitude of callousness?
A rabbi conducting funeral services for Leon Klinghoffer,

the victim of a horrible murder on the cruise ship Achille Lauro, refers to the case as a "holocaust of one." The media broadcasts this reference to millions of viewers. To the learned rabbi, it was just a rhetorical exaggeration. To the Klinghoffer family, I surmise, it was an embarrassment. But it is a distortion, nevertheless. Victims of the Holocaust had no funerals and no graves—and no rabbis to deliver eulogies.

We have no choice but to ignore, with disgust, frequent references in the media to the "Lebanon holocaust" or, most recently, to the "Maltese holocaust," the bungled attempt to rescue hostages on the Egyptair plane in Malta. . . .

[Also] the use of the Holocaust as a metaphor for assimilation is unforgivable. There is not even a remote equivalent to my mother's and my little sister's agonizing death in the Auschwitz gas chamber.

Abusing the Holocaust in every crisis, real or imagined, is tantamount to yelling "fire" in a crowded movie theater. If, God forbid, the real danger arises, no one will pay attention.

M&R 12:13, March-April, 1986

DEFINING THE HOLOCAUST

By Dr. Franklin H. Littell

At least half the letters which flood the office of the National Institute on the Holocaust/Anne Frank House display an appalling ignorance of the basic information of the Holocaust. Since almost all of them, with the exception of a small percentage of "poison pen" and threatening letters come from persons who are moved to learn more, we must assume that the public at large is even more ignorant.

A typical recent letter asks, "What are you doing about **other holocaust**s suffered by other nations?" (emphases added). Several ask about the "holocaust" of the Jews and millions of others killed by the Nazis. Some of them reflect absorption of Simon Wiesenthal's concept of 11,000,000 "victims of the Holocaust"—6,000,000 Jews and 5,000,000 gentiles.

All of this is profoundly misleading, and it prevents a real comprehension of the Holocaust and what its lessons are for Jews and other peoples.

The kind of thing involved is this: instead of speaking of the Exodus and what it has come to mean for Jews and other peoples, we are to spend our time comparing wanderings of the Hebrews with the wanderings of the Goths and Visigoths—not to forget the Huns from the Siberian steppes and the aborigines who are said to long ago have crossed the frozen Bering Straits to North America.

The Russians will talk only of the 22 million Russians who lost their lives during "the great Patriotic War" against Nazi Germany. And the Polish officials in Warsaw: they would talk only of the six million Poles who died at the hands of the Germans.

Thus, what the Jews who perished in the Holocaust were unable to attain in their lifetime, they have now acquired in death: they are counted as Russian and Polish "population losses."

The Marxists cannot cope with the Holocaust for the same reason as liberal Protestants, modern humanists, and other intellectual progeny of the Enlightenment. They can talk about "humanity," but appreciation of the particular escapes them. They can talk about "universal laws," but unique events are beyond their ken.

The Holocaust refers, speaking correctly, to the planned murder of six million Jews in Hitler's area of conquest (most of them in Eastern Europe).

Genocide, now a defined crime, refers only to the planned destruction of targeted groups of people. The Holocaust is a uniquely powerful illustration of genocide if genocide is on the agenda.

Mass murder, of which history has a surfeit (including the 20th century), includes phenomena beyond the parameters of Holocaust and Genocide.

It is now charged that modern war, which is directed primarily against civilian populations rather than against soldiers in uniform, is an incidence of mass murder. Yet the purpose of modern war, even the most ruthless execution of it, is not to destroy enemy peoples; the purpose is to comply their submission.

Omnicide is a term which enjoys some circulation, and it refers to nuclear warfare. . . . This realized eschatology— "Apocalypse Now"—has become a real possibility, a real accomplishment of modern science, and persons of conscience are concerned about it.

Yet, "omnicide" is not intended nor is it planned by individuals in power—not the dictators in the Kremlin, not the

administrators in Washington. Omnicide is not an extension
of genocide, and even less an expansion of the Holocaust.
Omnicide is, if it occurs, an extension of the logic of modern
war and militarism.

In June, 1985, there will be held in a suburb of Hiroshima, Japan, at the 40th anniversary of the atomic bomb,
a Second International Symposium on the Holocaust and
Genocide. The distinctions here made are important if such a
conference is not to slide into generalizations neither helpful
nor true.

The use of the atom bomb on Hiroshima and Nagasaki
was not "Holocaust." Neither was it "genocide."

Like the Exodus, rightly understood, it helps all people
of conscience to a new and more vivid appreciation of the
worth of human life.

M&R 9:14, March-April, 1984

THE HOLOCAUST AND
ISRAEL'S FOREIGN POLICY

By PROF. HENRY R. HUTTENBACH

One of the lasting consequences of the experience of
genocide is collective trauma, a permanent awareness of
existential danger, a deep-seated reflex which profoundly
affects all thought and action. Despite the passage of time,
the Jewish people suffer increasingly from the shock of the
Holocaust. Even those born after Auschwitz carry the psychological scars brought on by the cognitive encounter with the
Holocaust reality. Not only do all Jews identify with the victims, but more and more see themselves as potential victims
of a future outbreak of anti-Semitism in a world whose
capacity for genocidal behaviour has by no means diminished
since the end of World War II.

Not surprisingly, all kinds of defensive and precaution-
ary steps are taken to diagnose circumstances for their pre-
Holocaust content: the plight of Argentinian Jewry is a case
in point. Literally every instance of violence against Jewish
persons and property is automatically assessed in terms of
the physical assaults launched by the Nazis during the early
stages of their anti-Semitic campaign. Despite collective efforts
to remain calm and objective, Jews find it more than difficult,

if not impossible, to assess the dangers in the world around them without feeling the chilling influence of the long shadow cast by the Holocaust. For non-Jews to ignore the trauma of the Holocaust is to fail to comprehend the particularity of the Jewish psyche as it struggles to accommodate itself in the post-Holocaust era.

Not to take the Holocaust factor into consideration in the formation and execution of Israeli foreign policy will unavoidably lead to serious misunderstanding and miscalculation on the part of both the neutral observer and the involved diplomat. To assume that the foreign policy of Israel is forged like that of any other nation is to turn a blind eye to the single most operative mainspring in the thinking of its architects, the existential element, the struggle to preserve the Jewish state in order to guarantee the survival of the Jewish people.

To be sure, other countries have forged their foreign policies with an implacable enemy in mind, but never with the fear of complete extinction—both political and demographic —motivating their thinking. In the long and bitter history between Poland and Russia, both have had opportunities to invade one another and impose their will upon each other. Yet, despite ideologically extreme animosities—Catholic vs. Orthodox Christian, Soviet communism vs. Polish nationalism —neither people fear demographic annihilation at the hands of the other, if only because they sense security from the absolute size of their populations.

From its very inception, the Israeli State has had to contend with enemies that denied its legitimacy and were determined to erase it physically from the map. With almost every one in the original cabinet and decision-making organizations having experienced losses in the Holocaust, the initial response to the Arab determination to obliterate all vestiges of the Jewish state and its population could not but be one fanatically dedicated to the prevention of the repetition of genocide that had but a few years earlier wiped out a third of the Jewish people. The fighting units of the Yishuv and of the early Jewish state were increasingly replenished with survivors who fought with the additional conviction of having experienced genocide. For them, the Arab threat to wipe Israel from the map was more than rhetoric but the resurrection of a policy they had personally recently witnessed. Fresh out of the death-camps and with the shock of the past etched in their faces, the recent arrivals helped make the Holocaust a constant reference in the planning of the safety of the embattled Jewish State.

Though Ben-Gurion rarely made direct references to the Holocaust in his capacity as Israel's senior guiding political figure, he, nevertheless, characterized the country as a haven to all Jews from any future Hitlerian regime. By inference, Ben-Gurion made it clear that the existence of Israel would be dedicated to the continuity of the Jewish people whose very future was still being permanently threatened by the enemies of the Jewish state. Confronted by genocidally inclined foes, Israel could not afford a normal foreign policy stance. Regarded by its neighbors as an abnormality, as an illegal political entity, it was forced to devise a foreign policy based upon the lessons of the Holocaust experience.

In short, the essence of that policy was to assume that the Arabs meant what they said and, therefore, to act accordingly, international opinion notwithstanding. Israel could not and would not afford to risk how much of Arab propaganda to push Israel into the sea was bombast and how much was serious intention. In the past, waiting and hesitation (in part due to Jewish reluctance to believe that the Nazis meant to exterminate them, in part as a result of reliance upon the intervention of the rest of the world on their behalf) had cost countless Jews their lives. The same errors would not be committed by Israel's foreign policy elite; hence there was the strategy of preemption, a combination of unambiguous independence of action and overt self-reliance, two conditions tragically impossible for the Jewish masses facing the German death squads. Within the context of the state, however, sovereignty and defense forces gave the Jewish people sufficient flexibility to fight a genocidally motivated enemy commensurate with the perceived danger: a second Holocaust.

The possibility of a second Holocaust in the form of an Arab victory over Israel always loomed large in the calculations of the Israeli planners. Prime Minister Begin has, since May, 1977, made numerous public utterances in which he made it known that the memory of the Holocaust played a central part in his policy planning for Israel.

As long as Israel lives in the company of those striving towards another Holocaust, it has no alternative but to structure its foreign policy accordingly. As for the rest of the international community, both friend and foe of Israel, it will do well for them to acknowledge the dynamic anti-Holocaust character of Israel's foreign policy. To deny its centrality is to misread Israel's behavior and to underestimate that nature could not accept that. . . .

M&R 9:6, March-April, 1983

XIII. The Next Generation: The Children of Survivors

"And there took place a great miracle!" The immortal words not only recall the Feast of Chanukah, but today, mysteriously, seem appropriate to the rising phenomenon coinciding with the last years of the post-Holocaust decades.

For over 40 years, Holocaust survivors have carried the burden of preserving the memory of Auschwitz. As former "citizens" of hundreds of ghettos and "inhabitants" of a dozen Death Camps, the Survivors have borne the obligation of not letting the rest of the world forget. While living everyday lives as normally as possible, the survivors of genocide have had to cope with the abnormal role of being living witnesses. Since 1945, the majority has died; and it is only a matter of time before we shall find ourselves in the post-Survivor era, when nature will have gently stilled their persistent cry: "Remember the Six Million."

Just when it seemed that the Holocaust legacy would become a general heritage for all, there was born out of the very ranks of the dwindling Survivors those destined to carry the torch, their children. Over the past 20 years, propelled by their own inner dynamic, the offspring of the Survivors have organized themselves into the natural heirs of their parents' historic task. Spontaneously, as if in response to a common call, a growing number of the children of Jews who had miraculously escaped extermination, and who themselves were a product of that miracle of survival, have drawn together into a cohesive entity spread across six continents. Unanimously, they have agreed to continue the work their parents must inevitably abandon.

Nothing in our time speaks more eloquently the Jewish injunction—l'dor v'dor!—to pass the legacy on from generation to generation.

THANKS FOR GIFT OF LIFE

By Rabbi Bernhard H. Rosenberg

As a *ben yachid,* an only child of parents who survived the horrors of the Holocaust, I am constantly asked to comment regarding my feelings and sensitivities. I applaud those individuals who have painstakingly embarked on new avenues to communicate with children of survivors. Indeed, many may be in need of specialized advice to aid them in confronting their innermost anxieties and tensions. Sharing emotions, communicating one's fears, is of utmost importance. Some may, as psychologists have often suggested, sense pains of guilt. Others may seek to rebel against an environment which projects images of nightmares. Still others may avoid any conversion or situation which might awaken latent emotions.

I, for one, wish to share my personal thoughts regarding the issue of "children of survivors." I do not pretend to be either an authority on the subject, nor do I dare speak from psychological expertise. I merely wish to speak from the heart, as one child survivor to another, who cares and loves his brethren.

Many of us have been categorized as children possessing immense guilt. Others have attributed our zealousness for achievement due to an intense need for survival. Yet, others have been labeled as being overly concerned for their parents or, quite the opposite, rejecting parental authority and fleeing from the stereotyped image of Holocaust survivors.

I personally feel no guilt for having the God-given privilege of being alive. I mourn for my grandparents, uncles and aunts who perished at the hands of Nazi maniacs, often weeping for not having experienced their love. I cry in anguish when reminded that six million of my brethren, young and old, left this earth via gas chambers and crematoriums. I sense the pain of my family and friends who saw their elders shot before their very eyes and their babies hurled against brick walls and bayoneted. I experience deep anger when I view the numbers branded on the arm of my father. Yet, I thank God for sparing the lives of my beloved parents.

Yes, I blame humanity for remaining silent while my innocent brethren perished screaming in terror for someone to heed their outcries. Humanity, not God. We are not puppets to be controlled by our Creator. Humanity caused the Holocaust. People remained silent. Leaders of countries refused to intercede on behalf of the defenseless. Nazi maniacs, aided by the populace of bordering countries, destroyed our treasured martyrs.

Should I then hate humanity? Should I survive with anger in my heart, rebelling against the environment, rejecting those of other faiths and cultures? Perhaps I should walk along the rocky paths of society fearing what the future may bring.

I openly and candidly answer in the negative. No, I will not live in a shell of neurotic chaos. I will not reject society. I refuse to live in a world which rejects hope, receiving nourishment from the seeds of hatred.

I admire and respect my beloved parents, Jacob and Rachel, and honor them for their strength and courage. Even Auschwitz could not diminish their faith. They could have rejected God; instead, they encouraged their only child to enter the active rabbinate. They could have rejected humanity; instead, they aid others in their daily fight for existence. No, a world of anger and hostility is not our banner.

Refuse to discuss the Holocaust? Sweep these memories under the rug? No! This is not our mission to the world and ourselves. Let the truth be known! Let others realize what the world did to an ethical, moral and religious populace. Let them hear the testimony of valiant survivors. Let them see our courage.

Feel guilt for surviving, for speaking on behalf of children who were silenced—never!

I became a rabbi to aid the living, to insure our survival; to rekindle the Jewish flame. I am proud—proud of my heritage, proud of our strength, and proud of my beloved parents.

Some blame their parents for being overly protective. Some reject the wishes of their elders to grab hold of opportunities denied to them. I thank God every day of my life for the precious love received which many, unfortunately, will never experience.

Children of survivors, thank God for the gift of life! Love your elders for possessing *Yiddishe* hearts. Consult with them, cherish their advice. Walk proudly, speak with love, fight for Jewish survival.

SURVIVORS: AGONY AND RESOLVE

By Al Singerman

I am a child of concentration camp survivors. Not a very startling statement you may say, but until seven months ago I had not uttered those words to anyone. Not my brother, nor my cousins, whose parents are also survivors, ever dared speak about our parents as survivors. Yet, my entire life seemed to be absorbed in the anguish of my parents' suffering, in some distant memory of relatives inexplicably lost, relatives who perished before I was born but who insisted on making their lack of presence felt. My anguish was carefully kept within me, deposited in impregnable walls, as if a part of me knew that to release it meant losing control of overwhelming feelings I scarcely understood. Dealing with these feelings, and shaping them into a constructive resource, was as inconceivable to me as crossing the ocean that filled the gap between me and my parents.

What remains of my parents' wartime accounts is the bitter harshness with which they were told and the admonishments that I must not forget what happened. How could I forget? These accounts were reinforced by documentaries which I could not bear to watch but could not tear my eyes from. I dreamt of a skeleton descending upon me in the darkness. I often imagined myself in a gas chamber surrounded by suffocating people and would hold my breath until I burst because I was determined not to die. The worst visions, however, were the depictions of Jews humbly accepting their fate. This one perception, more than any other, caused me to be overwhelmed with rage, to shut myself off from any social or emotional contact, to wish I had never been born. For me the world was black and bleak; no sun could penetrate the threatening clouds. The manifestation of my trauma occurred when at the age of nineteen I quit college and enlisted in the infantry in 1966. I was intent on proving not only that I too was a survivor, but also that I was a Jew who could fight.

Fighting in and surviving Vietnam did little to help me understand my feelings about my parents and the Holocaust. It only brought me in closer touch with my rage. In one incident, when a Jewish friend who did not know my background began singing a German song I demanded that he stop. This rage consumed me and I didn't know what questions to ask or who to ask them of. Even the thought of reading about the Holocaust terrified me.

The change came for me in May, 1977, when I was interviewed by Helen Epstein for the June 19 article in the Sunday *N.Y. Times Magazine,* "Heirs of the Holocaust." It was disconcerting, but also comforting, to discover that other survivors' children who came from such diverse backgrounds shared many of my feelings. It seemed that there must be many of us who had reached the point where we were ready to explore, to confront, to attempt to derive some meaning out of this turmoil.

The desire to break this silence became even stronger than the pain that caused it. Together with Steven Schultze, also a child of survivors, and two psychologists, Yael Danieli and Florence Pincus, I formed an organization which we named the "Group Project For Holocaust Survivors and Their Children." Our main purpose is to form self-help and therapy groups where children of survivors can discuss their emotional reactions to the Holocaust.

Allowing myself to give voice to my feelings has enabled me to overcome my uncontrollable fear of everything associated with the Holocaust. I have read a number of books, especially those dealing with survival and resistance in the camps, but more importantly I have started asking my parents questions. Learning of resistance to the Nazis and the way Jews and whole populations were terrorized dissipated my perception of Jews dying like sheep, but learning of my father's attempts to escape from the Nazis, and the fire that lit up his eyes as he spoke about it, made me realize what enormous inner strength he must possess. For the first time in my life I felt a great pride in my father.

Participating in a group with other children of survivors has also caused me to give considerable thought to whether future generations will remember the lessons of the Holocaust and be prepared to prevent its reoccurrence. I see concerned Jews constantly urging us to take courses in Holocaust studies, for public schools to offer these courses in their curriculum. I am not opposed to these efforts, but I am certainly not convinced that courses on the Holocaust can effectively pass on its lessons. Tests, as in any other subject, give rise to learning dates and facts which are soon forgotten. But what truly disturbs me is that the Holocaust is being taught apart from the rest of history; children even have a choice to elect these courses, both in high schools and colleges. Furthermore, these courses tend to teach the Holocaust in a sterile atmosphere—

dates, figures, events. One's personal involvement is left at the door. Unless we start examining and understanding the Holo-caust with our emotions, all we will pass on to future genera-tions is numbers, and even Six Million will lose its significance fifty years hence. For this reason alone, these self-help groups (and many others around the country) are extremely impor-tant to my generation.

M&R 4:6, Jan.-Feb., 1978

SPEAKING IN RETROSPECT

By DR. PEARL BRANDWEIN

During the last few years, the tragedy of the Holocaust has been the subject of numerous documentaries, television shows, books, articles and scholarly publications whose goals have been to enlighten and to chronicle the genocide of a people—six million Jewish men, women, and children. The endless questions of how and why it happened continue to echo in our minds and hearts, yet the answers we are given always fail to address themselves to the essence of the tragedy which has become an integral part of every survivor's life. My own mother spent four years in a concentration camp, and those years not only made a permanent imprint on her psyche but on mine as well. Growing up in the shadow of her misery has not only affected me intellectually but also emo-tionally.

Although I was not present physically, I empathise with my mother's tragic life. My mother, always sheltered by her wealthy family because of her frail health, suddenly found herself thrust into the world all alone and unprotected at the age of twenty-one. Her mother and sister were killed, as were seventy members of her family. Without anyone to guide, protect, or help her, she managed to survive by struggling with starvation, disease, and imminent death for four years. I cry, then, not only for the martyrs but mostly for myself out of hopelessness, despair, and sorrow. They went nobly and heroically to their deaths, accepting their fate without ques-tion and placing themselves in God's hands.

I have always had a greater understanding and sense of purpose as a result of my mother's experiences. As the child of a survivor, I felt differently from my Jewish friends—not only emotionally but intellectually—when discussing the subject. Whereas they listened politely and described the tragedy of the millions who perished, their understanding is limited and their point of reference too narrow.

In retrospect, I realize that my accomplishments are really my mother's because I brought to fruition many of the things she herself had hoped to attain in her life. Her expectations and encouragement have led me to the top of my profession, while her love and unwavering support have seen me through many difficult times in my pursuit of academic excellence (M.A. in French, Ph.D. in comparative literature). Her constant striving for perfection has inspired me in every aspect of my life. Looking back, I find that I have inherited my mother's strength, resolve, insight, compassion and hope. I, too, therefore, consider myself a survivor. Whenever I feel sad, I only have to look at her and realize the power of the human spirit in facing the challenges of life and triumphing over them and the Holocaust in particular.

M&R 7:9, May-June, 1981

MY BUBBY IS A SURVIVOR

My bubby is a sorvivor and she's very specil to me. Sometimes she gets sad because of things that hapened many years ago. She lost most of her family in the notsy war. This made her very unhappy a specily arond the Jewish holidays. We always try too help her when she gets very sad. My Mommy and Daddy had to put her in the hospital when she felt so deprest and sad. My Bubby got better soon because she's realy a strong lady. She realy must be to have sorvived the notsy war. She came to America after the war and started a holl new life. She lorned a new langweg and picked up the peeses and started a new family. It must of been very hard for her to do. Bubby is a real specil person to be able to do all this. She is a real sorviver and I realy love her very much.

By MARISA GANIN

M&R 12:12, Sept.-Oct., 1985
Marisa is a second-grade student whose article about bubby (grandmother) is reproduced exactly as the wrote it.

IT'S IMPORTANT TO REMEMBER

By MICHAEL LEBOR

My Hebrew name is Mordechai Tzvi. We are a family of the Holocaust. My grandparents, Jack and Lillian Rozmaryn, are survivors of the Holocaust. I was named Tzvi for my great-grandfather, Jala Hershel Rozmaryn, who was a survivor of the Holocaust but passed away 17 years ago. I was named Mordechai Rozmaryn, for another greatgrandfather who perished in the Holocaust. My family name is Lebor, and my grandfather is here with us this evening. As a member of the British Army, he was a liberator of the Bergen-Belsen concentration camp.

As a third generation survivor, I have a responsibility to remember and help others remember this great tragedy that has come to be known as the Holocaust. . . .

We have been reading reports about a neo-Nazi group that is trying to tell the world that the Anne Frank story is not true but a mere forgery. Unbelievable as it may seem, there are people who are trying to convince the world that the Holocaust never happened. . . .

You in this assembly are living proof that this tragedy, unfortunately, did happen. We all have to make sure that everyone, Jew and non-Jew, knows that the Holocaust did take place and will always be remembered.

Along with the responsibility of remembering the past, it is our responsibility to make sure that this tragedy never happens again.

M&R 14:11, Sept.-Oct. 1987

XIV. The Holocaust Through the Eyes of Today's Youth

It is said that children suffer the most. That is, perhaps, because they are innocent and powerless. One of the bitterest consequences of the Holocaust is its legacy to the generations of youth who must inherit it as part of their heritage. The crime was committed, condoned, and/or observed by their parents and grandparents. Governments, whether democratic or totalitarian, republican or monarchic, socialist or capitalist, did little or nothing to prevent the mass murder of helpless Jews. Institutions and ideas to which today's children belong or subscribe—political parties, religions, the Red Cross, the Olympic Committee, universities, unions—participated in the crime of genocide or remained neutral.

How are they to come to terms with a past *cum* Holocaust? What lessons are they to draw from the event? Who can claim the authority to teach them, to show them the way, other than the dwindling ranks of the survivors themselves? What is there left to believe in after growing up under a sky polluted with the holy ashes of Auschwitz and on contaminated soil covering the putrid corpses of Bergen-Belsen. Can there ever be trust and love free from cynicism and despair after having sampled from the modern Tree of Knowledge nourished by the tears of Treblinka and Sobibor? Will the children's humanity survive?

The thoughts of the youth follow along with these selections. One must commend Sonja Spear's "A Day of Remembrance" (12:10 March-April 1986), winner of the First Annual Essay Contest of the United States Holocaust Memorial Council.

SHEDDING OF TEARS
FOR RIGHT REASONS

By Sara Silver

I have no right to be setting these words on paper. My only justification for uncapping my pen and letting it flow is that I am allowing it to spew forth only honest convictions. For what right have I to expound on the Holocaust? I, a teenager in New York in 1986—how can I allow myself to believe that I know what the Holocaust was?

As a child, I wrote many stories about the Holocaust. Each year around this time, my teacher would assign the class a creative writing piece about our impressions of "that awful era in Jewish history," and each of us would scribble out a few wavering lines about the horrors of life in a concentration camp and how it must never happen again. The only difference as the years went by was that the lines became less wavy and the language more sophisticated. But the initial content remained. The crumpled papers lying at the bottom of my wastepaper basket testify to the fact that this year I tried to do the same.

I tried to do the same until I dug down through the very deepest layers of my being to find out what I really knew and what I really felt about the Holocaust. And then I reached out and crumpled the papers gilded with glittery catch phrases, clichés, and banalities that had automatically come spilling out upon the mention of the trigger word "Holocaust." Because, suddenly, measured against the new truths unearthed, all the words accumulated upon this subject all these years represented nothing but a farce. For what do I, a neophyte molded by life's sands, know about such realities?

I have seen plenty of horror movies from World War II, and I have been moved by plenty of gruesome scenes. In grade school it almost used to be a contest as to who was affected by the Holocaust most. We proved to each other how upset we were and how awful we felt by how many tears were shed. And for someone to get up and walk out because they couldn't sit through any more—that was the ultimate proof of how deep their Jewishness reached within them. We

---

(The essay by Sara Silver, Yeshiva of Flatbush High School, Brooklyn, N.Y., won first prize in the 1986 competition of the U.S. Holocaust Memorial Council.)

284

really *were* upset by such movies. The tissues held ever-ready in my hand then collected honest tears. No one was pretending. But in those four words lies the tragedy: No one was pretending. Because when I go to the theater today, and the movie I choose to see is sad, I am not forcing those tears either. The very same hand that holds those tissues gathers the very same tears shed during the Holocaust movie and the movie seen for entertainment in the very same way. And I emerge from both movies feeling the same: a little melancholy, a little weepy, but harboring a feeling that I know will pass. But this is a dangerous attitude, for the Holocaust is not just another tearjerker. The reason I cry in other movies is that I am empathizing with the characters on the screen. I am feeling their plight and reacting to it. But how can I dare to react to a Holocaust movie in the same way, thus making a soundless statement that I am empathizing with the victims in the same way? How can I dare to presume that I, a relatively sheltered teenager, understand their plight?

I know nothing about suffering, and my head lowers in shame as the ink dashes across the page. My mind cannot begin to comprehend the starvation, the emaciation, the beatings, the cold, the shame, the terror, the stripping of identity suffered by my million brothers and sisters. And until now I could not accept that.

I shed no such tears about the Holocaust anymore, for it would be unjust to those who perished. I belong to a different generation—the survivors—and tears of empathy are no longer true or fair. The greatest Holocaust of all would be if I convinced myself I could share in the pain of those six million. I have no right.

What, then, must I extrapolate from history? I believe that I must remember and appreciate their pain always. But my real lesson must be taken from the miracle of each victim's bravery, for I am humbled before it. And, again, I am moved to recognizing that I can in no way hope to equal their bravery and faith, for in the face of such courage I am nothing. I am just a grain of sand among the infinite sands of life. But, yet, at the same time, I recognize that pebbles are built of many such grains, and boulders from many such pebbles, and mountains from many such boulders. And I believe that mountains of this kind are the ones that our brothers and sisters would have wanted us to build so that they shouldn't have died in vain.

A HOLOCAUST LESSON
FROM A GRANDFATHER

By Karen Kopp

The following is a true story. I'm sad to say that it took the tragedy of the Holocaust to make me realize how proud I am to be a Jew. I dedicate this story to my grandfather and also to all the relatives I will never know because of the insanity known as the Holocaust.

"Hey Karen, what's the difference between a Jew and a loaf of bread?" "I don't know. What's the difference?" I asked, half-expecting the perverted answed that came forth from my classmate's mouth. "A loaf of bread doesn't scream when you bake it in the oven!" he laughed with glee. I found myself laughing as well. It was a pretty good joke, actually, one that I would tell my parents when I got home.

What I have learned between that time and the present has been a maturing experience, and even now I yell at myself for the ignorance with which I grew accustomed for the first 16 years of my life.

I was born in Brooklyn, New York, the daughter of middle-class Jewish parents who had slowly but surely left the Jewish fold. Oh, sure, they turned the electric Menorah on for Chanukah, and they spent half a day in the synagogue during Yom Kippur, but that was about the extent of it. The funny thing was that their parents were Orthodox, having come over from Eastern Europe in the early part of the century. Somewhere, at some point in time, my parents had decided that religious devotion was "old hat," and my brothers and I grew up without that religious focus or devotion. Well, it was no big deal to a child of the seventies and eighties, where Bruce Springsteen and MTV ruled supreme. What was a "Jew joke" here and there? I was known to tell a couple of good Polish jokes myself. It was all in good fun.

One evening, my family and I visited with my maternal grandparents. It was always great fun to see them. The food was great, and there were always little presents put aside for my brothers and me.

During dinner, the topic of discussion turned to prayer

(The essay by Karen Kopp, Moore High School, Louisville, Ky, won second place in the 1986 competition of the U.S. Holocaust Memorial Council.)

286

in the public schools. I thought to myself that it would be a great time to tell my grandparents the joke I had heard in school a few days before.

"Hey, Grandpa." "Yes, Karen." "What is the difference between a Jew and a loaf of bread?" "I don't know." "A loaf of bread doesn't scream when you bake it in the oven!" A pained expression as I had never seen before came over my grandfather's face. He looked around the table at each member of my family and then excused himself from the table.

"What did I say wrong?" I asked my grandmother. "Karen, that joke was in very poor taste." Just, then, my grandfather emerged from his room and called to me. "Karen, please come into my study with me for a few minutes." I had no idea what he was planning to say to me. I was very nervous.

"Karen, I am going to tell you a few things and I want you to listen very carefully." "Alright, Grandpa." "When I hear jokes like the one you just told, it gets me very upset. I want to ask you something, young lady. You do know what the Holocaust was, do you not?" "Yes, Grandpa. It is what happened to the Jewish people in Europe, when Hitler tried to destroy them. He killed something like six million Jews." "That's right. But did you know that most of my family died in the concentration camps at Auschwitz and Bergen-Belsen," "Auschwitz? I heard of Auschwitz, but I didn't know any of our family was sent there."

"That's right, Karen. My cousins, my aunts, my uncles; they died because they were Jewish. Remember Uncle Moishe, who passed away about eight years ago? He was lucky. He was the only one who left the camps with his life. Uncle Moishe used to tell us that God spared his life so that he could tell the world about the atrocities that occurred right before his eyes. I think it's time I tell you about those atrocities. Maybe then jokes like the one you told won't seem so funny."

My grandfather went on to tell me about the young children whose heads were smashed against the wall for the amusement of the S.S., and about the horrible gas chambers in which people were packed together so tightly that when the doors of the chamber were opened the dead had to be disentangled from each other. He told me about the horrible mass graves, and the poor Jews who were made to dig them, brutally cut down once the task was completed. He told me of the Nazi scavengers who picked apart the bodies of the dead, stealing the only possessions they had left: their skin and hair. And, yes, he told me about the ovens, the final resting place of a long-suffering people. The cremations went on night and day, the black smoke billowing, a constant reminder of the death which pervaded all around.

My grandfather finished. "Grandpa, I'm so sorry," I said. "Karen," he said as he took my hand in his, "Agony and death is not something to joke about. Ours is a tragedy that must always be remembered so that it will never happen again. People laugh in ignorance. They just don't know or realize the pain and anguish we have endured. Because you are Jewish, you have an extra burden to carry. You will always have to live with the pain of knowing that your relatives, your people, were destroyed simply because they were Jewish."

Several days later, the same classmate came up to me and offered to tell me another one of his "Jew jokes." I was offended, and I was ashamed that I had ever allowed myself to become oblivious to my people's pain and to my family's, oblivious to a tragedy that deprived me of ever having the chance to know my aunts, uncles, and cousins.

I stopped him before he started, sat him down, and spoke with all my heart as my grandfather had spoken to me. Never again did I hear another "Jew joke" uttered from his lips.

M&R 13:10, Jan.-Feb., 1987

SURVIVOR'S PEN PALS

Dear Mr. Spanjaard:

Before I read your book, I never knew what a concintration camp was. I would always ask my mom or dad what they were. They always told me that they were to complicated for me to understand what they were. I used to play war with my friends and when I'd capture them, I put them into a small part of my backyard. I called this part a concintration camp. Then I read your book "Don't Fence Me in." I never knew what horror lies within a concintration camp, so now I don't even play war. Your childhood story really touched me in many different ways. I can't wait for your sequel to "Don't Fence Me in." It'll be the first book I'll buy.

Sincerely,

Mike

* * *

When you came to San Marcos . . . to give us a talk about your life, I loved it. It was very interesting and brought tears to my eyes.

I really thought my life was awful, but when I heard what you've been through, no comparison at all; I love living, but as you probably know, it's tough to be a teenager and sometimes I want to end my life so I won't have to live through these bad, terrible times. But when you came to speak to us, I thought about it, and I'm really happy to be alive! So thank you ever so much. I learned a lot. You didn't give up and now you seem very happy. Thank you;

If you ever have time, please write a letter and let me know how you're doing! Thanks again!

Stefany

(The above letters from junior high school children were received by survivor Barry Spanjaard, Canyon County, Calif. The letters are printed exactly as they were written.)

M&R 13:11, Jan.-Feb., 1987

SURVIVORS ARE APPRECIATED

I wanted you to know that you are doing a great favor to all of us by taking time out of your day to come and share your experiences with us. It was truly special. I know that all of your experiences cannot be taken away or forgotten, and only you know what it was truly like. Yet I now too, along with my fellow students, can only have an understanding of what the Holocaust really was.

I hope that you are able to put it behind you enough to enjoy your life now. Your presentation made me aware of how short life can be for some, and how important it is to enjoy it now. I wrote a poem which I hope you will like:

> Life was young and happy.
> All of it was taken away from me.
> Many died,
> Never seeing family again.
> Everyone —
> Women, children, and men.
> I was lucky
> And I'm still here
> With God on my side
> And always near.
> I am thankful to live
> Every lasting year.

(This above letter was received by survivor Eddy Wynschenk from Lisa Stamp, of the Independence High School, San Jose, Calif.)

M&R 12:6, Nov.-Dec., 1985

TILL THE SADNESS EVERYWHERE

(The poem was the winner in the 1983 competition of the Atlanta Bureau of Jewish Education).

Till the sadness everywhere
Amounts to nothing.
All the ugliness, all the filth
All the hatred and ignorance,
All the pain
Is meaningless, when the deaths are counted.

There are no words.
No ways to explain, no fresh air.
No smiles, no life,
Nothing.
Nothing to describe
What must be said.
What must be counted
And remembered
And mourned and feared.

The Holocaust.
The slaughter of our people.
The destruction
And the death.

Cry until the tears you have are used.
Mourn and be sad,
Be afraid,
Tremble and remember God,
And maybe die a little bit,
And you will know. . . .

JANA GOLDSTEIN

M&R 10:15, Sept.-Oct.,1983

WHAT DOES THE HOLOCAUST MEAN TO ME?

(The poem was written by a 12-year-old black student in the New York City Public Schools System.)

What does the Holocaust mean to me
Joy and happiness, a chance to be free?
A chance to be happy, in the few years to be.
Run in the sunshine,
See all you can see?
No, it's really not all that good.
In a gas chamber some of them stood
Thrown in a fire, burnt to a crisp
Running and hiding, taking a risk.
Flee child flee, run away.
Mama is caught, she will die today.
Hitler smiling, laughing with joy
While dreaming how to murder every girl and boy.
What shall we do Mummy?
What shall we do?
Father was captured and brother was too.
Run away Jews.
Run away all.
Hitler and his army are coming to call.
Hitler used his power to obliterate the Jews
Yanking out gold teeth and ripping off tattoos.
Many made attempts to shoot him in the head.
Almost everyone wanted him dead.
Mummy, Mummy take us home.
We dislike staying here all alone.
When will all of this be over?
Soon, my child, don't run a race.
Rest your sweet head on my shoulder.
Have faith, don't cry, it has to end.
But until that time, trust me as a friend.
Sleep my child, dream a happy, good thought.
Please, don't cry; we won't be caught.
Have faith.

MICHELLE HALL

M&R 10:15, Sept.-Oct., 1983

DEATH WAS ALL AROUND US

Death was all around us
and cries had filled the air
No one left their basements
No one even dared
When it all was over
our lively town had died
No dogs barked around us
No child even cried
We cleaned up all the ruin
and buried all the dead
And through those silent moments
Not a word was said
We tried to forget
what had happened here
They came and left a mark on us
That we'll remember with a tear.

AMY LASSER—8th Grade

M&R 3:8, May-June 1987

NOBODY CARED

The Holocaust is a fear.
It made me shed a tear.
The Holocaust is a danger,
It makes me full of anger.
The Holocaust was cruel,
It was a mighty duel.
The Holocaust, it kills,
It gives me the chills.
The Holocaust made the
Jews disappear
and what really gets me is,
nobody cared!

MELISSA HELFMAN—8th Grade

292

XV.
Zachor! Never, Never Forget!

The Holocaust survivor is haunted by the fear that the past, and, therefore, the Six Million dead, will slowly be forgotten, steadily fading into the background. Many more, of course, non-survivors, would be relieved if the memory of the ultimate political crime would simply fade away.

The call to remember has led to numerous solutions: a proliferation of survivors' memoirs; academic studies; Holocaust centers; Holocaust memorials; Presidential proclamations; and the annual 27th Nissan commemoration services. No opportunity is lost by those who recognize the Holocaust as an historic watershed to promote awareness of its significance and stimulate a sense of responsibility to keep the memory fresh from year to year. Much of the credit for success in this struggle to preserve the Holocaust past must go to *Martyrdom and Resistance* and its founder, Eli Zborowski, who, over the years, has never ceased in his crusade against forgetfulness.

Yad Vashem, the Israeli Remembrance Authority, is a unique institution and is the subject of an article in this section.

Another agency of remembrance, the U.S. Holocaust Memorial Council, is explored in a provocative article "Are We Erecting a Memorial for the Dead or Building a Monument for the Living," (Dr. Bernard Mandelbaum, 11:8 March-April 1985).

The call to remember has become a moral imperative, for to forget is a moral act, a value statement that there are more important things to remember, greater crimes to keep in mind, that the suffering of the Jews does not merit recollection. Bypassing the Holocaust is no amoral decision, and future generations should be sternly taught that in so doing, they join the ranks of the genocidists and the "neutral" bystanders.

REFLECTIONS AT YAD VASHEM

By Eugenia Nadler

Yad Vashem is located on the Mount of Remembrance close to Mount Herzl, not far from Theodor Herzl's tomb. It spreads over a valley and is surrounded by young and growing woods. Is this merely "landscaping"? Even before we are confronted with the indoor exhibits, we sense symbolism.

The woods commemorate all those forests which lent refuge to the victims fleeing from the demons; the woods, after they mature, will enclose within their area the sanctuary which must be assured as much quietude and isolation as possible. The last 800 meters which separate it from the highway, from the commonplace, from the busses, become a road of pilgrimage toward an experience which cannot be matched by personal toughness or any sort of immunity. The time that has passed since those events, the distance from them, the natural surroundings which ordinarily would have the effect of a cure—all of this fails. "Lasciate ogni speranza voi che entrate," as Dante was warning at the gates to his inferno. The contemporary inferno, seen at Yad Vashem, the product of factual data, not fantasies, overshadows the other one a thousand times.

Fire, burnout, ashes: these are elements that can be felt and seen, and that overwhelm us with their horror the moment when we cross the threshold of Yad Vashem's Memorial Hall. The half-darkness; the wooden ceiling appearing as if it had been blackened by fire, with an opening to the outside; the cider-covered basalt walls constructed of powerful rocks collected from the Biblical lands of the Galilee; the grayness of the mosaic floor consisting of six million individual little stones; the granite coverplace in the center bearing six wreaths, always fresh, create an atmosphere which allows for nothing else but mourning.

We are engulfed by this mourning unknowingly . . . unable to divert our gaze from the endless flatness containing enormous built-in tablets with the names of the largest concentration camps: Drancy, Bergen-Belsen, Chelmno, Belzec, Majdanek, Oswiecim, Mauthausen, Terezin, Stutthof, Sobibor, Treblinka, Ponary, Buchenwald, Babi Yar, Lwow-Janowska.

This article is translated from the Polish by Dr. Samuel R. Mozes, formerly executive director of the International Society for Yad Vashem.

My mother was seen in the camp at Lwow-Janowska. I now have a feeling that if that tablet were lifted, I would find her there. I have a feeling that here is the fulfillment of the many years of wanderings with my nostalgia and thoughts. I have a feeling that I am standing at my mother's grave. The walls around me acquire a new meaning. They cease to be a part of the structure and, because of their powerful stony nature, transform themselves into an armour protecting us from "all evil," that is, if there still is any kind of an evil left which was not experienced by those whose memory is here preserved for "all times."

We, the visitors, speak Polish to each other. We are bound by a common origin and a common fate. Are the others, like me, unable to contain a violent heartbeat? Do they experience, like me, contrary to the accepted idea, that time does not heal wounds? Do they also feel, like me, that we are standing in the largest cemetery known to mankind, a cemetery for six million, but without bodies buried in it? Are they living through a reaction similar to mine? And were this reaction, this shock, and this awareness intentional when Israel on September 19, 1953, decided in our Parliament to create an institution which was given the name Yad Vashem—literally "Monument and Remembrance," in accordance with the passage in the book of the Prophet Isaiah stating that a monument and remembrance represent a warranty more secure than one's own sons and daughters.

"So that it is not forgotten"—this is the principal motif of the concept and the implementation of Yad Vashem. The entire system: The Memorial Hall; the pavilion of names in black, with its index files arranged vertically, as if little coffins; the multilingual library containing 40,000 books in all contemporary languages of the world; the archives; the Museum; the synagogue; the research center; the section for the adoption of the destroyed communities and settlements, so as to create a permanent liaison between Israel and the Diaspora—all this represents one purpose alone: Not to forget!

It makes a lot of sense that around us assemble groups of school children, and among them children of concentration camp inmates. Here they learn about the past, here they perceive the value of their own homeland, here they find an answer to the anxiety which attacked them during the trial of Eichmann, which had reached beyond their understanding and to which they, unknowing, unencumbered, unrestrained, responded with the question: "And where at that time was our army?"

President George Bush—then Vice President—visited Yad
Vashem with Mrs. Bush in 1986, shown with (l. to r.)
Shimshon Eden, Yad Vashem secretary general; Dr. Yitzhak
Arad and Ambassador Reuven Dafni, chairman and vice
chairman, respectively, Yad Vashem Directorate.

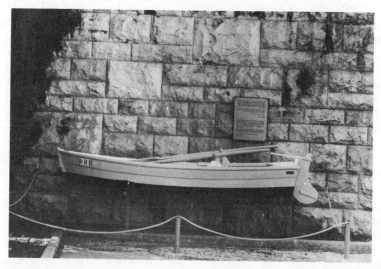

Boat at Yad Vashem used in the rescue of Danish Jewry.

It seems to me that, outside Poland itself, there is no place where so many Polish mementos may be found as in Yad Vashem. Here is what we see in the display cases: "A Call From Warsaw, 1943," an anthology of underground poetry; a pamphlet entitled, "Polish Children Suffer"; "The Tragedy of Warsaw and Its Documentation." Here we find the tragic appeals, from Zygelbojm to President Raczkiewicz, which ended with the former's suicide. In the archives will be seen the legacy of the historian Emmanuel Ringelblum, who understood the Poles so well. On the walls are shown old engravings of larchtree-constructed synagogues that were leveled down to the ground together with their congregations.

The Museum: In the large open space, one is compelled to stop in front of the "Ghetto Fighters," by Rapoport, the replica of the original monument which stands in Warsaw on the very spot of the actual events.

There, among the lawns and the flowers, among the colors and the smells meanders the Avenue of the Righteous Gentiles, getting longer from year to year, fuller every springtime. Is there any more convincing response to the evil of this world than belief in its goodness? Is it possible that there is deeper gratitude than the one which, according to the Talmudic dictum that "He who has saved one life, it is as if he was saved the whole world," inspired Israel to memorialize the the name of every Christian who was risking his own life to protect the hounded Jews?

The Avenue opens with the King of Denmark, Christian IX, in whose honor a tree was planted by the Danish ambassador to Israel. Next to the King is located the Pole, Bartoszewski, with an extraordinary personal record, and he is followed by names from all over Europe, including Poland, and a substantial number of priests and nuns. Altogether there are about eight hundred names. In each case there were several levels of investigation, hearings of witnesses and reviews of circumstances, before a decision was made to add the given name to this most noble of elites.

A freshly planted sapling has straightened out, has looked around its new environment, and has been greeted by the assembly of eight hundred leafy crowns, murmuring about the miracle of countermanded death, rustling about the regained freedom, about human kindness. After this sapling grows and develops, it too will enrich the vocal assembly by still another sound of voice, praising the triumph of man who loved his neighbor more than he loved himself.

M&R 10:6, May-June, 1984

PERPETUATING REMEMBRANCE: LEADERSHIP AT YAD VASHEM

If one were to chart the development of the International Society and American Society for Yad Vashem, the stunning growth would be immediately visible.

How far the Societies have come was dramatically clear at the Fourth Annual Dinner, which was held Nov. 13, 1988, at the Waldorf Astoria in Manhattan.

Now in their sixth full year, the Societies have become an impressive presence in the Jewish communal world. This is remarkable because it often takes many years before a Jewish organization makes an impact on the global scene.

The Societies began with meetings in living rooms, in parlors, in business offices. It was only in 1985 that the Societies were able to bring together sufficient numbers for an evening in a New York hotel.

Enthusiasm for the societies has continued unabated in the past two years, as the numbers at dinners increased and the list of VIP's on the dais expanded.

New heights were attained at the 1988 dinner, as a throng of near 1,000 crowded into the Waldorf. But the story goes beyond the numbers. What "makes the headlines" this year is the formation of the Young Leadership Society (YLS). More than just an added unit, YLS ensures that the commitment to remembrance is continual and never ending.

YLS is the gratifying proof of the maturation of the Societies, for which they have earned deserved acclaim as the educational and development arm of the Israel Remembrance Authority on the Mount of Remembrance in Jerusalem.

Understandably, the then and now of the Societies was a resounding theme at the Fourth Dinner, as speakers accented the growth of the American and International Societies for Yad Vashem.

Enhancing the theme of remembrance was the setting of the dinner during a period in which the world observed the 50th year of Kristallnacht, Nov. 9-10, 1938.

The nature of those who support the cause of remembrance was also illustrated in the persons of the honorees: one fled the onslaught of the Holocaust, while the other is an American, neither a survivor nor a child of survivors. Both have a common denominator: they are dedicated to remembrance because they realize the overwhelming importance of ensuring that there will never be another Holocaust. The message for the future was also eloquently articulated in the presence of Ambassador Ronald S. Lauder, who that night became the newest member of the Board of Governors of the International Society. His munificent support for Kristallnacht observance was a compelling story of the 50th year milestone.

The honorees are Marcos D. Katz and David Berg. Mr. Katz of Mexico City is a highly respected businessman and philanthropist who serves as a vice chairman of the International Society for Yad Vashem and a member of the International Board of Governors. Fleeing Cracow with his family in 1940, Mr. Katz has been in Mexico since 1947. He has been in the vanguard of leadership in the Jewish community in three continents. Especially noteworthy has been his leadership at Yeshiva University, the World Jewish Congress, and the Union of Orthodox Jewish Congregations of America.

An attorney from New York, Mr. Berg has been an energetic leader for many causes, in particular educational, cultural, and health institutions. These include Yeshiva University, National Israel Museum, the Jewish Theological Society, and Boys Town of Italy.

The keynote speaker was Dr. Joseph Burg, the revered Israeli political leader who was recently named chairman of the Yad Vashem Council. Among other speakers were Ambassador Lauder; Dr. Moshe Arad, Israeli Ambassador to the United States; Yochanan Bain, Israeli Ambassador to the United Nations; Justice Moshe Etzioni, of the Israeli Supreme Court; and Eli Zborowski, chairman, International Society for Yad Vashem.

The presence of Dr. Burg attests to the permanence and resolve of Yad Vashem. In introducing Dr. Burg, Ambassador Bain highlighted the former's record of achievement, as one who rescued Jews from the Holocaust in the D.P. camps; as a leader of Mizrachi Hapoel Hamizrachi; as a dynamic personality in Israeli political life. "Joseph Burg is a teacher, thinker, and doer," said Ambassador Bain, "who is the symbol of continuity and stability in the State of Israel."

Dr. Burg praised his predecessor at Yad Vashem. Gideon Hausner, who helped establish the International Society and resigned his post because of illness. Mr. Hausner will be remembered not only as the prosecutor in the Eichmann Trial but as the individual who did so much to elevate the cause of remembrance.

The inaugural of the Young Leadership Society and the presence of the new Yad Vashem chairman, Dr. Burg, underscored the message: the eternal mission of remembrance.

Dr. Burg was in both East and West Germany for Kristallnacht 50th year observances. His visit brought back memories, "I was in Berlin 50 years ago during Kristallnacht," he said. "To those who say we should close and forget the chapter of the Holocaust, I respond: 'My mother died in Theresienstadt. My family was deported.' All of this was not part of a general warfare. It was genocide. Therefore, it is our duty, those who remain alive, to remember and remind others, not to let others forget.

"We stand committed to fight a national Alzheimer's disease. We will remember what was and build what should be."

Before leaving for the conclusion of his U.S. visit, Dr. Burg told *Martyrdom and Resistance* that "Yad Vashem is vigorous and is pushing ahead on many projects and avenues of remembrance. We are especially confident in the future because of the consistent and heartwarming support given us by the American and International Societies for Yad Vashem. And, in particular, we are proud of the generosity of the younger generation because remembrance will be entrusted to them and we are confident they will meet the challenge handsomely."

Ambassador Lauder was welcomed to the Board of Governors by one of its members, David Chase, who was dinner chairman. The Ambassador gained international applause because he refused to attend the inaugural of Kurt Waldheim as President when he was envoy to Austria. "Ambassador Lauder has shown much imagination and creativity in initiating and underwriting remembrance projects," said Mr. Chase. "These programs, such as exchange projects or the wide network of Kristallnacht observances, are designed to fight anti-Semitism and to promote remembrance. We at Yad Vashem are proud that he is with us tonight and that he is in the fullest sense of the word one of us."

The remarks of the Ambassador centered on Yad Vashem as the model of remembrance, or remembering the dead. "It is an honor to be associated with Yad Vashem," he remarked "The cause of Yad Vashem is rooted in the Prophets. All its work is predicated on the duty not to forget. In the future we must keep to the pledge to remember and Yad Vashem is that powerful symbol of remembrance."

Reflecting on the Kristallnacht observances, the Ambassador noted, "'In a six-month effort we worked as a united force. We proved that we can accomplish a great deal when we work together. We must not allow even the smallest seed of anti-Semitism to take root. Words are not enough. Action becomes decisive. The fate of the world turned in 1938 only because we did not act."

Then, now, and tomorrow: the motif for the remarks of Eli Zborowski. At last year's dinner he challenged the next generation: "Our generation is prepared to hand the torch down to you. Please pick it up while its light still burns brightly. The answer came this year, Mr. Zborowski remarked. "The next generation is prepared to shoulder the burden of remembrance activities. The formation of the Young Leadership Society is exciting proof that the young people are prepared to meet the responsibility that we will always remember."

Speaking of Yad Vashem, he said that the remembrance authority "is more than bricks and projects, but it also has a *neshma*, a soul. It teaches martyrdom and resistance during the Holocaust, it instructs about the deaths of 1.5 million Jewish children, and it offers the most eloquent vehicle for the future so that we do not repeat man's inhumanity to man."

Mr. Zborowski also added his tribute to the visionary work of remembrance that had been demonstrated by Ambassador Lauder.

Graphic evidence that the torch of remembrance is being passed to the next generation was pronounced in the committed statements of its representatives Andrew Belfer and Yehiel Fromer.

Mr. Belfer spoke of his trip to Poland during Yom Hashoa 1988 as part of the "increasing focus of the second generations" on remembrance. "The trip to Poland was a painful journey," he said. "Seeing the places of suffering" from the past he turned to the future as he met with representatives of Yad Vashem to help ensure that such suffering is not repeated.

In his remarks, Mr. Belfer lauded the chairman of the American and International Societies, Mr. Zborowski, for his "dedication in preserving the past while keeping an eye to the future."

The past and the future blended with great emotion during a moving audiovisual on Yad Vashem. The drama of the project of the Valley of the Destroyed Communities brought home the point of preserving a heritage, a grandeur wiped out during the Holocaust. All the eloquence, all the voices of a choir, or all the scenes on screen can be reduced to one

theme: the Valley is "the definitive monument to a world
which is no more."

Chairman of the Young Leadership Society, Yehiel
Fromer vowed, "The Holocaust will not be forgotten or just
become another lost chapter in history books. We look forward
to creating, financing, and completing projects and activities,
all by YLS, under the umbrella and guiding hands of the Yad
Vashem Society."

Mr. Fromer added that the mission of YLS is a "process"
because it "must be ongoing forever, our children after us
and their children after them—as long as there is Jewish life
on this planet."

Several projects were targeted: educating the youth
around the world about the Holocaust, compiling teaching aids
for use in schools, and at Yom Hashoa observances, and in
1990, the wearing of the Yellow Star by "every Jewish child
—or as many children as we can reach."

The wondrous achievements of the Societies were touched
on by Sam Skura, general chairperson of the dinner. He traced
the beginnings of the Societies, with meetings at the homes of
Mr. and Mrs. Israel Krakowski, Mr. and Mrs. Isak Levenstein,
Mr. and Mrs. Sam Gross, Mr. and Mrs. Ben Mellon.. "The
first meeting was held in our own living room," he said, "with
a group of people that would have hardly filled a table or two
here tonight. But we were able to build a base of people who
were willing to provide financial support for some of the
projects that the Societies were undertaking and who helped
bring others into the organization as well. . . . We can look
back at the past and feel a full measure of pride in what has
been achieved so far. However, such reflections must wait
since there is still much to be done."

The sense of achievement Mr. Skura was referring to was
a result of such dedicated individuals as the honorees who
received the Remembrance Award for "inspiring leadership,
for motivating colleagues and others in engraving upon the
conscience of the world the lessons of the Holocaust and the
need for remembrance."

The award to David Berg was presented by Judge Etzioni,
who read a congratulatory letter from Israeli Prime Minister
Itzhak Shamir. Mr. Shamir said that David Berg's benefaction
"sets an example for others to follow. You gave and gave."

In his response, Mr. Berg stressed the importance of furthering the development of Yad Vashem, "which reminds us
not only of the Holocaust but of more than 2,000 years of
anti-Semitism." In particular, the honoree asked that the 1.5

million Jewish child victims be remembered. "They were destroyed," he said, "without having the chance to grow and create."

Ambassador Arad came to know the second honoree, Mr. Katz, while in the Israeli diplomatic service in Mexico. He described Mr. Katz as "dedicated to his family, people, and country." Mr. Katz was a very giving individual who has made education more accessible to countless individuals.

In his response, Mr. Katz recalled his youth in Cracow. "We must remember," he said, "because of the unbelievable losses we had. It is not possible to believe that people were killed simply because they were of a different religion." The honoree spoke with great emotion about his visit to the Children's Memorial, Yad Uziel, endowed by Mr. and Mrs. Abraham Speigel in memory of their son, killed at Auschwitz. "You hear the voices, the real names of children who were murdered," said Mr. Katz, "Rachel Klein, age 18, Moshe Rabinovitch, age 2. You realize that you must always remember."

The excitement of the evening was heightened by the announcement of major gifts by Mr. and Mrs. Sheldon Edelson and Mr. and Mrs. Abraham Speigel.

In addition, there were these significant developments: the designation of new benefactors—Mr. and Mrs. Ulo Barad, David Berg, Mr. and Mrs. Jack Burstyn, Mr. and Mrs. Israel Krakowski; the addition of trustees—Mr. and Mrs. Murray Alon, Mr. and Mrs. Charles Drukier.

The constant reference to American Society for Yad Vashem should not hide the achievements of the Canadian Society, whose exciting development was detailed by national chairman, Dr. Joel Dimitry, including a new chapter in Montreal.

While the phenomenal record of the Societies were applauded by the assemblage at the dinner, there were tributes from those not present, in the form of messages from dignitaries that were read at the dinner. Appropriately, the words of praise were read by representatives of the young leadership, Ira Drukier and Gail Hart.

There were messages from U.S. President Ronald Reagan, President-elect George Bush, Israeli Prime Minister Yitzhak Shamir, President Chaim Herzog, Foreign Minister Shimon Peres, and Deputy Prime Minister and Minister of Education and Culture Itzhak Navon, New York State Governor Mario Cuomo, Connecticut Governor William O'Neil, New Jersey Governor Thomas Kean, New York's U.S. Senator Patrick

Moynihan, New York City Mayor Edward I. Koch, New Jersey U.S. Senator Frank Lautenberg, Massachusetts U.S. Senator Edward M. Kennedy, former Secretary of State Henry Kissinger, Nobel Laureate Elie Wiesel.

Key roles at this most successful dinner were played by four committees: recruitment, program, dinner, and tribute. The chairpeople were Ulo Barad, Elinor Belfer, Joseph Bukiet, Yehiel Fromer, Sam Halpern, Isidore Karten, Mark Palmer, and Harry Wilf.

Among other program participants were Cantor Paul Zim, Rabbi Joseph Sternstein, and Rabbi Faivel Wagner.

M&R 15:1, Nov.-Dec. 1988

THE UNIQUENESS OF YAD VASHEM

By ELINOR BELFER

I am a second generation American married to a survivor of the Holocaust. Over the years, in very gradual, sometimes spontaneous, sometimes elicited recountings, my husband, Norman, told me of his ordeal and that of his parents, sisters, nieces, and nephews who perished at the hands of the Nazis.

My first perceptions of the Holocaust, therefore, grew out of Norman's experiences, as related to me and absorbed very intensely by me. The intrinsic wish and need to share all things with one's spouse create a powerful empathy.

Of course, I am shattered by the knowledge that people endured unspeakable horror solely on the basis of their religious heritage and geographical proximity to Hitler. Instantaneously, I felt amazement, admiration, and respect for the survivors I met and knew about, whose lives since their liberation have been shining examples of courage, achievement, and generosity.

Obviously, wherever we were born, our identities as Jews are derived from the collective past. The Holocaust is, therefore, a part of me and each of us. In this sense, we are all survivors. I felt a moral duty as well as a psychological need to join the physical survivors in their battle against forgetfulness and, even, malicious denial.

How can we build a future without reference to the past? How can viable political decisions be made by individuals or by nations without accurate acknowledgement of our past?

No matter how numerous and important our other affiliations. Yad Vashem stands as a unique responsibility for each of us as we aspire to a world that can learn from history. It is the special custodian and guardian of Holocaust memory, research, and archives.

Yad Vashem is not only a physical entity, an historic monument, a sacred place in Jerusalem, Israel. It is a profound experience to visit the remembrance authority.

Has there been anyone—the foreign dignitary on his requisite visit, the tourist from everywhere, the schoolchild—who has not emerged a different, more dimensional person than the one who entered Yad Vashem?

M&R 14:8, March-April 1988

YAD VASHEM OPENING EHRENBURG ARCHIVES

Twenty years after the death of Ilya Ehrenburg, the famous Soviet Jewish writer, researchers can gain access to developments during the Holocaust now that his archive has been opened at Yad Vashem.

In particular, the archive covers the Holocaust and the problems of the Jews in Nazi-occupied areas of the Soviet Union in the immediate post-war years.

Included is the original manuscript of *The Black Book*. There is detailed examination of anti-Semitic outbursts in the post-liberation period. The archive has a valuable collection of hundreds of letters written by Russian Jews to Ehrenburg. These Jews, concerned about the non-existence of organized Jewish institutions in the USSR, saw in Ehrenburg the only address for their varied requests and for the transfer of the documentation of their experiences during the Holocaust and the ensuing years.

Yad Vashem intends to publish a book containing the correspondence to Ehrenburg.

All the archival materials were forwarded to Yad Vashem

at Ehrenburg's request, for he saw the remembrance authority as the central institution in the world for the commemoration of the Holocaust. The person who delivered the materials to Yad Vashem and asked that it continue sealed remains anonymous, at his request.

M&R 15:8, Sept.-Oct. 1988

YAD UZIEL: MEMORIAL FOR 1.5 MILLION CHILDREN

By Dr. Isaiah Kuperstein

It is not immediately apparent to the eye. You come upon it almost by accident on the sprawling grounds of Yad Vashem. A quarry? A site?

From the distance stand neatly lined white rectangular pillars. There are twenty of them upon a hill, from small to large, projecting into the blue Jerusalem sky. They are curiously broken in half, reminiscent of traditional Jewish gravestones of children who die before reaching their prime. A cemetery?

As you approach, you come upon an arch over a stone walkway. To the right is a transparent glass sign. You have to come closer to read the carefully composed text. It says something about "this Memorial" to the one and a half million Jewish children who "perished" in the Holocaust . . . and the generosity of the Spiegels from Beverly Hills, California . . . in memory of their son Uziel, who was killed in Auschwitz.

Your face a descending stone walkway bordered by rough hewn words carved into the first of several horizontal beams. A commandment? An eternal message? Only if you can read Hebrew do you know that it says, "The soul of man is the candle of God," a verse from Proverbs. The horizontal beams cast their shadows upon the smooth stones in touch with your feet—lines which look like tracks, shadows of tracks. Where is it leading? And all you can see in front of you is an empty wall.

But no, there is more. The wall is just one side of an alcove; or do those stone benches indicate a resting area?

Suddenly you are momentarily trapped. Your descent is broken. And there on another wall is hung a metallic copper colored plaque which jars with the stone. On it is featured a frozen grimacing face of a boy whose eyes refuse to meet yours. The boy does not want you to see him, but, yet, you know that he knows you are there. This is Uziel. He died in Auschwitz in the Jewish month of Sivan. His eyes look strangely elsewhere, toward a door to the left. It is as if he is saying, you must continue, go on, do not wait.

You open the heavy iron door. And even before you enter you hear deep mournful sounds emanating from the dark depths of a chamber. The sounds are gasping, expiring, breathing, perhaps even wailing.

In the chamber you are suddenly confronted by large black and white photographs of boys and girls—perhaps a dozen of them. They look alive. They are like your own children come home from the playground. Who are they? Where did they come from?

You grasp the handrail for support, but also because you are about to enter a total pitch black darkness. And suddenly, without warning, a wondrous sight—four candles are reflected a million times through mirrors. You are surrounded by glimmering lights, stars. You are gazing in awe into the heavens and feel so small, insignificant. You have no contact and no reference. There is no floor beneath you; you are suspended in the darkness. All you are left with are your own thoughts as you hear the calm soothing voices of a man and a woman slowly reciting the names of children . . . Ruth, Asher, Joseph, Naomi . . . name, age, died . . . in English, Hebrew, Yiddish . . . without end.

You are so gripped by the moment that you want to stand there and wait until every name is recited, a million times. You try to count as many of those glimmering stars as you can, to leave with something captured. It is futile.

But as you turn to exit, you know that you will not remember their names, nor faces, nor understand why they had to die. You leave the place as suddenly as you found it. Once outside, you feel the burst of the bright and warm sun— a sun which bleaches out all your sighs, your wish to pay tribute, somehow, to those innocent lives.

What can you do? Nothing. But frozen in your mind is the image of thousands of flickering lights that burned out before their time.

YOM HASHOA: FROM FOREST HILLS TO THE WHITE HOUSE

By Eli Zborowski

As survivors we are grateful to the President of the United States, to Congress and to all those who have been actively involved in the institution of Days of Remembrance. The culmination was reached on Yom Hashoa with the holding of an observance in the White House.

The observance had its roots in the Warsaw Ghetto Uprising, which began on April 19, 1943. In 1953 the Israeli Knesset enacted the Holocaust and Resistance Law, which set aside the 27th of Nissan, on the Hebrew calendar, as an annual day of observance for the remembrance of all the Jewish martyrs of the European catastrophe and for tribute to the heroes of the Holocaust.

The choice of 27 Nissan was deliberate: as close as possible to April 19 and 8 days before Israel Independence Day. As survivors we well remember that Israel became a state right after World War II—on the ashes of Auschwitz, Treblinka, and Majdanek, and on the heroism symbolized by the flames of the ghetto revolts.

As survivors we also remember that during the war no country was willing to accept us, the persecuted Jews from Europe, within its boundaries. For that reason we appreciate so much more the existence of the State of Israel.

On Yom Hashoa, then, we are united with all brethren wherever they may be. And we are united by remembering our past. But not only the Jewish people must remember the Holocaust. It is a moral imperative for all humanity not to forget.

The observance of the Holocaust began quietly. In 1964 a small group of survivors—some presently working closely with the U.S. Holocaust Memorial Council—commemorated the first Yom Hashoa observance on record, outside of Israel, on 27 Nissan, at the Young Israel of Forest Hills, with the participation of the majority of Jewish communities, organizations, and institutions in the Borough of Queens. Since that historic event, every year a Yom Hashoa commemoration is held on 27 Nissan at the Young Israel of Forest Hills. The initiators of the Yom Hashoa observance in Forest Hills encouraged neighboring communities to hold their own observance. As a result we find today that on Yom Hashoa or on its

308

preceding evening, countless synagogues sponsor programs before fully packed gatherings throughout Queens, throughout New York City, throughout New York State, and throughout the United States and Canada, and the world.

A history of Yom Hashoa observance can not be meaningful or complete without speaking of the role of the American Federation of Jewish Fighters, Camp Inmates, and Nazi Victims. Organized in 1971 as a roof organization for survivors, the American Federation had as its main objective the permanent affixing of 27 Nissan, Yom Hashoa V'Hagvurah —and its corresponding day of the English calendar—as the annual day of observance for the martyrdom and heroism of the six million innocent souls who lost their lives simply because they were born as Jews.

The American Federation proceeded vigorously to carry out its objective. Upon its initiative a proclamation was issued in 1972 to observe 27 Nissan as a national remembrance date in conformity with Jewish communities throughout the world. National communities joined in endorsing the proclamation. The joint proclamation has been reissued annually ever since 1972, and today more than 80 national Jewish organizations cosponsor the proclamation.

M&R 7:6, May-June, 1981

THE PRESIDENT'S REMARKS FOR YOM HASHOA

Comments by PRESIDENT REAGAN

. . . This meeting, this ceremony has meaning not only for people of the Jewish faith, those who have been persecuted, but for all who want to prevent another Holocaust.

Jeremiah wrote of the days when the Jews were carried off to Babylon and Jerusalem was destroyed. He said, "Jerusalem weeps in the night and tears run down her cheeks." Today, yet, we remember the suffering and the death of Jews and of all those others who were persecuted in World War II. We try to recapture the horror of millions sent to gas chambers and crematoria. And we commemorate the days of April in 1945 when American and Allied troops liberated the Nazi death camps. The tragedy that ended 36 years ago was still raw in our memories because it took place, as we've been told, in our lifetime. We share the wounds of the survivors. We recall the pain only because we must never permit it to come again. . . .

I'm horrified today when I know that . . . there are actually people now trying to say that the Holocaust was invented, that it never happened, that there weren't six million people whose lives were taken cruelly and needlessly in that event, that all of this is propaganda. Well, the old cliché that a picture is worth a thousand words. In World War II, not only do we have the survivors today to tell us first-hand, but in World War II, I was in the military and assigned to a post where every week we obtained from every branch of the service all over the world the combat film that was taken by every branch. And we edited this into a secret report for the general staff. We had access to and saw that secret report.

And I remember April '45. I remember seeing the first film that came in when the war was still on, but our troops had come upon the first camps and had entered those camps. And you saw, unretouched—and no way that it could have ever been rehearsed—what they saw—the horror they saw. I felt the pride when, in one of those camps, there was a nearby town, and the people were ordered to come and look at what had been going on, and to see them. And the reaction of horror on their faces was the greatest proof that they had not been conscious of what was happening so near to them.

And that film still, I know, must exist in the military, and there it is, living motion pictures, for anyone to see, and I won't go into the horrible scenes that we saw. But, it remains with me as confirmation of our right to rekindle these memories, because we need always guard against that kind of tyranny and inhumanity. Our spirit is strengthened by remembering and our hope is in our strength. There is an American poem that says humanity, with all its fears and all its hopes, depends on us.

The hope of a ceremony such as this is that even a tortured past holds promise if we learn its lessons. According to Isaiah, there will be a new heaven and a new earth and the voice of weeping will be heard no more. Together, with the help of God, we can bear the burden of our nightmare. It is up to us to ensure that we never live it again. . . .

"NO RECONCILIATION WITHOUT REMEMBRANCE"

By RICHARD VON WEIZSAECKER

Today we mourn all the dead of the war and the tyranny. In particular we commemorate the six million Jews who were murdered in German concentration camps. . . . At the root of the tyranny was Hitler's immeasurable hatred against our Jewish compatriots. Hitler had never concealed this hatred from the public, but made the entire nation a tool of it. Only a day before his death, on April 30, 1945, he concluded his so-called will with the words: "Above all, I call upon the leaders of the nation and their followers to observe painstakingly the race laws and to oppose ruthlessly the poisoners of all nations: international Jewry." Hardly any country has in its history always remained free from blame for war or violence. The genocide of the Jews is, however, unparalleled in history.

The perpetration of this crime was in the hands of a few people. It was concealed from the eyes of the public, but every German was able to experience what his Jewish compatriots had to suffer, ranging from plain apathy, and hidden intolerance to outright hatred. Who could remain unsuspecting after the burning of the synagogues, the plundering, the stigmatization with the Star of David, the deprivation of rights, the ceaseless violation of human dignity? Whoever opened his eyes and ears and sought information could not fail to notice that Jews were being deported. . . . The nature and scope of the destruction may have exceeded human imagination, but apart from the crime itself, there was, in reality, the attempt by too many people, including those of my generation, who were young and not involved in planning the events and carrying them out, not to take notice of what was happening. There were many ways of not burdening one's conscience, of shunning responsibilities, looking away, keeping mum. When the unspeakable truth of the Holocaust then became known at the end of the war, all but too many . . . claimed that they had not known anything about it or even suspected anything.

There is no such thing as the guilt or innocence of an entire nation. Guilt is like innocence, not collective, but personal. There is discovered or concealed individual guilt. There is guilt which people acknowledge or deny. Everyone who

311

directly experienced that era should today quietly ask himself about his involvement then.

The vast majority of today's population were either children then or had not been born. They cannot profess a guilt of their own for crimes that they did not commit. . . . But their forefathers have left them a grave legacy. All of us, whether guilty or not, whether old or young, must accept the past. We are all affected by its consequences and liable for it. The old and young generations must and can help each other to understand why it is vital to keep alive the memories. It is not a case of coming to terms with the past. That is not possible. . . .

The Jewish nation remembers and will always remember. We seek reconciliation. Precisely for this reason we must understand that there can be no reconciliation without remembrance. The experience of millionfold death is part of the very being of every Jew in the world, not only because people cannot forget such atrocities, but also because remembrance is part of the Jewish faith.

(The address by the West German President was given May 8, 1985, the 40th year of German surrender.)

M&R 12:14, Sept.-Oct., 1985

POLAND OBSERVES 45TH ANNIVERSARY OF UPRISING

Plans are being shaped in Poland for the 45th commemoration of the Warsaw Ghetto Uprising. Officials and scholars, civic leaders and religious representatives, veterans from various Allied Armies that fought together against the Nazi beast, and youth the world over are joining ranks to pay tribute to the heroic fighters in the Ghettos.

According to Stefan Grayek, president of the World Federation of Jewish Fighters, Partisans, and Camp Inmates, a number of ceremonies will take place during April 15-19, with the participation of the World Federation and other international Jewish organizations.

These ceremonies include:

The opening of a Perpetuation Site in the Umschlagplatz,

from which the Jews were deported to Treblinka; a memorial gathering is being arranged at the site of the former Treblinka camp;

A scientific conference on the fighting of Jews and Poles against the Nazi occupiers, under sponsorship of the Polish Academy of Sciences, whose invitees will be historians and researchers from Israel, the U.S., and other countries.

The placing of wreaths at the Statue in Warsaw;

Gathering at the Great Theatre in Warsaw;

A visit by 1,500 Jewish youth from all over the world highlighting the observance of Yom Hashoa, corresponding this year to April 14, which will be held at Treblinka, the site of the German death camp and the crematorium, where over 800,000 Jews perished. Among those brought to Treblinka were most of the Jews from Warsaw and from other places in Poland and Jews from as distant as Paris, France;

The holding of the Quiz for World Jewish Youth on all facets of Jewish fighting during World War II, to be held on the very site of the "Jewish battlefield" in Warsaw, near the monument in memory of the Warsaw Ghetto Fighters.

Representatives of Jewish youth from countries like Rumania, Hungary, U.S.S.R. and from all over the Western world will participate together with personalities like Yitzhak Navon, educational minister of Israel and former President, as well as Edgar Bronfman, chairman of The World Jewish Congress.

It is expected that survivors will come in numbers to pay special tribute this year on the 45th Anniversary to their fallen comrades in the Warsaw Ghetto Uprising and to the hundreds and thousands of Jewish partisans who fought and fell in battle with the German oppressor.

The Polish authorities and the Israeli representative in Warsaw, Ambassador Mordechai D. Palzur, have expressed their interest in participating in the observance of the 45th Anniversary of the Warsaw Ghetto Uprising, which is the symbol of Jewish resistance and the Jewish contribution in the fight against Nazism, along with the Jewish participation in the Allied Armies, fighting together against the enemy.

M&R 14:1, Jan.-Feb. 1988

A PSYCHO-MORAL QUESTION

By Prof. A. Roy Eckardt

What does it mean to remember the Holocaust, the *Endlösung* ("Final Solution")? What is the purpose of remembering? Elie Wiesel has spent much of his life expressing such remembrance. Yet he himself has asked, "Remember what? And what for? Does anyone know the answer to this?" What are the virtues, the necessities in remembering? Would it not be better to forget? Again, there is the most vexing question: How is the Holocaust to be remembered?

Because of the very nature of the *Endlösung*, its remembrance tends to open up certain moral and psychological dangers. Death and destruction ever draw unto themselves human fascination. What horror tale can possibly compare to the Holocaust? It is replete with all the trimmings: piercing screams, silent but endless tears, rape, homosexual acts, flowing blood, rotting corpses. The greater the horror, the greater the opportunity for macabre pleasures. That a pornography of the Holocaust should have long since developed may revolt us, but it can scarcely surprise us.

The suffering of Jews has been so impregnated into our conscious and unconscious selves that our very study of it, our very attention to it, may well foster a kind of tacit or unconscious consent. . . . May not the remembrance of the Holocaust, especially in its temptingly obsessional aspects, kindle within itself a clandestine drive to repeat 1933, 1938, 1944? In gazing down into the abyss, may we not open the abyss within ourselves?

One member of the American clergy reported to my wife and me that several Christian participants in a visit to Yad Vashem, the memorial in Jerusalem to Holocaust martyrs and heroes, manifested hostility in face of all the remembering. (Would this hostility have surfaced if guilt were not somehow being summoned up?) A Roman Catholic priest who serves as an official Israeli guide told us that on one occasion some members of a group of German clergy declined to enter the Yad Vashem museum exhibit. They protested: "This has nothing to do with us." If the *Endlösung* is anti-Semitism in its final logic, may not the perpetuators of Holocaust memories be inadvertently keeping alive resentments and hatreds? May they not be acting, all unintentionally, in ways that sustain and aggravate *Judenfeindschaft?* This eventually becomes a special menace whenever charges of guilt are brought without proper discriminateness and care. At a Hamburg International Conference on the Holocaust and the Church Struggle in 1975, the first such assembly to be held on German soil, Caesar C. Aronsfeld of London objected to a concentration upon guilt and repentance. He contended that when people are forced to prostrate themselves or humble themselves, they will eventually turn upon the party they identify as making this demand. Nathan Rotenstreich of Hebrew University asserts that it is not easy to entertain or maintain feelings of guilt; they continually threaten one's pride and self-righteousness.

In addition, the plaint is often forthcoming that concentration upon the remembrance of the Holocaust is a waste of energy and has harmful consequences. Such effort only serves to keep us from helping to resolve the really fateful problems that today plague mankind and, if they are not solved, will lead to the extinction of man: the food shortage, overpopulation, pollution, wastage of the world's resources, annihilative weaponry—and, for that matter, additional genocides, not excepting potential genocidal acts against the Jewish people themselves. Every year, fifty million persons die of starvation —some eight times the number of Jews that were destroyed by the German Nazis.

A kindred attitude to this derives from a kind of baffled pragmatism: What, after all, can be "done" with the Holocaust? This outlook is exemplified in a statement from the German historian Golo Mann, son of Thomas Mann: "I think of Auschwitz once a week and have done so for thirty years. But you can't expect millions of Germans to don sackcloth and ashes and repent all the time. One likes to forget because what can you do with it?"

If there are psycho-moral dangers in remembering the Holocaust, there are counter-dangers in not remembering.

A former resistance fighter living in Israel, a man who himself advocates full discussion of the Holocaust, emphasized to us the unqualified right of individual survivors and their families to forget, if they so desire. Here is suggested one of the moral complications within public Holocaust observances in the State of Israel, from which, primarily due to the omnipresent "media," it is so difficult to escape. However, much depends upon who it is that is counseling forgetfulness, and to whom the counsel is directed.

There is all the moral difference in the world between a possible plea from a Jewish spokesman that his people ought to turn away from the horrors of yesteryear, and the actual pronouncement of the Chancellor of the *Bundesrepublik* that Germans have learned their lesson from the past. One may argue with the first party without necessarily charging him with an ideological taint or hypocrisy. With respect to the second party, the issue of self-deception and the deception of others is unavoidably raised. This other possible response is prompted as well by a moral reaction to the pervading public viewpoint within today's BRD that the "media" ought no longer dwell upon the Nazi atrocities. The same critical response may be called for against all those whose counsel of forgetting is demonstrably accompanied by insensitivity or by anti-Semitic attitudes.

In a word, there is a licit forgetting and there is a culpable one.

While the remembrance of the *Endlösung* carries psycho-moral dangers, a tacit or advocated forgetfulness bears equal or greater dangers. Personality wholeness and psychic health demand a reasonable harmony among the volitional, affective, and cognitive dimensions of the self. In a vital sense, this is also true at the collective level. In the words of Harvey Cox, "Psychiatrists remind us that the loss of a sense of time is a symptom of personal deterioration. . . . The same is true for a civilization. So long as it can absorb what has happened to it and move confidently toward what is yet to come its vitality persists." Alienation from its past induces decline and ultimately death.

One rejoinder to the counselors of oblivescence is that back-turning, suppression, and repression are aspirin tablets in the treating of cancer. The disease quickly reasserts itself, and when this occurs, the forms are often as terrible as before. Nor is the passage of years necessarily of help. Thus, Prof. Bastiaans found in many cases of the post-concentration camp syndrome among survivors, that the longer the lapse of time, the more serious the symptoms and the suffering. A final horror of the German Nazi system is its power to reach out beyond the generations it ravished, taking unto itself new victims. It is doing so at this very moment. Where, then, is the moral legitimacy in arguing that the Holocaust belongs to the past and ought to be forgotten?

M&R 4:3, March-April, 1978

INTERNATIONAL GATHERING UNITES SCHOLARS ON REMEMBRANCE THEME

By Dr. Michael N. Dobkowski

During the week of July 10-17, there was an extraordinary international conference sponsored by the Oxford Centre for Postgraduate Hebrew Studies, the Vidal Sassoon International Centre for the Study of Anti-Semitism at Hebrew University in Jerusalem, the Anne Frank Institute of Philadelphia and Elisabeth and Robert Maxwell of Pergamon Press. Convened in Oxford and London, the conference was entitled "Remembering for the Future: The Impact of the Holocaust and Genocide on Jews and Christians."

Some 600 academics from 24 countries gathered to listen to, discuss, and debate papers prepared by 300 scholars on a wide variety of themes relating to Christian-Jewish relations; the theological implications of the Holocaust; the challenge of the Holocaust to the Jewish community; the impact of the Holocaust on survivors and on the contemporary world; the roots of altruism and rescue; comparisons of the Holocaust to other genocidal actions; and identifying genocidal signals in the contemporary world. The participants listened to the insightful and inspirational words of such eminent authorities as Nobel Laureate Elie Wiesel, historian Yehuda Bauer, filmmaker Claude Lanzmann and theologians Franklin H. Littell and Emil Fackenheim.

What impressed us all about this "unique" event was the sense of purpose and dedication displayed by all: Christians, Jews, Holocaust survivors, Armenians, and Gypsies—to the principle of dialogue and mutual understanding. There were many disagreements, some frustrations, moments of tears, anguish and even anger, but in the end the scholars were united in their efforts to try to "understand" the Holocaust in its religious and historical contexts; to be true to the evidence so that revisionists and deniers will not enjoy intellectual legitimacy; and to further the cause of inter-faith dialogue and cooperation.

We also came away energized by the conviction that the recurring phenomenon of genocide calls for comparative study. We can no longer conceive of it as a random or even relatively rare historic phenomenon. Instead, we are compelled to look for patterns which lead to and are associated with these annihilations. Difficult as it may be to accept such a notion, we

A LEGACY RECORDED

must look upon the history and nature of societies giving rise to genocide as human-made and thereby influencable. We have to realize that mass murder does not occur in a vacuum.

Any other perspective would preclude the human agency necessary for destruction and necessary, conversely, to act to prevent it. By postulating that the social and historic circumstances making genocide possible are human-made, we must begin to penetrate the circumstances under which human beings have been annihilated in the past so that we can establish criteria for the prevention of similar destructions in the future.

To achieve this end, we need the input of scholars from a variety of disciplines and the using of a variety of techniques and sources. Certain insights that emerge from an examination of the Holocaust can and should be applied to a systematic, comparative study of genocide. We need to develop "early warning systems" that alert us to the possibility of genocidal actions in our own time. If the Holocaust has taught us anything, this conference revealed, it has taught us that certain target groups can become vulnerable to annihilation if the historical and structural conditions are ripe. Moreover, this vulnerability is enhanced when certain target groups are removed from the circle of obligation by being de-legitimized, and classified as the other, as an object with no rights; when they are symbolized as the source of evil or racial and religious corruption; when they are vilified in a concerted ideological attack; and when they are collectivized and isolated.

In 1959 Theodor Adorno wrote a sentence worth quoting: "We'll have come to terms with the past only when the causes that led to it will be abolished." To the extent that we can illuminate the shadows of the past, there is less likelihood that they will again fall upon the future. Correct action requires understanding. Whatever progress is made in this pursuit, and I think progress was made at this conference, will contribute to diminishing the possibility that we will engage in genocide in the future. In this approach the study of the circumstances that made the Holocaust possible becomes paradigmatic for studying other genocides—real or potential. This dialectical tension between the Holocaust and genocide (which has an omnicidal potential in the nuclear age) is the only way to relate the Holocaust to other genocidal events, preserving both its uniqueness and relevance. In this approach, finally, the study of the past carries with it a moral purpose, that is, for the sake of the future.

XVI.
The End of the 20th Century and Beyond

In 1995 the world will mark the 50th anniversary of the liberation of the death camps and the end of World War II. Throughout the past five decades, remembrance programs and centers have sprung up throughout the world and have flourished.

However, as we look ahead to the future, we can clearly see that there is no end to the problems we face, among them the Revisionists who deny the Holocaust, the racism and anti-Semitism on college campuses, the urgency of utilizing the experiences of survivors before they vanish.

To meet these challenges, major Holocaust facilities have been established, including those in Washington and Los Angeles. However, we still are convinced that Yad Vashem, the Israeli Remembrance Authority in Jerusalem, is the best guarantor that Holocaust remembrance will be fixed on the martyrdom and heroism of the Six Million and will offer the incisive lessons to prepare for the problems and concerns of the future.

Of note are these articles: "Addressing the Problems of African American Racism in Academia" (Barry Mehler 20:10 November-December 1993, January-February 1994); *Denying the Holocaust: The Growing Assault on Truth and Memory* (Deborah Lipstadt, 20:2, November-December 1993, Review, Diane Cypkin).

ON KRISTALLNACHT:
IT TOOK 50 YEARS TO SPEAK

By Hanna Goldsmith

I will try in capsule form to tell you about Kristallnacht. It took me 50 years to talk about it in public. It is hard for me to believe that 50 years have passed and that I am able to stand here to tell you the story. Many others were not as privileged.

We lived in the outskirts of Frankfurt. We received a phone call that my father should not get out of the house. The Nazis were arresting all Jewish men, taking them off the streets, buses, cars, and trains. They were burning the Torah scrolls and synagogues.

Our synagogue was built with maple wood, and since they could not burn this most beautiful synagogue, they used dynamite to destroy it.

It was a very busy time for the Nazis and a very bad time for us. They smashed all the windows of Jewish stores, went to the owners' homes, destroyed the furniture and threw it into the street.

We had heard the Nazis don't arrest men over 50 years, and since my father was over 60 years at the time, we felt a little relieved—but not for long. The next day we heard that all the presidents of all synagogues were going to be arrested. Since my father was the president of our synagogue for 35 years, we knew that they would come to us.

We were strict Sabbath observers. Our electric clock had just gone off when we heard the pounding footsteps— which I still can hear today—followed by knocking at the door.

I told them that this was our Sabbath and we were not allowed to turn on the lights. We had a night light, so it was not too dark. When they asked for my father, I told them that he was in bed, had a heart condition, for which the doctor had prescribed bed rest.

(The above are excerpts from the Kristallnacht program at the Jewish Community Center in Reading.)

Determined To Save Father

That makes no difference, they told me. He had to come along. I also told them that my mother was paralyzed and needed 24-hour care. I made up my mind to save my father. But they told me that my mother's condition had nothing to do with my father. It had a lot to do with my father, I told them, and, moreover, I informed them that they could take me, but not my father. After about fifteen to twenty minutes, they informed me that they would think about the situation. They then left.

We were relieved, but not for long. A half-hour later we heard again the marching of the SS. Looking behind the drapes, I could see many people who were waiting to see if my father would be arrested.

Several SS men entered the house once more, and began the process again. They insisted that they had strict orders to arrest my father. In response, I stood firm that my father was under strict doctor's orders not to leave the bed. Moreover, my father had done much for the community, and many of the citizens were good friends with my brothers. I must have been very convincing because they departed without my father.

The tension eased, but we still suffered along with the others. My brother-in-law was arrested.

After several days had passed, the men were still detained in the convention hall. Then we heard that they had been shipped to Dachau, Begen-Belsen, and other concentration camps.

It is important for me to tell you so that you all know: in that turmoil and confusion, there were Christians who put their lives on the line. Our tailor, who had many Jewish customers, took in 30 men, fed them, and sheltered them in his apartment until it was safe for them to return to their homes.

A YOUTH VISITS POLAND: LEAVES WITH COMMITMENT

BY DEBBIE TAUBENBLATT

While I was on my way to Poland, many thoughts entered my mind. Like all of you, I had seen countless pictures and movies, heard testimonies of survivors and tried to visualize that which is too horrifying to imagine. This time I knew it would be different. I would be seeing it through my own eyes, not those of my elders recalling the nightmares which they'd rather forget. I was nervous, yet awaiting desperately to see the terror that our people were faced with. The first concentration camp we visited was Auschwitz. The tales suddenly became reality and the horror was no longer just a far away tale. The realization that I was on the exact ground that my family, our families, stood on, forty years before as they were endlessly terrorized by the Germans, sent chills through my spine.

The Auschwitz we can visit today is really a reconstructed version of the Nazi death camp that stood forty years ago. It now stands with bricks, windows and doors, when all that stood then were sealed wooden shacks. Surrounding me were miles and miles of fields. . . .

On Yom Hashoa, more than 2,000 marched in what was called the March of the Living. It was ironic, for the road on which we were marching was then the actual road to death. As we began to march, hand in hand, snow began to fall, and in my mind all I kept hearing were the screams, the cries of the children, the helpless mothers pleading for their lives, for their babies' lives, as they were forced to watch their loved ones fall.

Entering Birknau the chill was unbearable. I could not help but think how anyone survived in their bare flesh when I, fully clothed, was freezing. From there we went to a memorial service in the commemoration of all who perished. As the speaker began to speak about Israel, the sun suddenly began to shine brightly. It was errie, and we all got the feeling that it was more than a mere coincidence.

Our next stop was Majdanek. The night before going

Debbie Taubenblatt of Forest Hills, N. Y., was among the 2,000 students who were in Poland for Yom Hashoa 5748 and took part in the March of the Living from Auschwitz to Birkenau.

we were all warned and spoken to about this camp. I didn't think anything of it. I didn't believe there was a diversity among death camps; after all, how much worse can one be from the other? I had no idea what was in store for me. Upon entering, we stopped at the first memorial and this time it was my turn along with the people on my bus to give the service. I felt as though I was doing something special—something to perpetuate the memory of those who died in Majdanek. . . .

Majdanek, centered in the middle of the city Lublin, was left untouched. There were barracks and barracks filled with shoes, caps, brushes and clothing. We saw actual bones and ashes—we entered the gas chambers that still had the blue gas on the walls. The room, which was built to fit maybe thirty to fifty people, accommodated 300, doomed to death. . . .

Today, in our free world, there are still people who deny this great trauma, who say the Holocaust never took place. However, I saw that not only was it real but it was seen by many others. Majdanek was in the center of a town, meaning the Poles could actually look out their windows and see the flames rising from the crematorium chimneys. If they didn't see the inside of the camp, they most certainly saw the Jews marching through the city—beaten to death on their way to Majdanek. The trains stopped three miles away from the camp, so the Jews had to walk the rest of the way. But the population closed their eyes and there was silence. . . .

The end of my trip was soon approaching. I couldn't help but feel joy overwhelm me at the thought of leaving. I wanted to get out, put all this behind me. But like the survivors themselves, who tried for so many years to shut out the pain, the feeling of guilt was insurmountable. How could I feel this way? I felt terrible inside—the Jews had no choice! They could not leave; they had to remain and endure the brutality which would lead to death or to deep, unhealable scars. I felt revenge come over me, I was helpless: what could I do? I realized then that my only task was to never forget. I cannot help all those who died.

I can not ease the pain of those who survived. I can only make sure that when there are no more of that eyewitness generation to tell their tragic story firsthand, I will perpetuate their memory.

INAUGURAL CEREMONIES AT VALLEY OF DESTROYED COMMUNITIES

REMARKS OF ELI ZBOROWSKI
(Chairman, International Society for Yad Vashem)

The year of 1989 marks the 50th anniversary of the outbreak of World War II, the German attack on Poland, the outset of the Holocaust, the beginning of a saga of Jewish suffering with no parallel in mankind's history. The collective memory of that tragedy is more acute, more visible in the Jewish homeland than anywhere else in the world.

The Martyrs' and Heroes' Remembrance Law of 1953 obliges the people of Israel to commemorate the greatest tragedy in our history. Yad Vashem became the national Remembrance Authority on the basis that of that law and in the spirit of the Hebrew dictum articulated in *Isaiah*: "I will give unto them in my house and within my walls a *place and a name* [Yad Vashem]."

Yad Vashem, home for Six Million Souls, will now house the Valley of the Destroyed Communities as well. The Jewish people the world over recognize that the State of Israel is the most meaningful and lasting response to the Holocaust. To build and maintain a memorial in Israel, to help and support Yad Vashem is to ensure that the Jewish tragedy be remembered and lessons be drawn from authentic historical material.

In no other part of the world is the story of our tragedy, the Holocaust, told by survivors, by historians, and by a new generation of lecturers, as authentically as it is taught here at Yad Vashem.

Here on Har Hazikaron in the Eternal Capital of the Jewish People, the City of Jerusalem, I must reflect upon my own hometown, one of the 5,000 Jewish Communities destroyed in the greatest catastrophe to befall mankind. Zarki, a small town near Czestochowa, is the place where I was born and raised. Now there are no Moshelech and no Shlomelech in my hometown and none in the 1,415 Jewish communities that existed within the prewar Polish borders, where they dwelt and where Jewish life had flourished for 1,000 years.

Our community had religious, educational, charitable institutions that took care of every facet of Jewish life. Can we imagine, can we comprehend the magnitude of 1,000 *shtet* and *shtetlach* with their vivid and flourishing centers, with their Hasidim and Misnagdim, Zionists, and Bundists, religious and secular institutions.

Polish Jewry was one big center of Jewish creativity. When I returned to my *shtetl* after the liberation in January 1945, I realized that Zarki, my home town, remained. It is there, but Dzurik, its Yiddish name, is gone forever, together with the rest of Polish Jewry.

We, together, with our children—the future generations— will visit Jerusalem, pay homage to this Valley, pay respect to the names of the communities, remember them: how they lived, created, and perished.

Every town with a Jewish community will have its home here.

Many communities were wiped out and there are no remnants of a living Jewish soul. All in all, a total of 5,000 Jewish communities were hit and erased from the map of Europe.

We, the International Society for Yad Vashem, have joined Yad Vashem in a partnership to erect this Valley in which every community, be it small or large, will have its name engraved in Jerusalem stone and its history housed in the Beit HaKehilot, the Home of Communities. In this House we will gather, computerize, store, and disseminate every bit of historical information available on each *shtetl*, the life there, the problems and sufferings, the greatest days and moments of creativity.

This knowledge honors and commemorates each town and will remain an immeasurable source for teaching future generations. We, in turn, feel honored and privileged to have the opportunity to be a partner in this monumental task, as every Israeli is honored to share in Yad Vashem.

The International Society's officers on the dais are the driving force behind the campaign outside Israel and have been outstandingly generous, but credit belongs in equal measure to the more than 20,000 supporters who participate with their donations, large or small, whether they are here with us today or thousands of miles away.

Today, on this solemn day, we take an oath to remember the teachings and values that were once dear and precious to them, our forefathers. We will fulfill the commandment: "V'Shinantam L'Vanecha"—"And you shall teach your children."

We will teach our children. We will not forsake this institute of learning which we hold so dearly to our hearts. We will build and support Yad Vashem with all its educational facilities. We will strengthen the World Center for Holocaust Research and Studies so that mankind will learn from its history how to prevent recurrence of such tragedies. We have gathered here today to sanctify this site. Hundreds and thousands of Jews from all corners of the world have come to Jerusalem to Yad Vashem, to witness the consecration of Polish Jewry, once the educational center and the primary source for Jewish teaching for centuries.

We pray from the holy place that the hands of those who work for the cause of remembrance be strengthened, and that their endeavours touch the consciousness of every corner of the globe. We need Yad Vashem; world Jewry needs Yad Vashem. We wish you success, for therein lies our success, in ensuring that the memorial flame of the Holocaust will not be extinguished.

M&R 16:11, Nov.-Dec., 1989

VISITING THE VALLEY: SADNESS AND LOVE

BY ESTHER FARBER

We stood quietly on a hilltop at Yad Vashem, looking down into this national museum's newest, though yet unfinished, memorial to the six million victims of the Holocaust.

Small wildflowers, new life, pushed up among the terraced hillside of Jerusalem stone, while far below us, rose up the walls of The Valley of the Destroyed Communities. Columns of massive stone blocks, jagged and roofless, lifted skyward. The overall structure depicts the map of Europe as it was at the time of World War II. The pillars and walls symbolize the countries that contained the 5,000 Jewish communities that were totally annihilated in the Holocaust.

We maneuvered down a winding path among construction materials and unset slabs of stone and marble, until we reached the bottom and entered the memorial. A totally new perspective. Now we were looking up at the massive walls open to the sky. We were no longer in our beloved Jerusalem, but standing inside of Hungary, Poland, Austria, Germany, Czechoslovakia, and Russia. On the rough hewn stones and polished marble were carved the names of the communities.

As we walked through, I became lost in the maze, in the history, and in my memories. I searched the pillars, scanning the etched names, hoping to find my birthplace, Bratislava, Czechoslovakia.

My father was born in Satmar and raised in Topolcany. My mother was born in Lemberg and grew up in Vienna. Both my sister and I were born in Bratislava. Had my father's family survived, I would have had ten aunts and uncles instead of only the two who escaped when we did. I had seven cousins on my father's side, ranging in age from three to thirteen, all of whom were put to death in the camps.

I passed Berlin, Leipzig, Munich, Warsaw, Lodz, and Lublin, impatient and intent on finding one of my family's home towns. Knowing that our time was over, I almost gave up and started to head back to the entrance. There would be other visits, other years. Then, one of my friends came through a passageway and said, "I just saw Czechoslovakia, there to the left. I'll go with you."

We hurried back into the labyrinth and came to Hungary. Now there was a flash of recognition as I saw "Topolcany," my father's home. We took a picture to bring home to my dad. In the adjacent space was Vienna. Another photo. Finally we came to Bratislava, and as I posed beneath the column, my feelings crowded in at once. With barely time to explore what I was feeling, we walked away to rejoin our group.

Thinking back, the experience of standing inside The Valley of the Destroyed Communities was an awesome one, a mixture of sadness and love. I felt the presence of my lost family who had only known me until December 1939, when I was a toddler, and who are now only shadows to me. Of the six million Jews, the five thousand communities, those few had held me and played with me. They were my powerful connections. I felt thankful that my parents had managed to escape to America, and grateful for the many years of life I have enjoyed. How lucky we were!

And then I thought of my three wonderful grown up sons, who got the chance at life and made so much of it, and I could no longer hold back the tears. How blessed I feel to have been spared, to have given life to three bright and accomplished members of a new generation, all of them committed to the vitality of Judaism. They and I stand in place of those who perished.

M&R 18:9, May-June, 1992

PILGRIMAGE TO VALLEY
OF DESTROYED COMMUNITIES

By Dr. Luba K. Gurdus

Yad Vashem's newest Holocaust memorial, The Valley of Destroyed Communities, will be inaugurated in October, during the Feast of Sukkot. Embedded in its rocky hillside, the gigantic memorial has developed into a uniquely engrossing landmark, dramatically underscoring the enormity of Holocaust devastation.

Viewed from a distance, this open-air memorial suggests a labyrinth of truncated masonry shells wound around square spaces. But the symbolism and architectural merit of the memorial can only be fully realized in the very heart of the structure. Extending over a span of six acres, it was largely preconditioned by the regional typography and accordingly developed by two leading Israeli architects, Lipa Yahalom and Dan Zur, who succeeded to evoke the memorial's symbolism through a dramatic "descent" into the valley, suggesting the abyss of the Holocaust, and subsequent "ascent" into the heart of its adopted homeland.

Surrounded by an area of afforested hillside, the extensive memorial will have its own House of Communities, "Beit Hakehilot," where visitors will find exhaustive documentation on the destroyed Jewish centers from Yad Vashem and "Avotaynu," keeping records on 21,000 pre-Holocaust Jewish communities.

Eli Zborowski, chairman of Societies for Yad Vashem commented on Beit Hakehilot:

"In this house we will gather, computerize, store and disseminate every bit of historical information available on each shtetl, the life there, the problems and sufferings, the greatest days and moments of creativity."

Trekking through the "courtyards" of the Valley, I realized that each belongs to a family of countries distinguished by major urban centers engraved in bold letters on rough hewn blocks, flanking huge marble slabs in various sizes and colors, engraved with concentrations of Jewish towns, villages and shtetls surrounding the larger cities.

My euphoria reached its peak in Poland's major "courtyard" with "Warawa," prominently engraved on a huge wall facing on the opposite side my family's birthplace Bialystok, flanking a marble tablet with a long litany of familiar communities: Narew, Zabludow, Slonim. These names were often mentioned by my father, whose uncles and cousins died. On a high lintel of the passageway to the adjoining "courtyard," is the city of Lublin, which became the symbol of our own Holocaust calvary.

Aroused by emotions, I followed Poland's inexhaustible concentrations before I trekked to the south with Czechoslovakia, Hungary and Rumania, the east with the territories of the "Einsatzgruppen" and their mass grave at Babi Yar, and the north with Vilna, Kovno, Riga, and vicinities, cradles of Jewish religious and secular scholarship and endeavor.

Driven by indelible recollections, I turned to the west and brought my tantalizing journey to an end in the "courtyard" of Troudheim, the center of Norwegian Jews, whose dramatic rescue inspired the subsequent rescue efforts of the Scandinavians.

Thousands of communities, millions of human beings, turned into dust and rubble, have reclaimed for posterity in a reborn Jewish state, the State of Israel. Names of communities, eternalized in stone, will serve as poignant reminder of a sea of humanity which populated them over a millennium.

The Valley will become a place of pilgrimage for world Jewry seeking out the communities of their forebears, adopted by a reborn homeland: a place for the entire world to see, study and remember.

M&R 19:9, Sept.-Oct., 1992

PLACE TO REMEMBER, REFLECT, WEEP FOR WHAT'S LOST

By Dorothy Fuerst

Yad Vashem: memorial and remembrance. How can we remember and memorialize best those who were lost to us in that terrible time we call the Holocaust?

Dr. Yitzhak Arad, chairman of the Yad Vashem Directorate, has spent his professional life and has put to himself the task of how to express and memorialize that inexpressible loss. For many years Yad Vashem, under Dr. Arad's leadership, had directed its effort to show, as he explained, "how the destruction was carried out," to gather together the physical evidence of the means of destruction: in remembrance of those men and women and children who were destroyed."

Twelve years ago, Dr. Arad, inspired by a vision outlined by Eli Zborowski, turned his attention to "what was destroyed," to remembering, to memorializing the 5,000 Jewish communities in the Diaspora which had sustained and supported Jews in their physical and spiritual lives for hundreds of years. How does one memorialize in stone the 5,000 living, breathing communities, which, until the Holo-

caust destroyed them, constituted Jewish life across Europe?
Dr. Arad did not want tombstones, although what he
had to represent was death. The problem, therefore was, how
to represent the devastation and destruction of 5,000 centers
of Jewish life. Dr. Arad invited landscape architects in open
competition to plan a memorial to the last communities of
Europe; over 70 accepted the challenge. The plan for the
Valley of the Destroyed Communities had to provide for
communities as large as Warsaw or Vilna and as small as
the ones in Tirana, Albania, to represent all of Europe, symbolize an end yet stand for eternity. The winner of the contest was Dan Tsur, from the office of architects Lipe Yahalom
and Dan Tsur.

The Valley of the Destroyed Communities is designed
according to the map of Europe, beginning in the north, in
Oslo, Norway, progressing south to the Netherlands and
Belgium. To France, across to Eastern Europe to Poland,
where 1,600 Jewish communities were lost and are inscribed,
to Southern Europe, through Yugoslavia and south to the
two Jewish communities in Albania: light colored, massive,
natural hewn stones, rough alternating with smooth form
walls, one section drawing one along to the next.

Deep into the heart of each stone is engraved, in Hebrew
letters and Latin, the name of each village, town and city
in which there was a prewar Jewish community with a rabbi
and ritual slaughterer (shohet). Some stones are crowded
with names: small communities such as Piestany, Trnava,
Modra, Malacky, Stupava–small town life where families
and friends' lives were intertwined for generations and
generations. On some stones only one name is engraved:
Warsaw, Vilna, Berlin, Bratislava, large, thriving communities which exuded big city life and the vitality of Jewish
culture. All are gone.

In planning the Valley of the Destroyed Jewish Communities, Dr. Arad has had another mission in mind. "In
order to understand what was destroyed, we must speak,
teach about and study what was destroyed." Annually, Yad
Vashem has published studies of the devastated Jewish communities of Europe. However, these scholastic studies have
not had the popular circulation that Dr. Arad feels they
deserve. Therefore, at Dr. Arad's insistence, in the Valley
of the Destroyed Jewish Communities, there will be a Beth
Hakehilot, the images and the histories of the destroyed communities of Europe will be available for them in all their
myriad facets.

The construction of the Valley of the Destroyed Jewish Communities of Europe cost between $13 to $14 million, including provisions for infrastructure, such as access roads and electrical power lines which were necessary. Some of the money was provided by Landsmanschafts, community groups which wanted to perpetuate the memory of their towns. Some cities in Europe, particularly in Germany, contributed money to memorialize the Jewish communities in their midst which were exterminated. The largest contributor, by far, however, was the International Society for Yad Vashem, under the leadership of Eli Zborowski.

Walking through the Valley of the Destroyed Communities of Europe is a reminder of the Wailing Wall: massive stones, one above the other, with wisps of green, starting to grow between the rocks, signs of ongoing life. The smell of pine in the air. The stones of the Valley are open to the Judean sky, washed by the rain in the winter, warmed by the rays of the sun in the summer. The Valley is lit by man-made light at night, a place to reflect, perhaps to weep— the Valley of the Destroyed Jewish Communities of Europe: a place of memorial and remembrance.

M&R 19:9, Sept.-Oct., 1992

VISION OF EZEKIEL REALIZED AT VALLEY OF THE COMMUNITIES

By CAROLA GREENSPAN

Our first visit was to Yad Vashem and the Valley of the Communities. We were given a short introduction by the present members of the board of Yad Vashem and led by buses up the hill to look down at the Valley. It is impossible to put into words the feeling, when you are standing on top of that hill and have before you in stone the horrors of our destruction.

It is compared to the vision of Ezekiel's Valley of Dry Bones. Through this association the meaning of this symbol is just like in Ezekiel's vision: the bones will rise from the pits. So did the remnant emerging from the Holocaust embody the rebirth of the State of Israel. We were symbolically the first pilgrimage to Beit HaKehilot, where Cracow is prominently represented.

We were addressed by the new Director of Yad Vashem, Avner Shalev. All the speakers stressed the urgency of second generation involvement, to carry on the legacy of the Holocaust. To my great surprise, there was a concert scheduled at the Valley—the first concert to be held at Beit HaKehilot, a concert at a cemetery.

It was extremely difficult for me sitting there, surrounded by walls where each stone represents a lost life—and listen to music! But as I sat there surrounded by hundreds of people from all over the world in that cool breeze on a beautiful Jerusalem evening, I somehow became a part of that celebration of life, expressed under most confusing circumstances. I tried to understand that in our tradition we celebrate death and life: we celebrate Yom Hashoa and Yom Haatzmaut!

That evening in the Valley left an unforgettable impression . . .

M&R 20:8, Jan.-Feb., 1994

YAD VASHEM TEACHING SEMINAR HAD A POWERFUL IMPACT

By PNINA SPETGANG

This past summer I was among the 35 participants attending the Yad Vashem seminar "Teaching the Holocaust and Anti-Semitism" in Jerusalem.

All participants chose to spend three weeks of their summer vacation learning of the past, examining moral dilemmas of Jewish victims and leadership, confronting the evil perpetrated by human beings through lectures, films, exhibits, study guides and through personal testimonies of Holocaust survivors.

All educators are committed and dedicated to teach the

A LEGACY RECORDED

future generations so that this grim period in Jewish history will not be repeated to any group of individuals. Professor Yehuda Bauer, Shalmi Barmore, Sergio Della Pergola, David Bankier, Mordechai Paltiel and Yitzhak Arad were only a few among the many well-renowned members of the course faculty.

In addition to the formal lectures, we benefited from the informal discussions we led with each other. These were the most important and precious times we spend together, debating, challenging and questioning the validity of the issues studied.

One of the most important aspects of this course was the integration of Jews and non-Jews attending the course. This combination marked the first step in understanding each other, developing close friendships and future networking.

Aside from the intellectual aspect of this Seminar, living in Jerusalem for such an extended period of time was a spiritual experience for me.

The Seminar culminated in a service of remembrance "Lest We Forget." The service opened by reading victims' names who perished in the Holocaust. Readings from "Scrolls of Auschwitz" and "The Last Will and Testimony of Chelmo" were read by some participants others read their own personal reflections. Ani Ma'amin, Kel Maleh Rahamim, Kaddish and Hatikvah were sung by all.

During my life I attended many memorial services, but this one had a special meaning for me. The emotional impact was felt by everyone present. May the memory of all individuals who perished in the Holocaust be of blessed memory.

M&R 19:9, Jan.-Feb., 1993

YAD VASHEM SEMINAR
IS MEANINGFUL EXPERIENCE

BY ROZ ARZT

Austrians, Americans, and a few Israelis took part in the seminar. They included community leaders, teachers, lawyers, authors, reporters, members of the clergy, and recorders of testimonies of Holocaust survivors. Three who participated were Christian ministers. Many were children of survivors. One of them had fled from Poland to the Soviet Union and spent the war years in Soviet forced labor camps.

Intensive workshops designed to prepare the participants to present and teach the material upon returning to their communities were interspersed among the lectures, films, discussion groups, visits to museums and meetings with survivors.

The excellent lectures from Israel and abroad, the caring and responsible guidance of the Yad Vashem administration, the varied approaches to the subject matter and the personal and moving closing ceremony—planned and carried out by the participants—all made the course an unforgettable intellectual and emotional experience.

We began the course as 21 separate people. As we dealt with the intensive and sensitive presentation of a very difficult period in human history, we became an integrated and mutually supportive group.

M&R 16:8, May-June, 1990

YAD VASHEM PUBLICATIONS HELPFUL IN FAMILY HISTORIES

BY MIRIAM WEINER

Virtually everyone who visits Jerusalem comes to Yad Vashem, the world's foremost institution for Holocaust research and scholarship. There, they see and feel the horrors of the Holocaust through the exhibitions, memorials, documents and photos. In addition to the museum and memorials, Yad Vashem encompasses other equally important departments, including the libary, archives, education and research center, and publishing division.

In tracing family history, eventually each person wants to know what happened to their ancestral town during the Holocaust. The Yad Vashem publications represent a primary source for such information.

In 1970, Yad Vashem published the first volume of *Pinkas Hakehillot* (Encyclopedia of Jewish Communities). To date, 11 more have followed, covering Poland, Germany, Hungary, Netherlands, Romania, Yugoslavia and Latvia/ Estonia. Each volume in this on-going series is of use to historians, genealogists and anyone who wants to know the detailed history of their ancestral town.

These comprehensive volumes commemorate the Jewish communities destroyed during the Holocaust, beginning with a history of the Jewish presence and accompanied by maps, photographs of synagogues and other well-known buildings along with pictures of communal leaders and rabbis. Statistical tables trace the Jewish population. The extensive bibliography leads the reader to other sources.

What makes this series so valuable is that many of the localities included here are very small. Often, the entry represents the only available source of information. The series is published in Hebrew, although most volumes include an English index.

If one's ancestors came from the Soviet Union and served in the military, one may find extensive biographical information in *Under Fire: The Stories of Jewish Heroes* of the Soviet Union, compiled by Gershon Shapiro. The book is a collection of 150 biographies (with photos) and descriptions of the heroic deeds of Jews who were awarded

the distinction of "Hero of the Soviet Union" during the
war between Germany and the Soviet Union (1941-1945).

If one's family came from Romania, *Resisting the Storm:
Romania, 1940-1947, Memoirs* is a "must." In addition to
the name index, the place index enables one to immediately
focus on the area where one's family once lived. The book
includes many photos and documents from the memoirs of
Alexander Safran, former chief rabbi of Romania during
the most tragic years of this community: the destruction
of the Bessarabia and Bukovina Jews and the rescue of the
Jews from only Romania and South Transylvania.

Vilna was known for generations as the "Jerusalem of
Lithuania" due to its vibrant Jewish cultural life. For those
with roots in Vilna, see *Ghetto in Flames: The Struggle and
Destruction of the Jews in Vilna in the Holocaust*, by Yitzhak
Arad, chair of Yad Vashem's directorate. Anyone whose family came from Lithuania is likely to find references to their
ancestral town in the place index. The well-documented chapters are augmented with extensive photos, maps, statistical
charts and a detailed listing of archival material, all providing a vivid description of the fate of the Jews of Vilna and
a history of one of the largest ghettos.

Each year, Yad Vashem publishes another volume of
Yad Vashem Studies, containing a wide range of papers,
documents and book reviews dealing with various aspects
of the Holocaust written by scholars from Israel and abroad.
Twenty volumes have been published to date. One branch
of my family came from Shepetovka in the Volhynia district; therefore, a research paper by Shmuel Spector in Vol.
XV was of particular interest to me. This was "The Jews
of Volhynia and Their Reaction to Extermination," which
formed the basis for his subsequent book, *The Holocaust
of Volhynian Jews: 1941-1944*.

A unique chronicle of the Nazi extermination of more
than six million Jews and other "undesirables" can be found
in *The Pictorial History of the Holocaust*, a joint publication of Yad Vashem and Macmillan, Inc., edited by Yitzhak
Arad .This oversized book is an extraordinary compilation
of photos, maps and explanatory text.

The more than 400 photographs from Yad Vashem's
archives and private collections were taken at a time when
such photography was against the law in Germany and
other occupied territories.

These publications are found in many Judaic libraries

or may be purchased at Yad Vashem's bookstore. To order
by mail or to request a listing of titles, write to Yad Vashem,
P.O. Box 3477, Jerusalem 91034 Israel. Specify if the listing
of publications in Hebrew or English is preferred.

M&R 17:8, May-June, 1991

RIGHTEOUS GENTILES: QUALITY, NOT NUMBERS

By Dr. Mordechai Paldiel

There are those who respond to the assertion on the
significance of the Righteous Program at Yad Vashem, the
official Holocaust remembrance authority, by asserting,
"You're exaggerating and making an issue where none exists."

Recently in Lyon, France, a Belgian survivor of Auschwitz passionately related to a lecture I gave by claiming
that placing an emphasis on the righteous citizens who saved
Jews creates a false impression, as though people were
standing in line for the opportunity to help Jews. And we
know this to have been quite otherwise.

There is, of course, a measure of truth in these statements, but the issue is not one of numbers but the qualitative significance of these figures.

For some people, the story of the little goodness emanating from the pits of hell of the Holocaust raises anguished
fears that the frightening story of the Shoah itself will
somehow be distorted and trivialized, and perhaps be replaced by the relatively few stories about the righteous. But
the fears are unjustified. The case is quite otherwise.

The teaching of the Holocaust produces a sharper impact on those who did not witness it, when spiced with the
humanitarianism of the Righteous Gentiles. In order for the
Holocaust story to be viable for future generations, it needs
the little positive ingredient of the Righteous Gentiles.

Mordechai Paldiel is director of Yad Vashem's Department of
Righeous Gentiles.

Hence, the need for righteous stories to show how the individual can and did respond to the Nazi-type inhumanities, how a Christian ought to practice true Christianity ... devoid of hatred and animosity, and how one can and should assert one's humanity.

If only for this reason, the deeds of the Righteous Gentiles are an indispensable element in the teaching of the Holocaust—to demonstrate man's failure against the background of the righteous and, simultaneously, by desribing the simplicity of their deeds and lives, making it possible to identify with these heroes of the human spirit, and thus preclude a situation where the likes of Hitler stifle and paralyze our nature-given humanitarian responses.

But there's also a moral dimension to the teaching about Righteous Gentiles: it is that those who, like Hobbes and Freud, condemned man for his failures, and damned him as a savage brute bent on destroying everything that stands in his path of self-gratification—they don't tell the whole story.

There's an additional, not-yet-fully explored dimension, to man: of gratuitous love to one's fellow man without consideration of reward to himself—at times to help even at the risk of the life and freedom of the helper. This dimension needs to be further cultivated so that it may eventually evolve into a balancing counterweight to the destructive forces inherent in man's nature.

M&R 17:8, March-April, 1991

REFLECTIONS FROM POLAND
ON AN ANNIVERSARY

By Selma Schiffer

The balcony of the Nozyks Synagogue in Warsaw was filled to capacity. Sitting there that April morning, I was struck that in all the voices merging around me not a word of Polish was to be heard.

Selma Schiffer is the Executive Director of the Societies for Yad Vashem.

Dominant to my ear, rather, was the harsh, yet melodic
Hebrew being spoken by young Israeli women of every
color—white, black, and in between. They made for a strikingly
visual ingathering of the Jewish people from everywhere.
That they should now be on that balcony was no less a
miracle to me than any of which on Passover we say,
"Dayenu!"

The journey to Twarda Street and the Nozyks Synagogue
began two days earlier at Kennedy International Airport
in New York City, where I had boarded the Lot Polish
Airlines flight that took me non-stop to Warsaw. There I
joined the other members of the delegation representing the
American and International Societies for Yad Vashem taking part in the ceremonies commemorating the 50th Anniversary of the Warsaw Ghetto Uprising.

A bare listing of the events cannot convey the emotions
they evoked, the thoughts they inspired:

April 17. Sabbath morning services at the Nozyks
Synagogue, destroyed during the Nazi years and now rebuilt.

April 18, the 27th of Nissan, the day set by the Knesset
of Israel as Yom Hashoa for Jews worldwide, was commemorated at Treblinka, an event organized by the World
Federation of Jewish Fighters, Partisans and Camp Inmates,
which is headed by Stefan Grayek. The Chairman of the
American and International Societies for Yad Vashem, Eli
Zborowski, a former underground fighter himself, was one
of the speakers. And then in the evening, at the Cultural
Palace of Warsaw, the city was host at a special program
that included a performance by the Kaminska Yiddish
Theatre.

April 19. Many of the participating organizations, including the American and International Societies of Yad
Vashem, placed wreaths at the foot of the Monument to the
Heroes of the Uprising. A visit to Mila 18 followed, after
which the Governments of Israel and Poland took part in
an evening ceremony dedicating the Monument commemorating the historic occasion of the Warsaw Ghetto Uprising
that began April 19, 1943.

April 20. The American and International Societies for
Yad Vashem delegation was invited to join Prime Minister
Rabin and his party for a tour of Auschwitz and Birkenau.

All the events were listed on the program I received.
It was simple enough, of course. A black and white recita-
tion of the days and times the events were to take place.
But for the mind and the heart, there was no black and

white, and no program could schedule the emotions, the thoughts, the feelings of those days, feelings that I, as an American Jew whose grandparents left Poland long before the rise of Nazism, had up to now known only second-hand.

On Saturday morning I entered the Nozyks Synagogue through the rear because the front entrance had been defaced so often that not even a good scrubbing could erase the defilement. But the enduring scars of hatred only added to the sense of wonder I felt at being in a synagogue in Poland 50 years after the virtual annihilation of the Jewish people. Sitting there with the women of Israel, with Jewish women from Canada, South Africa, Latin America, Australia, England, France and other countries in Europe and elsewhere, I felt a sense of destiny—irrational and inexplicable, but joyous and proud.

And as I looked down at the scene below, I felt a sense of awe, too. For there were the old men of Poland. There were the young jean-clad Israelis. There were the unmistakable Western delegates to the anniversary commemoration. All together—in the main sanctuary down below and up here in the balcony—the scene was one of strength, of continuity, of faith.

And then there was the Chief Rabbi of Poland, quietly at his place near the Ark, orchestrating the proceedings. That scene within a scene—the rabbi directing the service—brought to my mind the Saturday mornings my grandfather would take me to *shul* with him in Brooklyn. For me, at that moment in time and place, Nozyks Synagogue merged with the *shteblich* in Brooklyn, with the grand synagogues of London, Paris and Berlin, and with all the *shtetlach* no longer here to welcome the Sabbath Bride. Yes, Warsaw was far away from Brooklyn in time and distance, but the memory it stirred is part of the glue binding me with remembrance.

It was the next day at Treblinka, where nothing remains but the monuments to the sound of the dead that the awesome reality settled deep inside of me. It remained with me at Auschwitz and at Birkenau, and it will now always be engraved on my consciousness and spirit. As I walked through the camps, it was as if I had become transformed. It wasn't today; it was 50 years ago, and I was there with my suitcase, there with my husband. And there was my hair, my grey hair, my glasses, and my toothbrush all gathered together. Yes, I could have been there, and that makes me a survivor, too, and so compelled to testify.

The speeches by President Walesa, Prime Minister Rabin, and Vice President Gore delivered no unexpected surprises. They honored the past, and they spoke of hope for the future. But nothing they had to say, not all the stories about Holocaust memorials and their uses. Not all the scholarly treatises and agonized philosophizing and theorizing on authentic memory and the Holocaust—none of it really gets to the heart of it. All objectivity fades away and all I feel standing in front of the crematorium at Birkenau is my mind. All I see are the railway tracks next to the town road, the neat houses lining it now, even as then, the houses that witnessed the human freight passing by.

Looking back now, I want to believe that the Polish people yearn to reconcile. One by one, their leaders spoke of it as the day of Yom Hashoah came to a close. But nothing spoke louder than the hope spelled out by the picture of the Chief Rabbi of Poland and the Archbishop of Warsaw sitting side by side on the night of April 18, 1993.

When all the words and prayers were said, after the ceremonies were over, Kaddish sad, memories recalled, tears shed, what I remember is that on the first night of Passover in 1943 a shot rang out in the Warsaw Ghetto. The Jewish people stood together in armed resistance against ther enemies. That was when Israel was reborn in our time.

It is the legacy that now belongs to all Jews everywhere.

M&R 19:6, May-June, 1993

REMEMBERING COMMON HISTORY, COMMON TRAGEDY

We are assembled here for a special moment. Fifty years ago on Sunday, April 18, at this hour, a decision was made. The commandant of the Jewish fighting forces issued an order to defend the Warsaw Ghetto. . . .

The world looked with surprise . . . and kept silent. Closed in the ghetto, condemned to death, people rose to

---

(The above remarks were made during the 50th anniversary ceremonies in Poland by Andrzej Zakrzewski, Minister for Polish-Jewish Relations.)

resist. In deepest despair, they found courage to oppose the inhuman verdict, in order to manifest the right to choose their own end and die with dignity, with honor.

And then came the final, heroic day. The Ghetto defenders were dying—lonely, without support of the world, which looked from afar, indifferently....

We are here to remember, 50 years ago, as we looked on the greatest crime, perpetrated in world history. They sought to liquidate a nation on its own soil. A tremendous common grave was dug up. The Star of David was painted on the armbands you wore in the ghetto. "I believe that in the future in Poland, this Star, this band will be the highest medal awarded to the bravest," wrote Julian Tuwim in the text *We Polish Jews*....

Our neighbors were buried here, our brothers with whom we lived together ... We had good times together; however, there were also very difficult times ... Memories of those good and bad times were deeply embedded within us when the Holocaust came.

A half century ago, the enemy committed as cruel a crime as possible. He took away a part of us, our close ones: neighbors, citizens. This empty place constantly reminds us of the extent of this tragedy. Not all wounds are healed today. The Holocaust still hovers over everything....

We remember our common history and we remember our common tragedy.

However, we cannot cry anymore over the event. We have to transform the memory into new values.... We must wage war with the bestial instincts within. Dangerously, the world today is forgetting past experiences, which make possible the repetition of past experiences. We, who lost one-fifth of a nation, see that even today hate generates a new harvest.

I, therefore, close with the words of a Pole and a Jew, a poet, whose work we will admire in a monument: "Become, therefore ... the living force behind the battle for goodness and justice in this world."

AT TREBLINKA:
MARKING THE REVOLT

REMARKS BY ELI ZBOROWSKI

We came assembled here from different parts of the world to pay respect and honor to the heroic fighters of the Warsaw Ghetto at the fiftieth anniversary of the first armed resistance to the German occupation. We congratulate Stefan Grayek, leader of the Warsaw Ghetto uprising and the World Federation of Survivors, of which he is the president, for their role in organizing this event, for having brought us to Treblinka, to mark the Fiftieth Anniversary of Jewish resistance to inhumanity and tyranny.

The uprising in the Warsaw Ghetto inspired other ghettos, such as Czestochowa, Bedzin, Bialystok and others, to revolt against the enemy. Even in the death camp of Treblinka there was armed revolt. The Jewish partisans fought along with other underground fighters and at times as Jewish units and today we honored their glorious deeds.

But resistance also manifests itself in many other ways—in non-violent ways, where the victim uses courage, decency, and humanity to frustrate the aggressor's designs and robs him—the aggressor—of his "victory."

We are all aware of cases where parents or children, with the possibility to escape, refused to leave their loved ones and chose to die together, thus defying the basic instinct of nature, which calls for self-preservation at any cost.

In this moving moment my memory takes me back to my hometown Zarki near Czestochowa, from where the entire Jewish community was dragged to this place—to this death camp—Treblinka. The two spiritual leaders, the Rabbis in our community, sacrificed themselves and chose to accompany their fellow Jews to certain death, although they had the possibility at that time to escape. And so did my 29-year-old aunt Yaffa Salcia, who chose to go with her parents, my grandparents.

These acts, too, were part of Jewish resistance. Yes, we remember this and more.

The remarks were delivered at the Treblinka Commemoration, part of the 50th anniversary celebration in Poland of the Warsaw Ghetto Uprising.

Observing the fiftieth anniversary of Jewish multi-faceted resistance, we must recall and pay honor to the righteous among the nations for their role in saving Jewish lives. Knowing the unfriendly and hostile environment under which we lived during the occupation, we begin to appreciate more fully the risks they took and the courage and nobility of their actions.

But, my friends, our remembering will mean little in the course of history if we are not successful in ensuring that future generations also remember. Are they ready and equipped for this task? Do they have the resolve to stamp out with promptness and vigor, to relentlessly destroy the evil forces which continue to this day to pursue their evil goals?

The presence of so many youngsters, our children and grandchildren—many thousands came from the four corners of the earth to mark the fiftieth anniversary of Jewish resistance on Yom Hashoa V'Hagvurah in Treblinka—gives us hope that the message and the command of Zachor will be carried from generation to generation.

In closing my remarks I want to quote the last call made by ZOB, the Jewish Fighting Organization, signed by Mordechai Anilewicz, the commander of the Warsaw Ghetto uprising.

His declaration to the outside world ended with these words: "The struggle against our common enemy is for our and your freedom, za nasza i wasza wolnosc—for our and your human, social and national honor. Long live freedom."

Let us and future generations live up to the expectations of these words and let us be worthy to have lived to the fiftieth anniversary of Jewish resistance in that darkest period of human history.

In the spirit of remembering let us resolve that we will carry the torch that was lit in the Warsaw Ghetto.

A NEW GERMANY OR A REVIVAL
OF THE OLD HITLER DAYS

By Charles R. Allen, Jr.

On the eve of unification, the preponderant American view of the new Germany and its prospective role in world affairs was positive, if not outright enthusiastic.

Writing under the headline "Germany Flexes Its Muscles, And Rightly, So!" the former Reagan diplomat Jeanne Kirkpatrick, wrote, "No one should be surprised if [a unified] Germany would once again be the strongest nation on Continental Europe [and] pursues [its own] independent policy."

Not to worry, she added: "The Germany that has enjoyed 40 years of democracy and prosperity will surely be interested in preserving and extending them."

An editorial in *The Wall Street Journal* cautioned against ". . . the politics of paranoia and confrontation" if a "new Germany" would emerge again as a "great power." "German policy is not basically nationalistic," the influentnal paper concluded.

Writing in *The New York Times*, the eminent Yale historian Dr. Henry Ashby Turner, Jr., found "no grounds for expecting Germans of the future to behave as those of the past." He rejected as "hackneyed" any notion of "an indelible national character," saying with confidence, "we need have no fear of a 'xenophobic Germany.' "

President George Bush welcomed the unification, commenting that people "ought to forgive" the Germans for the Holocaust. "I'm a Christian," he told *The New York Times*, ". . . forgiveness is something I feel about."

In its lead editorial of May 20, 1990, the *Times* sounded a veritable benediction: "The Germany of 60 years ago was a deeply dissatisfied society, embittered by what many people felt was an unjust settlement of World War I, battered by depression and disdainful of a then-fragile democratic tradition. But not today. Self-confident, Germany is more likely to flex its muscles in the economic realm. Such assertiveness may breed resentment, but will contribute to, not threaten, the long term peace in Europe."

The singularly most significant voice in this debate, however, was all but ignored by the world media. . . .

Nobel Laureate Elie Wiesel went a step further, proposing a formal presence of Jewish representatives at all negotiations leading to Germany's unification. William Proxmire, the former U.S. Senator from Wisconsin who single-handedly led the United States to adopt the United Nations Convention Against Genocide, concurred. He emphasized that such a proposition was not designed to impose the sins of German fathers onto subsequent generations, but to rivet into the memory of the unified German leaders "the clear recollection of Hitler's terrible crime of genocide."

The prophetic voice of the survivors was not heeded in 1949 by the architects of the two postwar Germanys, West and East. Nor were they heard at the official unification of Deutschland on October 3, 1990. Little wonder the new Germany was born amidst extraordinary eruptions of violence, racism, anti-Semitism on both sides of the demolished Berlin Wall. Neo-Nazi skinheads marched with banners calling for "Ein Volk! Ein Vaterland! Ein Deutschland! Deutschland Uber Alles!" Young German fascists beat and killed foreign workers from Asia, Africa, and southern Europe. The far-right Republikaner Party, led by a Waffen SS veterans, made strong showings in local and regional elections.

What do these right-wing stirrings portend? Is this the prelude to a popular Nazi revival? Certainly, we must take these menacing fringe groups seriously, but the greater threat lies closer to the political center, as evidenced by that nation's failure to exorcise Nazism from the German Weltanschauung.

From its start in 1949, much of West German society was dominated by officials of the former Nazi regime. Dr. Hans Globke, the most powerful political figure during the long administration of Konrad Adenauer (1949-1963), authored the legal Commentary of the 1935 Nuremberg Laws, the "legal" basis of the Third Reich's institutionalized anti-Semitism that culminated in the Holocaust. Wanted by several countries for crimes against humanity. Globke managed to escape prosecution.

The entire command of the "new" West German army, from the 1950s through the early 1970s, had served in the German General Staff under Hitler. New evidence has surfaced about a secret conference of former high-ranking World War II officers held in the early 1950s under the leadership of Hans Speidel, former Wehrmacht general and later German army general. The conference resolved that "pardons for war criminals" and an "end to defamation of German soldiers" was a prerequisite for any "military contribution" by the Federal Republic of Germany to Western defense against Communism. Thus Hitler's military escaped prosecution for war crimes and helped lay the groundwork for rearmament.

Combine this failure to punish war criminals in the Federal Republic with the systematic denial of the Holocaust in the "anti-Fascist German Democratic Republic" and the result is what novelist Gunter Grass called "the German amnesia."

What, then, can we expect from unified Germany? An analysis of Germany's burgeoning weapons industry may provide an answer. From 1983 to 1990 the United States and the Soviet Union dominated the $327 billion conventional weapons market. The principal purchasing nations were Saudi Arabia, Iran, Syria, Iraq, and Libya. Germany, a relative latecomer into this market, realized some $8.62 billion in 1990, fifth place. Industry leaders in Germany have indicated their determination to capture second place in the near term, and then seriously contend with the United States for domination of the world armament markets.

Daimler-Benz, producer of Mercedes-Benz automobiles, ranks high among these nakedly ambitious German arms manufacturers. The corporation's Nazi past has been recently documented by Prof. B. P. Bellon in *Mercedes in Peace and War* (Columbia University Press, 1991). In the 1920s the firm bragged in an internal memo: "We help to motorize the [Nazi] movement." Daimler-Benz was the chief source for transporting Hitler's ground forces during World War II, aiding in the implementation of the Holocaust. Yet none of its executives were charged with war crimes. In fact, the major trucking contract awarded by the U.S. Army of Occupied Germany went to Daimler.

The New York Times (April 9, 1989) summed up Daimler's position in the current corporate arms race: "Daimler has taken control of AEG . . . Germany's No. 3 electronics; MTU, the nation's largest jet engine company; and Dornier, a major aircraft manufacturer . . . [and is] also seeking control of Messerschmidt-Boelow-Blohm . . . Germany's largest aerospace company. MBB makes helicopters, warplanes, and military electronics, and owns 38 percent [of] Europe's Airbus Industrie aircraft consortium."

The *Times* concluded: "In creating the biggest German military group since the House of Krupp . . . after W.W. II, [Daimler-Benz] is boldly showing that . . . German arms makers are no longer content to remain tiny compared with their European and American rivals, Daimler would receive more than 40 percent of [Germany's] annual weapons procurement program and more than half of [its] military research and development budget."

Even more ominous is Germany's trade in weapons of mass destruction and terror. . . .

Of the 207 firms that supplied Saddam Hussein with missiles, long range cannon, poison gas, Scuds, nuclear weapons, and ballistic rockets, 41.6 percent were German. On February 21, 1992, the Associated Press reported that three German firms had sold and maintained "equipment for producing nuclear weapons" to Hussein and "the detonator for the Scud-b missile used by the Iraq during the Gulf War."

In *The Death Lobby, How the West Armed Iraq*, K. R. Timmerman reported that in 1980 there were unconfirmed reports that Iraq was developing a nuclear bomb capability from "6 tons of depleted uranium purchased [by Italian sources] from the [government backed] West German consortium NUKEM."

The Italian traders feared that "NUKEM might not deliver the plutonium once the true customer [Iraq] was discovered by the giant German consortium." "But [the Italians] needn't have worried about NUKEM's scruples," continues Timmerman. "The consortium was a wholly owned subsidiary of the German chemical giant Degussa, which had invented and manufactured Zyklon B, the powerful cyanide gas that streamed out of the showerheads in Hitler's death camps, killing millions of European Jews. Degussa had also played a key role in the Nazi effort to build an atom bomb.

"As the Third Reich was going up in flames, Degussa's chairman, Hermann Schlosser, donated 45,000 reichmarks to Hitler's SS. Thirty-five years later, Schlosser was still on the Degussa board, and in 1987 he was awarded the German Federal Merit Cross for his services to industry."

Schlosser himself was a ranking member of Heinrich Himmler's "Circle of Friends," made up of Germany's captains of industry and finance. Schlosser held an honorary rank of SS-Standartenfuehrer (Col.). He was never charged with war crimes.

M&R 19:4, Nov.-Dec., 1992
M&R 19:4, Jan.-Feb., 1993

CAMPUS ANTI-SEMITISM
A GROWING PROBLEM

The history of the Third Reich shows an organized program of anti-Jewish legislation and practices in education—on all levels. For that reason, there is widespread concern and wariness about a burgeoning problem: anti-Semitism on campus.

In its annual report, "Audit of Anti-Semitic Incidents," the Anti-Defamation League of B'nai B'rith spotlighted the sharp increase of on-campus incidents.

Recent articles in *Jewish Week* by Naomi Godfrey detailed the breadth of concern on this issue.

Jeffrey Ross, director of the ADL department of higher education/campus affairs, noted that reported incidents are underreported because colleges seek to avoid negative publicity. Moreover, reportage often has a reverse effect by producing an imitation of the outbreaks elsewhere.

"The most serious campus incidents were anti-Semitic vandalism targeting Hillel buildings, other on-campus centers of Jewish student activity and Jewish religious displays or monuments," the ADL report stated.

Ross classified Anti-Semitic incidents into five categories: ideological anti-Zionism, "country club" and "gutter" anti-Semitic prejudice, a fusing of anti-Zionism and anti-Semitic rhetoric, academic neo-Nazism, and JAP-baiting.

Ideological anti-Zionism, observed Ross, is "a world view that not only denies the right of Israel to exist as a Jewish state, but sees the earth threatened by a diabolic conspiracy of Jewish and non-Jewish Zionist agents."

At the University of Nebraska, for example, a letter to the campus newspaper charged that Prof. David Wyman, a respected non-Jewish Holocaust scholar who had spoken at the school, was a "Zionist agent" spreading the "Holocaust myth."

Old-fashioned bigotry is the best way to describe "gutter" or "country club" anti-Semitism. At the University of Kansas, the Hillel Organization received a missive that read: "Dear Jew, we the concerned farmers of USA do not want you here. You control our banks, our media, and our way of life. Jew boy, get out."

As an example of the fusion of anti-Zionism and anti-Semitism, Ross cited the Organization of Arab Students at the University of California at Riverside, who produced fliers alleging that Israeli foods are made with the blood of Arab children.

Holocaust revisionists, who deny the Holocaust, seek to build credibility through academic neo-Nazism, by enlisting academicians to advance these theories.

"The ugly phenomenon of 'JAP-baiting' has become widespread on many campuses, a behavior manifested by both Jews and non-Jews," said Ross. "The 'Jewish American Princess' stereotype blends anti-Semitism with misogyny and Jewish self-hatred, depicting Jewish women as 'self-centered, overindulged, undersexed, and subject to the conspicuous display of an avaricious materialism.' "

What can be done to combat bigotry? Frustration seems to be the reaction, a refusal to admit the problem and an inability to meet the problem. "I don't think a lot of us want to admit there's a problem," said Jennifer Marks, president of Hillel at the University of Kansas. "Therefore, a lot of people don't know what to do. We need people who are willing to come here and speak to us and tell us what to do. I think if students saw the professionals reacting to it, it would make it a lot easier for us to react to it."

The Student Governing Board of the North American Jewish Student Appeals (NAJSA) has submitted a resolution for consideration by the General Assembly of the Council of Jewish Federations. The resolution asks for support of the organized Jewish community to fight anti-Semitism on campus.

"We think students need the tools to counter propaganda and hate—students don't necessarily come to campus prepared for these attacks," said Bennett Graff, NAJSA Board President

Aside from condemning these outbreaks and countering these developments, NAJSA leaders stressed that "Jewish identity should be explored and experienced in positive ways."

CAN AFRO-AMERICANS
BE CALLED RACISTS?

BY DR. ROY SCHWARTZMAN

I write this article not as a Jew, yet nonetheless as a person of faith; in reason, faith that intelligence will not waver indefinitely after it has been ignited. When I read and hear the anti-Semitic invective spewing from the lips of Louis Farrakhan's disciples, it does not undercut my religious faith or make me fear to be a Jew. It erodes a bit of the hope that drove me to be an academic. I hoped that on college campuses and in young minds lay the foundation for replacing racism with ethical commitments that transcended the boundaries we so often erect and hide behind.

The anti-Semitic currents flowing from the Nation of Islam are especially disturbing because of how they swell in intellectual centers. Yet, the infection of universities and young black intellectuals with anti-Semitism raises hope for containment and cure no less than it injures confidence in the morality of intellectuals. If rational, intelligent people fall prey to anti-Semitism, then rationality and intellect might stem the rising tide of hatred.

I will not repeat the now familiar anti-Semitic epithets so forcefully hurled by the likes of Khallid Abdul Mohammed. My task is to propose responses that go beyond revealing factual inaccuracies about Judaism, selective memory that obliterates Jewish contributions to civil rights, and the crude stereotypes pinned to Jews. Instead, I want to show the people who utter these remarks that they are racist and counterproductive to the cause of black empowerment.

The standard defense African-American anti-Semites use against the charge of racism is, "I can't be racist. Racism implies empowerment. Since I am not empowered, I can't be a racist." This contention sounds like a perfectly logical enthymeme. But it is a logical fallacy, disproven argumentatively and historically.

The denial of racism rests on the assumption that it is impossible to be racist unless one is empowered. This is historically false. Adolf Hitler launched his most virulent attacks against Jews long before he became Chancellor of Germany. When Hitler's speeches became the focus of international attention, he toned down his public anti-Semitism to avoid alienating foreign powers and losing potential allies. Far from being a sign of power, anti-Semitism—like other bigotry—traditionally has been used by politically or socially marginalized groups to ascend the ladder of power. Hitler referred to the Jewish "pestilence" (July 28, 1922 and September 18, 1922) long before the Nazi party assumed national prominence. The infamous characterization of Jews as bacilli occurred in *Mein Kampf*, written while Hitler was in prison after the failed Beer Hall Putsch. A prison cell hardly qualifies as a position of power. Could Hitler be racist only if he occupied a seat of power?

No person or group has a monopoly on anti-Semitism. While racism is always a form of repression, the racist need not employ physical subjugation. The Klu Klux Klan has long consisted of the economically and socially dispossessed. KKK members fear anyone they think threatens their tenuous toehold on social advancement. Klan members enjoy a position of power only insofar as they wield the clubs and shotguns. Put a weapon in anyone's hands and that person is empowered to oppress others. But this empowerment is illusory. Force is not power, because true power involves voluntary consent.

The denial that blacks can be racist conveniently immunizes African-Americans from any accusations of racial misconduct. This immunization has a side effect: blindness. Anyone's categorical denial of racism authorizes all behaviors and all languages under the blinding cloak of self-denial. Anyone can be a racist All too often, most people have practiced some form of racism. An anti-Semitic or anti-black remark still hurts even if unaccompanied by a bludgeon. Racism is a remarkably democratic disease. Anyone can suffer from it. Racism can infect the unemployed, homeless, illiterate as easily as the Fortune 500 CEO. Virtue cannot lie only with those who lack the tools to institutionalize hatred.

REVISIONISM PAINS SPIRIT OF HOLOCAUST SURVIVORS

By Dr. Jacob Felberbaum

Long before the grim statistics on the Nazi efforts to finalize—as quietly as possible—the solution of the Jewish problem were known, we sensed that the crime committed must have been enormous. One popular historian just before his death in Majdanek (recorded by Alexander Donat) understood that the truth would depend on who would write the history. "Should they [the Nazi] write the story of this war, our destruction will be presented as one of the most glorious exploits in world history. But if we write the story, we will have the thankless task of providing to the disbelieving world that we really are Abel, the murdered brother." And how right he was!

The existing evidence of committed crimes is so overwhelming that till today it has been impossible to study the records in their totality especially before the Russians opened their massive files in Moscow. There exist additional troublesome problems in writing about historical events when personal emotions of the writer are involved. We refer to the materials left by the victims. After all we are concerned with not so distant events and a survivor would not be human if he would not have any feelings after a loss of his family.

Barbara Tuchman approaches this problem as follows: "I am not saying that emotion should not have a place in history. On the contrary, I think it is an essential element of history. . . . History, one might say, is emotion plus action recollected or, in the case of latter-day historians reflected on in tranquility after a close and honest examination of the records. The primary duty of a historian is to stay within the evidence."

The problem with the revisionists is that they summarily dismiss the facts as hoax, quote out of context, twist the truth and finally reverse the roles of the perpetrator and the victim: the Nazi becomes the innocent victim.

The irony of the indecent denial of the fact of the genocidal Nazi policits is the impact it has on the spirit of the survivors. After the painful loss of a family, scores of friends, the liquidation of the place they once lived in, everything is being declared as a big lie. Their most personal memories are being disputed and forced to roam within new imaginary dimensions of a nonexistent world where those long lost may still live. Hope is a very strange feeling, that feeds on any, no matter how irrational idea. Eventually, however, the naive must return from the hypocritical twilight zone to this real cruel world of historical truth.

M&R 20:5, Sept.-Oct., 1993

TRANSMITTAL OF THE HOLOCAUST KEYNOTED BY AHARON APPELFELD

BY DOROTHY FUERST

In a three-day conference dedicated to and entitled *The Individualization of the Holocaust*, Aharon Appelfeld gave the keynote speech and addressed himself not only to the subject and title but also and simultaneously to the question of the hour. Now that the survivors of the Holocaust are slowly departing this world; now that the eye-witnesses will no longer be able to bear witness, through their testimony of their silent presence, how will we be able to "continue the story of the Holocaust without them? How can we preserve the individuality and the intimacy that survivors gave to this most terrible event in our collective history?" How can we transmit it to future generations? How will they understand the Holocaust?

The highly stimulating conference was sponsored by the Eli and Diana Zborowski Interdisciplinary Chair in Holocaust Studies at Yeshiva University. The chair has sponsored varied conferences and programs through the years, in addition to inaugurating Holocaust courses. The conference took note of these achievemnts with the presentation of an award to Eli Zborowski.

Appelfeld traced the path of the literature of the Holocaust from its very beginnings, as it was created in the crucible of agony and destruction in Warsaw and Lodz, and other ghettoes. These were testimonies, journals, poems, prose, expressing the wrenching anguish of the soul and, at the same time, looking for a new definition of man just as their world was going up in flames around them. As hunger gnawed at their insides, as disease stalked them, as death surrounded and claimed victims all around them, and as one transport after another took the Jews around them to their destruction, the poetry and prose of the ghettoes sought to "anchor itself in spirituality, to seek a new definition of man, to find its place in a world going up in flames."

The extermination of European Jewry followed a systematic pattern, Mr. Appelfeld noted. First one was deprived of one's house, one's home environment, then of one's personal belongings; one was confined to infested and overcrowded ghettoes, separated from family members, and, finally, what remained was a famished body moving from place to place, "devoid of the Divine Image." It was the eradication of the self. The journals written during the Holocaust were the "most furious outcries of the soul; a last effort to preserve a shred of the self before it was taken and destroyed."

The flames of the inferno destroyed many, perhaps most of the writers. Few survived. The survivors, after the war, could not bring themselves to look back into the flames and write about what had happened to them, artistically, spiritually. As Appelfeld has said elsewhere, "Artistically, it is impossible to deal with it directly. You cannot look at the sun; the temperature is too high. The Holocaust is like that. You cannot speak; you cannot utter, you cannot feel. You must degrade it to some extent in order to speak of it."

The survivors spoke in the beginning of what had happened to them. Each survivor found that the cruelty inflicted upon him had a rival and often was even surpassed by the barbarity, the cruelty, the torment inflicted upon the other survivors he met. These spoken exchanges, Mr. Appelfeld pointed out, were the beginning of the survivors' awareness, his arousal, the "first stirrings of perspective." Then, miracle of miracles, the survivors began to re-enter normal life. This was indeed a miracle, for, instead of mad, insanity, after living as they had been forced to live for years, "eating like an animal, living like one, crawling like one, seizing whatever came to hand," after the most terrible experiences that man can be subjected to and still survive, the survivors became part of normal society. The survivors

took refuge in life. Indeed, says Appelfeld, they plunged
into life.

In time, the survivors accepted the need to record what
had happened. There was an imperative urgency about recording in detail the depravity, the barbarity, the evil in-
flcted, the torment, the agony suffered, but these were
chronicles of what happened. In his review of the literature
of the Holocaust, Appelfeld pointed out that in these
chronicles we should seek innerness, spirituality, a new
definition of man, which characterized the literature written
during the Holocaust. It is a form of chronicle, concealing
more than they reveal: wounded feelings, fear to stand
naked," Appelfeld says, for what the survivors had undergone remained an oppression and secret.

Memory, commemoration were the motifs of survivors.
Survivors ensured in their accounts that the events were
told in proper order in precise detail. Places and names
were meticulously recorded. Memoir followed memoir, scholarly article followed scholarly article as the decades passed.
Now the record stands approximately complete. Not that
there are no areas which have escaped scrutiny, for lack
of witnesses or issues which have not yet been clarified. For
the most part, however, the general picture is complete.
"The story of the Holocaust is gradually assuming the patterns given to it by the witnesses, Mr. Appelfeld pointed out.

Having traced the literature of the Holocaust so far,
Appelfeld then returned to the penultimate question. "Now
that the survivors are slowly departing and eyewitnesses
will no longer be able to bear witness, how can we continue
the story of the Holocaust without them. How can we
preserve the intimacy and the individuality that survivors,
by their presence, gave to this terrible period in human
history?"

Appelfeld presented his answer to this problem. "Now
is the time to add an upper floor to the structure the survivors have built." To the historical question of what happened and how it happened, we must now ask, "What is
the way it must have happened?"

It is the beginning of a new approach to the study of
the Holocaust, a new dimension; an approach, however,
which has been used since the beginning of time. Appelfeld
used the Bible as a point of reference and example for its
individualization of historic events. The journals recorded
history. Now is the time for vision; for interpretation; for
artistic presentation; for individualization for this most ter-

rible event in history, so that we can present and relate to
individuals of flesh and blood, without idealization, the
Holocaust in all its complexity, in all its shadings of good
and evil. The truth must be laid bare. "The truth must be
laid bare. There were also collaborators among the victims,
informers and evil people." The complexity of this evil must
not be concealed.

It is the time for new formats to be used: prose, poetry,
visual arts, Mr. Appelfeld explained. It is by using these
forms and through individualization that we can try to
arrive at the essential truth and the profoundest meaning of
that inferno of Jewish existence which we call the Holocaust.

M&R 20:11, Nov.-Dec., 1993

OUR GRANDCHILDREN: THOUGHTS ON THE THIRD GENERATION

BY PAULA MANDELL

Unforeseeable, but it's happening: the pilgrimage to the
Washington Holocaust Museum upstages that of the number
of visitors to tour the White House, the Arlington Cemetery
or the Lincoln Memorial. The recent new movie about the
Holocaust relating the story of Oskar Schindler, savior of
1,200 Jews in World War II, inserts the audiences squarely
into the crime of the century, and prompted President Clinton
to talk about this firm's meaning today.

In September 1993, the most dramatic rebuttal of those
pseudo-scholars who claimed that the gas in camps was for
delousing and the Final Solution was a Zionist Myth came
out in the form of a book published in Paris by Claude
Pressac entitled, *The Crematorium of Auschwitz: The
Machinery of Mass Murder*. The author, using newly available documents taken by the Soviets from Auschwitz, describes with chilling objectivity the floor plans and the
ventilation system of the gas chamber, and reproduces order
forms for furnaces. This evidence cause a blow to the
Holocaust deniers.

Moved and awakened to the horrors of World War II,

the one person of five who did not believe according to the
latest poll taken by the American Jewish Committee, the
twenty percent of the American population who doubted
the possibility of the Holocaust ever having occurred, will
be able to give credence to the records of history. [The
poll's inaccuracy has since been stated.]

We the survivors listen to their comments of disbelief
and astonishment triggered by this latest resurgence of
Holocaust accounts. It follows as if a missing piece of a
puzzle would turn up: the mention of Yugoslavia. I find
myself often emphasizing the underlying difference. Holocaust account turns into motion a science of dehumanization and a factory of death. In Yugoslavia an eruption of
long suppressed anger, hate, and desire for revenge, vented
toward brother, neighbor and friend, has been propelled by
the newly won freedom in Eastern Europe.

Many a time this explanation is handed over to our
grandchildren who, in contrast to our roots, are products
of a different world, progressive times, and dissimilar environment. Therefore, their perception is branched out differently from ours. Facing the above, I recently witnessed
an episode that underlined the above observation.

Several weeks ago, I dropped into a friend's house. There
I found myself in the midst of a heated discussion between
the grandfather and his grandson. The topic was familiar:
a clash of two cultures came to a fore, the former lecturing
the youngster on how things ought to be: the latter, insist-
ing on the merits of the status quo. For us, the survivors,
it is most difficult to shed the ingrained attitudes and
opinions developed in our formative years while living in
Eastern Europe in a host country unfriendly to Jews. To
many positives bestowed upon us, we nod our head with an
affirmative, yes, for these are values stemming from tradition, religious beliefs and age old morals that were ham-
mered in us from dawn to dusk. This, we live, this we
breathe, this we think. Still, de ought to allow ourselves
to widen our horizon. To flex the straight jacket of intolerance and stagnation.

In contrast to us, this Third Generation in its formative years breathes freedom. There is the opportunity to
pursue the very best in human potential. They can soar to
the heights, and are free to actualize their aspirations. Let
us rejoice in that and realize that the goal to pursue happiness is the road we never touched in our formative years
and therefore leap for joy in theirs.

360 A LEGACY RECORDED

We relish on being witness to the budding of our grandchildren. Each and everyone of them with wide open eyes
listens to our horror stories. Many of them travel to Poland
and into that innocent and ideal youth trickles the perception of cruelty done to man against man, and the inhumanity
meted out to the families of their grandparents. They are
eager to go time and time again as though to pay dues for
the good life fate has bestowed upon them. There they
look, shake their heads in disbelief, and ask, "How could
all this have happened?"

In an article entitled, "Message from the Third Generation," by Jennifer Hamburg, she writes about two events
that solidified her mission as a Jew and a third generation
survivor. First, was the impact of her visit to Yad Vashem.
Second, the frightful possibility of David Duke's successful
election to the office of Gevernor of Louisiana. She writes,
"It was at this time I began to realize how ignorant many
people are, including myself, of the intolerant past Duke
had and tried to mask. I have come to realize that I hold
an important role in overcoming the ignorance, indifference,
and complacency as it relates to the Holocaust."

Our children and grandchildren inherited from us the
bloody pages of Jewish history and anti-Semitism from the
world around them.

For a glimpse at the attitude of a third generation person, let us see how Jennifer Gruber expresses herself. She
is a granddaughter of Holocaust survivors on her maternal
and paternal sides, and she writes as follows: "My attitude
is, if you are motivated, you can accomplish anything.
Friends are a big part of my life. My family members molded
me into the person I am. I have a lot of respect for my
parents and grandparents. Amid my strivings and goals on
the threshold of young adulthood stepping into responsibilities of independence loom the memory and horrors my grandparents went through. I have been in Poland with them in
June 1992. In my diary, I recorded what I have seen and
felt there. In years to come, I'll read it to my children and
eventually will hand it to them."

Jennifer told me that she has read the diary to her
classmates.

Michael, her brother, has been in Poland twice and
plans to go the third time. His insatiable eagerness is coupled
with incomprehension of the wrong done to his ancestors.
"My culture is American. My background is Jewish Eastern
European," he once told me. Michael devours all informa-

tion connected with the history of the Jews. "I want to spend part of my college years in Israel. I have this calling within me," he reiterated. He shows the films of his trip to Poland to all his friends at college.

It is evident that the memory of the Holocaust touches young adolescents in different ways. Several weeks ago, an acquaintance of ours celebrated the Bar Mitzvah of their son David. During the prayers and ceremony, David expressed the wish to invoke the name of a child who perished in the gas chambers of Auschwitz. It's remarkable because David's ancestors were never directly touched by the horrors of the Holocaust. The solemnity of the moment moved everyone of us, as though the soul of the young child of five would come to life and hover above each one of us.

The Holocaust memory is etched deeply in the collective consciousness of the Third Generation. Though the American culture permeates every aspect of their young lives, individualism and freedom of choice inevitably awakens a desire to be whole and self-sufficient. Still, the ties to ancestral history is strong and enduring.

Amid all intricacies of the American enlightenment, the above testimonies of the Third Generation provide ample proof that the ever thinning thread of the Holocaust memory is inextricably woven into their lives.

M&R 20:5, March-April, 1994

Marvin and Celina Zborowski Lectures

REMARKABLE QUALITIES OF THE SURVIVOR THEME AT QUEENS

By Dorothy Fuerst

Studies of the Holocaust generally concentrate on the time of the terror: how, when, where and why. The "why" can perhaps be fathomed. When the post-Holocaust period focused on the Holocaust, it was always in terms of "Never Again." Never again shall anti-Semitism be allowed to rear its evil presence, unchallenged.

A LEGACY RECORDED

This year, the annual Celina and Marvin Zborowski lecture at Queens College, concentrated on the survivors and the survivor's experience in their post-Holocaust world. Prof. William B. Helmreich, author of *Against all Odds*, expressed the essence of his findings in the thought, "It is not a story of remarkable people, but a story of how remarkable people can be."

The message, therefore, is for every man. Survivors, Professor Helmreich pointed out, survived because of luck, or because they were fated to survive. Certainly, nothing they did, or could possibly have done, determined their survival. It was determined for them by circumstance, by their tormentors, by sheer luck. How "lucky" were the survivors if they carried with them the sights and sounds of the crematoria, the long years of hunger, the excruciating pain of loss, of suffering without end? Lucky is relative.

The story of how they proceeded with their post-Holocaust lives teaches all of us a lesson in how to deal with adversity, how to put searing pain and loss, bitterness and anger and despair, behind us, or at least on the side, while we get on with our lives.

In his study of the survivors, Professor Helmreich found that certain traits helped the survivors build new lives on the ruins of their former lives. "Don't look back" clearly has to be a cardinal rule. "Compartmentalize." This happened, then, in the past. "It has nothing to do with my new life." And there is more: Flexibility in new situations; assertiveness; determination that one can do the job; optimism; belief in the future; street smarts; the ability to make a decision in a split second.

Does this mean that the survivor has divided his/her life into two separate parts, divided by a plexiglass wall, through which he/she can see but cannot be touched and cannot touch the former self? Not at all. At moments when one least expects, the past touches the survivor. In the depths of the night, dreams come to haunt the survivor. A smell of chloride, a sound of dogs barking jolt the memory and the two lives are one, but upon recovering from his jolt, his personal reminder, the survivor looks forward once again, putting his faith and hope into a new and unknown future.

Professor Helmreich found in his study that only 10 percent of the 140,000 survivors who came between 1946 and 1953 needed psychiatric intervention for emotional dysfunction. Perhaps that mirrors the emotional needs of the general population: 90 percent of the survivors did not. For the rest of us, facing loss and adversity, *Against all Odds* serves as a beacon, a torch to show us the way.

The fascinating narrative of Professor Helmreich added another chapter to the Marvin and Celina Zborowski lecture series. They have brought outstanding scholars and personalities who have informed and enchanted audiences on a variety of themes.

M&R 20:13, May-June, 1994

REMEMBER! REMEMBER!

I survived, I am glad;
And still, I am sad,
Why did I survive the Holocaust hell?
Is it because I have to tell?

How women, men and children were killed,
How six million voices were stilled?
The victims' crime: they were born a Jew.
They were human beings like me and you!

Auschwitz, Birkenau, Treblinka, Sobibor:
These names we can't afford to forget, to ignore.
In these death camps, six million of our people,
        their lives were lost!
We have to remember, remember the Holocaust.

EDDY WYNSCHENK

M&R 8:12, Sept.-Oct., 1981

SOME FINAL WORDS:
M & R–A GLOBAL REACTION

By CHARLES R. ALLEN, JR.

It has happened in Moscow, Paris, Berlin and London. It has happened in Toronto, Montreal, Vancouver, San Francisco, Chicago, and Sarasota, Florida.

I've been stopped on subways, buses, in airport terminals amid the babble of different tongues and in newspaper editors' offices, radio broadcasting booths and network TV studios when people ask: "What is that publication?" "What's it about?" Where can I get it?"

I'm talking about *Martyrdom & Resistance*, of course, and the not infrequent meetings I've had with *M & R* at home and abroad.

I also have had warm, exciting and always instructive, stimulating meetings with *M & R's* readers, contributors, and supporters across the United States and Canada. (On a few occasions, as I shall briefly relate, I've even had some equally instructive exchanges of *M & R's* detractors both in person and over the radio/TV airways.)

It has also been my happy lot to introduce *M & R* to the young: students at colleges, high schools, synagogues and youth groups gathered at conferences, retreats, or—even better—impromptu-rap sessions. In recalling the images of these exchanges, some remain indelibly inscribed on memory even as to their very feel timbre and, ultimately, meaning.

On the eve of Yom Hashoa in San Francisco this year, I spoke informally (but at length, as we dialogued far into the night) with nearly one hundred survivors—many of them husband and wife, along with their children—at the Holocaust Center Library and Research Center of San Francisco, certainly one of the major resources of the Holocaust in the country.

Suddenly, after looking out over the audience, I realized that dozens of my new friends were holding—even at one point, brandishing a rolled-up copy to drive home a point—copies of *Martyrdom & Resistance*.

The latest issue? Of course, they chorused. "Now let me

Charles Allen, author-lecturer, is internationally known for his writings on Nazi war criminals.

say a few words about this particular review," one said as she launched into a learned assessment of a recent volume on Jewish resistance during the Holocaust. She spoke with evident expertise and fervor: deported from Holland to the Warsaw Ghetto where she fought in the 1943 uprising, she "escaped to the Aryan side" and made her way to partisans with whom she fought to the end of the war.

"Martyrdom and Resistance," she said, "is one of the few publications that pays attention to the history of the Resistance by the Jews."

After our dialogue, we all repaired to San Francisco's magnificent Grant Park overlooking the Bay of that beautiful city. Mists drifted over the water, a lone freighter made its way out to the sea, an unseen fog-horn echoed mournfully, the chilly air caused us to move closer holding hands in a half-circle, as the rabbi read the kaddish by the light of the eternal flame of remembrance.

In company with the survivors and the children of the second generation, the origins, purpose and responsibilities of *Martyrdom & Resistance* are manifest.

. . . I am on a flight headed for a lecture in New Orleans. A young man returning home after the end of the college term sees me reading a copy of *M & R*. He asks to see it. I give it to him. Hours later as we deplane, he wonders if he can keep the copy. I say sure. "Terrific reading," he says. "Not easy either. I'll have to study it." He tells me he is not Jewish. "Neither am I," I reply.

. . . In 1986, the Boston College Law School hosts the "First International Conference on The Holocaust and Human Rights Law." The qualitative level of both audience and speakers is very high. They are concerned with the precedents and developments in both American and international law. In the audience and on the panels of this highly important symposium are Federal judges, present and former government prosecutors of suspected Nazi war criminals living in the United States, distinguished faculty from Harvard, Wellesley, the Fletcher School of Law and Diplomacy at Tufts University, Yale, Williams, and the University of Chicago.

As the only non-lawyer on the panel titled "The U.S. Response to War Criminals and Persecutors: An Overview and Evaluation," I draw specifically from some of my writings in *M & R* for my own paper: "Tensions Between Immigration Concerns, Prosecutions and National Security Interests: An Evaluation and Analysis."

At lunch, a Federal jurist inquires about *M & R*. He later

tells me that he finds my essays on I. G. Farben, Auschwitz and the corporations profiting from the Holocaust are "very important, as is this (*M & R*) publication."

When I put a stack of *M & R*s on the literature table, the students snap them up.

. . . A letter arrives from an international lawyer practicing in Milwaukee, Wisconsin. He tells me that he had seen me on television, talking about *Martyrdom & Resistance*. He himself is a scholar and commentator on the law and the Holocaust. I send him some back copies. He replies: *M & R* has proven "exciting and invaluable" both for his own work and the Milwaukee intellectual community.

. . . It's a stint being on a five-hour radio talk-program on the NBC affiliate in Tampa, Florida. During the course of what was a brilliantly mounted program by its young producer, we opened with an astounding recording made at the 1940 surrender of Paris to the Nazis. We discussed at length *M & R* and its features.

The initial call-ins reflect positive and rational interest in the paper. Then a harsh, manic voice comes on. "I've seen your Jew-Commie rag," he rasps. "You better wise up. This is KKK territory. There was no crematorium at Dachau. I seen it myself. Auschwitz is a lie. . . . Hitler just didn't finish the job. But we will, and start tonight!" There are no incidents.

. . . I am in Moscow in the winter of 1986-1987. I give a ninety-minute paper at an international conference marking the 40th year since the Nuremberg War Crimes Trials. There are nearly 400 delegates from 28 nations, including observers from Israel. In Europe and the U.S.S.R., the event is major news, meriting extensive media attention for an entire week.

I devote a considerable portion of my paper arguing the necessity to specifically and fully acknowledge and deal openly with the genocide of European and Soviet Jews by the fascists.

I further argue that world Jewry and a large portion of the world itself has come to call the genocide of the Jews The Holocaust. Out of respect, out of historical accuracy and in the spirit of the "new thinking" (*novya glasnost*), I urge the Soviets to acknowledge and openly explore what has been hitherto ignored.

Insofar as I know, this has been the first time the subject has been publicly so addressed. The reaction from the audience, particularly the younger cadres among the writers, journalists, diplomats, scholars and scientists, is very positive. I give out many copies of *M & R* to members of the ultra prestigious U.S.S.R. Academy of Science. A measure of its effect may be gleaned from a remark by a young Leningrad historian and expert on the SS Einsatzgruppen: "This is a most realistic publication with excellent information." I smile and give him a subscription coupon.

... I receive a phone call from a young professor at Tufts University. Dr. Jerry Meldon is a very interesting scholar who teaches (chemical/electrical) engineering and is also a Holocaust scholar in his own right. He proposes to create a special course on the question of the post-Holocaust presence of actual Nazi war criminals in the United States.

I help him with the syllabus. The president of Tufts is Dr. Jean Mayer, who himself fought in the French Resistance. He unreservedly supports the project. This distinguished school launches the first such course by an American University. Describing *Martyrdom & Resistance* as "an invaluable resource," the school orders the microfilm of all back issues and urges the students to subscribe.

I am invited to deliver a late spring lecture before Dr. Meldon's special elective. As I enter the classroom, I have yet another encounter with my valued companion and teacher: at each student's chair is a copy of the latest issue of *Martyrdom and Resistance*. Our discussion is lively, the vigor of the young and inquiring minds reaching out for sustenance to remember and learn the lessons of the immortal Holocaust.